D1826723

RELIGIOUS TRANSFORMATION IN SOUTH ASIA

OXFORD HISTORICAL MONOGRAPHS

Religious Transformation in South Asia

The Meanings of Conversion in Colonial Punjab

CHRISTOPHER HARDING

OXFORD
UNIVERSITY PRESS
Great Clarendon Street, Oxford OX2 6DP

Oxford University Press is a department of the University of Oxford.
It furthers the University's objective of excellence in research, scholarship,
and education by publishing worldwide in

Oxford New York

Auckland Cape Town Dar es Salaam Hong Kong Karachi
Kuala Lumpur Madrid Melbourne Mexico City Nairobi
New Delhi Shanghai Taipei Toronto

With offices in

Argentina Austria Brazil Chile Czech Republic France Greece
Guatemala Hungary Italy Japan Poland Portugal Singapore
South Korea Switzerland Thailand Turkey Ukraine Vietnam

Oxford is a registered trade mark of Oxford University Press
in the UK and in certain other countries

Published in the United States
by Oxford University Press Inc., New York

First published 2008

British Library Cataloguing in Publication Data
Data available

Library of Congress Cataloging in Publication Data
Data available

Typeset by Laserwords Private Limited, Chennai, India
Printed in Great Britain
on acid-free paper by
Biddles Ltd., King's Lynn, Norfolk

ISBN 978–0–19–954822–4

1 3 5 7 9 10 8 6 4 2

For my grandparents

Preface

This book emerged from a very broad postgraduate interest in that modern meeting and mingling of European and Asian religious cultures which has affected everything from philosophy and popular religious experience on both continents to social work and policy, political ideology, and ideas about mental and spiritual health. I focused my attention upon a single set of circumstances within this far larger scheme: religious transformation and the meaning of conversion in the lives of oppressed rural groups in north-west India, European Catholic and Anglican missionaries whose attention, allegiance, and resources—in the broadest sense of the word—they sought, and the various local individuals and groups who led, mediated, or opposed this encounter.

The lives of ordinary people do not, of course, require crowbarring into a particular narrative in order for historians to take an interest in them. But where rural Punjabi converts in the late nineteenth and early twentieth centuries are concerned, the fact that conversion to Christianity compounded an already marginal economic and social status—since it was looked upon by many groups in India as a kind of apostasy of national identity—renders their story significant as a dimension of 'subaltern' experience in modern South Asian history still relatively ignored by secular historians.

In addition, for a historical context where mission work is frequently discounted as an epiphenomenon of colonialism, and conversion is seen in terms of a relatively undifferentiated activist missionary effort and a passive, barely sincere convert body rendered vulnerable by poor circumstances, a critical focus upon agency, strategy, and frames of reference in conversion—on all sides—is urgently called for. Understanding convert agency is a tall order, not least because of a lack of documentary sources generated by converts themselves. This book explores the potential of a comparative analysis of third-party—mainly missionary—sources in accessing converts' worlds, but future research in this area might profitably make systematic use of oral and musical histories (including hymns and songs penned by converts) in adding new dimensions to our understanding here.

Finally, although recent public discourse has revolved around rather narrow political or institutional constructions of 'religion', where the writing of social history is concerned a fuller and more open-ended reconsideration of the many roles played by religious impulses and ideas in human experience is currently under way. This book is offered as a modest contribution to this; focusing upon themes which operate on a more intimate level than national stories and interests, from the dynamics of small communities to inter-regional connections based on personality and aspiration.

For all the benefits of a broad approach such as this, it makes for a baptism of fire where a first academic enterprise is concerned. As a result, I owe an unusually great many debts of gratitude for academic, linguistic, financial, and personal support. For unfailing guidance in my studies at the University of Oxford I should like to thank Judith Brown, along with David Washbrook and Nandini Gooptu. John Webster and Fr. John Rooney have also been extraordinarily generous with their time, encouragement, and bibliographical assistance. Imre Bangha persevered in teaching me Hindi and Urdu, while Anne-France White assisted me with French translations.

Br. Xavier Vadakkekara and his colleagues in Delhi, Uttar Pradesh, and Punjab offered me the warmest of welcomes in India, allowed me to shadow them in their work, and helped me to arrange interviews with Christian families in Kalmar, Sarekhas, Dugri, and Sayekar villages in Kartarpur district, Punjab. I should like to thank the people of those villages, for their hospitality, openness, and patience with my language skills; above all I am grateful for their letting me hear their stories, family histories, and music, and for giving meaning and reality to this study. I am very grateful also to Capuchin houses in Antwerp and Rome for their hospitality and warm assistance, in particular Fr. Jean-Pierre Tytgat and Frs Kamiel and Stan Teuns in Antwerp, and Br. Benedict Vadakkekara in Rome.

For sponsorship in the form of a Masters followed by a Doctoral Studentship I am grateful to the Arts and Humanities Research Board, now the Arts and Humanities Research Council. For permission to reproduce archival and published material I thank the Belgian Province of the Capuchin Order in Antwerp and the administrators of the General Archives of the Capuchin Order in Rome; the Church Missionary Society and United Society for the Propagation of the Gospel; the British Library; and Princeton University Press. I should also like to thank the staff of the Indian Institute Library in the Bodleian Library, the Bodleian Library of Commonwealth and African Studies at Rhodes House, the History and Theology faculties at Oxford University, and the Special Collections at Birmingham University, all of whom were consistently patient with me and extremely helpful. For seeing this book safely through to production I am grateful to Laurien Berkeley, and to Seth Cayley, Kate Walker, and Mikki Choman at Oxford University Press.

For personal as well as academic support over the course of a steep learning curve I am grateful to a huge number of people, in particular Crispin Bates, Nandini Chatterjee, Martin Conway, Pete Huddlestone, James Milner, Izabela Orlowska, Kabir Singh, and Ian Talbot. Most of all, I owe thanks to my family, especially Kae, whose love and patience withstood my infuriating pace and style of working and who has been told so many times that this book is finally finished she could be forgiven for thinking I had published an entire series by now.

C.H.

Edinburgh
January 2008

Contents

Maps

Figures

Tables

Abbreviations

ABC	Archives of the Belgian Capuchins
ACMS	Archives of the Church Missionary Society
ASPG	Archives of the Society for the Propagation of the Gospel
BL	British Library
CEZMS	Church of England Zenana Mission Society
CMC	Central Mission Council (CMS)
CMR	*Church Missionary Review*
CMS	Church Missionary Society
CTS	Catholic Truth Society
DC	district commissioner
DMC	District Mission Council (CMS)
DMN	*Delhi Mission News*
GACO	General Archives of the Capuchin Order
ICS	Indian Civil Service
OFM	Order of Friars Minor
OIOC	Oriental and India Office Collections
PN(D)CC	Punjab Native (District) Church Council (CMS)
PUP	Punjab Unionist Party
Rs	rupees
SBCP	Society for Bettering the Condition of the Poor
SCPF	Sacred Congregation for the Propagation of the Faith
SPG	Society for the Propagation of the Gospel

Introduction

> The distance to travel was no less than 110 English miles. It was winter, extraordinarily cold, with the north wind blowing fiercely. To crown it all torrential rain had made all the paths impassable. Two nights were spent under the stars; a third in a goat's stable too small to accommodate the entire convoy. Our Christians enveloped themselves carefully in their traditional cover and huddled up against each other to protect themselves against the cold. Yet still . . . they suffered enormously.
>
> (Godefroid Pelckmans, *Dix Années d'apostolat au Pundjab*)

For six days in January 1893 three Punjabi Catholic families and a couple of Belgian Capuchin priests trekked across Punjab to a barren area of land that was to become the Catholic village of Maryabad. Allusions to the Exodus in this Capuchin account are revealing of the self-image treasured by the young Belgian missionaries, breaking new ground for Catholicism in Asia and leading people from slavery to freedom. For the three Punjabi families, representing hundreds of thousands of other labourers and village servants seeking association with Christian missions across the province, these six days were part of a far broader, independent attempt to migrate from one state of being to another—a journey with more than its fair share of suffering and inhospitable terrain.

From the last decades of the nineteenth century urgent and unprecedented demands among oppressed peoples in rural Punjab and elsewhere in India drove what came to be called 'mass conversion movements', launching a revolution in South Asia's 2,000-year Christian history. For all the scale, drama, and lasting controversy of a subaltern Christian movement approaching half a million members in Punjab alone by the end of the 1930s, a great deal in fact turned on a varied range of tempestuous local relationships between converts and mission personnel, based upon uncertain—sometimes unspoken—and constantly evolving terms.

These local relationships are the focus of this book, which places two rather different mission organizations in comparative perspective: the (Catholic) Belgian Capuchins and the (British Evangelical) Church Missionary Society (CMS). The aim is to bring into relief the role of personalities, aspirations, culture, class, and theology in generating the diverse mission presentations of Christianity and the ambitious convert and mission ideas about religious transformation and the meaning of conversion which shaped an unpredictable encounter in Punjab, from first contacts to the forging of new, post-conversion communities.

Despite the success of Henriette Bugge's comparative approach to mission and conversion in south India, in which she looked at the (Catholic) Missions Etrangères de Paris and the Danish Lutheran Mission,[1] the preponderance of Protestant missions in Punjab, combined with comparatively small numbers of Catholic conversions (though considerable in absolute terms), has until now meant that the mission of the Belgian Capuchins—the group given sole responsibility by Rome for the evangelization of Punjab in the late nineteenth century—has not been studied by a historian unconnected to any Church or mission organization.[2] Moreover, sustained analysis of the relevance of missionary backgrounds to their work in India has, despite calls from anthropologists and historians like Andrew Porter, remained limited.[3] Important exceptions such as a study on South Africa by Jean and John Comaroff notwithstanding,[4] there remains little of the kind of

[1] Henriette Bugge, *Mission and Tamil Society: Social and Religious Change in South India 1840–1900* (Richmond, 1994).

[2] To the best of my knowledge, and that of the archivists in Antwerp and Rome, this is the case. The scholarship and personal assistance of Fr. John Rooney has, however, been indispensable in my use of archival material relating to the Capuchins.

[3] See e.g. Andrew Porter, 'Cambridge, Keswick and Late Nineteenth Century Attitudes to Africa', *Journal of Imperial and Commonwealth History*, 5/1 (1976), and id., 'Evangelical Enthusiasm, Missionary Motivation and West Africa in the Late Nineteenth Century: The Career of G. W. Brooke', *Journal of Imperial and Commonwealth History*, 6/1 (1977).

[4] Jean and John Comaroff, *Of Revelation and Revolution: Christianity, Colonialism and Consciousness in South Africa* (Chicago, 1991). Other useful studies which have looked at the domestic backgrounds of mission societies include Max Warren, *Social History and Christian Mission* (London, 1967) and Stuart Piggin, *Making Evangelical Missionaries, 1789–1858* (Abingdon, 1984).

investigation to which another powerful interventionist force in Indian society, the Indian Civil Service (ICS), has been subjected.[5]

Many of the themes addressed in this volume flow from the notion of 'religious transformation'. Firstly, transformation from what to what? How did convert understandings emerge of where they had come from and what they were to become through association with Christianity? How did CMS and Capuchin missionaries construct their own understandings of the lives and recent past of their expanding flocks, and towards what kind of future did they hope to see converts move?

Secondly, how appropriate is it to describe the transformation sought by converts as 'religious'? The epithet of 'rice Christian' was applied to poor rural converts at the time of the mass movements, by commentators who saw their conversion as a pathetic, cynical, and even 'denationalized' attempt to gain material advantage. Indeed, of all the avenues towards liberation explored by disadvantaged groups in modern South Asian history—education, social and political organization, adoption of the symbols and social behaviour of the powerful, peaceful demonstration, and violent insurrection—conversion to Christianity has arguably been treated in general historical discourse as the least honourable and courageous. Moreover, the treatment of mass-movement converts from the time of their conversion to the present day, in many parts of South Asia, has been such that conversion turned out to be less an escape from subalternity than an intensification of that status.

Given these accusations and outcomes, it is important to find ways of addressing the question of motivation in mass-movement conversions, but without simply wielding the analytical knife to segregate 'religious', 'social', and 'material'. There is a need to develop an alternative approach to investigating this emergence of a subaltern movement, through an open-ended evaluation of what the terms 'religious' and 'conversion' actually meant in the mass-movement context. This was, after all, a period of the most intense competition in rural and particularly urban Punjab—as elsewhere in India—among social reformers offering multidimensional social visions and programmes, taking in basic education, social welfare, the status of women, new philosophical directions, and the pruning of what different individuals and groups regarded as

[5] See Clive Dewey, *Anglo-Indian Attitudes: The Mind of the Indian Civil Service* (London, 1993).

undesirable aspects of local or national socio-religious culture.[6] Where does conversion to Christianity sit here? As a protest against caste and the prevailing social system in general? As a strategy to move up within or to rework that system, rather than repudiate it?

Thirdly, questions about 'religious' transformation might equally be asked of missionaries. Recent scholarship by John Webster, John O'Brien, and Jeffrey Cox has gone some way towards reversing the popular impression that missionaries targeted the poor and vulnerable in Punjab and elsewhere as easy pickings, and has shown instead how missionaries themselves were targeted by individuals and organized delegations from among these exploited rural communities.[7] How did this state of affairs affect missionary views of their task in Punjab? Did the poverty of catechumens and converts demand a shift in their notion of religious transformation? Were missionary ideas here essentially uniform, with only cosmetic points of difference between denominations, or did their visions for religious transformation reflect particular, distinctive moments in the theological, social, and cultural development of their respective mission organizations, and of the societies from which they came.

Transformation also prompts questions about agency: what were the roles of local Punjabi leaders, ordinary converts, other villagers, foreign missionaries, and Indian (usually Punjabi) catechists and other mission-Church employees in driving the mass movements? How much was shaped by shared purpose and how much by conflict?[8] There was certainly no shortage of the latter, as converts demonstrated independence from their village communities through the act of conversion itself (sometimes literally parading the fact when Christian festivals or other special occasions allowed), and through weathering landlord anger and

[6] See Kenneth W. Jones, *Socio-Religious Reform Movements in British India* (Cambridge, 1989), and id., *Arya Dharm: Hindu Consciousness in 19th Century Punjab* (New Delhi, 1976); Richard G. Fox, 'Urban Class and Communal Consciousness in Colonial Punjab: The Genesis of India's Intermediate Regime', *Modern Asian Studies*, 8/3 (1984); Charles Heimsath, *Indian Nationalism and Hindu Social Reform* (Princeton, 1964); Susan Bayly, *Caste, Society and Politics in India from the Eighteenth Century to the Modern Age* (Cambridge, 1999).

[7] John C. B. Webster, *A History of the Dalit Christians* (San Francisco, 1992); John O'Brien, *The Construction of Pakistani Christian Identity* (Lahore, 2006); Jeffrey Cox, *Imperial Fault Lines: Christianity and Colonial Power in India, 1818–1940* (Stanford, 2002).

[8] This book uses the term 'mission-Church' to describe evangelistic and pastoral structures in Punjab that were staffed and controlled jointly—although not equally—by European and Punjabi personnel.

violence in response to their new affiliation. They underscored their autonomy from the missions too on regular occasions, from daily disagreements over ceremony and behaviour to threats of apostasy and the withholding of rent payments from missionary landlords in newly created Christian villages.

The key to tackling these basic concerns and the array of questions which flow from them is to approach the convert–mission encounter as one defined primarily by presentation and perception on all sides, and to focus accordingly upon the particular contemporaneous interests and frames of reference of Punjabi converts and of CMS and Capuchin mission personnel. What follows in this chapter is an introduction to each of these groups and the ways in which this book seeks to address the particular questions and methodological challenges associated with them. First of all, however, a brief overview of the movements themselves will serve as a useful starting point.

CONTOURS OF THE MASS MOVEMENTS, *c.*1860–1930

Large-scale religious conversion was not a new feature of South Asian life in the nineteenth and twentieth centuries. Waves of conversion across the subcontinent to Christianity, Islam, Sikhism, Buddhism, and Hinduism date back at least as far as the 1500s and they continue to occur in twenty-first-century India, where legal, political, and violent physical repercussions against converts attest to the seriousness of the social challenge they are felt to represent. However, while India was under British rule, mass conversions towards Christianity took place on an unparalleled scale, mainly among low-caste rural peoples and overwhelmingly towards a range of mission societies that were newly arrived in the country. Beginning in the south as early as the 1790s and peaking in a number of regions across India between the 1860s and the 1920s, these mass movements prompted concern among a number of religious reformers, social critics, officials, and nationalist politicians.

From villages around Tirunelveli to Telegu country and Tamil Nadu, low-caste interest in Christianity was first noted by organizations like the (Lutheran) Royal Danish Halle Mission and the (Anglican) Society for the Promotion of Christian Knowledge. The result was a rise in Protestant Christian numbers in Madras Presidency to 75,000 in 1851 and then to 300,000 just forty years later, matched by similar growth in the Catholic Church.[9] Patterns were noted at the time—and have been traced more thoroughly in recent years—of individual local leaders, often the first to convert, spreading some kind of knowledge about Christianity and creating demand for education and for association with the missions. Small-scale education, sometimes in the open air or in cattle-sheds, was organized in response. This was run and frequently paid for by converts, and helped to give shape and a degree of permanence to these initial bursts of interest. Violence often followed, at the hands of local landowners who feared for their dominant local position and the cultural fabric which supported it.[10]

The interaction of caste and denomination added both complexity and controversy to the movements. The subcontinent had become something of a denominational patchwork quilt by the mid-nineteenth century, and there was serious disagreement among American and European Protestant missionaries over how to engage with the issue of caste. Some compared it with English notions of class. Others insisted that its roots lay so deep in the country's socio-religious DNA that the kind of top-down social osmosis through which some believed Europe to have embraced the Christian faith could simply not work in India. Attitudes hardened to the point where serious conflict flared up among Protestant missionaries and among Indian Christians from the 1820s onwards.[11]

At the local level a particular denomination sometimes became associated with a certain caste, to such an extent that other social groups of similar status would gravitate towards different missions or would avoid Christianity altogether in order to emphasize a distinct identity.[12] Converts were known to shift between denominations, depending upon their level of satisfaction either with their mission's local representatives or with the mission itself. Protestant organizations regularly claimed that Catholic missions profited cynically and disproportionately in this

[9] Figures quoted in Bugge, *Mission and Tamil Society*, 143. See also Sathianathan Clarke, 'Conversion to Christianity in Tamil Nadu: Conscious and Constitutive Community Mobilization towards a Different Symbolic World Vision', in Rowena Robinson and Sathianathan Clarke (eds), *Religious Conversion in India: Modes, Motivations and Meanings* (Oxford, 2003).

[10] On these themes, see the Introduction and survey chapter in Robert Frykenberg (ed.), *Christians and Missionaries in India: Cross-Cultural Communication since 1500* (Cambridge, 2003); id., 'Christian Missions and the Raj', in Norman Etherington (ed.), *Missions and Empire* (Oxford, 2005); Webster, *A History of the Dalit Christians in India*.

[11] See Duncan Forrester, *Caste and Christianity: Attitudes and Policies on Caste of Anglo-Saxon Protestant Missions in India* (London, 1980).

[12] Ibid. 83–4.

way since they were less strict in what they required of their members. It is difficult to gauge how far this was actually true, but it seems clear that, in any case, theological and other distinctions between denominations were generally distorted by converts' own socio-religious ideas and expectations and by the lack of sustained and in-depth contact between trained mission personnel and convert communities. So many Christians in early twentieth-century Punjab were unaware even of the name of their denomination that census officials had to ask local clergy to provide Christians with a piece of paper bearing the required information.[13]

The local mission agent was a key point of contact between converts and foreign missionaries, and a pivotal figure in managing disagreements and determining outcomes. The sheer diversity of roles played by these male and female mission agents—from peripatetic catechists and classroom teachers to medical workers and legal representatives—combined with the weight of local initiative, calls into question the significance of 'foreign' agency in the mass movements. It might even be argued that foreign missionary contributions were limited to providing administrative aid (including heavy financial input), together with the kind of occasional social interaction that some converts sought as a public advertisement of their raised social and religious status as Christians. Rural converts certainly trumpeted these connections from time to time: on one occasion Punjabi Catholics alerted fellow villagers to the presence of their visiting bishop with a volley of gunfire.

Unfortunately, details about mission agents, an important and diverse group, remain in disproportionately short supply.[14] Mission employers observed very little of their work, since huge distances in central Punjab meant that only sporadic contact between missionaries and convert communities was possible. On top of this, local agents' relatively humble place in mission-Church hierarchies, the conspicuous desire of many missionaries to emphasize their own efforts, and a generally low view of the quality of local compared with European personnel conspired to reduce their presence in missionary reports, letters, and diaries. The foreign female missionary effort is often similarly eclipsed,[15] and it is this vacuum of solid illustrative material that has helped to

[13] *Census of India 1891, Punjab Report*, pt I, 98.

[14] For recent work on mission agents, see Webster, *A History of the Dalit Christians in India*; Bugge, *Mission and Tamil Society*; Cox, *Imperial Fault Lines*; Heike Liebau, 'Country Priests, Catechists and Schoolmasters as Cultural, Religious, and Social Middlemen in the Context of the Tranquebar Mission', in Frykenberg (ed.), *Christians and Missionaries in India*.

[15] For more on this point, see Cox, *Imperial Fault Lines*.

prolong the life of an erroneous popular image of white European and American men as the mainstays of Christian mission in South Asia.

A common theme since the late nineteenth century has been discussion of the complex issue of motivation in conversion. It was perhaps indicative of the rather limited relationship that missionaries were able to have with the majority of rural converts that these early discussions were heavy with personal anecdotes and theological speculation and contained precious little evidence of extended conversations with converts themselves. This went on to affect the post-conversion stage of the mass movements. Mission strategies for Christian community-building were rooted in Western theological and cultural concerns, such as those raised in Bishop Waskom Pickett's book *Christian Mass Movements* (1933), rather than in a solid awareness of what converts hoped to gain from being part of such communities.[16] One advantage of this state of affairs for historians, however, is that problems arising within these new Christian communities offer valuable hints to the various motivations at work among both converts and mission personnel from the outset of the mass movements.

These questions of motivation overlap with a broader, final issue in the mass movements: legitimacy for converts, particularly where compatriots perceived a conflict between Christian conversion and nationality or where critics from majority Christian cultures set out to distinguish 'genuine' expressions of Christianity from flawed ones. In general terms, as Gauri Viswanathan has pointed out, the implications of conversion for politics and political identity run deep: conversion alters demographics, challenges 'national' cultures and the communal function of religion, and forces civil and political authorities to enter religious debates where minority rights are threatened.[17] In the Punjabi context in particular, urban converts who sought, in the 1920s and 1930s, to forge positive political connections and to assume the role of political intermediaries between the British Government and Indian nationalists found the flipside of their perceived neutrality in major communal issues to be a certain marginality and expendability in the eyes of the main parties. For some, they were politically suspect by virtue of their closeness to what was seen either as a Western religion or at the

[16] J. Waskom Pickett, *Christian Mass Movements in India: A Study with Recommendations* (New York, 1933).

[17] Gauri Viswanathan, *Outside the Fold: Conversion, Modernity and Belief* (Princeton, 1998), pp. xi–xvii.

very least as one that had made unwarranted headway in India thanks to a Western imperial presence.[18] In general historical writing on South Asia, too, a primacy of the political paradigm—combined perhaps with the difficulty of analysing religious experience itself, as opposed to its historical ramifications[19]—has led to an almost undifferentiated 'missionary' type being identified with colonialism, while conversion to Christianity among the poor is seen as predictable colonial fallout and is rendered a mere footnote.[20]

Connections between mission work and 'colonial power', broadly conceived, in fact have a long and complex European pedigree. Seventh-century religious orders formed dioceses in newly conquered European territories, delivering up local populations for conversion and bolstering new rulers' claims to have lifted them out of barbarism and towards 'civilization and the opportunities of salvation'.[21] Similar services were later offered at the time of Spanish conquests in Latin America. But there were always ambiguities and conflicts in the relationship between missionaries and political authorities. In Latin America missionaries were both standard-bearers for the religious and intellectual culture on which expansionary powers based their claims of superiority and, at the same time, guardians of European moral conscience. For instance, the Dominican friar Antonio de Montesimos castigated Spanish notables and a local governor in Hispaniola in 1511 for their 'detestable wars [against] innocent people': 'are they not human beings?' he asked; 'have they no rational souls? Are you not obliged to love them as you love yourselves?'[22]

In late nineteenth-century India, missionary talk of 'providence' in geopolitical matters, enthusiastic sponsorship of Western education and associated values, and supercilious moral condemnation (not to

[18] Gerald Studdert-Kennedy, *British Christians, Indian Nationalists and the Raj* (Delhi, 1991), 123–6; John C. B. Webster, 'Punjabi Christians and the Indian Nationalist Movement, 1919–1947', *Indo-British Review*, Special Issue, 15/1 (1988), particularly pp. 128–9.

[19] Rustom Bharucha, *The Question of Faith* (New Delhi, 1993), 14. See also the discussion in Viswanathan, *Outside the Fold*, especially pp. xi–xvii.

[20] Robert Frykenberg has sought to counter the continued 'conflation' of Christianity with colonialism while Jeffrey Cox has argued that a 'master narrative of imperial and western expansion' and more recent Saidian narratives have tended to make do with an assumption that missionaries were complicit in the broader imperial project, perhaps even serving as its ideologues-in-chief; Frykenberg, Introduction, in Frykenberg (ed.), *Christians and Missionaries in India*, 6–10; Cox, *Imperial Fault Lines*, 9.

[21] Paul Johnson, *A History of Christianity* (London, 1976), 134.

[22] Repr. in Gustav Gutierrez, *Las Casas: In Search of the Poor of Jesus Christ* (Maryknoll, NY, 1993), 29.

mention lurid caricaturing) of local cultures and religions contributed to suspicions about them as the shock troops of modern colonialism. Similarly, there were Evangelical officers in the ICS whose friendships with like-minded missionaries led them to offer considerable private support for missionary efforts (they could do little in their professional capacities to help[23]), including contributing funds, visiting mission projects, attending public baptisms for converts, and helping to generate donations at home in England.[24] On the other hand, mission groups like the Belgian Capuchins were at pains to distance themselves from the Raj, promoting themselves instead as counter-cultural and sometimes actively criticizing what they saw as the wrongly ordered priorities of the British in India. Some Evangelical missionaries too were dubious about official involvement in their work, believing mission efforts in previous centuries such as those of the Jesuits to have suffered as a result of ties to political power.[25] These anxieties were vindicated by the inclusion of churches, converts, and missionaries on the list of targets whenever twentieth-century Indian nationalism burst the peaceful banks which Gandhi and other nationalist leaders intended for it.

The greatest real advantages enjoyed by missionaries in late nineteenth- and early twentieth-century India came as a result of subtler connections between mission and empire, revolving around some Indians' identification of missionaries and Christianity with European scientific, cultural, and technological achievements, and political–military power. These connections were loudly advertised by missionaries themselves, when it suited them. A missionary working for the (British Anglican) Society for the Propagation of the Gospel in north India proudly recorded in his notes that with the help of a small globe he had informed his village audience that the vast British and Russian empires were built on a rejection of idolatry and an embrace of Christianity.[26] Missionary propaganda such as this caused problems of legitimacy for converts not just where accusations of foreign political agency in evangelism were concerned, but also in terms of the image of Christianity

[23] See Cox, *Imperial Fault Lines*, particularly pp. 31–8.

[24] Such men were in a very small minority by the 1920s, with the prevailing view being that mission activity strengthened the emerging nationalist cause. On the ICS, see Studdert-Kennedy, *British Christians, Indian Nationalists and the Raj*, particularly pp. 4–6, and Dewey, *Anglo-Indian Attitudes*.

[25] Andrew Porter, 'Religion and Empire: British Expansion in the Long Nineteenth Century, 1780–1914', *Journal of Imperial and Commonwealth History*, 2/20 (1992), 377.

[26] See Ch. 3.

as a foreign faith, coming to India from Palestine only via definitive cultural and philosophical modification in Europe—this despite Christianity's long history on the subcontinent, according to some accounts stretching back as far as the apostle Thomas but certainly pre-dating the Christianization of many parts of Europe.[27]

Having introduced some of the main themes associated with the mass movements—through to these final, broad implications for conversion—we turn now to the more specialized focus, upon grassroots conditions and personalities, undertaken in this book.

CONVERTS IN RURAL PUNJAB: LABOURERS, CHRISTIANS, 'CHUHRAS'?

Punjab, situated in the north-west of the Indian subcontinent (see Map I.1), was one of the most religiously eclectic regions of the country in the nineteenth and early twentieth centuries. Long a melting pot of Hinduism, Islam, and Sikhism, in the nineteenth century it was abuzz with religious revival, the rhetoric of socio-religious reform, and the fevered activity of a wide range of Christian mission organizations. Once missions started to note large-scale rural interest in Christianity, from the 1860s onwards, it quickly became apparent that the vast majority of those seeking some kind of association with Christianity were from low-status social groups—primarily what was described at the time as the Chuhra caste, from which around 95 per cent of rural converts to Christianity in Punjab were said by the late 1930s to have come.[28]

[27] See Frykenberg, Introduction and survey chapter, in Frykenberg (ed.), *Christians and Missionaries in India*. Evidence for a ministry of St Thomas is contained in stories handed down in South Indian Christian communities, passages in the early third-century document Acts of Thomas, and references in the works of prominent early Christian writers like Origen and Jerome. Suggestions that Thomas pursued additional mission work around Taxila are supported by modern archaeological discoveries near Taxila of coins bearing the name of a local king, Gondaphorus, who is referred to in the Acts of Thomas. For more information on the Thomas Christian tradition, see the relevant entries in Scott Sunquist (ed.), *Dictionary of Asian Christianity* (Grand Rapids, Mich., 2001), and the discussions in Susan Bayly, *Saints, Goddesses and Kings: Muslims and Christians in South Indian Society 1700–1900* (Cambridge, 1989), 241–57, which locate the tradition in its South Indian cultural context.

[28] E. D. Lucas and F. Thakur Das, *The Rural Church in the Punjab* (Lahore, 1938), p. viii.

THE PUNJAB

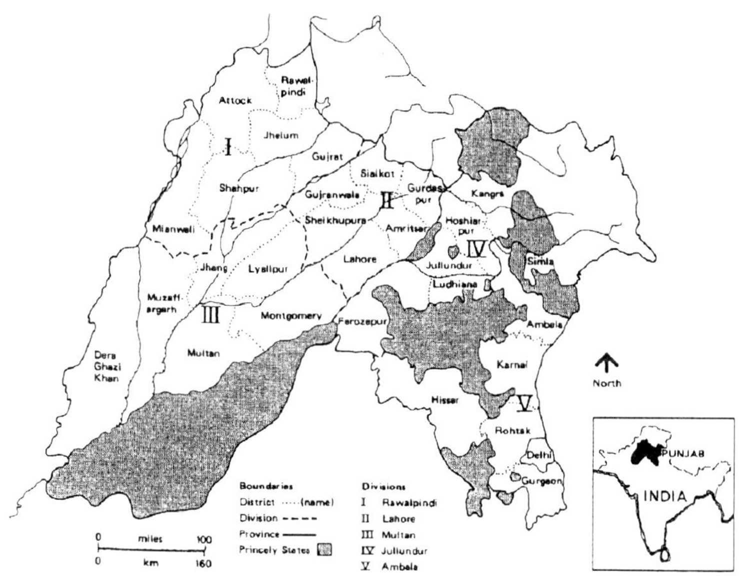

Map I.1. Punjab, *c.*1947.

Source: Imran Ali, *The Punjab under Imperialism, 1885–1947* (Princeton, 1988)

There are a great many problems with the word 'Chuhra': it distorts the self-ascription of the people themselves, its etymology is uncertain and the colonial British and missionary role in perpetuating its use contentious, its accuracy in describing a single social group in this period is debatable and probably unknowable, and finally, in many quarters of modern India and Pakistan it has become a term of abuse.[29] The use of the word 'Chuhra' in the writings of the CMS, the Capuchins, and the colonial British—ubiquitous and rarely questioned or disputed—is of interest to the question of how the CMS and Capuchins came to construct their ideas about who precisely their converts were, and from what kind of lives and prospects they were transforming them. But it is also of course disappointing, since it makes it all the more difficult to reconstruct convert lives and thought.

[29] John O'Brien has noted that in early twenty-first century Pakistan some Christians deny their caste background altogether, claiming instead to be Jats or Rajputs; O'Brien, *The Construction of Pakistani Christian Identity*, 459.

In order to avoid simply reproducing colonial-era discourse here, and in an effort to recover something of the multiple and shifting identities which drove the conversion encounter on all sides, this book employs an additional range of external designations and socio-religious self-ascriptions, including 'labourer', 'low-caste', 'convert', 'Lal Begi', and 'Bala Shahi'—the latter two derived from the names of local deities and heroes. The status of the term 'Christian', external in origin yet appropriated by rural Punjabis as part of their ambitions for religious transformation, is integral to the internal dynamics of mass conversion and is discussed throughout the volume.[30]

Uncertainties over nomenclature reflect the broader problem of a basic lack of information when it comes to the lives and perspectives of those in rural Punjab who took an interest in Christianity. Documentary source material generated by converts themselves is almost non-existent, owing not just to their low levels of literacy in the late nineteenth and early twentieth centuries but also to missionary processes of information-gathering. Whereas missionaries recorded and sometimes published testimonials or short biographies relating to some of their handful of educated urban converts, the far larger numbers of lower-status rural converts tended to be considered as a group. Missionaries appeared to find nothing particularly instructive or revealing about their journeys towards Christianity—it is open to question, of course, how much missionaries actually knew—and so a great deal more space in missionary writings, both public and private, is given over to generalities about the character of 'this people' or 'this class of people', together with missionary aims for their future.

As a result, it is rare to find individual names mentioned in missionary sources, and few of the questions which interest historians a century later were usually asked of converts—even by missionaries like Fr. Felix, of the Capuchin mission, or the Revd J. Youngson, of the Church of Scotland, who doubled as amateur local historians or anthropologists. Instead, the most influential CMS and Capuchin views of converts were amalgamations of first-hand experiences corrupted by language problems and a hectic schedule of village itineration, colleagues' anecdotes, contemporary European writing on Indian society, analogy with the rural poor of Britain or Belgium, and genuine (though, to present-day sensibilities, paternalistic and prejudicial) philanthropic and spiritual concern. This presents the historian seeking to glean information about

30 For a recent survey of historical and anthropological debates here, see ibid.

mass-movement converts from mission records with serious difficulties, which are discussed below in the context of the CMS and Capuchin missions.

One of the main areas of convert life which I seek to access here, and which is addressed in Chapter 1, is their socio-religious world and its connections with the wider world of the village. This was the context in which concepts of Christianity were communicated and refashioned, and decisions were made to convert. It also provided the model for establishing early relationships with the missions. Again and again in the mass movements the sheer unprecedented nature of events for all concerned can be seen throwing converts as well as mission personnel back upon prior experience in an effort to make sense of the situation and to formulate strategy. For converts, existing relationships of (profoundly uneven) interdependence in the village seem to have provided a basic paradigm for dealing with the missions, although as a complement to this the content of their private pre-Christian religious beliefs and ceremonies—what little can be uncovered—provides important insights into the patterns of thought and expectation which also appear to have played a role in their approach to the missions.

Another set of questions where rural Punjabis are concerned is whether mass-movement conversions carried inner meaning for individuals—as the Evangelical CMS in particular clearly hoped—or whether they were meaningful primarily in terms of identity at the family or wider community, *biraderi*, level. If the latter, then what was the role of socio-economic conditions in determining the timing and scope of the mass movements? Might conversion first and foremost have been a form of social protest, with the key moment in 'conversion' for converts themselves not their baptism but rather the earlier decision to seek association with the missions, whether taken collectively or by a particular leader?

Standing back from the movements to examine why they occurred when and where they did, Duncan Forrester has offered an economic hypothesis, suggesting that some rural low-caste peoples were rendered uniquely vulnerable by a gradual disintegration of old patterns of village interdependence in the late nineteenth century. The resulting weave of 'spiritual, psychological, social and material [needs]' pushed low-castes into the arms of new patrons.[31] This argument is problematic in the case of Punjab, however, since a detailed socio-economic study of the

[31] Forrester, *Caste and Christianity*, 74–5.

village of Vilyatpur by Tom Kessinger has cast doubt on the idea that old village ties were really dissolving in north India in this period.[32] Forrester's argument has been modified by John Webster, who has suggested that only a small minority of low-caste Punjabis were exposed to 'new orientations and new life-styles' outside their village or locale at this time. Yet as 'men of standing in their local communities', often moderately wealthy and well-travelled traders or local leaders, they were able to ensure a respectful audience for new and potentially beneficial ideas. Much of the important work of evangelization was thereby accomplished with neither the knowledge nor the participation of foreign missions, resulting in a pattern of expansion that baffled missionaries at the time.[33]

The details of communication and decision-making remain opaque, however. One of the possibilities addressed in this work is that although rural low-castes were largely removed from the emerging urban public arena of newspapers, journals, professional circles, societies, and conferences which helped to support the activities of social reformers and reform groups, a notion of community 'uplift' may nevertheless have filtered through to them via the leaders described by Webster and via the outside groups, missions included, who claimed to be taking an interest in their welfare in this period. In that case, meaning in the mass movements could in part be located in convert desires for 'uplift' of some sort, with a basis both in their socio-religious culture and recent experience and in European rhetoric of social uplift which was introduced into Punjab by missionaries and others.

Another possibility under consideration is that, from initial community decisions regarding Christianity, private interest and conviction in individuals may have followed. This is particularly significant because, alongside socio-economic causes and routes of communication which emphasize community and male community leaders, we must add the personal influence of ordinary women and men who held sway within their families. There is evidence to suggest, for example, that Catholic girls marrying into non-Catholic families were responsible for the conversion of many members of those families.[34] In any case, as a number of mission personnel recognized at the time of the movements, any pervasive spiritual dimension would be most likely to develop over

[32] Tom G. Kessinger, *Vilyatpur 1848–1968: Social and Economic Change in a North Indian Village* (Berkeley, 1974).

[33] Webster, *A History of the Dalit Christians in India*, 52–4.

[34] See Ch. 4.

time, with 'conversion' in this sense taking not days or weeks but years or perhaps generations.[35]

Finally, what place in the convert–mission encounter ought to be accorded the trained, organized, and paid local agents of mission? Recent scholarship on both India and Africa has drawn attention to the pivotal role, in perception and presentation, of this professional 'native agency' alluded to in the previous section: clergy, rural catechists and a range of teachers, medical staff, and general assistants. Important work on these figures by O. U. Kalu, Adrian Hastings, John Webster, Henriette Bugge, Heike Liebau, and Jeffrey Cox has depicted these agents as socio-cultural, religious, and linguistic interpreters, with pastoral responsibilities among converts and an important function in providing an intelligence network for missionaries.[36] This book explores catechists' training, workload, and loyalties, and the extent to which they embodied the traumas and compromises of the conversion movements. We must allow, however, for the possibility that these agents were *not* the linchpins that their job descriptions might suggest. Their individual dispositions and their treatment at the hands of their employers had the potential to produce anything from pride and creativity in their work to a sense of mere wage labour.

BELGIAN CAPUCHINS AND BRITISH EVANGELICALS

There were missionaries in Punjab from at least the early 1800s, but by the turn of the twentieth century there were more than thirty Christian groups at work in the area, from (American) United Presbyterians and Baptists to Methodists, the Church of Scotland, the Belgian Capuchins,

[35] See, on this question, John C. B. Webster, 'Christian Conversion in the Punjab: What Has Changed?', in Robinson and Clarke (eds), *Religious Conversion in India*, particularly p. 352.

[36] O. U. Kalu, Introduction, in Kalu (ed.), *The History of Christianity in West Africa* (London, 1980); Adrian Hastings, *The Church in Africa: 1450–1950* (Oxford, 1994); Webster, *A History of the Dalit Christians in India*; Bugge, *Mission and Tamil Society*; Liebau, 'Country Priests, Catechists and Schoolmasters as Cultural, Religious, and Social Middlemen in the Context of the Tranquebar Mission'; Cox, *Imperial Fault Lines*. In the Punjabi context, Cox has drawn attention to the numerical predominance of women in the missions (both Punjabi agents and foreign missionaries), a fact disguised by male dominance of missionary record compilation, writing, and publication. Ibid., particularly pp. 5 and 76–84.

and the Salvation Army.[37] These last two were notorious for ignoring the comity agreements which were supposed to set territorial boundaries for different missions' spheres of evangelization. This was arguably a function of their effective status as the underdogs of Christian mission in the province—the Salvation Army heavily working-class and the Catholic Capuchins the clear denominational and cultural outsiders, a position used by the latter to enhance the down-to-earth image which they sought to project in Punjab, living among the people (see Fig. I.1). This was in conscious contrast to the majority of Protestant missionaries, whom the Capuchins saw as better-funded, too fond of secular Western dress, and too prone to hobnobbing in high colonial society when they ought to have been getting their hands dirty in the villages. Accusations of what was known (in an extension of the biblical metaphor of 'flock') as 'sheep-stealing' tended to be made disproportionately against the Capuchins, and not without reason: the Capuchins were open about the fact that they regarded Protestant converts as 'fair game'—more so, in fact, than non-Christians. Whereas the latter were destined for limbo, Protestants were considered heretics and as such were headed straight for hell.[38]

The Belgian Capuchins' association with the north-west of the subcontinent, which continues to this day, began in the late 1880s following the ending of old disputes between Portugal and the papacy and the establishment of a Catholic 'Hierarchy' in India in 1886. The Friars Minor Capuchin were a sixteenth-century offshoot of the Franciscans, the Order established by Francis of Assisi in the thirteenth century which emphasized the personal example of a spiritually engaged life over and above the finer points of theology: Francis had worried that these might stifle prayer and endanger the virtues of simplicity and poverty in which he saw a crucial redemptive quality.[39] The Franciscans had been the first Order whose Rule made explicit mention

[37] See Cox, *Imperial Fault Lines*, 2, for a useful table of mission organizations active in Punjab around this time.

[38] The emergence of inter-mission bodies and a sense of ecumenism among Protestant denominations in the 1910s and 1920s had the effect of worsening relations in the short term, with Catholic missionaries even less inclined to give quarter to Protestant mission-Churches.

[39] See OFM International Mission Council, Mel Brady, Anselm Moons, Andreas Müller, and Flavian Walsh, 'Listening to Francis of Assisi on Mission', *Spirit and Life: A Journal of Contemporary Franciscan Studies*, 6 (1994); Cuthbert, *The Capuchins: A Contribution to the History of the Counter-Reformation*, 2 vols (London, 1928).

Fig. I.1. The first Capuchin residence in the village of Adah, *c.*1890. One of the two Capuchins pictured is likely to be Fr. Lievin (see Chapter 2).

Source: ABC, Photographic Archive

of evangelization beyond Christian lands,[40] and the work of Franciscan and Capuchin missionaries owed much to the evangelistic technique pioneered within Europe in earlier centuries of implanting monastic houses in new areas: generating a new community around themselves and helping to displace pre-existing religious attachments by forging deep new associations between the Christian liturgy and local festivals and seasons.[41] The Belgian Province of the Friars Minor Capuchin, formed in 1586, had drawn its first recruits from among the gentry of the region, and three centuries later its austere romantic ideal continued to attract well-educated men, often from the countryside, in addition to strong financial support from wealthy Belgian Catholics.[42]

Under the terms of the Hierarchy the Belgian Capuchins were entrusted with a new Catholic diocese of Lahore, which extended as far as Kashmir in the north, Bahawalpur in the south, the rivers Chenab and Jhelum in the west, and Kangra, Ludhiana, and Ferozepur in the east and south-east (see Maps I.1 and 2.2). Before 1884 any mission area given to the Capuchins would have been administered centrally by the General of the Order in Rome, but under new rules the entire responsibility for mission work now fell to a particular province of the Order. The Capuchin Provincial in Antwerp thus had effective control over all decisions about who would go to Punjab, how they ought to be trained, who would return home, and how funds would be collected

[40] Francis created the Rule for his Order after hearing a sermon on the 'Great Commission'—the command to go out and preach the Gospel that Jesus was believed to have given to his disciples: 'These twelve Jesus sent out; but first gave them their instructions . . . Preach as you go, telling them, the kingdom of heaven is at hand. Heal the sick . . . cleanse the lepers. Do not provide gold or silver or coppers to fill your purses, nor a wallet for the journey, no second coat, no spare shoes or staff; the labourer has a right to his maintenance. Whenever you enter a city or village, find out who is worthy to be your host, and make your lodging there until you go away . . . Go therefore and make disciples of all nations, baptising them in the name of the Father and of the Son and of the Holy Spirit, teaching them to observe all that I have commanded you' (Matt. 10: 5–11, 19–20). See Juniper Cummings, 'Saint Francis and the Missions', *Spirit and Life: A Journal of Contemporary Franciscan Studies*, 6 (1994), 27. See also Hilarin Felder, *The Ideals of St Francis of Assisi* (Paderborn, 1951), 317. Francis himself travelled to Damietta, the front line of the Crusades, while other friars worked along the North African coast. John of Piancarpino was the first Papal Envoy in Asia, bringing a letter from Pope Innocent IV to Genghis Khan in 1246. By 1305 John of Monte Corvino had baptized 6,000 Chinese and translated the New Testament and Psalter into the vernacular. Charles V. Finnegan, 'Franciscan Evangelization: A Brief Historical Overview', *Spirit and Life: A Journal of Contemporary Franciscan Studies*, 6 (1994), 6–10.

[41] See Stephen Neill, *A History of Christian Missions* (Harmondsworth, 1964), 77–80.

[42] Cuthbert, *The Capuchins*, i. 221, 344; Daniel D'Souza, *Capuchin Missions in India* (Karnataka, 1997), 204.

and distributed.[43] The Bishop of Lahore and his Council were all drawn from among the Belgian Capuchin Order by the early twentieth century, overseeing a Catholic population estimated at 1,840 Europeans and Eurasians and fewer than 700 Indians in 1891. The archives of the Belgian Capuchins are based at their provincial headquarters in Antwerp and at the Generalate in Rome, and include letters between European missionaries and their superiors in Lahore, Antwerp, and Rome; reports, statistics, and short profiles of some of the missionaries; a number of rare publications; and a large selection of photographs.[44]

The CMS presence in Punjab pre-dated that of the Capuchins by some thirty-five years. They were invited into the province by British military officers as a 'thank-offering to Almighty God for His late mercies'—a reference to the annexation of Punjab in 1849[45]—and enjoyed official support in its unofficial capacity: private financial donations, logistical expertise in locating and constructing urban mission infrastructure, and the kudos of close association with imperial power. The main decision-making body in Punjab was the Corresponding Committee, whose membership reflected the nature of the CMS mission as a joint lay–clerical undertaking. The Corresponding Committee was answerable ultimately to CMS headquarters in Salisbury Square, London. The Society's archives are held in the Special Collections of the University of Birmingham, and comprise correspondence within Punjab, and between Punjab and Salisbury Square, as well as regular annual letters from missionaries to the Secretary of the Society.[46] Records of internal CMS decision-making processes are also available, together with a range of CMS publications (which contain detailed statistics for mission personnel, conversions and finances) and a range of missionary articles and official reports from the field.

[43] The Provincial's role in distributing funds was shared with the Bishop of Lahore.

[44] Two particularly significant publications, produced by the Belgian Capuchins themselves, are G. Pelckmans, *Dix Années d'apostolat au Pundjab* (Bruges, 1900), Headquarters of the Belgian Province of the Capuchins, Antwerp, Archives of the Belgian Capuchins (ABC), and E. Blondeel, *In Het Land Der Vijf Rivieren* (In the Land of Five Rivers; Antwerp, 1938), ABC. An additional Capuchin publication, covering the work of the worldwide Capuchin Order and held in most Capuchin houses, is the annual journal *Analecta Ordinis Minorum Capuccinorum* (Rome, various years).

[45] See Eugene Stock, *History of the Church Missionary Society*, 4 vols (London, 1899, 1916), ii. 205.

[46] It was conventional for the annual letter of missionaries, and other letters sent to the London headquarters of the Society, to be addressed to the Secretary of the CMS. In order to conserve space, correspondence references feature 'CMS Secretary' in place of the incumbent's name.

Both sets of archives, and mission archives in general, are appealing for their size, their standard of organization, and the detailed reflection they offer from women and men who were generally well educated, had more sustained contact with certain areas of rural Punjab than most British officials, and were less bound than the latter by political concerns in terms of how they acted and how they recorded their experiences. The challenge for historians and others now accessing these archives lies in testing how far mission sources can be decoded, interpreted, and squeezed for valid meaning where authentic convert perspectives are concerned, and in doing so help to answer present-day questions about the mass movements. There are limits here, and even where analysis of rare convert narratives—i.e. convert accounts of their own lives—has been successful in locating the heavy stylistic footprint left by missionary editors, serious concerns remain. These include the lack of contextual biographical detail for converts, missionary selection of convert interviewees and contributors (in many cases employees of the mission), converts' immersion in missionary language and concepts, and self-consciousness and possible self-editing on the part of converts, who usually knew that their comments were intended for an audience of mission personnel or Western donors.[47] Attempts at recovering convert voices in missionary sources tend, as a result, to be more successful in discovering common patterns in the missionary 'containment' of convert voices than they are in revealing concrete new information about how converts themselves thought and felt. This is of use in itself, however, helping to update the almost homogenized missionary image which still persists in popular imagination.

The approach to the missions and their archives taken in this volume centres around establishing key information about the backgrounds and frames of reference of CMS and Capuchin missionaries, from where a more informed comparative analysis of their writings becomes possible. This includes, firstly, an exploration of the nature and implications of fissures within the missionary 'type': between Catholic and Protestant mission societies; between policy-makers in Europe and missionaries 'on the ground' in Punjab; between the prioritization of expatriate and

[47] A case in point is a document penned by Ta'unga, a Rarotongan from the Cook Islands, which contained precisely the kind of grizzly account of cannibalism which missionaries might be expected to want to hear; Peggy Brock, 'New Christians as Evangelists', in Etherington (ed.), *Missions and Empire*, 140–1. For a recent attempt at recovering lost convert voices in this way, see Gareth Griffiths, '"Trained to Tell the Truth": Missionaries, Converts, and Narration', ibid.

Eurasian Christian society and the seeking out of 'the heathen'; between an emphasis upon urban proselytization and cultural–intellectual influence, and the advocacy of a simpler, rural base for new Indian Churches.

Secondly, possible origins of mission attitudes and strategies in Punjab are sought in the nineteenth- and twentieth-century experiences of European Churches. From basic theology and the rhetoric of social and spiritual uplift to ideas about education, total Christian formation, 'community', and legitimate authority within new Churches, European models and dilemmas will be shown to have informed the work of missions in India in important ways.[48] This is particularly significant in the mass-movement context as missionaries' experimental responses to an unprecedented situation not of their own making may be seen to have drawn heavily upon their understanding and interpretation of various aspects of European Christian experience. Hence, labouring families in Punjab came to share rural England's experience of aggressive and defamatory attacks upon private and nonconformist religious cultures, which were feared by established Churches as expressions of dissent, and as a rejection of external socio-religious authority.

This approach is complemented by the use of a number of other contemporary sources: the archives of the Society for the Propagation of the Gospel,[49] a number of Government of India documents (including the Punjab Reports of Indian Censuses, Reports of the Director of Public Instruction in Punjab, and District Gazetteers[50]), and the private papers of two ICS officers with a particular interest in rural Punjab: Lieutenant Frank Brayne and Sir Malcolm Darling.[51] Interviews have also been conducted with South Asian Christians and Church personnel, both in

[48] Whereas Henriette Bugge's assessment of South India supports this idea, John Webster has highlighted the significance of the Indian context for organizations like the CMS, particularly the 'ethos of the Raj itself and of the civil service'. See John C. B. Webster, 'British Missions in India', in Torben Christensen and William R. Hutchison (eds), *Missionary Ideologies in the Imperialist Era: 1880–1920* (Aarhus, 1982), and, most recently, id., *A Social History of Christianity: North-West India since 1800* (Delhi, 2007).

[49] The archives of the Society for the Propagation of the Gospel (SPG), which operated around Delhi and in south Punjab in our period, are held at the Bodleian Library of Commonwealth and African Studies at Rhodes House. They are particularly useful for the annual letters of missionaries and the quarterly newspaper *Delhi Mission News*.

[50] These sources were consulted at the British Library and at the Indian Institute (Bodleian Library).

[51] These papers were first looked at by Clive Dewey (see Dewey, *Anglo-Indian Attitudes*).

Indian Punjab and in the United Kingdom.[52] Finally, an analysis of post-conversion events—in particular early attempts to build Christian communities, including small Christian villages—is used as a way of gaining insights into pre-conversion motivations and expectations.

The structure of this book reflects its primary concern with the contextual frames of reference through which the various groups introduced in this chapter engaged one another. Chapter 1 explores a range of socio-economic and religious dynamics in rural Punjab which help to explain the outlook of low-caste Punjabis and their interactions with mission personnel. Movements for socio-religious reform contributed to a particular sense of social dynamism in parts of the Punjab countryside from the late nineteenth century. The notion of 'uplift' with which many reformers were concerned, from the Arya Samaj (a reformist movement within Hinduism) to the ICS officer Frank Brayne and the low-caste socio-religious and political group Ad Dharm, represented something of an intellectual continuum linking different social classes in Europe and India. Although low-caste communities are usually seen as targets rather than sources of uplift initiatives, their syncretistic and highly political private religious culture in fact reveals concerns that match the very essence of uplift: a combination of basic welfare, local power relations, and existential questions about individual and community survival. This had important ramifications for low-caste dealings with mission personnel who held a range of strong beliefs of their own concerning the meaning of uplift.

Chapter 2 looks at how two starkly differing forms of Christianity took root in the province: British Evangelical Protestantism and Belgian Catholicism. Investigating national and social backgrounds, theological convictions, and personal quirks—as well as a range of often colourfully expressed tensions surrounding money and policy—the discussion sets out to assess the importance, for the convert–mission encounter, of the fissures in the missionary 'type' mentioned above. The second half of the chapter introduces four rural mission stations as case studies: the

[52] These informal interviews (hereafter Punjab–UK interviews) were conducted with Protestant and Catholic families in the villages of Kalmar, Sarekhas, Dugri, and Sayekar in Kartarpur district, near Jalandhar City, and with a former resident of Clarkabad village (see Ch. 5) who now lives in the UK. Key topics included family history, village relations, religious beliefs, and forms of worship. Interviews were also conducted with Fr. Michael Ani, Catholic historian and parish priest of Jalandhar Cathedral, and Babu-ji Younis, a Catholic catechist in Kartarpur district.

CMS stations of Tarn Taran and Narowal, and the Capuchin stations of Adah and Sahowala.

Having built up this initial picture of low-caste Punjabi and missionary lives and attitudes, Chapter 3 looks at the ways in which Christianity was communicated across vast expanses of rural Punjab, the reaction of missionaries once they became aware that a large-scale movement of poor rural workers towards Christianity was afoot, and the various ways in which they sought to order and teach those entering the mission-Churches. Convert perceptions about Christianity at this early stage are crucial. Was there a tendency among converts to view it as a collection of ideas and resources from which they could pick and choose, or rather as a cohesive whole that would have to be either accepted or rejected in its totality? The role played by catechists in these early years of the mission–convert relationship is examined, from their training and workload to varying perceptions among missionaries and converts about what their main duties ought to be and how satisfactorily they were executing them.

Chapter 4 looks at missionary and convert attempts to construct a Christian community life in the wake of the mass movements. Frustrations on all sides are highly revealing of the expectations with which mission personnel and converts entered uncertain associations with one another. From contests over the question 'What does it mean to be a Christian?' and attempts by the CMS and the Capuchins to win influence in scattered convert communities the focus shifts, in the final chapter, to the Christian village experiment. Brand new villages, constructed by the missions on land reclaimed through canal irrigation in western Punjab, offered missionaries control of the natural, socio-economic, and religious environment in engineering the ideal Christian communities of the future. Free now of old, oppressive village ties that they had once hoped simply to renegotiate, the small numbers of converts who moved to the new villages had high expectations of their own. The CMS village of Clarkabad, pictured in Fig. 5.1, and the Capuchin village of Maryabad had the potential finally to stretch the mission–convert relationship to breaking point.

1

The Meaning of Uplift in Punjab

At the core of 'uplift' in rural Punjab was a desire for regeneration. How this manifested itself in concrete strategies depended upon two things: the nature of the problem and the experience and particular social (often socio-religious) critique that different reformers applied to it. Reformers could broadly agree that Punjabi villagers faced low standards of living and education, and that systems of village interdependence were not working to the advantage of all. The finger of blame, however, was pointed variously at a neglectful government, international economic change, overbearing landlords, carnivorous moneylenders, recalcitrant labourers (uninterested in the lessons of modern agricultural science), and an entire godless ensemble of Punjabis in need of Christian teaching.

It was not surprising, then, that uplift in Punjab took the form of a spectrum of different initiatives rather than any single strategy. Something of a broad common thrust can nevertheless be discerned, since many reformers were similarly motivated—not least by a self-image as the shapers of an ideal modern society—and often borrowed from each other's work. Punjab in the late nineteenth century was an increasingly vibrant and open market for new ideas, thanks to a proliferation of journals, newspapers, public lectures, bazaar preaching, societies, schools, and social events. Processes of exchange, challenge, and assimilation were more marked in urban than rural areas, but migration and trade across the province ensured that even those rural communities that lacked daily exposure to this world were nevertheless connected with it.

In this way nineteenth-century European notions of social reform, characterized by a genuine concern about poverty combined with a projection of middle-class values, found their way to Punjab both as abstract attitudes and as actual social practice, through the uplift efforts of ICS officers like Frank Brayne and of various European missions. Here they chimed with the outlook both of a new Punjabi urban middle class, taken up by the reformist Hindu Arya Samaj, and of various groups lower down the social ladder.

This reformist milieu in the province arose not just from a self-image as social leaders but also through a universalist conviction that what was good for one social group was good for another. So, for example, Frank Brayne and a great many European missionaries believed that the rural poor of Punjab were afflicted by essentially the same problems as the rural poor at home in England and elsewhere in Europe. Tried and tested methods of European social work were never far from these reformers' minds. This was hardly surprising in the case of CMS and Capuchin missionaries, most of whom arrived in Punjab with no experience of missionary work (or even travel) in other parts of the non-European world. Similarly, Indian groups like the Arya Samaj hoped, in time, to offer the benefits of their newly codified social values to those—low-castes among them—whom they sought to uplift.

One effect of this universalist and frequently moralizing tone of reform was to underline a tension, in both the European and Punjabi contexts, between those who by virtue of wealth, education, class, caste, religion, or nationality were external to the group whose regeneration they sought, and those who were firmly part of that group. Conflict surrounding this 'outsider–insider' distinction and the related problem of legitimacy for reformers could be partially offset, however, where the interests and aspirations of outsiders and insiders temporarily coincided. In limited ways, for example, Arya Samaj and low-caste Hindu agendas very briefly brought the two groups together, as was the case for middle-class reformers and labourers in rural England.

These dynamics of reform are key to an understanding of the ways in which rural Punjabi converts may have viewed their association with the missions. They are brought together in the pages that follow as an examination of the meaning of uplift in the Punjabi context, beginning with economic and socio-religious conditions in central areas of the province. The primary focus here, as far as limited sources allow, is upon low-caste life and 'Chuhra' religion in particular. A number of Victorian intellectual and practical roots of uplift are also considered, along with their export to Punjab and the uses to which they came to be put by a variety of aspiring reformers—all battling to win supremacy for a particular notion of uplift and a particular social vision.

'GOD HAS SAVED US FROM THEIR POWER': INTERDEPENDENCE IN RURAL PUNJAB

Village Economy and Society

Following annexation in 1849, Punjab found itself subject to a British administration which put a premium on rural peace, maintained through influential district commissioners in cooperation with local elites. The region was an important agricultural producer, particularly for export, and advances in farming techniques and agricultural science became objects of imperial inquiry. Substantial investment was made in canal irrigation, over 10 million acres of land being irrigated by 1931.[1] Punjab also became significant to the British as a prime recruiting ground for the Indian Army, due to the province's geographical location (particularly its proximity to Afghanistan), loyalty at the time of the 1857 uprising, and the supposed martial prowess of its people, noted by the British during the Anglo-Sikh Wars.

Map I.1 shows the main administrative divisions of Punjab under British rule. The precise borders of the province fluctuated over time but natural boundaries existed in the form of mountains to the north, desert to the south, and rivers to the west and east (the Indus and Ganges, respectively). The area of central Punjab around Sialkot and its nearby military cantonment was highly fertile and populous, attracting the CMS and the Capuchins as well as American and Scottish Presbyterians. To the south-west lay the canal areas where Protestant and Catholic missions established Christian villages from the late nineteenth century onwards.

Table 1.1 shows some major demographic features of Punjab in this period. It was a predominantly rural society, slow to move to the towns and cities and slow to acquire literacy. Shifts in religious affiliation show a relative decline in Hindu numbers at the expense of Islam, Sikhism, and—most strikingly, in proportional terms—Christianity, whose numbers increased almost tenfold in the space of fifty years. These shifts are further illustrated in Fig. 1.1.

[1] *Census of India 1931, Punjab Report* (Lahore, 1933), pt I, 52–3.

Table 1.1. *General statistics for Punjab, 1891–1941*

	1891	1901	1911	1921	1931	1941
No. of towns	178	171	139	146	177	202
Urban population	2,413,704	2,325,467	2,211,964	2,212,191	3,067,464	4,359,964
No. of villages	34,664	32,663	33,421	34,119	34,630	35,256
Rural population	18,453,143	18,004,872	17,762,992	18,472,833	20,513,388	24,059,855
Hindu	7,743,477	7,874,413	6,682,818	6,579,260	6,328,588	7,550,372
Muslim	11,634,192	10,825,698	10,955,721	11,444,321	13,332,460	16,217,242
Sikh	1,389,934	1,517,019	2,093,804	2,294,207	3,064,144	3,757,401
Christian	53,587	65,811	198,106	329,050	414,788	486,038
(Indian)	18,514	36,571	157,609	303,336	392,144	467,135
(European, Eurasian)	35,073	29,240	40,497	25,714	22,644	18,903
Literate males	675,941	744,174	717,384	755,344	1,097,044	2,272,650
Literate females	18,206	34,631	57,461	78,148	150,713	765,500
Illiterate males	10,421,196	10,198,531	10,274,683	10,550,921	11,783,466	12,809,600
Illiterate females	9,584,821	9,353,003	8,925,428	9,300,611	10,549,629	12,107,700
TOTAL POPULATION	20,866,847	20,330,339	19,974,956	20,685,024	23,580,852	28,418,819

Note: Figures are given for British territory only, and those from 1901 onwards exclude North-West Frontier Province. From 1911 a new definition for 'town' was employed which demanded 'distinct urban characteristics' rather than simply a population in excess of 5,000. For this reason the figures for towns and for urban population fell in 1911. In order to conserve space the categories given here for religious community are limited to the three largest religions in Punjab, along with Christianity. Other categories appearing in the Census during these years included Parsi, Jew, Jain, Buddhist, and Arya (Samaj).

Source: *Census of India 1891–1941. Punjab Report, Part II (Statistical Tables).*

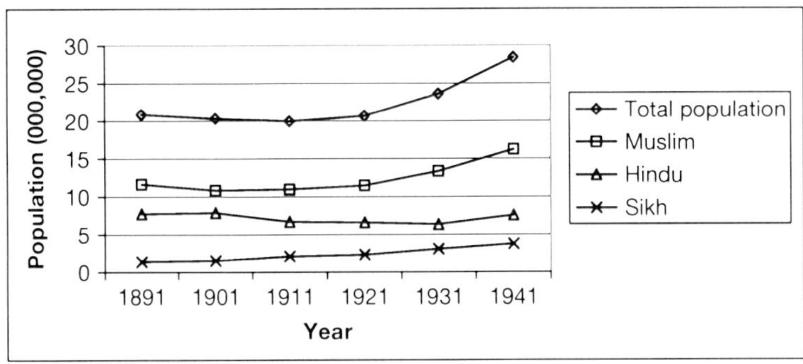

(a) Muslim, Hindu, and Sikh

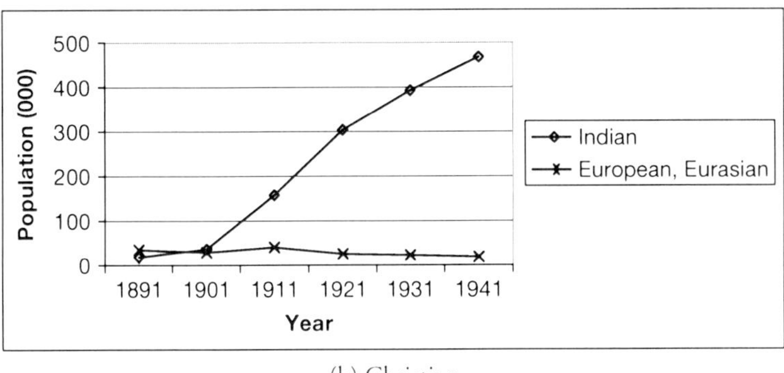

(b) Christian

Fig. 1.1. Religion in Punjab, 1891–1941. These figures are for the British territory only, and those from 1901 exclude the North-West Frontier Province. *Source: Census of India 1891–1941, Punjab Report, Part II (Statistical Tables)*

Land lay at the centre of economic activity in Punjab's villages, a financial asset for a lucky few and a source of income and employment for almost all. It was also a key factor in shaping local structures of authority and status. In Sialkot district five categories were used to describe different types of landholding. The patriarchal or landlord type, where an entire village might be owned by a single person (a founder or conqueror), usually developed into a 'communal' or 'joint stock' holding, where the land was managed cooperatively by the patriarch's heirs after his death. A third, 'divided' type arose if this joint stock was shared out among the heirs. It became a fourth, 'customary' type if population growth and migration required a replacement of familial with customary regulation. A fifth and final type existed where possession of the land became the sole basis for regulation, and all sense of familial or customary regulation had died out.

Smallholdings of the fourth or fifth types were the most common form of tenure since the population was large, marriages occurred at a relatively young age, and emigration was negligible in this period.[2] The passage of time tended to erode familial dominance of holdings in a given village, but landownership in Punjab nevertheless remained the virtual oligopoly of a handful of castes. As late as 1938 Jats, Rajputs, and Arains together still owned over half the cultivated land in the province.[3]

Although the size and shape of villages in Punjab varied greatly, and the British admitted to using 'village' simply as a term of convenience for census and land revenue purposes,[4] it was generally the case that the layout of villages and different types of housing reflected basic social distinctions, grounded in villagers' relations to the land. Larger villages in particular exhibited a strong tendency towards segregation based on caste. Where possible, moneylenders and merchants sought housing in the centre of the village, in order to provide security for themselves and their assets. Low-caste families were often forced to live in a small hamlet on the outskirts of the village, with a separate well.

The houses themselves were a further reflection of socio-economic differentials. In most villages of Sialkot district the houses of wealthier residents were constructed with mud and plastered with mixtures of clay, cow dung, and chopped straw.[5] In newer villages, houses might be built with sun-dried brick. Depending on the natural resources available, planks of wood or pieces of stone might be used to strengthen the structure of large houses. The additional security requirements of wealthy villagers were served by the building of a high wall of burnt brick around the house, creating an enclosure.[6] Poorer villagers had to content themselves with simple reed huts, comprising a single room which was sometimes shared with livestock. Their houses were simply furnished, typically with a grain jar, a smaller

[2] See *Gazetteer of the Sialkot District 1894–5* (Lahore, 1895), 85–7.
[3] Lucas and Thakur Das, *The Rural Church in the Punjab*, 2.
[4] *Census of India 1911, Punjab Report* (Lahore, 1912), pt I, 21.
[5] Lucas and Thakur Das, *The Rural Church in the Punjab*, 4.
[6] *Census of India 1911, Punjab Report*, pt I, 25.

jar for molasses, a wooden box for clothes and ornaments, and some cooking pots.[7]

Village life was governed to a great extent by the seasons, with a rotation of spring and autumn crops. Everyone had a well-defined economic role—even children, who tended livestock and assisted in planting, harvesting, threshing, and making crude sugar. Of the five main social groups in Punjabi villages—landlords, peasant cultivators, tenants, village servants, and landless labourers—the two lowest groups were reliant upon other members of the village for work and a share of the harvest. The place of low-castes in these 'interlocked' social and economic structures was usually as the *sepidar*s (customary employees) of higher-caste families.[8] This meant that they provided services directly to particular agricultural families in return for a percentage of the family's harvest or a fixed sum.

For men and women of the Chamar and, to a lesser extent, the Chuhra castes, these services often included field labour, and the division of time between agricultural work and 'traditional' caste occupations was highly variable. In Vilyatpur village, in Jalandhar district, Chamars worked in the fields only when their patron families required them to: in peak seasons or for specific, labour-intensive tasks such as weeding. Elsewhere Chamar men worked almost constantly in the fields, while women did any leatherwork which was required. Although these were generally long-term relationships, *sepidar*s might nevertheless move from one village to another, depending upon the availability of work. Other village servants, including potters, dyers, goldsmiths, and drummers, enjoyed a partial freedom from these ties by plying their trades in surrounding villages when they had time.[9]

In Sialkot district Chuhras were the second most numerous caste after the Jats. British officials enumerated them in two separate groups, according to whether they worked primarily as labourers or as 'sweepers' (disposing of human and animal waste). Vijay Prashad has argued that this was a compromise on the part of local officials, who were aware that 'sweeping' played only a minor role in the daily lives of most Chuhras yet were limited by standard census classifications.[10] '*Athri* Chuhras' denoted labourers, working the land and tending the cattle of (usually)

[7] *Gazetteer of the Sialkot District 1920* (Lahore, 1921), 67–8.

[8] Lucas and Thakur Das, *The Rural Church in the Punjab*, 2.

[9] Kessinger, *Vilyatpur*, 58–61, 75.

[10] Vijay Prashad, *Untouchable Freedom: A Social History of a Dalit Community* (New Delhi, 2000), 28.

just one peasant family in return for food, clothing, and a small share of the harvest.[11] '*Sepi* Chuhras' worked as sweepers to two or more families: cleaning toilets, making dung fuel, assisting with cattle, and running messages.[12]

Authority in the village rested with a headman, a hereditary position which, in the period under British rule, became nominally subject to the approval of the district commissioner (DC). Matters of revenue and crime—the two major concerns of the British in rural Punjab—were dealt with by the DC through the local *zaildar*, an official elected for the purpose by the headmen of a group of villages, or *zail*. Village politics was largely an extension of socio-economic relationships: in villages where one caste group was dominant, other groups in the village had no real political autonomy, and participated according to social ties with dominant families.[13] This was equally true in the rare cases where the dominant group was low-caste. Violence by dominant groups was not uncommon and there was often no effective recourse to external justice or arbitration.

Authority within the caste group was primarily a matter for the *panchayat* (a ruling 'council of five') and the range of sanctions at its disposal, facts of life among low-castes to which foreign Christian mission personnel adapted with varying degrees of success. Marriage too was of central importance to a given family's standing in the community, and is illustrative of the notion of *izzat* (honour, or status within the community) that was key to social relations in Punjabi society. Given the paucity of first-hand source material, any attempt to construct a sociological account of low-caste Punjabi life in the convert generation would be hazardous to say the least. There are, however, certain basic insights that are both reasonable and necessary to bring to bear, and one such is the premium placed by a great many Punjabis, including those of low caste, upon the maintenance of proper relations within the family and wider community, understood in terms of *izzat* and *be-izzati*, the latter meaning loss or diminution of *izzat*. These operated both across the entire village community and also within a given social group. 'Though we are poor,' one elderly man told researchers from Forman Christian College in Lahore, 'yet we marry our sons and daughters in a

[11] *Gazetteer of the Sialkot District 1894–5*, 98. [12] Ibid. 98–9.

[13] Kessinger (*Vilyatpur*) cites M. N. Srinivas, 'The Social System of a Mysore Village', in McKim Marriott (ed.), *Village India: Studies in the Little Community* (Chicago, 1955), 18.

manner that would bring credit to us . . . after all the izzat of the biradari has some meaning. . . even if we cannot afford, yet we must spend'.[14]

Among Chuhras, marriage involved a bride price rather than a dowry, and took place when a girl was between 5 and 8 years of age.[15] For all rural Punjabi families the process of betrothal was complex, involving the initial sending out of a priest or barber by a girl's father, followed by gift-giving, announcements, and finally the wedding itself. The detail of the customs and procedures varied, but high costs (relative to the means of the families) were universal. Births and deaths involved similarly intricate—although less costly—processes of informing, gift-giving, and the observance of rituals. The ceremonial value attached to clothes and jewellery, in addition to their functions of beautifying, indicating status and storing acquired wealth, meant that, much to the distaste of a number of reformers, large sums tended to be spent by people of almost all social classes on items like rings, bracelets, armlets, and necklets.[16]

Patterns of Conflict and Change

Socio-economic research conducted by students at Forman Christian College in 1938 offers a snapshot of rural Punjab at the end of our period. Debt, and the crippling terms on which it was contracted, remained the most serious problem for low-caste people, as for many other groups in the village. Causes of debt included heavy expenditure on marriage, pilgrimage, litigation, and jewellery, and the continued fragmentation of small landholdings as a result of inheritance customs.[17]

Care should be taken with this kind of microanalysis, however. It is indicative of the ideologically slanted accounts of rural poverty to which many uplift groups in Punjab adhered, playing down conflicts between different socio-economic groups in the province. In reality there was frequently disagreement, for example, over wages—reduced in real terms when profits were down—and over low-castes' rights to collect wood for fuel, to graze cattle, to use the village well, and to receive food, clothes, and tobacco as part of the *sepidari* relationship. Tensions were particularly high in times of famine, with a Karnal

[14] Lucas and Thakur Das, *The Rural Church in the Punjab*, 36.
[15] J. Youngson, 'The Chuhras', *Indian Antiquary*, 35 (1906), 85.
[16] *Gazetteer of the Sialkot District 1894–5*, 48–9.
[17] Lucas and Thakur Das, *The Rural Church in the Punjab*, 34–7.

district settlement report in the late 1880s claiming that Chuhras were even being deprived of their right to collect the carcasses of dead animals.[18]

These long-running conflicts were exacerbated by a second crucial factor: the disastrous effects of British agricultural policy in some quarters. This policy was part of a combined socio-economic and political strategy aimed at the formation of an insulated, conservative, loyal, and productive countryside as the bedrock of a stable and prosperous region. Its success was evident in the cultural distance which opened up between a highly educated, self-conscious, and (to varying degrees) anti-British urban middle class, swift to take advantage of new administrative posts and commercial opportunities, and generally collaborative rural landowning and cultivator classes who formed the pro-British Punjab Unionist Party (PUP) in 1923.[19]

Although some rural elites were grateful for freedom, under British rule, from old fears of arbitrary extraction by rival powers and for a relative rise in income, their continued support was nevertheless carefully cultivated by the British through protectionist legislation, a relative lowering of land revenue payments, and a range of perks including durbar seats, gifts of guns and swords, and exemptions from the ignominy of court appearances.[20] Early Punjab administrators were steeped in Victorian Romanticism and went to great lengths to bring what they saw as 'manly' agricultural groups like the Jats on-side, compiling detailed lists and histories of major families and offering them influential positions such as honorary magistrate, municipal commissioner, and police inspector.[21] Younger members of this elevated group could

[18] Reported in Lucas and Thakur Das, *The Rural Church in the Punjab*, 32.

[19] On urban Punjab, see Fox, 'Urban Class and Communal Consciousness in Colonial Punjab', 461.

[20] David C. Potter has pointed to the increasing politicization of ICS officials' work as a result of this need to find and retain collaborators. Such was the scale on which political 'bargains' were struck that Indians effectively ruled each other at the district level, unless problems with revenue or local order emerged. David C. Potter, *India's Political Administrators* (Oxford, 1986), 43. For a detailed account of British efforts to recruit collaborators in Sindh, see Sarah F. D. Ansari, *Sufi Saints and State Power: The Pirs of Sind, 1843–1947* (Cambridge, 1992). See also Prakash Tandon's personal account of this period: *Punjabi Century, 1857–1947* (London, 1961).

[21] At least two-thirds of these administrators were also Evangelicals, prompting the official biographer of the CMS to describe Punjab as a 'land of promise', ruled by 'devout Christians'; Eugene Stock, *History of the Church Missionary Society*, 4 vols (London, 1899, 1916), ii. 200–2. On early British administrative culture in Punjab, see Peter van

look forward to a suitably elite education at an establishment such as Aitchison College in Lahore.[22]

This system of collaboration generally worked well for the British in the countryside, with the PUP successfully holding off both the Indian National Congress and the Muslim League until the early 1940s. However, Punjab's economy suffered badly as new proprietary rights to land, the movement towards a monetary economy (through the collection of government taxes in cash), and higher prices for land and produce led many landowners to make ambitious and ultimately disastrous credit decisions. Landowners who had used their land as security on personal debt were ruined, as new civil and penal codes facilitated an alarmingly efficient process of land alienation to urban creditors. Civil debt cases multiplied after 1860, and by 1876 the administration felt the need to monitor the phenomenon by differentiating, in annual reports, between transfers to 'agriculturalists' and 'non-agriculturalists'.

With 500,000 acres a year being transferred to non-agriculturalists by 1886[23] and spiralling litigation and violence threatening the ruination of their rural establishment, the British came up with the Punjab Alienation of Land Act in 1900, effectively putting a stop to the transfer of land to castes designated 'non-agricultural'. In practice, however, this simply meant that the moneylending business changed hands, with wealthy agriculturalists now offering even harsher terms of credit than their urban predecessors. By 1929 peasant debt in the province stood at Rs 330 *crores*, the equivalent of each person in Punjab owing in excess of an entire year's income to moneylenders. The Punjab Provincial Banking Commission discovered that moneylending to agriculturalists was now Punjab's largest industry.[24]

It was indicative of the way village interdependence operated that landowners and cultivators now passed these problems on, as far as possible, to labourers and others who were locked into their service. This tactic was actually facilitated by the British in three ways: by their acceptance that certain social groups naturally performed subordinate,

den Dungen, *The Punjab Tradition: Influence and Authority in Nineteenth Century India* (London, 1972).

[22] I. Talbot, *Punjab and the Raj, 1849–1947* (New Delhi, 1988), 49–50, 57. See also Sir Lepel Griffin, *Panjab Chiefs* (Lahore, 1865).

[23] N. Gerald Barrier, *Punjab Alienation of Land Bill of 1900* (Durham, NC, 1966), 23.

[24] Ibid. 161.

assisting roles in cultivation; by their designation of low-castes as 'non-agriculturalists'—despite being aware that caste names were rarely a precise reflection of everyday work;[25] and by their flawed assessments of the customary arrangements which regulated village interdependence. These assessments, recorded in the village administration document, the *wajib-ul-'arz*, were often based on the word of landowners and tenants, who told officials what to record. Low-caste groups, usually ignorant of Urdu and unaware of their customary rights, were rarely involved in these crucial processes of information-gathering and were ill-positioned to argue their case in village disputes.[26]

Alongside these major socio-economic dynamics, which wove the Punjabi rural poor into vulnerable positions in the fabric of national and global economics, were a number of smaller-scale and locally variable patterns of change. A gradual early twentieth-century shift from *sepidari* relationships to the payment of annual and later daily cash wages was experienced by some low-castes, particularly Chamars, as steady economic liberation and greater potential for diversifying the work that they did. For many others with a limited range of work experience and low social status, however, the same trend towards casual cash labour meant becoming dangerously exposed and insecure.

Evidence given at the turn of the twentieth century by a Punjabi Christian pastor, the Revd Mian Sadiq, suggested that the socio-economic position of Chuhras in particular was actually in decline at this time. Families were squeezed between increasingly unsympathetic landlords and corrupt 'lower [revenue] officials', with some families forced into theft and vagrancy in order to feed themselves.[27] Capuchin missionaries picked up on this, claiming that many of the (Chuhra) converts sent to the new Catholic village of Maryabad in the 1890s were being saved from 'lives of thieving' forced upon them by their landlords. Even where menial was exchanged for non-menial labour the social stigmatization experienced by low-castes continued, at least in the short term. Caste prejudice could be eased by the renunciation by low-castes of behavioural traits deemed 'unclean' by other villagers, such as eating the flesh of animals that had died naturally rather than

[25] Vijay Prashad has shown that the decision in favour of the designation 'non-agriculturalist' for these groups was politically motivated, against low-caste acquisition of land; Prashad, *Untouchable Freedom*, 37–8.

[26] Ibid. 30–1.

[27] Archives of the Church Missionary Society, University of Birmingham (ACMS), *Proceedings of the Punjab Native (District) Church Council, 1899* (Lahore, 1900), 21.

being slaughtered in the proper manner, but poverty often made such modifications of diet impossible.[28]

The diversification of employment among Chuhras in the early decades of the twentieth century, which is apparent in census reports, gazetteers, and a number of studies, should not necessarily therefore be taken as a sign of improved economic fortunes. In many cases it was a forced response to deteriorating conditions of *sepidari* service.[29] In Sialkot district one of the biggest changes in the early twentieth century was the increased availability of construction and maintenance work on the rail, canal, and road infrastructure, much of which was taken up by low-caste workers. Sialkot's Chamars took to trading in skins, leather, and furs in this period, inspiring a new employment category in the *Gazetteer* in 1911. At the same time the number of Chamars involved in leatherworking fell (from 8,203 in 1904 to 1,766 in 1911), possibly suggesting a partial displacement of menial work with trade and non-menial labour. By 1931 enough people held second and even third jobs to warrant another new category in the *Gazetteer*.[30]

Even where low-caste people did experience positive social change, anecdotal evidence collected by British officials such as Sir Malcolm Darling suggested that, if anything, this reinforced rather than reduced competitive social distinctions. They continued to sit on the floor at village meetings, for example—'to show', according to one landlord, 'the difference between them and us'.[31] In a village where menial workers maintained a separate bank from local landlords, Darling was told that

[28] See Lucas and Thakur Das, *The Rural Church in the Punjab*, p. iii. An observer in the 1920s described Chuhra families driven by 'gnawing hunger . . . cutting off and carrying away parts of a dead ox, while fifteen or twenty scrawny dogs and a host of vultures crowd near, waiting for their turn' (H. J. Strickler, 'The Religion and Customs of the Chuhra in the Punjab Province, India', MS, 1926, 6, repr. in John C. B. Webster, 'Dalits and Christianity in Colonial Punjab: Cultural Interactions', in Judith M. Brown and Robert Eric Frykenberg (eds), *Christians, Cultural Interactions and India's Religious Traditions* (London, 2002), 94). O'Brien has pointed out that to describe this as the eating of 'carrion' is misleading, since the word 'carrion' implies decaying flesh, whereas low-castes in fact ate the flesh only of animals that had died very recently of natural causes—this 'natural' death sometimes hastened through the use of arsenic; O'Brien, *The Construction of Pakistani Christian Identity*, 494–5.

[29] Such was the case with Chuhra families who migrated to find work in cities such as Delhi. See Nandini Gooptu, *The Politics of the Urban Poor in Early Twentieth Century India* (Cambridge, 2001), and Bayly, *Caste, Society and Politics in India from the Eighteenth Century to the Modern Age*.

[30] *Gazetteer of the Sialkot District 1931* (Lahore, 1932).

[31] See Malcolm Darling, *Rusticus Loquitur, or, The Old Light and the New in the Punjab Village* (London, 1930), 65, 135.

'God has saved us from their power; we would rather get thirty rupees from our own bank than fifty from theirs.'[32]

This theme of separation as a group was in part the product of exploitation within the village system. Yet it was clearly elaborated by low-castes themselves as a form of collective defence and assertion, shaping both their attitudes towards village politics and their fundamental world-view. It is to this latter area of low-caste life, and to the beliefs, prayers, and rites through which it was expressed, that we now turn.

Religion and Low-Caste Identity

The first comprehensive assessment of religious practice in the villages of Punjab was made by an ICS officer, Denzil Ibbetson, and appeared in the Punjab census report of 1881 as a special appendix.[33] The account was read widely by ICS officials and also by Christian missionaries. Although Ibbetson's analysis was seriously let down by his use of nineteenth-century British Protestantism as a yardstick by which to judge Punjabi religiosity (Hinduism's catholicity, elasticity, and apparent lack of a strong ethical code were taken as proof that 'India's conscience [was] young'[34]), it nevertheless provided valuable observations on village religion's blend of Hinduism, Islam, and Sikhism with older animist forms of worship.

Ibbetson found that a major feature of rural Punjabi religion was a pantheon of 'pure' and 'impure' gods and godlings who bore little relation to those found in the sacred texts of Hinduism, Islam, or Sikhism. Villagers had heard of Śiva, Vishnu, and Ram but regarded them, in Ibbetson's view, as 'too high company', their day-to-day world dominated instead by propitiatory offerings to these lesser deities.[35] H. A. Rose (Punjab Census Commissioner for 1901) later concurred with Ibbetson's findings, describing the resulting morality as 'not high'.[36]

[32] Malcolm Darling, *Wisdom and Waste in the Punjab Village* (London, 1934), 273.

[33] *Census of India 1881. Punjab Report*, pt I, *Appendix B: Extracts from Mr. Ibbetson's Report on the Punjab Census, noting peculiarities of the Hindoo and Mohammedan religions, as practised in that Province* (hereafter Appendix B). Another collection of extracts from Ibbetson's report was published in 1883: Denzil Charles Jelf Ibbetson, *Outlines of Panjab Ethnography* (Calcutta, 1883).

[34] Appendix B, p. vi. [35] Ibid., p. viii.

[36] *Census of India 1901, Punjab Report* (Simla, 1902), pt I, 160. Rose nevertheless noted a certain 'altruism' that operated within a given social group, something which interested him as a possible reason why there appeared to be little enthusiasm or call for Western-style public bodies in the province. Ibid.

This dichotomy of 'pure' and 'impure' was present also in ancestor worship, as a distinction between the benevolent and the unsettled dead. The latter were either men who had died without leaving a son, or men and women who had failed to settle into a second life. Villagers generally believed low-castes the most likely to become unsettled or 'malevolent' after death, and for this reason they insisted that low-castes be cremated or buried with their faces down, so that their spirits could not escape. Ibbetson noted that 'riots have taken place, and the magistrates have been appealed to, to prevent a Chura [*sic*] from being buried face upwards'.[37] The impression of serious local disagreement on this point is enhanced by an account given by a group of Chuhras to the Revd J. Youngson, of the Church of Scotland mission, in which they emphatically stated that Chuhras were *not* buried facing downwards.[38]

The available evidence suggests two major dimensions to village religion. The first was an acute awareness of the determining role of supernatural forces in people's lives and environment. The second was the association of religious affiliations and practices with individual and group identity. Both were apparent in the persistent problems which census officials reported with low-caste returns, particularly the groups they insisted were Chuhras. In 1881 it was found that a large number of these people had returned themselves as Chuhra under the headings of both caste *and* religion, while others gave 'Lal Begi', 'Bala Shahi', or 'Balmiki' in the latter category. These last two names derive from the same individual: Balmik (the Punjabi version of Valmik), traditionally regarded as the author of the Ramayana and claimed in low-caste mythology as an ancestor, and around whom the Balmiki (or Bala Shahi, in its Islamicized form) religion developed. Lal Beg is thought to have been a mendicant preacher of the Mughal period who built on this religious cult of Balmik, attracting his own followers in the process.[39]

At the next census nearly half of Punjab's 1,224,966 Chuhras gave as their religion a category not recognized by officials. The Census Commissioner, E. D. MacLagan, admitted that the returns left him and his staff 'rather more confused than we were before'. Rather than allocate more funds to clarify the situation he entered everyone as 'Hindu'.[40] Thirty years later, Chuhras remained 'the chief disturbing element in

[37] Appendix B, p. xi. [38] Youngson, 'The Chuhras', 310.

[39] This is by no means certain, however, and in some sources Balmik and Lal Beg are viewed as one and the same person. For a discussion on this point, see O'Brien, *The Construction of Pakistani Christian Identity*, 124–36.

[40] *Census of India 1891, Punjab Report* (Calcutta, 1892), pt I, 200.

the return of religions in the Punjab, on account of the flexibility of their religion'.[41] By this officials meant not merely the opaqueness of low-caste religion, as it appeared to them, but also an accretive tendency in the construction of ritual and myth noted by Ibbetson and others.

It is impossible to be certain about the social forces which contributed to this process of assimilation of ideas from Hinduism, Sikhism, and Islam, but the most likely explanation is that it occurred both under pressure from local elites—with low-caste communities, as suggested by Mark Juergensmeyer and John Webster, acquiescing to an extent in the domination of the local religious environment by their employers[42]—and as a more independent and self-conscious process, over centuries, of understanding and emphasizing distinctness as a group through religion. This latter process drew in religious signs, symbols, and beliefs present in the village environment to form a unique world-view that incorporated a mythical account of how low-castes had arrived at their current low social status. The names of figures invoked in Chuhra songs—Nanak, Brahman, Ram, Allah, Krishna, Joseph, Moses—offers an indication of the size of this conceptual palette from which low-castes drew in their 'tactical consumption' of local religion.[43]

[41] This time special instructions were issued in advance to Census officials to list all Chuhras as Hindus who did not use any of the other main faith categories to describe their religion; *Census of India 1921, Punjab Report* (Lahore, 1923), pt I, 178. The All-India Census Report of the same year claimed that the Census was not concerned with personal religion, but rather with 'religion in its communal aspect'; *Census of India 1921, India Report* (Calcutta, 1924), pt I, 108.

[42] Low castes modified customs (shifting between burial and cremation, for example; *Census of India 1901, Punjab Report*, pt I, 111), changed their names, and in some instances converted to one of these religions. Hari Lal, an elderly Chamar interviewed by Juergensmeyer in the 1970s, wore all the outward signs of a Sikh, including the turban, long hair, and beard. Yet Lal's knowledge of Sikhism was poor and he insisted that the Chamars of the village were not really part of the Sikh community since it was an upper-caste body only. In fact, as Juergensmeyer discovered during the course of his interviews, a low-caste man might go as far as giving his name variously as Ram Chand, Ram Singh, and John Samuel, depending on whether he found himself in Hindu, Sikh, or Christian company. See Mark Juergensmeyer, *Religion as Social Vision: The Movement against Untouchability in Twentieth Century Punjab* (Berkeley, 1982). John Webster has described a patron–client relationship between powerful local figures and low castes requiring favour, respect, or protection; Webster, 'Dalits and Christianity in Colonial Punjab', 95.

[43] It is difficult to imagine a more apt description of the accretive process than this, from O'Brien, *The Construction of Pakistani Christian Identity*, 621, based on M. de Certeau's phrase 'the tactics of consumption'; M. de Certeau, *The Practice of Everyday Life* (London, 1984). For a more in-depth analysis of the various sources upon which low-caste mythology drew, see O'Brien, *The Construction of Pakistani Christian Identity*, 97–138.

To the frustration of amateur anthropologists at the time, however, Chuhras were unwilling to give details of many of the songs which invoked these names—especially those that denounced mainstream religion and predicted future liberation—for fear of high-caste reprisals.[44] The Revd Youngson was nevertheless successful in locating a rare manuscript in a village in Sialkot district, which contained a number of Chuhra genealogies and songs, the latter sung at life-cycle ceremonies and regular acts of worship. One of the songs was to Bala Shah, according to legend born a Brahman and then tricked by his brothers into performing ritually polluting work:[45]

On the Resurrection Day you will be called blessed.
The followers of Ram and Rahim will hide themselves then.
I will send them to hell.
Making paradise beyond, I will show it to you.[46]

For European observers the salvific theme in songs of this sort suggested a closeness of Chuhra religion to Christianity. The Capuchins claimed that Chuhras in Punjab with whom they were acquainted expected their 'hour of rehabilitation' imminently, and from outside their own community.[47] This fits with similarly millenarian ideas among low-castes elsewhere in India. Followers of the Yogi Pothuluri Virabrahman cult among the Madigas of Telegu country lived in expectation of the end of caste altogether, and its replacement with equality.[48] Here as in Punjab such ideas were eagerly taken up by missionaries trying to convince potential converts—as well as donors at home in Europe—that Christianity was the fulfilment of low-castes' existing religious orientation.[49]

This self-image of a distinct community, embattled yet proud, was further expressed in a collection of beliefs and forms of worship which a recent study has attributed to multiple layers of religious influence over many centuries, from old animist formulations to later contact with

[44] Prashad, *Untouchable Freedom*, 69–71.

[45] Different versions of this central element in low-caste myth were recorded by official and missionary observers in Punjab, including both the CMS and the Capuchins.

[46] Repr. in Youngson, 'The Chuhras', 350–1. 'Followers of Ram and Rahim' referred to Hindus and Muslims, respectively.

[47] ABC, L781, Letter from Regular Superior to Provincial, 6 Aug. 1912.

[48] See Forrester, *Caste and Christianity*, 91.

[49] It was largely for this reason that Belgian Capuchins and other missionaries took an interest in low-caste religion, confident that Christianity could build upon and perfect existing religious traditions in India long before such an idea was formally developed by twentieth-century theologians.

Hinduism, Islam, and Sikhism.[50] The result was a form of religion very much concerned with the present life, forged over a long period of socio-economic marginalization and its attendant socio-religious pressures and compromises.

Among the most visible aspects of this religion were the open-air shrines to Bala Shah, made up of a mound of earth or brick, up to 6 feet high. At their consecration a number of objects were temporarily buried inside the shrines: gold, silver, and copper knives (one of each), a goat's head, and a coconut, all bound with a single piece of red cloth. Thereafter, at weekly acts of worship held on a Thursday, oil lamps were placed in the shrine and sacrifices were offered.[51] Chuhra converts to Islam (known as Musallis or Kutanas) and to Sikhism (Mazbis and Rangretas) seem to have continued to adhere to these beliefs and forms of worship in some measure, although it is difficult to gain an accurate sense of the extent. Marriage and funeral rites for Musallis and Kutanas appear to have been performed by Muslim *moulvies*, for example.[52] Complications surrounding the eclectic religious lives of low-castes proved to be a major source of confusion and misunderstanding among Christian missionaries, as subsequent chapters will show.

Table 1.2 illustrates in the context of Sialkot district the close links between religion and caste suggested above, and provides an idea of the extent of change in our period. The figures cover the major religions of the district and the particular affiliation of Chuhras and also Chamars. Against a backdrop of falling Muslim and Hindu figures between 1901 and 1921 large numbers of Chuhras dramatically altered the way in which they identified themselves to census officials. Usage of the caste name 'Chuhra' dropped from 63,811 to 1,231 over this twenty-year period, while the number of Christians in the district increased by 50,327.[53]

Alongside the subordinate role of low-castes in the village economy went a sense of separateness, reinforced by factors beyond their control: local

[50] See O'Brien, *The Construction of Pakistani Christian Identity*.

[51] Youngson, 'The Chuhras', 340, 355. O'Brien notes that even in 2006 Thursday remained the day for worship of Bala Shah in Pakistan, even among some Christians; O'Brien, *The Construction of Pakistani Christian Identity*, 294–5.

[52] W. P. Hares, 'Mass Movements and their Consequences', *CMR* 64/765 (Jan. 1913), 30; Youngson, 'The Chuhras', 310.

[53] Census officials in 1921 and 1931 were told not to insist that Chuhra converts to Christianity give a caste name if they did not want to; *Census of India 1931, Punjab Report*, pt I, 334.

TABLE 1.2. *Caste and religion in Sialkot district, 1881–1931*

	1881	1891	1901	1911	1921	1931
Religion						
Hindu	299,311	371,265	302,012	242,325	174,303	206,395
Muslim	669,712	685,342	716,953	604,801	580,532	609,633
Sikh	40,195	49,872	50,982	81,761	74,939	94,955
Christian	1,535	11,668	11,939	48,620	62,266	66,365
Indians	253	9,711	10,662	46,267	n/a	n/a
Europeans, Eurasians	1,282	1,957	1,277	2,353	n/a	n/a
Religion by caste						
Chuhra	78,980	18,419	63,811	23,895	1,231	1,688
Hindu	19,617	n/a	12,240	20,061	1,048	312
Muslim	59,363	n/a	51,571	3,803	169	30
Sikh	n/a	n/a	n/a	31	14	n/a
Christian	n/a	n/a	n/a	n/a	n/a	1,346
Chamar	10,672	12,791	8,157	8,045	8,639	6,594
Hindu	8,051	9,680	8,134	7,905	8,402	4,713
Muslim	2,621	79	23	n/a	n/a	1,364
Sikh	n/a	90	n/a	140	237	510
TOTAL POPULATION	1,012,148	1,119,847	1,083,909	979,553	937,823	979,617

Note: n/a = not available. The presence of a 'Chuhra Christian' Census figure in 1931 is unusual, since Chuhra converts to Christianity were usually no longer enumerated as 'Chuhra'. The table does not provide as accurate an indication of Chuhras' exchange, en masse, of their caste name for that of 'Christian' as it might. There was a general fall in the population at this time, largely the result of migration to nearby canal colonies. There was also a rise in Sikh numbers, reflecting some of the uplift and conversion work undertaken by local Sikh groups. There were also new conversions and reconversions to Islam and to Hinduism.

Source: *Census of India 1881–1931, Punjab Report, Part II (Statistical Tables)*; *Sialkot District Gazetteer*, 1904, 1912, 1936.

economic and power relations, provincial politics, British agricultural policy, social and socio-religious exclusion. In addition, low-caste people themselves played a role in delineating, contextualizing, and taking pride in who they were. Chuhra census returns and a range of other indicators suggest forms of identity that were limited and local, varying from family to family or perhaps village to village,[54] but nevertheless drawing on a shared tradition and featuring a private rejection of higher-caste values.

Looked at as a form of self-uplift—offering a blend of psychological amelioration, the underpinning of a combative group identity, long-term

[54] Detailed information on this point is in frustratingly short supply.

survival, and even salvation—Chuhra religion suggested an ambivalence about dealing with outside groups. On the one hand there was a keen awareness of the potential for exploitation, but on the other there existed themes of salvation from without, together with long experience of socio-economic patronage and interdependence.

'Outsider' reform groups, including missions, therefore faced a complex situation in trying to get their messages across. There was room for dialogue, but since reformers seldom start work with a blank slate, there existed the danger that a particular view of the world and concept of positive social change would colour reformers' interactions with low-castes, and possibly compromise any potential for success.

FROM LONDON TO LAHORE

Victorian Connections

> Two nations between whom there is no intercourse and no sympathy; who are ignorant of each other's habits, thoughts and feelings as if they were . . . inhabitants of different planets.
>
> Benjamin Disraeli, describing the gap between rich and poor in Britain.

The Society for Bettering the Condition of the Poor (SBCP), established in 1798, set the tone for the uplift consensus which emerged in later decades. Its members believed that the poor should be equipped to help themselves, through the inculcation of essential values of 'industry, prudence, foresight, virtue and cleanliness'.[55] This was the agenda of a generation of reformers who had learned the value and rewards of education and hard work in a rapidly evolving society, full of new opportunities. They were in sympathy with the relatively recent science of political economy, which was wary of government interference in industry and commerce and which suggested that poverty could be an important spur to initiative and hard work; the SBCP even took Adam Smith's saying 'the desire implanted in the human breast of improving its condition' as its motto. The wealthy should not, it was believed, be

[55] Introductory letter to the Reports of the SBCP, repr. in Boyd Hilton, *Age of Atonement* (Oxford, 1988), 99.

taxed in order to support the poor, and voluntary private benevolence ought to be carefully directed.[56]

The SBCP was led by Evangelicals, including Thomas Bernard and William Wilberforce MP, and by the mid-nineteenth century Britain's ambitious middle and upper-working classes were increasingly laying claim to the Evangelical spirit as the most suitable expression of their socio-religious outlook. In its early days in the eighteenth century the Evangelical movement had not been popular. An Evangelical MP, Sir Richard Hill, had made a habit of quoting the Bible in the House of Commons, to 'prolonged roars of laughter',[57] while the Revd George Whitefield reportedly 'drove fifteen persons mad' with his first sermon in 1736.[58] Yet by 1850 around one-third of Anglican clergy were Evangelicals and the movement's presence was felt in Parliament, in British universities and cities, and in the wider world, through new mission organizations such as the CMS.

The activism and sense of personal responsibility that characterized the revival had the effect of sanctifying the contemporary socio-economic hierarchy and protecting the role of the successfully industrious in forming and maintaining it. Uplift came to be seen as part of this duty: simultaneously an affirmation of middle-class leadership in society, a response to social problems that genuinely stung people's consciences, and a learning of the lesson in social politics provided by France in 1789.

The mainstays of this kind of uplift were a basic education and a healthy domestic life, provided largely through private philanthropy and a great deal of enthusiastic and sometimes poorly coordinated voluntary work. Rather than equip people to leave the factories and the fields—the sources of Britain's recent economic advances—education for the poor focused upon inculcating the values championed by the SBCP and teaching children to read their Bibles. Sunday schools proliferated, with attendance figures rising from 2 million in 1851 to 5.7 million by 1881.[59] Edwin Chadwick, one of the architects of the 1834 Poor Law, saw education of this type as 'prevention': the forestalling of the occurrence of 'any conception in the mind which can lead to the

[56] D. W. Bebbington, *Evangelicalism in Modern Britain: A History from the 1730s to the 1980s* (London, 1989), 121.

[57] Quoted in Paul Johnson, *A History of Christianity* (London, 1976), 370.

[58] Quoted in Stock, *History of the Church Missionary Society*, i. 35.

[59] Edward Royle, 'Evangelicals and Education', in John Wolffe (ed.), *Evangelical Faith and Public Zeal: Evangelicals and Society in Britain, 1780–1980* (London, 1995), 121.

commission of a criminal act', including 'offences against the common morality' such as vagrancy and trade unionism.[60]

Attention to domestic life was similarly characterized by measures that suggested a contemporary mindset unconcerned with distinguishing between social support and social control. Inquiry and intervention ranged from surveys of family conduct, housing, and sanitary conditions to investigations into the effect of cramped housing upon the sexual activity of inhabitants.[61] Malthusian concerns about population expansion—in particular the multiplication of the wrong sort of people—combined with a general view of moral restraint as the supreme Christian virtue to produce a level of objectification and invasion of privacy unthinkable in the case of middle-class households.

Women greatly outnumbered men in all aspects of uplift, from the provision of food, shelter, clothing, domestic advice, and medical care to Sunday school teaching and doorstep preaching. They were largely untrained, although married women adapted their household management skills to the task of uplift and the London Bible and Domestic Mission pioneered the employment of working-class 'Bible-women' to reach communities that found middle-class piety objectionable. These Bible-women were the first paid agents of British social work, fulfilling the function, within a class paradigm, for which 'native agency' later became essential in foreign missionary work.[62]

Working-class participation here was the exception rather than the rule, however. Despite the popularity of the notion of self-help, reformers' sense of personal responsibility and the mixture of compassion, disdain, despair, and fear with which they viewed their subject matter convinced most of them that social reform would be unsound and unpredictable unless its leadership remained in middle-class hands. Even the fathers of English socialism, Charles Kingsley, Frederick Maurice, and John Ludlow (the last famously criticizing Victorian uplift for helping people *in* their poverty rather than *out* of it[63]), displayed ambivalence with regard to working-class organizations such as the Chartists.

[60] A. P. Donajgrodski, '"Social Police" and the Bureaucratic Elite: A Vision of Order in the Age of Reform', in Donajgrodski (ed.), *Social Control in Nineteenth Century Britain* (London, 1977), 66.

[61] Ibid. 64–5.

[62] See below, Ch. 2 onwards. On Bible-women in Britain, see Kathleen Heasman, *Evangelicals in Action: An Appraisal of their Social Work in the Victorian Era* (London, 1962).

[63] Quoted in John C. Cort, *Christian Socialism: An Informal History* (Maryknoll, NY, 1988), 140.

It was indicative of resistance to radical socio-economic change among a great many Victorian social reformers that Maurice's Workingmen's College in London employed John Ruskin to teach men about art rather than politics.[64]

Uplift in the countryside was of a similarly outsider and palliative nature, premissed upon an idealized, hierarchical community—in this case a single landowner overseeing a harmonious moral and social order, guaranteeing regular church attendance and banishing pubs to a good distance.[65] Since many landowners shared Lord Derby's view of the countryside as 'a dull place',[66] it usually fell to local gentry and clergy to act as 'moral guide and true friend' to those 'living under every temptation to sensuality':

> It is only thus that their particular errors can be understood and combated, right reasoning set before them, and right feelings substituted for wrong ones. The mind and heart of the uninstructed expand themselves under such intercourse, in obedience to the natural craving of the human understanding for communion with an intelligence superior to its own.[67]

Rural uplift was also spurred by the Anglican Church's desire to stem the success of Methodism by reconnecting with its countryside base. Activist clergy set about refurbishing churches, making house visits, and establishing Sunday schools and sometimes day schools. Biblical metaphors of 'flock' and 'children' were used to present the social hierarchy in a benign and unassailable light,[68] while attempts to neutralize folk culture were epitomized in the turning of raucous harvest celebrations into a harmless Church-sponsored service and supper at which farmer and labourer were brought together to celebrate another year's successful battle against the elements.[69]

The intersection of Nonconformist religion with working-class radicalism in this period suggests that an Anglican clergy drawn from the

[64] A minority of activists worked to support social reform legislation in local government, but basic problems such as low wages were rarely dealt with; Heasman, *Evangelicals in Action*, 46–7, 68.

[65] The agent for the estate village at Sandringham boasted that villagers would have to walk at least 2 miles to find a pub; Alun Howkins, *Reshaping Rural England: A Social History* (London, 1991), 26.

[66] Quoted ibid. 75.

[67] Hugh Tremenheere (a Victorian reformer described by Donajgrodski as a 'traditionalist'), quoted in Donajgrodski, '"Social Police" and the Bureaucratic Elite', 62.

[68] Howkins, *Reshaping Rural England*, 68–70.

[69] In 1862 Convocation at Canterbury issued an order of service for harvest time; ibid. 72.

ranks of politically conservative university graduates, and whose social proximity to local gentlemen worked against their professional duty of associating with labourers, must have made for unconvincing agents of reform.[70] Few parsons seemed inclined to 'go local' as effectively as Joseph Spence, who became well known in South Lindsey for his zealous use of what was rather haughtily described as the 'vulgar idiom'.[71]

The result was that the element of social coercion implicit both in the clerical house visit (at once alms-giving and inquiry into domestic conditions) and in the selective dispensation of food supplies, coal, clothes, and blankets, was rendered all too obvious to labouring families, causing significant resentment. Even the observations of clergymen claiming in-depth knowledge of the labouring classes amounted to nothing more than the view—later reproduced in rural Punjab—that 'country-folk . . . pray like children and play like children. Play and prayer alike [ought to] be simple and wholesome.'[72]

The Anglican ideal of happy rural interdependence was felt to be an attempt to obscure the distinct socio-economic interests of labourers. Alternative labourer religion was, like its Punjabi counterpart, characterized by a profound impenetrability to external inquiry, reflecting origins in a distinct subaltern identity governed by labourers' relationships with both the natural and socio-economic environments. External observers in both England and Punjab viewed labourer religion as intellectually interesting—even poetic and suggestive of a 'nearer apprehension of the spiritual world'[73]—but at the same time backward and threatening.

In the English context, the increasing success of Primitive Methodism in tapping into and expressing labourer religiosity was a cause of concern for non-labouring rural classes. In addition to providing an alternative spiritual life, Primitive cottage-chapels gave labourers the sense of solidarity and common cause (so far achieved only by urban migrants) and the experience of public speaking, organization, and fundraising that contributed to the formation of labour unions and participation in local government towards the end of the nineteenth century. The fear

[70] On Nonconformist religion and working-class radicalism, see Eric Hobsbawm, *Primitive Rebels: Studies of Archaic Forms of Social Movement in the Nineteenth and Twentieth Centuries* (Manchester, 1959).

[71] See Jim Obelkevich, *Religion and Rural Society: South Lindsey, 1825–1875* (Oxford, 1976).

[72] A. H. Baverstock, *The Failure of the Church in the Villages* (London, 1913), 30–7.

[73] Henry Winn, an observer and diarist from Whitby, quoted in Obelkevich, *Religion and Rural Society*, 259. In Punjab the Revd S. Ghose noted 'stray bits of poetry' in Chamar religion; S. Ghose, 'Work amongst Chamars', pt II, *DMN* 2/4 (Oct. 1898), 44.

that these developments inspired in other villagers brought constables, mobs, and even the army into a battle to eradicate the Primitives from the rural landscape, underlining Primitivism's status as a 'Church of the disinherited'—a phrase used by H. Richard Niebuhr to describe a situation in which Protestant Christianity fails to overcome social divisions.[74] In this sense Primitive Methodism did for rural labourers exactly what Evangelicalism had done for the generation of ambitious middle classes described above: it expressed and catered for the needs and aspirations of a specific, independently minded social group.

Rural labourers' response to Victorian uplift was a rejection of the messenger rather than the message. Radical chapels echoed middle-class aspirations in maintaining strict standards of 'sobriety, neatness, plainness in dress and good behaviour',[75] while a disowning of 'plebeian' culture and the promotion of an ethic of honest work and pay became the foundation of the working-class self-image.[76] For women this was a mixed blessing (the ideal of the domesticated housewife began to replace that of the active field labourer, although women did achieve influence as Primitive preachers[77]), but the establishment of Allotment Committees by local government in the early twentieth century represented the beginnings of labourer control in matters of land and other areas of politics. Here was a form of self-uplift that promised a degree of freedom from external standards of correct behaviour.

Victorian uplift contained an element of clear cynicism and socio-economic self-interest, in the sense that major economic inequalities went virtually unchallenged, just as socio-economic surveys like that of Forman Christian College in Punjab tended to underplay the iniquities of the bigger political picture. However, for at least some of those who took an interest in urban and rural poverty what really motivated them was a social and often a religious conscience, closely bound up with a need to understand and to perfect both themselves and the world in which they lived. Frequent allusions by social reformers to the successes of science in achieving a degree of mastery in the world are particularly

[74] H. Richard Niebuhr, *The Social Sources of Denominationalism* (Hamden, Conn., 1954), 20–30.

[75] Alun Howkins, *Poor Labouring Men: Rural Radicalism in Norfolk, 1872–1923* (London, 1985), 52–3.

[76] Howkins, *Reshaping Rural England*, 223. By the 1880s the average Oxfordshire pub was apparently marked by relatively sober and peaceful socializing; Obelkevich, *Religion and Rural Society*, 86.

[77] R. W. Ambler, *Ranters, Revivalists and Reformers: Primitive Methodism and Rural Society, South Lincolnshire, 1817–1875* (Hull, 1989).

telling in this regard. Such social ideals had in common with religious ones the implication of universal applicability. This opened the way for competition despite the fact that a combination of imitation and shared basic aspirations meant that disparate groups in England ended up championing very similar strategies of uplift.

Punjab Pioneers? Lieutenant Frank Brayne and Sir Malcolm Darling

Lieutenant Frank Brayne and Sir Malcolm Darling served as ICS officers in Punjab in a period when the Service was on the wane in terms of influence, independence, and quality of manpower. Increasing bureaucratization, new political pressures in Delhi and London, the financial costs of the First World War—which had left 200 posts unfilled by 1919—and the preference of British graduates for lucrative domestic over fading foreign opportunities left most civil servants in Punjab striving simply to hold the provincial administration together and generally cynical of any grand plans that harked back to the 'good old days' of the early Punjab administrators. Brayne and Darling were exceptions to this rule.

Frank Brayne is notable in particular for his 'Gurgaon Experiment', launched during his time as District Commissioner there in the 1920s. In many ways his work embodied the 'industry, prudence, foresight, virtue and cleanliness' of the SBCP, as well as the ambition and voluntarism of his Evangelical (clerical) family in nineteenth-century rural England.[78] Brayne's was a forthright and intolerant style, lambasting senior ICS officials as 'unsympathetic', 'out of touch', and suffering from such an obsessive fear of Indian nationalism that they were ignoring a rural population in dire straits.[79] This dislike and disdain of many of his colleagues—vigorously reciprocated[80]—nevertheless paled in comparison to the harsh words reserved for sections of Punjab's rural population. Villagers in Gurgaon were guilty of 'bad farming methods',

[78] For more on Brayne's family background, see Dewey, *Anglo-Indian Attitudes*, 31–7.

[79] Frank Brayne, *Village Uplift in India* (Allahabad, 1927), 40–1.

[80] A friend advised him in the early 1930s of the 'appalling amount of venom which is expressed with regard to you . . . I wonder whether you have a single real friend in the Punjab secretariat'; Letter from H. H. Peterson (Secretary, YMCA, and Director, Broadcasting Station, Lahore) to Brayne, 13 Apr. 1932, BL, OIOC, Brayne Papers, fo. 34H.

keeping 'filthy villages', wasting their wealth on marriage and jewellery, resisting change, and blaming Providence for what was really their own 'stupidity'.[81] Gerald Studdert-Kennedy has suggested that Brayne's focus on individual responsibility—a testament to his Evangelical roots—left him bemoaning not merely the parlous state of people's education but also their supposed lack of the 'individual personality's power of judgement'.[82]

Such language was all the more objectionable to Brayne's critics in light of the fact that Gurgaon suffered from notoriously unreliable rainfall. To blame the indolence and ignorance of villagers in such circumstances suggested that Braynean uplift placed self-referential ideology over practical assistance. His School of Rural Economy, which opened in October 1925 with forty-seven students, underlined this, advocating uplift strategies imported directly from England and using texts written by Brayne himself. Brayne even published a book, *The Indian and the English Village* (1933), discussing English solutions to rural problems.[83]

Some of the School's work was undoubtedly sound—including initiatives in agriculture, first aid, infant welfare, and public health—but Brayne's hortatory style, insensitivity, and desire for centrality (epitomized in his open envy of what he saw as Christian missionaries' unfettered power to lead rural communities[84]) won him a great many opponents—from villagers themselves to urban critics in Punjab and further afield. He refused to listen to villagers' complaints that the cost of a new iron plough was too high, for example, nor could he be persuaded to drop his claims that heavy expenditure on marriage and jewellery was simply a waste of money and a distraction from the plight of oppressed women and unwashed children.[85]

As with many of his Victorian antecedents in urban and rural England, Brayne seemed to believe that it was in the nature of the poor to resist attempts at their betterment. His advocacy of agricultural credit societies owed as much to his belief that Punjabi villagers could not be trusted with money as it did to the need for safeguards against moneylenders.[86]

81 Brayne, *Village Uplift in India*, 9.

82 Studdert-Kennedy, *British Christians, Indian Nationalists and the Raj*, 136–144.

83 Lala Deshraj, 'Is it Village Uplift?', *Young India*, 17 Oct. 1929, Brayne Papers, fo. 48C.

84 'Practical Christianity', article notes, *c.*1933, Brayne Papers, fo. 39E.

85 Brayne, *Village Uplift in India*, 19.

86 Miscellaneous (untitled) article notes on rural uplift, *c.*1933, Brayne Papers, fo. 39B.

Brayne also shared his predecessors' hope that society's elites could be co-opted to the reforming cause, beginning, in the Punjabi context, with the setting of an example by English officers of how to cultivate small gardens in order to produce fruit and vegetables for the family.[87]

Brayne was generally as contemptuous of financial realities as he was of reticent ICS men and unthinking villagers. An anonymous letter to the Editor of the *Lahore Tribune* on 1 February 1928 revealed that people in Gurgaon had been made to wait 'years and years' for the final payment of their bills or salaries. Roads were badly out of repair and the sanitation of the villages remained miserably poor despite a very expensive health department. Brayne kept a 'disproportionate' staff for propaganda purposes, with Rs 40,000 spent on printing expenses alone during his Gurgaon campaign. The letter-writer saw Brayne's style of leadership as simply egotistical. Brayne had published *Village Uplift* from district board funds, and was in the habit of naming new buildings after himself, or after members of his own family.[88] Having placed himself at the core of uplift, any achievements quickly withered once he left Gurgaon.[89]

Although Gandhi took great interest in Brayne's ideas—writing to express his support[90] and giving *Village Uplift* a review in *Young India* which Brayne described as 'the best which any of my books have received, either in India or outside'[91]—he was nevertheless critical of some of Brayne's methods, in particular the expectation that reform could have permanence when it 'came not from within but was superimposed from without'. Brayne's system of village education was 'perfectly sound and difficult to improve upon', yet he had 'relied more on money for the success of his experiment than upon his faith in himself and the people'.[92] While Gandhi was not without appreciation and sympathy for the Christian element in Brayne's ideas, in particular the notion of

[87] Brayne Papers, fo. 29.

[88] *Lahore Tribune*, 1 Feb. 1928, Brayne Papers, fo. 46. Brayne's propagandist agricultural event the Palwal Show featured the Brayne Challenge Ploughing Belt and the Harry Cup for Gurgaon District Wrestling Championship, named after his son. Brayne was also accused of running another of his institutions, the Domestic School of Economy (established in 1926), on the basis of personal recommendations rather than proper entrance criteria; Brayne Papers, fo. 48C.

[89] Brayne Papers, fo. 46.

[90] Letter from M. K. Gandhi to Brayne, 25 Dec. 1934, Brayne Papers, fo. 36A.

[91] Undated draft of a letter from Brayne to M. K. Gandhi, *c.*1935, Brayne Papers, fo. 36B.

[92] M. K. Gandhi, 'Village Improvement', *Young India*, 14 Nov. 1929, Brayne Papers, fo. 48D.

individual regeneration, he could not accept the imposition of uplift from outside.[93]

Like Brayne, Sir Malcolm Darling prided himself on his personal contacts with villagers, and although his published accounts of horseback tours through Punjab suggest a keener sense of local and global economic forces and a more pragmatic approach than Brayne's, the two men's recommendations for uplift in Punjab did not differ substantially.[94] There was little discussion of the broader socio-political picture in Punjab and India as a whole, and no committed moral or legislative case was made for low-caste uplift. Profound socio-economic inequalities inherent in the *sepidari* system were denounced simply on the basis that the employment of menials militated against rural productivity and cooperation by allowing cultivators to view manual labour as beneath them.[95] Instead Darling focused on the 'recklessness' of litigation, elaborate marriage arrangements, and possession of jewellery, which suggested to him that rural Punjabis had yet to learn the difference between 'productive and unproductive expenditure'.[96] He advocated cooperative credit societies, just as Brayne did, and wrote openly of the need for 'moral progress' among villagers,[97] there being an 'intimate connexion between character and sound finance'.[98]

Darling also shared Brayne's advocacy of a simple agricultural education, both as a boost for rural uplift and as an alternative to the literary education that created, in wealthier village families, aspirations for urban

[93] L. M. Bhole, 'A Gandhian Critique of Planned Development in India', in B. P. Pandey (ed.), *Gandhi and Economic Development* (London, 1991), 5.

[94] Darling's major works included *Rusticus Loquitur* (London, 1930), *The Punjab Peasant in Prosperity and Debt* (London, 1925), and *Wisdom and Waste in the Punjab Village* (London, 1934).

[95] Brayne, *Village Uplift in India*, 139. Brayne thought that low-castes should be 'steadily drafted off to the canal colonies, given land and sent to re-instate themselves in the world' (Brayne Papers, fo. 29), while Darling simply noted gradual natural improvements in their social standing in some parts of Punjab.

[96] Brayne, *Village Uplift in India*, 327.

[97] Darling, *The Punjab Peasant in Prosperity and Debt*, 276.

[98] Darling, *Rusticus Loquitur*, 326–7. Cooperative societies were a success, with the amount of available credit expanding from Rs 30.29 *lakhs* in 1911 to Rs 817.91 *lakhs* by 1931. Within twenty years 17,000 such societies had been established in Punjab, and another 80,000 elsewhere in India; *Census of India 1931, Punjab Report*, pt I, 33. S. K. Bajaj has suggested that Darling's focus upon 'local factors' such as peasant behaviour, in the face of macro-economic imbalances which the British were not prepared to address, was merely a 'pious hope', and was based upon assumptions rather than solid evidence; S. K. Bajaj, 'Malcolm Lyall Darling: A Study of his Perspective', *Punjab Past and Present*, 14/1 (Apr. 1980), 177–81.

jobs that simply did not exist in sufficient quantities. Disappointed school-leavers were too often forced to return to the village, where villagers saw them as physically and mentally unfit for cultivation work.[99] Darling's educational philosophy was distinct from Brayne's, however, in that it did not view a sound practical education and professional aspirations for the future as mutually exclusive. Darling suggested that the middle-school curriculum feature agriculture, sanitation, and rural economics *alongside* literary subjects, and he petitioned the Punjab Government to focus its funding more upon primary and secondary than tertiary education.[100]

Finally, Darling's hope that popular religion would take a positive lead in protecting India from the possible corruptions of economic change suggested a link with Victorian notions of individual responsibility in subjecting economic laws to those of morality and proper conduct. Darling even wrote of a 'Gospel of Sufficiency and Service' as a middle way between the poverty of traditional village life and modern economic and technological development. 'Since [the villager's] needs will be few . . . he will learn to desire quality rather than quantity.'[101]

There is much to distinguish Darling from Brayne—class, social goals, grasp of economics, religion—but both men represent a significant survival of Victorian uplift ideals into early twentieth-century Punjab. A strong sense of normative and self-referential social reform pervades the writings of both men, at the expense of a vigorous and detached appraisal of the Punjabi context. The nature of their employment of course served as a limiting factor here, but even when such connections are put aside—and Brayne rarely paid them much heed—clear social and intellectual themes remain that were redolent of an earlier era in Britain and were closely related to the reform ideas of the Arya Samaj and the Ad Dharm.

Indian Movements for Reform: Arya Samaj and Ad Dharm

A wave of Indian reformers and reform organizations emerged during the nineteenth century that embodied a blend of Indian religious tradition and certain aspects of contemporary European culture, both

[99] Darling, *Rusticus Loquitur*, 358.

[100] Darling, *Wisdom and Waste in the Punjab Village*, 326–9.

[101] Presidential Address to India's Society of Economics, Lucknow, 1927, Darling Papers, fo. LXII/2.

secular—including the positivist philosophy of Auguste Comte—and Christian. In general these movements were dominated by high- and middling-caste men and women from areas with a long-standing British presence (Bengal and Bombay in particular), and featured, as Richard G. Fox has put it in the case of Punjab, an 'ideology, social program, ritual assemblies and educational institutions' that served the specific material and psychological needs of a new urban middle class.[102]

The improvement of the conditions of the rural poor was just one area that gained the attention of these reformers. Others included *sati*, infanticide, and issues of marriage age and remarriage. Although many of these reformers operated within a high-caste Hindu cultural framework, similar debates about 'modern' forms of social and religious practice emerged in Indian Islam, in Sikhism, and—increasingly in the twentieth century—among various caste groups.[103] The notion of regeneration was taken up almost universally as a means of improving the social status and professional prospects of members of the religious or caste group concerned. Newspapers, journals, and public meetings proliferated, in what has been seen as the precursor of the mass nationalist, communal, and caste-based political movements that emerged in the middle decades of the twentieth century.[104]

Our focus here is on the vision of uplift offered in Punjab by two of the most influential reform organizations of the late nineteenth and early twentieth centuries: the Arya Samaj and the Ad Dharm. Swami Dayananda Saraswati, founder of the Arya Samaj, made the full spiritual and intellectual journey from an orthodox Hindu background and education to acquaintance with all the reforming ideas of the mid-nineteenth century, through contact with Indian reformers, Christian missionaries, and British officialdom. The reformed Hinduism that Dayananda brought to Punjab in 1877 was intended as a pure, Vedic tradition, stripped of what he regarded as unnecessary post-Vedic

[102] Fox, 'Urban Class and Communal Consciousness in Colonial Punjab', 473.

[103] For an account of a highly influential low-caste reform agenda in western India, see Rosalind O'Hanlon, *Caste, Conflict and Ideology: Mahatma Jotirao Phule and Low Caste Protest in Nineteenth-Century Western India* (Cambridge, 1985), particularly pp. 50–88, 206–20. On socio-religious movements in Punjab, including branches of the Bengali Brahmo Samaj and the new Anjuman-i-Himayat-i-Islam (Society for the Defence of Islam, founded in 1866 in Lahore), see Jones, *Socio-Religious Reform Movements in British India*.

[104] See e.g. Carey Watt, 'Education for National Efficiency: Constructive Nationalism in North India, 1909–1916', *Modern Asian Studies*, 31/2 (May 1997), particularly pp. 367–74.

accretions including polytheism, the Puranas, and the high status of priests. The complex *jati* system of caste was rejected in favour of the Vedic notion of four *varna* groups to be linked to conduct rather than to birth. Equality for women was promoted through rights, education, and higher marriage ages. Arya Hinduism was also combatively exclusive and nationalistic, rejecting religious syncretism as nonsensical: religions were 'night and day' to each other, according to Dayananda.[105]

It was in Punjab that these ideas first found broad support, among a new generation of Western-educated middle classes to whose social and professional aspirations Dayananda's streamlined, rationalist, and highly ethical form of Hinduism strongly appealed.[106] An Arya *samaj* (a branch, or local association) was established at Lahore in June 1877. A set of 'Ten Principles' was drawn up which, while Hindu in essence, was expressed in a Victorian reformist idiom. The 'primary aim' of the Samaj was 'to do good to mankind . . . to ameliorate the physical, spiritual and social condition of all men', understood in social and educational rather than political terms. Principle Nine stated that 'no one ought to remain satisfied with his own welfare . . . the welfare of the individual should be regarded as contained within the welfare of all'.[107]

In action too the Samaj behaved very much like a Victorian reform society, using journals and fundraising meetings to publicize a blend of modern ideas about health, hygiene, and an ordered society with a rediscovery of core religious and moral values. Public life was reformed and sanitized, religious ceremonies drastically altered, and 'obscene' songs repudiated. The eating of meat and drinking of alcohol were viewed with conscientious distaste.[108]

The uplift of the rural poor in Punjab was clearly not an urgent priority. An Anglo-Vedic School came first, established in Lahore in 1886 with the aim of offering professional-class supporters a government-standard yet culturally sound education for their children. Only then did leaders of the Samaj begin to react to the drift of disillusioned rural low-caste Hindus towards better prospects in Islam, Sikhism, and Christianity, and even then only with the minimum measures required to placate low-castes who were calling for higher socio-religious status.

[105] Quoted in Heimsath, *Indian Nationalism and Hindu Social Reform*, 122.

[106] See Jones, *Arya Dharm*, particularly pp. 59–61.

[107] Repr. ibid. 321.

[108] Jones, *Arya Dharm*, 95. See also Fox, 'Urban Class and Communal Consciousness in Colonial Punjab'.

A *shuddhi* (purification) ceremony was invented in the mid-1890s, and was sometimes carried out for hundreds of low-caste people at a time. It involved no questioning of candidates about their beliefs and no religious instruction. Instead, following tonsure (for women there was a bath and a change of clothes), candidates were given a mark on their forehead and handed a copy of the *Bhagavadgītā*. Some received dinner, a small picture of Krishna, a packet of cigarettes, and a brief exhortation to pray twice a day, abstain from alcohol, and defend the temple.[109] According to the President of the All-India Shuddhi Sabha, the Samaj 'purified' around 60,000 to 70,000 Punjabis in this way between 1901 and 1910.[110] Only in rare cases was education in special Arya Samaj schools offered.[111]

Even this limited work with low-caste groups encountered strong resistance in rural Punjab. In March 1903 a crowd of 3,000 Meghs in the Sialkot area seeking *shuddhi* was reduced to a group of just 200 through the intimidation of Muslim village headmen, whose *sepidar*s the Meghs were.[112] Another 36,000 Meghs who did go through the ceremony around this time later suffered intimidation at the hands of village leaders, including the laying of false charges against them. They continued to be refused access to wells, sometimes with violence, and in extreme cases they were forced to leave their villages. Rajputs in the village of Pattansen who were tried and convicted for beating a group of them claimed that they had acted in response to a change in their *sepidar*s' attitudes. The Rajputs had previously been called 'Gharib nawaz' (Protectors of the Poor). They were now greeted with a simple 'Namaste'.[113] This suggests that in parts of central Punjab even uplift initiatives that were of little material significance could nevertheless have a profound effect if they were viewed as radical in socio-religious terms. Serious opposition to *shuddhi* voiced by members of the Sikh, Muslim, and orthodox Hindu communities appears to bear this out.[114]

And yet, although Arya conversion figures soared from 213 in 1911 to 50,884 in 1921, the attitude among higher-caste Aryas themselves

[109] James Reid-Graham, 'The Arya Samaj as a Reformation in Hinduism: With Special Reference to Caste', Ph.D. thesis (Yale University, 1943), 504.

[110] S. K. Gupta, *The Scheduled Castes in Modern Indian Politics: Their Emergence as a Political Power* (New Delhi, 1985), 134.

[111] See Lala Ganga Ram and Lala Charu Dass, *The Uplift Movement at Sialkot, Punjab* (Calcutta, 1914).

[112] Ibid. 5–9. [113] Ibid. 12–18.

[114] Reid-Graham, 'The Arya Samaj as a Reformation in Hinduism', 441.

was, according to British official observers, one of 'apathy' at best.[115] The majority of high-caste Arya Hindus appear rarely to have mixed with new low-caste members.[116] It is impossible to know the degree of satisfaction experienced by the majority of 'purified' low-castes, but there is significant evidence of some disillusioned low-caste Aryas leaving the movement to start organizations of their own.

This happened just as the widening of the electoral franchise under the Montagu–Chelmsford reforms of 1919 was serving to heighten the anxieties of Hindu, Muslim, and Sikh leaders at the apparently wavering loyalties of hundreds of thousands of low-castes. One of the new organizations was the Ad Dharm, established in 1926 by educated members of the Chamar caste who saw independent politics rather than the apron strings of the Samaj as the key to genuine uplift. Early leaders of the movement such as Swami Shudranand had been educated by the Samaj and had even worked as *updeshaks* (Samaj missionaries).[117] They now made use of this education and organizational training in the service of an insider uplift movement, designed to harness low-caste socio-religious identities in order to win political power. This was done through appeals to rural low-caste religion, using Ravi Das (a sixteenth-century Chamar *bhakti* poet–saint) as a figurehead and role model. In urban Punjab they promoted a set of practical ethical standards designed to appeal to a 'new species of lower caste entrepreneur'.[118]

Here was a pattern familiar from both the English and the Indian reform contexts: a new group taking a set of values already in circulation and reinventing them for a particular audience and purpose. Major features of the Ad Dharm cause included an improved status for women and a rejection of drinking, gambling, and bride money.[119] A dedicated newspaper, *Adi Danka* ('Drum of the Adi People'), was established, along with an executive committee which took care of correspondence, financial records, and mail campaigns to stimulate support for rallies.[120]

[115] *Census of India 1911, Punjab Report*, pt I, 152. Conversion figures for 1921 taken from Reid-Graham, 'The Arya Samaj as a Reformation in Hinduism', 432 and 442.

[116] Reid-Graham, 'The Arya Samaj as a Reformation in Hinduism', 519.

[117] Shudranand himself always denied that he had worked as a Samaj missionary but Mark Juergensmeyer was inclined to believe the testimony of another Ad Dharm leader, who suggested otherwise; Juergensmeyer, *Religion as Social Vision*, 37.

[118] Ibid. 83–8, 44. [119] Ibid. 121–3.

[120] Ibid. 55–6. Emigrant Punjabi Chamars as far away as Singapore, the United States, and New Zealand contributed to the cause and were represented on the managing committee. More than Rs 12,000 was donated from New Zealand in the Ad Dharm's first few years. Ibid. 59.

Samaj-style missionaries and preachers were employed. A final thematic continuity with other forms of uplift was the seemingly inevitable alienation of a lower social group—in this case Punjabi Chuhras and some Chamar sub-castes, who could not be persuaded to join the Ad Dharm in large numbers. Retaining legitimacy as 'insiders' was always a sensitive issue for Ad Dharm leaders, and the collection of money at mass rural rallies, for example, was arguably more important as a reinforcement of the movement's grassroots credentials than as a fundraising initiative.[121]

Ad Dharm leaders also worried that their numbers in the all-important census might be pushed down as a result of competition from the Arya Samaj. The latter's offer of improved social interaction with high-caste Hindus has been shown above to have been largely hollow, but it nevertheless had an appeal at the time. The Samaj might also lure rural low-castes away with pecuniary incentives or perhaps, given the many similarities of organization and presentation between the Arya Samaj and the Ad Dharm, some people might fail to distinguish between the two groups when the moment came to choose. Interestingly, the anti-Ad Dharm content of Samaj newspapers and lectures in the late 1920s and early 1930s indicates that they were as worried about the Ad Dharm as the Ad Dharm were about them. Despite these potential difficulties, and the hostile activities of Christian and Akali Sikh representatives, in Jalandhar and Hoshiarpur 80 per cent of Chamars returned themselves as 'Ad Dharm' at the 1931 Census.[122]

CONCLUSION

The 'outsider' uplift initiatives looked at in this chapter, often the product of an aspiring new group of people and bearing the stamp of their culture and values, had a significant socio-religious impact upon low-caste communities in some areas of rural Punjab. And yet ultimately they failed to effect thoroughgoing material change, not because low-castes automatically rejected external help or advice but because in these

[121] Ibid. 58. Nandini Gooptu has suggested that urban Adi Hindu leaders were generally able to retain the support of low castes, despite the formers' education, since they were recognized as having shared social origins with their audience; Gooptu, *The Politics of the Urban Poor in Early Twentieth-Century India*, 160.

[122] See Juergensmeyer, *Religion as Social Vision*, 49–74.

cases it was predicated upon visions of social improvement at odds with low-castes' own experience of poverty and powerlessness. Where outsider uplift had as its aim the better functioning of an existing interdependent social order, a broad generalization holds for insider uplift in the rural English and Punjabi contexts in that it saw society as defined by fundamentally conflicting economic imperatives. Real socio-economic gains were therefore to be achieved independently rather than handed down.

The journey from early nineteenth-century Britain to the Punjab Census of 1931 suggests that the most significant legacy of outsider uplift initiatives lay not in the direct results they achieved but rather in their constituent parts—education, forms of organization, notions of respectable living—that the rural poor found useful in their independent efforts to balance the social scales. This is an important dynamic to bear in mind where low-caste Punjabis' petitioning of Hindu, Muslim, Sikh, and Christian groups for attention in the late nineteenth century is concerned. They may well have been motivated by a desire for access to some or all of these useful constituent parts, rather than by an interest in the socio-religious whole. Equally, converts to Christianity may not actively have distinguished between the parts and the whole.

The success of Christian missions in exporting their world-view—and not merely a collection of skills and tools that came with it—would depend upon a convincing engagement with the socio-economic predicament faced by low-caste Punjabis, deeply intertwined as it was with their religious outlook. This implied a challenge for the missions far greater than simply transcending language and idiom. The backgrounds and personalities of the missionaries and the way they conceived their priorities and chose their friends in local society might well make the difference between success and failure.

2

British Evangelicals vs Belgian Catholics

RIGHT from the outset the Church Missionary Society (CMS) and the Belgian Capuchins offered highly distinct and competing forms of religion in Punjab. Through the basics of institutional expression like gender, clothing, comportment, language, organization, and architecture the two missions spoke volumes about themselves before so much as a single missionary mouth was opened. The CMS and the Capuchins also wove themselves into European–Punjabi society in very different ways. The CMS enjoyed a thirty-five-year head start in urban Punjab, where they formed close relations with a number of British officials and built a modest network of urban institutions and largely middle-class converts. The Capuchins were distinctly ambivalent about Britain's imperial project in India, in sympathy with some aspects of a *mission civilitrice* but as loyal Catholics culturally opposed to others. They enjoyed far less developed local networks than their CMS counterparts and often lamented among themselves the disadvantages under which they laboured, in a hostile environment made doubly heathen by having Protestants in charge of it.

The comparative exploration of these two Christianities that follows looks at relationships with political power and access to secular patronage of various sorts, mission finances and pastoral priorities, and the impeding effect on mission work of internal difficulties and disagreements—personality counted for as much in CMS and Capuchin circles as in any other organized venture. The four mission stations upon which subsequent chapters focus are also introduced: the CMS stations at Tarn Taran and Narowal, and the Capuchin stations at Adah and Sahowala.

ROOTS AND RIVALRIES

The Roots of Capuchin and CMS Mission in India

As with their Protestant rivals, Catholic fortunes in India were determined to a great extent by events thousands of miles away in Europe. Catholic mission had been invigorated in the sixteenth century by Portuguese and Spanish expansion and by a Counter-Reformation spirit from the 1560s onwards. At the same time as the Catholic Church set about reasserting itself as the true fount of Christian authority, the Vatican sought greater control over missions through the establishment of the Sacred Congregation for the Propagation of the Faith (SCPF) in 1622.[1] Although the SCPF shaped policy at a general level, missionary appointments and on-the-ground activity were determined within religious Orders and by local conditions in the mission territories. There were frequent contradictions. The SCPF desire that non-European clergy be trained as quickly as possible—a response in part to uncertainties in Europe—was all but ignored by most mission groups in regions like India. Similarly, the tone of preaching and teaching on the subcontinent was often far removed from the SCPF command for missionaries to adapt to local cultures as far as possible.[2]

By the time the Belgian Capuchins received their Punjab commission more than 200 years later, the Church's position in Europe had deteriorated greatly, losing wealth and prestige to Napoleon, credibility in the face of new intellectual ideas, and political influence at the hands of newly emerging Protestant powers. Hopes of Catholic reform were dashed by nineteenth-century papal encyclicals that effectively rubbished the idea of rapprochement with modern Europe. Rationalism as the

[1] Ludwig Freiherr von Pastor, *The History of the Popes from the Close of the Middle Ages*, 40 vols (London, 1901–53), xxvii. 132–4.

[2] '[Introduce] only the faith, which does not despise or destroy the manners and customs of any people . . . but rather wishes to see them preserved unharmed . . . Do not draw invidious contrasts between the customs of the peoples and those of Europe; do your utmost to adapt yourselves to them' (Instructions issued to Vicars Apostolic by the SCPF, 1659, quoted in Neill, *A History of Christian Missions*, 179). This new enthusiasm for the ordination of indigenous clergy arose in part from fears, inspired by events in Protestant Europe, that hostile governments in mission territories could easily 'arrest, drive out or put to death' foreign missionaries. Indigenous priests would be able 'more easily to remain in concealment' (Articles of Association of the Missions Etrangères de Paris in 1663, quoted in Neill, *A History of Christian Missions*, 180).

ultimate epistemological standard was vociferously and consistently condemned,[3] and having famously described a 'great war being waged against the Catholic Church', the *Syllabus of Errors* in 1864 put a red line through liberalism, freedom of worship, 'immoderate freedoms of opinion', licence of speech, 'love of novelties', freedom of publication, and state-directed education.[4]

Even Pope Leo XIII, 'the social Pope', offered a vision of reform closely akin to Victorian uplift. His encyclical dealing with industrial society (*Rerum Novarum*[5]) reaffirmed the existing socio-economic hierarchy and rejected socialism's attempt to battle nature's indiscriminate gifts of 'capacity, skill, health and strength'. Leo instead exhorted employers and employees to make 'free [wage] agreements' that would satisfy the 'frugal' and 'well-behaved' worker, and rejected social welfare as an incursion into the Church's historical domain of provision for the poor.[6]

Mission was seen by Leo as a way of bypassing problems in Europe and asserting the Church's universality, promising—along with a renewed popular interest in Francis of Assisi—to raise Catholics above the mundane and selfish disappointments of politics and everyday industrial life.[7] Leo had much to say on the subject of how missionaries should be trained. In the encyclical *Depuis Le Jour*, addressed primarily to the French Church, Leo described the role of Catholic clergy and Religious in bringing the conciliatory spirit of *Rerum Novarum* to the field and workplace:

> You go to the people, to the workers, to the poor. You endeavour by all means in your power to help them, raise them in the moral scale, render their lot less hard. To this end you form meetings and congresses; you establish homes, clubs, rural banks, aid and employment offices for the toilers. You labour to introduce reforms into economic and social life, and in the difficult

[3] Pius IX, *Qui Pluribus*, 9 Nov. 1846 (Vatican, 1846).

[4] The *Syllabus* was published as an attachment to the encyclical *Quanta Cura*; Pius IX, *Quanta Cura*, 8 Dec. 1864 (Vatican, 1864).

[5] The title of the encyclical was significant since the papacy's understanding of 'Rerum Novarum' was 'Revolutionary Things', a distinctly provocative title in late nineteenth-century Europe.

[6] Leo XIII, *Rerum Novarum*, 15 May 1891 (Vatican, 1891).

[7] Paul Sabatier's biography of Francis of Assisi (1894) received a wide readership, while earlier in 1882 Leo XIII had invoked the saint's apolitical legacy in *Auspicato Concessum* (Vatican, 17 Sept. 1882). Similarly, Charles de Montalembert's *The Monks of the West* (Edinburgh, 1861) played on the romantic attraction of monastic life. See Bernard Aspinwall, 'Changing Images of Roman Catholic Religious Orders in the Nineteenth Century', in Ecclesiastical History Society, *Monks, Hermits and the Ascetic Tradition* (Padstow, 1985).

enterprise you do not hesitate to make serious sacrifices of time and money; and with the same scope you write books and articles in the newspapers and reviews.[8]

Clergy and Religious were warned against the current European spirit of independent action, and were exhorted instead to follow the instructions given by their superiors, and to guard against 'perilous innovations in speech, manners and associations'. *Depuis Le Jour* ended with a rallying cry for the defence of the Church against her enemies, and a call for a pastoral style of which Francis of Assisi would undoubtedly have approved:

In all things give an example of good works; that is, of active and exemplary life, animated by a true spirit of charity and guided by the maxims of evangelical prudence—of a life of sacrifice and toil, consecrated to the welfare of your neighbours, not with earthly views or for a perishable reward, but with a supernatural object.[9]

The Belgian Capuchins were also obliged to act upon Leo's policies regarding evangelization, which set the standard for Catholic missions until the 1930s. The encyclical *Paternae* (1899) advocated the use of newspapers and journals in publicizing the mission cause and attracting donations, in conscious emulation of (and opposition to) Protestant and secular publications.[10] *Ad Extremas* (1893) reiterated the SCPF's early emphasis upon raising indigenous peoples to the priesthood as a way of connecting more fully with indigenous cultures and securing the mission effort against possible hostility towards foreign missionaries. Leo called for diocesan seminaries to be established in mission territories at the earliest possible opportunity.[11]

By this time, French, Belgian, Irish, and Dutch missionaries had come to form the core of an increasingly active Catholic mission effort, boosted in India with the signing of a concordat between Rome and Lisbon. This brought an end to old rivalries over ecclesiastical jurisdiction and allowed Leo to establish the new 'Hierarchy' in 1886. Eight archdioceses were created—Goa, Agra, Calcutta, Madras, Bombay, Pondicherry, Ceylon, and Verapoly—to be overseen by an Apostolic Delegate to the East Indies.[12] Members of religious Orders now had

[8] Leo XIII, *Depuis Le Jour*, 8 Sept. 1899 (Vatican, 1899). [9] Ibid.
[10] Leo XIII, *Paternae*, 18 Sept. 1899 (Vatican, 1899).
[11] Leo XIII, *Ad Extremas*, 24 June 1893 (Vatican, 1893).
[12] Leo XIII, *Humanae Salutis Auctor*, 1 Sept. 1886 (Vatican, 1886).

the opportunity to become archbishops and bishops in India, and the number of European religious and secular clergy on the subcontinent soon started to rise—from around 1,765 Catholic priests in India in 1884 to 2,150 in 1913 and 3,280 in 1922.[13]

The freedom of action which came with sole responsibility for evangelization in the diocese of Lahore suited the independent spirit of a Belgian Capuchin Order shaped both by its Franciscan inheritance and by the socio-political cauldron that was nineteenth-century Belgium. By this time Belgium was fifty years into its life as an independent modern nation. The freedoms of religion, press, education, and association enshrined in the 1830 Constitution had apparently 'scandalized' Pope Gregory XVI,[14] but the next few decades were in fact kind to Belgian Catholicism. Vocations to the priesthood and to religious Orders soared—the latter from 4,800 women and men in 1829 to 18,000 in 1866[15]—and parish life was reinvigorated by the establishment of new monasteries and confraternities. Popular Catholicism in the countryside translated into parliamentary success for Catholic parties (partly thanks to an electoral system weighted in favour of rural power[16]), and these quickly set about embedding Catholic influence in Belgian society, from national ceremonies to the armed forces, education, and even the courts.[17]

The national atmosphere in which this was accomplished, however, and in which future missionaries to Punjab were raised, was one of constant battle with liberal and socialist groups who feared the corrosive effect of extensive Catholic influence. A sense prevailed of conflict across all areas of public life, from parliament and schools to trade unions, cafés,

[13] Capuchin Mission Unit, *India and its Missions* (New York, 1923), 145.

[14] Bernard A. Crook, *Belgium: A History* (New York, 2002), 64.

[15] Ellen L. Evans, *The Cross and the Ballot: Catholic Political Parties in Germany, Switzerland, Austria, Belgium and the Netherlands, 1785–1985* (Boston, 1999), 25, 136. This figure rose to 30,000 by 1890, and fourteen years later the value of Belgian Church property was around £50,000,000; D. C. Boulger, *Belgian Life in Town and Country* (London, 1904), 123.

[16] Els Witte, 'The Battle for Monasteries, Cemeteries and Schools: Belgium', in Christopher Clark and Wolfram Kaiser (eds), *Culture Wars: Secular–Catholic Conflict in Nineteenth-Century Europe* (Cambridge, 2003), 105.

[17] Ibid. The Church was particularly quick to establish its dominance in state education, from primary school all the way up to university; J. C. H. Blom and E. Lamberts (eds), *History of the Low Countries* (New York, 1999), 314–15. See Ch. 4. On new forms of Catholic influence in Belgium in the inter-war period, see Martin Conway, 'Building the Christian City: Catholics and Politics in Inter-War Francophone Belgium', *Past and Present*, 128 (1990).

and cooperative insurance and credit societies.[18] Revivified religious Orders were heavily involved here, supplying thousands of teachers to Belgian schools (where, thanks to the Church's political strength, Catholic religious education was made compulsory[19]), and running local relief committees, orphanages, hospitals, and other institutions in the Belgian countryside.

Rural Belgium was at this time home to more than half the population, with living conditions that were among the worst in Europe. Tens of thousands of people died from starvation, typhus, and cholera here in the late 1840s alone.[20] As the Church sought to recall its medieval prerogative in providing relief here, members of religious Orders easily undercut both state and privately run welfare rivals by working for free and establishing mini-industries like lace-making and laundry to help cover institutional costs.[21] They prided themselves on personal connections with the rural poor and focused in particular upon the welfare of the young.[22] A contemporary observer, D. C. Boulger, attributed the political and cultural success of the Belgian Church by the early twentieth century to its 'dominant influence over the youthful mind', which it maintained 'by keeping up a direct interest in and practical control over the individual during his worldly career'.[23]

Early Capuchin mission in Punjab came to be defined to a great extent by the attitudes, expertise, and perspectives derived from this kind of politicized socio-religious work in Belgium. Race and culture did not render the rural Punjabi context unique as far as Capuchin missionaries were concerned. Instead these factors pushed rural Punjabis towards the more urgent end of a spectrum of human poverty already well established in Capuchin minds when they left Belgium for India. Capuchin strategies in Punjab also owed much to the charism of their Order and its particular manifestation in modern Belgium.

[18] R. Seebohm Rowntree, *Land and Labour: Lessons from Belgium* (London, 1911), 476–7.

[19] The number of male and female Religious serving as primary school teachers by 1912 was 18,000; Crook, *Belgium*, 80.

[20] Ibid. 69. A reliable, cheap railway network was allowing large numbers of workers to remain in the countryside and commute to urban jobs; H. Hearder, *Europe in the Nineteenth Century: 1830–1880* (New York, 1966), 126.

[21] Rowntree, *Land and Labour*, 483. In the orphanages religious Orders charged even less than their usual low rate if those sending the orphans to the institution allowed them to remain there until they reached adulthood; ibid. 486. See Chs 4 and 5 on Capuchin orphanages and industrial schools in Punjab.

[22] This extended to apprenticing young boys into factories and providing them with their first tools.

[23] Boulger, *Belgian Life in Town and Country*, 122.

They preferred to form potential missionaries in Antwerp, equipping them there with the necessary 'apostolic zeal and spirit of initiative' rather than send them to a proposed Capuchin training institution in Rome.[24]

New Protestant Churches from the sixteenth century onwards were initially too preoccupied with fighting for their own survival to consider the establishment of overseas missions. When it began, Protestant mission work was nevertheless remarkably quick to gather pace in India, sometimes following early English traders to areas like Bengal and at other times operating entirely independently of any European trading or military presence. An Anglican establishment emerged in the wake of East India Company expansion in India, with a Bishop of Calcutta in place from 1814 and the diocese of Lahore established in 1877, encompassing all of Punjab, Kashmir, Sindh, and Delhi.

The CMS had been founded in 1799 in the context of a new Evangelical spirit in Europe and Britain, its first missionaries sent to the subcontinent in the year that the see of Calcutta was created. Although it moulded itself around Anglican structures in India, establishing a Punjab Corresponding Committee not long after the diocese of Lahore was put in place, the CMS was firmly rooted in the voluntarism of ordinary people, and members regularly expressed disappointment at the slowness of Anglican institutions in India to take up evangelization among Indians.

Like the Capuchins, the CMS had had to fight for influence at home, where public suspicion of Evangelicals and derision of working-class 'consecrated cobblers'[25] had made for a tough first few years for the Society. However, the Archbishop of Canterbury, originally so lukewarm about the CMS that the organization had almost died at birth, was finally brought on board by 1841 (an office of vice-patron was created especially).[26] By this time the CMS had been assiduous in building up contacts in Parliament and elsewhere, particularly among those with influence in overseas affairs.[27] Thomas Babington, the former

[24] Letter from Provincial to General, (date illegible) 1920, GACO.

[25] The phrase was first used by the satirist the Revd Sydney Smith of William Carey, the shoemaker-turned-missionary whose work in Bengal went on to have an important impact on mission in India and elsewhere.

[26] This was held by every subsequent Archbishop of Canterbury.

[27] The first President was Admiral Lord Gambier, famed for his naval successes against Napoleon in 1807 and 1809; Stock, *History of the Church Missionary Society*, i. 108.

Governor-General of India, became a Vice-President of the CMS in 1812, and by 1841 he was joined by no less than a marquis, three earls, a viscount, six lords, and four heads of Oxbridge colleges.[28] A special Patronage Committee dedicated itself to obtaining 'the support of influential persons', and the official CMS biographer later conceded that without such people 'many of the Society's early enterprises would not have been possible'. Favours received included the gaining of passage for missionaries on government ships, letters of commendation from the Colonial Office in London, and the inclusion in the 1813 East India Company Charter Bill of a resolution in favour of mission work.[29]

Alongside its Patronage Committee the CMS organization in Britain comprised a General Committee, responsible for finding and training missionary candidates, an Accounts Committee, and a Funds Committee.[30] In the mission territories Corresponding Committees were responsible for establishing mission posts, constructing buildings, and managing missionaries and catechists.

Punjab was relatively hospitable from the start, the CMS mission arriving in Amritsar in 1852 following a request from British veterans of the Anglo-Sikh Wars seeking to establish a mission as a 'thank-offering to Almighty God for His late mercies'.[31] John Lawrence, chief commissioner of Punjab, was among those at an inaugural meeting in 1852, while his brother Henry promised an annual subscription to the mission of Rs 500.[32] In stark contrast to its Capuchin counterpart, the CMS mission in Punjab was always a joint lay–clerical undertaking. Evangelical laymen outnumbered missionaries throughout the nineteenth century,[33] supplying crucial financial and logistical assistance. Rs 20,000 in anonymous sums and Rs 10,000 in small collections was received in 1852 alone, with a further Rs 25,800 and £3,000 added to this the next year. Government engineers designed and built houses and schools in support of catechists during the 1850s[34] and the second Lieutenant Governor of Punjab, Sir Robert Montgomery (after whom a CMS-run Christian village was later named) used his influence to have churches in all CMS mission stations built—using Rs 60,000

[28] *History of the Church Missionary Society*, i. 373.

[29] Ibid. i. 103–109.

[30] Ibid. i. 110–1.

[31] Ibid. ii. 205. Amritsar was chosen because American Presbyterians were already at work in the provincial capital, Lahore.

[32] Robert Clark, *The Missions of the Church Missionary Society and the Church of England Zenana Missionary Society in the Punjab and Sindh* (London, 1904), 3.

[33] Stock, *History of the Church Missionary Society*, ii. 65.

[34] Ibid. ii. 206–10.

from the province's Public Works budget.[35] This use of funds was permissible under government rules, since the buildings would be part of the infrastructure of European colonial society, but Catholics in Punjab were convinced that CMS projects were receiving approval far faster than their own.[36] In general there was a sense among Capuchin missionaries of being locked into a heroically unwinnable game of institutional catch-up, from a hopelessly backward position and lacking both resources and useful contacts.

CMS strategy in Punjab was decided largely between London and the Punjab Corresponding Committee, and, as the subsection below entitled 'Internal Tensions' will show, there was great variation of opinion among missionaries and converts about how the CMS ought to proceed. In theological terms, Evangelical mission was constantly evolving and had no basis in carefully worked-out theory until well into the twentieth century. Here again the CMS was worlds apart from the Capuchins. The latter experienced disagreements among themselves and with others in the Catholic Church about whose responsibility it was to organize, fund, and direct evangelization. Yet these occurred on a relatively narrow scale and in the context of papal authority and a sacramental community, unified and international.

For the CMS, questions about the missionary role were far more open and fundamental. Religious authority rested with Scripture, and the role of the Church lay in bringing the individual to a saving relationship with God, through an appreciation of Scripture and encouragement in the living of a disciplined life. But given the crucial emphasis on 'the Word', just how far evangelization ought to incorporate basic or advanced literacy for those requiring it remained an open question. So too with the issue of leadership in new Christian communities and the task of scriptural definition and exegesis: did authority precede exegesis or proceed from it in these circumstances? A proliferation of different readings of the Bible would surely present serious difficulties for the notion of Christian 'community', so what claim could an evangelizing group have upon the evangelized?

[35] Clark, *The Missions of the Church Missionary Society and the Church of England Zenana Missionary Society*, 237, 35.

[36] Only a vigorous press campaign by Catholics in Lahore finally succeeded in extracting the funds for St Anthony's Church (1899) from what they saw as the tightly clenched Protestant fists of Punjab officialdom; Leo van Ninove, *The Capuchin Mission in the Punjab: With Notes on the History, Geography, Ethnology and Religions of the Country* (Mangalore, 1910), 89.

The Raw Material: Spending Power, Policy, and Personnel

The CMS in Britain first raised money through annual subscriptions, receiving between 200 and 300 of these in its first five years. It gradually became more aggressive, targeting clergy who were known to be sympathetic to the Society, and asking them by means of circulars for contributions to the missionary effort. By 1814, £13,200 was received annually in this way, rising to £30,000 per annum in 1820 under a new system of 'Associations' (local fundraising branches of the Society). From the 1830s onwards these funds were supplemented by legacies and by increasing sums from missionary boxes. Other major sources of income for the CMS included funds given to support specific regions or aspects of mission work.[37]

Publications were an important way of gaining public support for mission work and thus generating income through all these channels. The CMS was very active, after 1840, in publishing accounts of its work and making appeals for funds, carefully identifying different audiences and producing appropriate publications. The *Church Missionary Gleaner* became the popular monthly magazine of the Society from 1841, featuring articles on various aspects of the missions, letters from missionaries, recent news from the field, information on candidates and vacancies, and work among the young. The *Church Missionary Juvenile Instructor* was aimed at children and the *Church Missionary Intelligencer* at adults seeking more in-depth coverage of the mission effort, from analysis of major questions facing the mission to specialized notes on India, Africa, and East Asia. *Mercy and Truth* was first published in 1897, as the mouthpiece of the CMS Medical Mission. By the turn of the century the Society was spending more than £5,000 annually on publicity of this sort.[38]

Table 2.1 shows the receipts of the Society from 1900 to 1935, the relative value of different sources of income, and total expenditure. Two significant features of the figures are the proportion of income generated in Britain compared with that generated in the missions, and the frequency with which expenditure approached or outstripped

[37] Benefactors sometimes supported an individual mission station, missionary, or catechist, receiving personal thanks in the respective personnel's annual letters.

[38] Figures compiled from the *Proceedings of the Church Missionary Society for Africa and the East* (London, various years) (hereafter *Proceedings of the CMS*). Many of these publication titles changed in the early twentieth century. *The Gleaner* became the *Church Missionary Outlook* in 1922, *The Intelligencer* became the *Church Missionary Review* in 1907, and *Mercy and Truth* was called the *Mission Hospital* after 1922.

Table 2.1. *CMS receipts and total expenditure, 1900–1935 (£ s. d.)*

Receipts	1900	1905	1910	1916	1920	1925	1930	1935
Associations	167,628/13/7	171,243/19/4	169,636/2/5	183,035/3/6	270,032/16/4	307,937/8/9	304,796/0/8	276,573/7/9
Benefactions	32,888/14/2	30,602/16/7	41,060/9/6	45,366/15/5	79,660/14/2	48,361/19/2	47,088/16/11	26,739/18/10
Annual subscriptions	3,740/10/7	5,167/3/3	4,976/11/2	6,987/14/3	6,008/11/1	5,358/18/5	10,245/11/3	10,284/14/11
Individual collections	242/10/10	347/18/80	261/17/2	247/10/8	301/5/4	263/9/4	163/16/9	154/8/11
Legacies	32,883/19/7	43,008/15/10	53,221/5/2	43,110/8/8	52,310/0/9	34,255/15/11	78,721/3/9	69,052/15/9
Foreign contributions	621/11/11	2,022/16/10	490/12/10	1,030/0/9	4,208/18/6	2,247/19/0	1,862/12/7	1,468/4/5
Receipts in the missions	2,480/12/3	4,544/7/4	3,513/11/6	2,545/14/2	2,600/7/1	2,810/3/9	3,160/7/6	1,216/8/8
Interest and dividends on investments	6,097/16/6	3,207/12/9	4,698/15/8	4,325/8/8	5,499/9/2	6,023/13/11	5,178/17/10	n/a
Appropriated receipts	52,195/14/5	74,235/0/10	94,116/6/0	94,947/12/0	133,840/3/7	34,713/4/2	166,506/9/0	n/a
(of which medical mission)	10,594/6/9	26,605/11/10	38,898/9/11	42,886/10/1	52,478/13/5	13,822/15/9	n/a	n/a
Special appropriated receipts	4,601/15/3	n/a	n/a	n/a	n/a	n/a	n/a	n/a
Special funds/ Misc. receipts	80,324/9/7	9,905/16/10	38,317/16/9	10,876/8/2	n/a	n/a	125,791/0/8	n/a
Peace Thankoffering Fund	n/a	n/a	n/a	n/a	113,430/18/10	n/a	n/a	n/a
TOTAL	450,442/10/3	346,057/12/10	395,615/10/4	393,280/10/7	668,554/14/11	461,863/0/6	493,943/15/7	404,046/12/7
Total expenditure	450,442/10/3	400,860/18/6	403,747/6/0	368,869/1/10	558,722/7/6	524,062/9/0	493,509/14/5	409,395/8/3

Note: n/a = not available. The surplus in 1920 was almost wiped out by the need to cover an accumulated 'adverse balance' of £81,544, as well as depreciation in securities held by the Society; *Proceedings of the CMS 1920–1* (London, 1921), sect. ii, p. 3. 'Benefactions' were listed as 'donations' after 1920.

Source: *Proceedings of the CMS* (London, various years).

receipts. These two factors had had a strong impact on the development of CMS mission policy from the 1850s, when a decline in the Society's finances encouraged greater emphasis upon a policy formulated by the Secretary of the Society, Henry Venn, of encouraging self-supporting, self-governing, and self-propagating 'Native [national] Churches'.[39] Henry Venn, son of one of the CMS's founders, John Venn, hoped that these new Native Churches would represent an indigenous expression of Christianity, both as a sign of true, Evangelical conversion and as a way of freeing missionaries—and mission funds—for evangelistic rather than pastoral work.

This was to be the start of debates about how new Churches should be supported and managed, splitting opinion from the late nineteenth century onwards among European donors, Indian and European mission personnel, and converts themselves. The stakes were raised in the early decades of the twentieth century when financial retrenchment—following CMS spending of around £2.5 million in the 1890s—coincided with the onset of the mass movements. Inevitably the meaning of conversion in these movements, the duties of foreign missionaries, and the long-term prospects for new Christian communities were considered against this pressing economic backdrop. By the time the Society's finances recovered, in the early 1940s, the mass movements were all but over.

The CMS's cash-flow problems in the late nineteenth and early twentieth centuries make it all the more surprising that their Punjab mission continued to rely heavily upon expensive European personnel, as Table 2.2 suggests. By 1909 there were approximately thirty-three European clergy working in Punjab, together with twenty-five male European lay missionaries, forty-three wives of missionaries, and twenty-nine single female missionaries, a total of 130 Europeans, costing around £86 for each missionary per year (this was the lowest amount on which a European was thought able to 'subsist').[40] This contrasted with just £37 each, per annum, to support Indian missionaries—yet only twenty-one were employed at this stage.[41] Staff was distributed

[39] Stock, *History*, i. 482–3.

[40] Letter from Bomford to CMS Secretary, (undated) 1888, ACMS, G2/I4/O 1888, n. 170.

[41] Figures taken from *Proceedings of the CMS, 1909–10* and *1910–11* (London, 1910, 1911). In reality the figure for Europeans was probably slightly higher than £86, since a small fraction of the European personnel (the *Proceedings of the CMS* do not give precise details) were in Punjab at their own or a sponsor's expense, while missionary couples were cheaper to support than two single men or women.

TABLE 2.2. *Expenditure of the CMS on its Punjab and Sindh mission, 1904–1934 (£)*

Expenditure	1904	1909	1913	1919	1924	1929	1934
European missionaries	11,275	11,155	11,085	11,290	10,832	13,892	9,442
Buildings, land purchases, New Works	101	1,227	n/a	n/a	n/a	92	35
Medical mission establishments	4,661	4,288	2,570	4,274	2,417	2,823	1,455
Grants to native church council	252	n/a	n/a	n/a	n/a	n/a	n/a
Native missionaries	707	775	890	807	1,672	2,001	n/a
Native agents	1,117	1,740	1,517	1,551	1,980	2,308	3,101
Schools	2,658	2,568	2,811	2,883	3,441	2,229	1,893
Secretariat expenses	407	475	469	366	651	766	740
Mission servants	401	431	285	299	372	366	203
Itinerating	561	360	334	231	425	364	499
Travel (within India)	303	294	253	197	135	193	71
Travel (to and from Europe)	n/a	n/a	n/a	3,782	1,951	1,692	928
Exchange losses	n/a	n/a	n/a	8,649	1,650	−162	−102
Other	2,454	2,486	7,325	6,894	7,990	4,016	4,127
TOTAL	24,897	25,799	27,539	41,223	33,516	30,580	22,392

Note: n/a = not available. Statistics from 1913 onwards were given by the CMS as round figures. In 1934 'native missionaries' were included in the 'native agents' category. In the 'exchange losses' category, negative figures appear where a profit was made on currency exchange.

Source: *Proceedings of the CMS* (London, various years).

across twenty-three mission stations and eight branch stations by the early twentieth century. Central stations were grouped around Lahore and Amritsar—including Jandiala, Narowal, Tarn Taran, Batala, and Clarkabad (see Map 2.1)—while so-called 'frontier stations' ran along the border with North-West Frontier Province.[42]

In addition to Indian missionaries, 133 lay 'Native Agents' were employed in 1909, at a comparatively inexpensive £13 each per annum.[43] The scope of their work was, however, limited by mission policy and by European missionary superintendence. Despite the aim of encouraging new Churches to become self-sufficient, the belief remained strong in the CMS that European workers were preferable to Indian ones. Even the modest rise in the number of Indian workers at this time was prompted more by a fall in European missionary vocations than by an increased sense of confidence in Indians' abilities. Indian recruitment did not even keep pace with these falling numbers of Europeans. From 1902 to 1912 the number of CMS converts in Punjab tripled and the number of European missionaries fell by four, yet the number of Indian missionaries increased by just two. Gordon Hewitt, a recent official biographer of the CMS, has suggested that had European missionaries in Punjab been in closer touch with the declining fortunes of Christianity in England they might have looked earlier and more urgently at Indian recruitment.[44]

The broad significance of financial questions across the mission-Church in Punjab was felt by Punjabis and Europeans alike. Discussions at the Punjab Native Church Council (established in 1877 to encourage local responsibility in mission-Church affairs yet effectively subordinate

[42] Amritsar was of particular importance to the CMS leadership as the prime religious and commercial centre for a Sikh population thought more likely than either Hindus or Muslims to be sympathetic to the claims of Christianity—and perhaps even to become hard-core evangelists (in keeping with the contemporary British view of the Sikhs as a martial race, there were hopes that Sikh converts would become, as Clark put it, 'soldiers of the Cross'); Clark, *The Missions of the Church Missionary Society and the Church of England Zenana Missionary Society in the Punjab and Sindh*, 22.

[43] This tentative figure is arrived at through calculations based on Table 2.2. Although an approximate figure of £13 holds until 1914, after this date the number of agents employed by the CMS in Punjab and Sindh began to rise out of all proportion to the amount spent on them. Since catechists often worked in a variety of capacities, it is possible that some were paid from school or other funds. Given the importance of catechists among rival Protestant and Catholic missions, and their relatively short supply, it is unlikely that the cost of their employment dropped significantly in the period under discussion.

[44] G. Hewitt, *The Problems of Success: A History of the Church Missionary Society, 1910–1942*, 2 vols (London, 1971), ii. 31.

Map 2.1. Principal CMS mission stations in central Punjab. From Sialkot, in the north, moving south and south-west, may be seen the main CMS stations with which this book is concerned: Narowal, Tarn Taran, and Clarkabad.

Source: Robert Clark, *The Punjab and Sindh Mission of the Church Missionary Society* (London, 1885)

to a veto-holding European chairman and to London[45]) frequently turned to matters of income and their relation to the question of independence for the Punjabi Church. The Revd Dr Imad-ud-din, one of the most prominent Punjabi clergymen of his day and the first Indian Christian to receive the degree of Doctor of Divinity, blamed 'illiberal' attitudes towards giving among Punjabi Christians for the local Church's lack of financial independence.[46] Others among the predominantly urban middle-class delegates, including the Revd Wadhawa Mal, preferred to blame the CMS, and in particular its premature establishment of large, expensive institutions—such as elite schools—and its appointment of Punjabi pastors for Christian communities that could not afford to support them.[47]

The CMS missionary the Revd T. Bomford shared the view that mission policy was misplaced, driven not just by financial questions but also by the Society's perennial concerns about institutional security and profile. Bomford claimed the CMS had overextended in Punjab, throwing away good opportunities in the process,[48] and had insisted on locations associated with the British Army where missionaries would simply be 'lost . . . in a crowd of Europeans'. Similarly, he criticized CMS bureaucratic structures, saying that these tended to be 'an imitation of the government system'.[49]

The CMS were certainly ambitious. The Society had hoped to overturn the post-1857 British policy of non-interference in religious matters, and when this failed had nevertheless followed its domestic pattern of establishing and maintaining influential connections—much

[45] 'It is an obvious fact', the Revd H. U. Weitbrecht complained in the late 1890s, 'that the most advanced Church Councils in India are just as much under the control of Salisbury Square as the weakest or most recent. They may contribute more money but they have no more power to modify their constitution or to . . . acquire property without an order from London' (*Evidence of Reverend Dr Weitbrecht to the CMS Centenary Commission*, *c.*1897, ACMS, G/CCb 4/2c, pt 2). The PNCC sources used here are English versions of the Council's Urdu proceedings, produced by the CMS and based on delegates' own translations of their Council speeches.

[46] ACMS, *Proceedings of the Second Meeting of the Punjab Native Church Council, 1877* (Lahore, 1878) (hereafter *First Meeting*, *Second Meeting*, etc.), 70.

[47] Paper given by the Revd Wadhawa Mal at the Twenty-First Meeting of the PNDCC, ACMS, *Twenty-First Meeting of the PNDCC, 1897* ([Lahore?, 1898?]), 31. Jeffrey Cox has described the CMS in Punjab as 'inveterate institution builders' (Cox, *Imperial Fault Lines*, 27).

[48] T. Bomford, 'The Development of the Church in India', *CMR* 71/829 (Mar. 1920), 8.

[49] Letter from the Revd T. Bomford to CMS Secretary, 16 Nov. 1896, ACMS, G2/14/O 1896, n. 21.

to the distress of anxious senior government officials in Lahore and Delhi. The baptism of six Indians at Amritsar in May 1859 was attended by the local Commissioner, Deputy Commissioner, Assistant Commissioner, and the commanding officer of a local Sikh regiment. When the Viceroy heard about the incident, he wrote a letter to the secretary of the Punjab Government demanding to know why the men had been present. The secretary replied, on behalf of the Commissioner, Mr Cust, that he maintained 'his right to attend on the religious ceremonies of his own Church, so long as . . . principles of toleration are not compromised'.[50]

The matter was eventually settled in favour of the men's right to attend such occasions, but the perception clearly existed in some Indian quarters by the early twentieth century that Protestant missions worked in collusion with the Government to promote and preserve British rule. B. D. Basu's *Rise of the Christian Power in India*, first published in 1923, chronicled the East India Company's '[destruction] of the trade and industries of India' and gave centre-stage to what Basu saw as the self-conscious yet highly hypocritical and sanctimonious Christianity of Company Men—linking them with their avaricious co-religionists: the Portuguese, the Danes, the Dutch, and the French.[51] The brand of vociferously imperialist Christian apology deemed most offensive by people like Basu had largely subsided by the 1920s, but nationalists remembered and invoked it nonetheless, both as a stick with which to beat the British and as a rallying cry to a first generation of mass support.

The advantages for the CMS of connections to authority in fact lay less with government officials than in the meaning of the gospel message in the light of European power and achievements. While Rome had rejected much of the modern world, Protestant Christianity had 'not only accepted it but to some extent claimed paternity'.[52] Railways, the telegraph, education, and industry all bolstered Protestant missionaries' self-image and, they believed, their case in the towns and villages.

[50] Clark, *The Missions of the Church Missionary Society and the Church of England Zenana Missionary Society in the Punjab and Sindh*, 231.

[51] B. D. Basu, *Rise of the Christian Power in India* (Calcutta, 1931), 976, 17–31.

[52] Johnson, *A History of Christianity*, 462. The subject of relations with the governments of mission territories was debated by Commission VII of the World Missionary Conference at Edinburgh in 1910. A general principle emerged that 'the aid of the secular arm or of official favour should not be invoked for purely spiritual work', yet it was agreed that missionaries could legitimately 'appeal to the civil power or to the civilized world' in support of their cause; *Resolutions of the CMS Committee on the Report of Commission VII of the World Missionary Conference*, repr. in W. Mackworth-Young, 'Missions and Governments: Commentary on Resolutions Proposed with Reference to Report of Commission VII of the World Missionary Conference', *CMR* 62/744 (Apr. 1911), 207–9.

Through a combination of Evangelical conviction and highly selective references to recent European learning they sought to present European civilization as an unadulterated boost for the claims of Christianity.

Although in their official capacities there was little they could do for the CMS, the importance to the mission effort of ICS officers acting as private individuals was attested to by their exchange with CMS missionaries of laudatory published accounts of each other's toils in Punjab. One ICS officer, James Robert Maconachie, penned a virtual hagiography of his CMS missionary friend Rowland Bateman in 1917, dedicating it to 'the younger men of the empire, now proving their manhood on the blood-stained battlefields of a Holy War'.[53]

If CMS policy was capable of influence by financial concerns, security requirements, realities on the ground in Punjab, and a constantly evolving mission theology, then when it came to personnel at least the Society was sure it knew what it wanted. One of the first secretaries of the Society, Josiah Pratt, described his perfect missionary candidate in 1816: 'An honest zeal springs up in a man newly awakened to feel his own obligations to Redeeming Mercy, to communicate the knowledge of Salvation to others. Missionary Sermons, or Meetings, or Publications, awaken his attention to the awful state of the Heathen World.'[54]

Although Pratt promised that the CMS would not 'undervalue men of a heavenly character though not of a superior mind', the Society was clearly proud of its 'University men'. In the early nineteenth century the missionary movement had been a convenient social escalator, but in the second half of the century the proportion of missionaries from working-class backgrounds (including drapers, blacksmiths, railway clerks, warehousemen, and domestic servants[55]) declined rapidly in favour of ordained graduates.

Nor did this mean that young men's motivations in choosing the missionary life were now entirely beyond reproach. Those whose chosen career paths had been thwarted or had proved unsatisfactory might enter the ministry and then a mission society as a way of guaranteeing a certain professional status. Evangelicalism recognized that social and

[53] Robert Maconachie, *Rowland Bateman: Nineteenth Century Apostle* (London, 1917). The CMS reciprocated by remembering Maconachie's publicity and fund-raising work for the Society during the last years of his life with an article, 'In Memoriam: Robert Maconachie', in the *Church Missionary Review*; *CMR* 73/840 (Dec. 1922), 302.

[54] Quoted in Stock, *History of the Church Missionary Society*, i. 122–3.

[55] L. Nemer, *Anglican and Roman Catholic Attitudes on Missions: An Historical Study of Two English Missionary Societies in the Late Nineteenth Century, 1865–1885* (St Augustin, 1981), 77.

spiritual ambition need not be mutually exclusive, but its demand of a deep self-understanding and openness of conscience was evident in the recruitment process in Britain as it was in the official requirements to be met by candidates for baptism in Punjab.

The heavy presence, in responses to CMS recruitment questionnaires, of biblical language and popular Evangelical platitudes makes it difficult to gain reliable access to candidates' thinking.[56] Stuart Piggin has suggested that although 'economic security' motivated a number of candidates in the late nineteenth century, it was more often the case that entrance into mission work actually entailed considerable financial and professional sacrifice. Other possible factors at this time included romantic notions of overseas adventures, a utilitarian–Evangelical desire to make oneself useful and to engage in the kind of work which best suited one's natural gifts, a desire to 'civilize', according to public notions of the time, denominational rivalry (particularly opposition to Catholicism), and finally the notion of being called to missionary service as part of one's own conversion.[57]

While successful missionary candidates rarely required much preparation for the mission field if they had been to university and had trained for the ministry, non-graduates were sent by the CMS to the Church Missionary Institution in Islington, otherwise known as Islington College. English, Latin, Greek, logic, mathematics, and divinity were taught at the College, which opened in 1825, along with Hebrew, Arabic, Sanskrit, and Bengali (depending on the students' mission destination) and around 100 basic medical lectures.[58] In the 1860s the curriculum was broadened to include the theology necessary to engage representatives of Islam and Hinduism.[59] Training continued in the mission territory itself, and it was claimed by one CMS missionary in 1882 that the standard of Hindustani among the Society's missionaries in Punjab exceeded that found among ICS officers.[60] Students at the College were

[56] Piggin, *Making Evangelical Missionaries, 1789–1858*, 125–8.

[57] Ibid. 128–49.

[58] Stock, *History of the Church Missionary Society*, iv. 470.

[59] The CMS tried to institute examinations in these religions but this did not work. Instead, they incorporated an element of religious learning into the two-level language examinations that were set for missionaries. By the turn of the century, however, there were still few missionaries with a detailed knowledge of Indian religions. Most could simply 'quote a few aphorisms' (Responses of the Revd H. G. Grey to the Questionnaire set by the Centenary Review Committee, undated (received in London 1 Sept. 1897), ACMS, G2/I4/O 1897, n. 330).

[60] Letter to CMS Secretary (sender unknown, Peshawar), 23 Aug. 1882, ACMS, G2/I4/O 1882, n. 162. At the same time, the missionary stressed that language learning

mostly of British origin, although candidates from mission territories in Africa, India, China, and North America were increasingly accepted.[61]

CMS recruitment strongly reflected both the strength and the location of Evangelical influence in Britain, peaking during the last two decades of the nineteenth century and drawing particularly heavily upon the University of Cambridge. This is clear from a breakdown of the educational backgrounds of male missionaries added to the CMS's roll in the period January 1895–April 1899:

Cambridge University	40	
Oxford University	10	
Dublin University	8	
Durham University	3	
London University	2	
Scottish universities	5	
The Royal University of Ireland	1	
St John's Hall, Highbury	3	
Islington College	55	(31 clergy, 24 laymen)
From Australia, Canada, etc.	20[62]	

There was no comparable institution to Islington College for women until the 1890s, when public opinion, combined with numerous requests from women for independent work, forced a shift upon the CMS. The Society had initially been reluctant to employ women as missionaries, working with the Church of England Zenana Mission Society (CEZMS) and the Zenana Bible and Medical Mission to provide CMS missions in India with the required female staff.[63] As the CMS began to accept the principle of sending out female missionaries of their own, they used 'training homes' run by private individuals, such as Mrs Pennefather and Mrs Bannister. Mrs Babington and Mrs Handley Moule (wife of Bishop Moule, whose theological writings were used in the training of CMS catechists) meanwhile exercised considerable influence at Cambridge in introducing suitable female candidates to the CMS.[64]

In 1891 a CMS training institution for 'a less educated class of women' was finally opened, at Highbury, and from 1917 onwards the

should not take precedence over 'daily and hourly' engagement with the people of India. There was no point in missionaries striving for 'excellence as oriental scholars'.

[61] Stock, *History of the Church Missionary Society*, ii. 74.

[62] Ibid. iii. 704. Differing social and institutional backgrounds had the potential to breed tensions in the mission field. See below.

[63] The *zenana* was a secluded quarters reserved for women.

[64] Ibid. iii. 371.

Society took on the task of training its own female missionaries at Kennaway Hall. By the time of the First World War the role of female missionaries had been solidly established, although women struggled to receive equal treatment in the running of the Society itself. A decision in 1914 that women could eventually be ceded up to a third of the seats on the Committees for Correspondence, Funds, and for the Annual Report (but no seats on the General Committee[65]) represented slow progress, but the minority report of the subcommittee considering the matter revealed objections even to this. It noted that 'the general trend of Holy Scripture places the responsibility of government in the hands of men only'.[66] Female influence continued to be limited to the Women's Committee (Foreign), which had been set up in 1912 to 'consider general foreign matters affecting women'. Business was referred to it by other committees and its members were appointed by the all-male General Committee.[67]

The first personnel sent by the Belgian Capuchins arrived in Lahore on 9 March 1889 (see Fig. 2.1), their determination to set up a mission among Punjabis apparently a source of some amusement to the outgoing Italian Capuchins, who assured them that not even the domestic staff of the mission buildings could be made to convert.[68] Catholic mission work in Punjab had so far been confined to the European and Eurasian populations, including military personnel, with the salaries of Catholic chaplains paid by the British Government since 1858.

British officers had gone to pains to restrict Catholic clergy to towns and cantonments, and they failed now to muster much enthusiasm for the idea of Catholic evangelism among Punjabis. The deputy commissioner of Sialkot warned the Capuchins in August 1889 of the danger of one mission society being played against another by individuals who sought material advantage rather than Christian teaching.[69] The

[65] 'Church Missionary Society: Representation of Women on Committees, Reports I and II, February 1914', ACMS, G/AP2.

[66] Ibid.

[67] *Proceedings of the Committee of Correspondence of February 6, 1912, to be presented for confirmation to the General Committee of February 13, 1912*, ACMS, G/AP2.

[68] J. Rooney, *Into Deserts: A History of the Catholic Diocese of Lahore, 1886–1986* (Rawalpindi, 1986), 15.

[69] Letter from Deputy Commissioner, Sialkot, to Fr. Clement, 4 Aug. 1889, repr. in Ninove, *The Capuchin Mission in the Punjab*, 77.

Fig. 2.1. The first group of Belgian Capuchins sent to Punjab, 1889. Back row: Br. Leopold de Turnhout, Br. Edmond de Turnhout, Br. Theodore de Bruxelles, Br. Felix d'Anvers. Front row: Br. Leopold van Ninove, Fr. Desiree de Mons, Fr. Antoine d'Anvers, Fr. Arsene de Emblehem.

Source: ABC, Photographic Archive

reply from the Capuchins was that villagers' requests for attention could not be ignored, and that no financial benefits would be offered them.[70]

Listed in the Appendix at the end of this book are the first Capuchin missionaries to arrive in Punjab in 1889, and personnel arriving in subsequent years. Maps 2.2 and 2.3 show their principal areas of operation. The friars sent out to Punjab by the Belgian Province were, on the whole, rather young. The youngest, Br. Felix, was 21 years old and the average age in the initial 1889 group was just 28. Most friars had joined the Order as young men of around 18 or 19 years of age. Their formation encompassed a novitiate of around one year, after which they made their profession of vows. In most cases, training for the priesthood followed soon afterwards, and the majority of friars were ready for ordination by the age of 25 or 26.

Although those who went to Punjab usually did so within a couple of years of ordination, it can be seen from the Appendix that the initial intention was for friars to go to Punjab *before* ordination. A seminary was established at Dalhousie, with theological, language (Urdu and Punjabi), and cultural instruction attended to by Fr. Godefride, with Fr. Arsene as his assistant.[71] In 1891 there were four Belgian friars living in the seminary, and it was hoped that future Indian candidates for ordination would eventually be trained there.

The Belgian Capuchin desire to run things their own way has already been commented upon. They had, however, to bear in mind the teachings of Pope Leo XIII mentioned above, regarding the missionary life, which fortunately were very much in line with the Capuchin charism and the lessons of modern Belgian life.[72] And yet although the Capuchins were rarely to be found openly straying from the line set down by Pope Leo XIII in *Paternae* and *Ad Extremas*, which included the requirement to prepare indigenous peoples for the priesthood,[73] it was to be a striking feature of Capuchin mission between the 1880s and Indian independence that this kind of training was almost never discussed.[74] There appeared to be little in the Capuchin understanding of Catholic theology and mission strategy that rendered such questions as urgent as they were in the CMS mission, nor were there forums equivalent to the Punjab Native Church Council in which these things could be discussed.

70 *The Capuchin Mission in the Punjab*, 81.

71 Rooney, *Into Deserts*, 17.

72 See above, from Leo XIII, *Depuis Le Jour*.

73 See above.

74 See Ch. 5, on the slow and uneven evolution of Capuchin and CMS missionary thinking in the twentieth century.

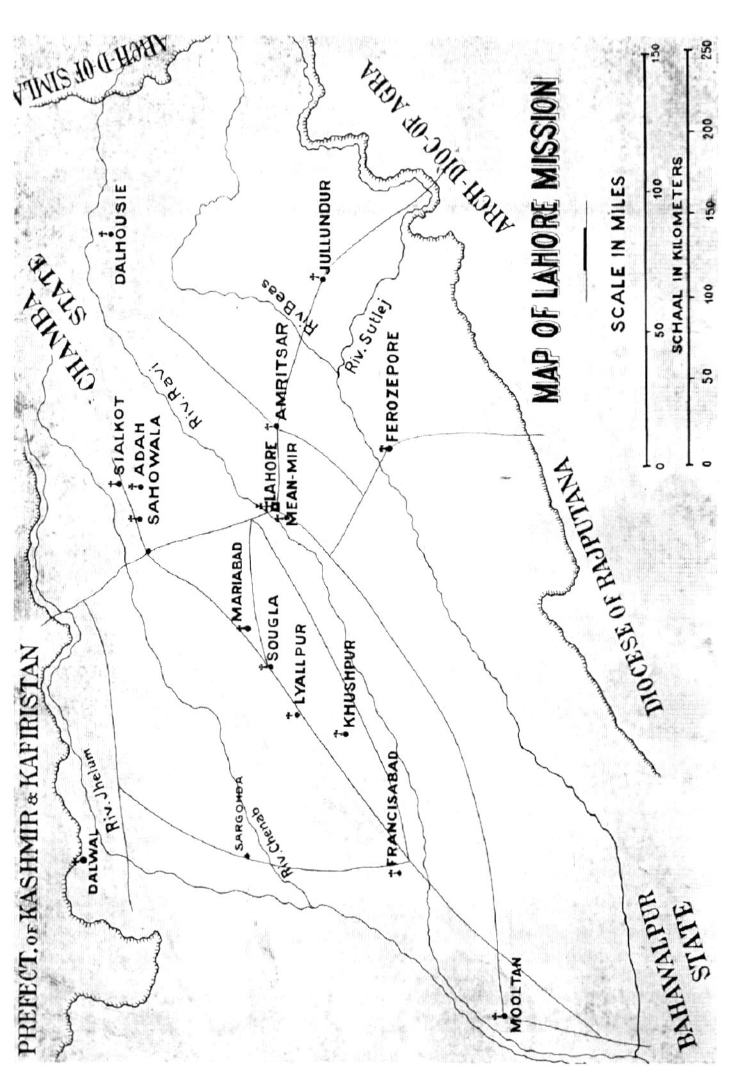

Map 2.2. The Belgian Capuchin Lahore mission.
Source: ABC, Photographic Archive

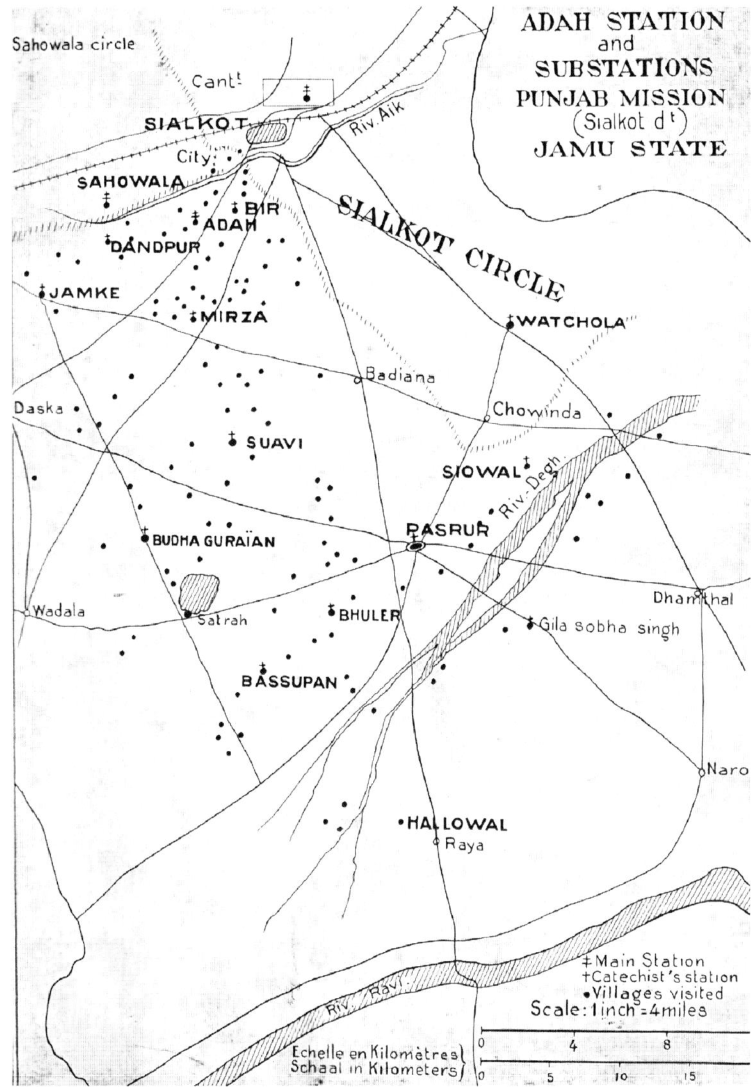

Map 2.3. The principal Capuchin mission and catechist stations around Sialkot, including villages visited.

Source: ABC, Photographic Archive

There was no set length of service for Capuchin missionaries, and a friar might expect to work in the mission indefinitely unless old age, exhaustion, or proven unsuitability for the work led to him requesting—or being requested—to return to Belgium. In the period covered by the lists of Capuchin missionaries shown in the Appendix (1889–1930), twenty-two returned to Belgium and nineteen died in India. The conditions of work took a heavy toll on missionaries' health, and this may well have been a factor in the Provincial's sacrifice of experience in favour of youth when selecting friars to send to Punjab. The lifespan of missionaries ranged from that of Fr. Rochus, who left Antwerp at the age of 22 and never celebrated his twenty-third birthday, to Fr. Arsene, who joined the mission at the age of 26 and lived to be 95.[75]

As a proportion of the number of Capuchin friars in the Belgian Province, the missionary effort in Punjab was considerable. The Belgian Catholic resurgence of the mid-nineteenth century had brought large numbers of new recruits for the Capuchins: their numbers rose from just seven friars in 1825 to 114 by 1860. By the time the first missionaries left for Punjab in 1889, there were 137 friars in the Province, rising to 446 by 1930.[76] On the basis that almost all new recruits were under the age of 25 and therefore potential candidates for mission work (factors such as long-term ill health, which may have rendered some in this age group ineligible for mission work, are difficult to assess given the available biographical data), it is possible to discern a regular percentage of eligible new recruits sent to Punjab in this period (see Table 2.3).

TABLE 2.3. *Percentage of eligible new recruits sent to Punjab, 1891–1930*

Decade	No. of new recruits	Percentage sent to Punjab
1891–1900	135	14.8
1901–1910	143	12.6
1911–1920	117	11.1
1921–1930	169	14.0
AVERAGE		13.0

Source: Teuns, *Historische Ledenlijst*, 20–250.

[75] S. Teuns, *Historische Ledenlijst Minderbroeders-Kapucijnen, 1802–1995* (Sint-Truiden, 1996), 109.

[76] Ibid. 8–12.

Friars' pastoral responsibilities among civilians and military personnel led many Capuchin mission stations to be established close to British army cantonments, as well as towns with sizeable European and Eurasian populations. The early Capuchin mission stations are listed in Table 2.4, along with the Catholic populations of each station in 1891. They are divided, as in the Capuchin sources, into European–Eurasian and Indian populations.

Such was the small number of missionaries at this point that only at Capuchin Houses in Lahore, Sialkot, and Dalhousie was there more than one Capuchin priest. Elsewhere, a single priest shared a small house with a Capuchin brother still in training for the priesthood. Although Capuchin work among Europeans and Eurasians lies outside the scope of this volume, it is important to note that the Capuchins were as strident in their criticism of the morals and behaviour of soldiers as they were of rural Punjabi converts. They believed that Catholic soldiers from deprived backgrounds in Ireland and urban England (and frequently without access to Catholic priests or church services while on military duty) lapsed terribly—into drunkenness and sometimes into Protestantism. Many knew almost nothing of the Catholic faith, and Capuchin friars worked to prepare them for the sacraments of Reconciliation and the Eucharist.[77]

TABLE 2.4. *Catholic populations in early Capuchin mission stations, 1891*

Mission station	European and Eurasian (unspecified)	European	Eurasian	Indian
Lahore	900	n/a	n/a	50
Sialkot	150	n/a	n/a	12
Villages in Sialkot area	0	n/a	n/a	800
Myanmir	80	n/a	n/a	0
Multan	n/a	180	0	6
Amritsar	n/a	80	n/a	8
Jalandhar	n/a	150	n/a	0
Tirozepur	100	n/a	n/a	6
Dalhousie[a]	200	n/a	n/a	5

Note: n/a = not available.

[a] Summer only.

Source: GACO, Letter from Provincial to General, [1920].

[77] *Report of the Mission of Lahore for the Year 1891*, ABC, L88.

In addition to the Capuchins, there were thirteen female religious working in Punjab at this time, from the Franciscan Convent of Jesus and Mary in Lyon.[78] In Lahore the sisters ran a middle school and high school for European and Eurasian girls, as well as the Sacred Heart School for 'native girls of high caste' and St Joseph's Orphanage, which doubled as a school for orphans and non-orphans alike. The Capuchins later claimed that although they disliked the European racial prejudices which dictated this segregation in education, they saw no way around it. No comment was made, however, on the caste prejudice implied by the opening of a school for high-caste girls. The Sisters of Charity, from Ghent, operated in Punjab from 1897, running middle schools in Multan and Dalhousie and eventually taking over the management of St Joseph's Orphanage.[79] Major urban institutions run by the Capuchins themselves included St Anthony's School for European and Eurasian boys and St Francis's combined school and orphanage for Indian boys, both situated in Lahore.[80]

A Catholic diocesan synod held in January 1890 to decide upon 'strategies and policies' was one of the rare occasions when the training of an indigenous clergy was seriously discussed[81]—fully in line with SCPF policy and with Leo's *Instructions to the Missions* three years later, in which he also urged evangelization in villages, where he thought people would have had less contact with a corrupt Western world.[82] All these projects required funds, however, and the Capuchin mission, like the CMS, found itself constrained by its finances and influenced by those who held the purse strings. As Table 2.5 shows, a large proportion of Capuchin funds was supplied by 'external benefactors' in Belgium, with a stable additional source of funds available in the stipends paid to Capuchin military chaplains. The latter, however, were seen as lost labour to an indigenous mission that was perpetually short of hands. Moreover, two-thirds of missionary chaplains' earnings went to the Bishop of Lahore, and there was no guarantee that this money would be spent on mission projects.[83]

[78] The number of female religious rose to 53 by 1909; Ninove, *The Capuchin Mission in the Punjab*, 193.

[79] Ibid. 190–1.

[80] Ibid. 190.

[81] Rooney, *Into Deserts*, 18.

[82] Leo XIII, *Instructions to the Missions*, 19 Mar. 1893 (Vatican, 1893), quoted in Letter from Ladiolas-Michel, Archbishop of Thebes (Apostolic Delegate), to the Bishop of Lahore, 6 Aug. 1893, ABC, L121.

[83] The statistics usually show this as a reduced (one-third) sum appearing as a Receipt, although for some years (1925, for example) the full figure appears in the Receipts with two-thirds of the sum then shown in Expenses. See Tables 2.7 and 2.8.

Table 2.5. *Receipts of the Capuchin mission in Punjab, 1900–1935 (Rs, annas, paise)*

Receipts	1900	1905	1910	1915	1920	1925	1930	1935
Stipends for Masses	5,443/8/3	5,027/9/11	8,341/12/0	3,081/13/10	11,715/4/6	2,778/0/0	5,656/11/0	7,779/7/4
Alms from external benefactors	9,401/11/4	n/a	n/a	n/a	n/a	n/a	507/0/0	6,903/2/0
From various indigenous sources	n/a	n/a	n/a	n/a	n/a	n/a	390/0/0	3,443/13/0
Alms received from Provincial	n/a	n/a	2,717/1/0	n/a	n/a	n/a	6,540/8/0	4,997/8/0
Alms received from General	n/a	n/a	294/6/0	1,697/15/0	n/a	n/a	n/a	n/a
Belgian Mission Fund, Lahore	n/a	n/a	n/a	n/a	1,228/11/0	347/7/0	n/a	n/a
Quota from military chaplain wages	1,837/8/0	2,950/0/0	3,720/8/8	3,256/0/0	8,365/4/0	15,727/0/0	11,618/3/9	15,253/10/0
War bonus to military chaplains	n/a	n/a	n/a	n/a	994/15/0	n/a	n/a	n/a
Other alms, legacies, etc.	779/4/0	4,256/10/6	4,912/1/0	1,593/0/0	3,625/3/0	8,859/13/0	6,274/0/0	32,732/18/0
Carried over from previous year	2,529/7/4	12,234/4/5	8,144/10/6	15,325/10/3	19,035/11/7	22,757/5/5	9,091/9/0	17,581/14/1
TOTAL	19,991/6/11	24,490/1/11	28,130/11/2	24,954/7/1	44,964/15/0	50,496/9/11	40,006/1/9	88,692/8/5

Note: n/a = not available. The categories used are my own amalgamation of changing categories employed by the Regular Superior. The lack of regular categories or published records for Belgian Capuchin finances in Punjab has resulted in an incomplete table, although the totals and surpluses shown are those given by the Regular Superior. Stipends for Masses all came from Belgium, as did the great majority of alms from external benefactors (the sources do not reveal how much exactly).

Source: Letters and Reports of the Regular Superior to the Provincial and SCPF.

Punjabi contributions amounted to very little in the mission. They were not even listed separately in financial statistics until 1930, and references to financial self-sufficiency occurred far less frequently in Capuchin than in CMS correspondence. Although the promotion of financial self-sufficiency in mission territories was an important point of Catholic mission policy (the Apostolic Delegate warned presciently in 1893 that if Europe were to suffer a 'long war' or 'some other catastrophe' then European parishes could no longer be relied upon for funds[84]), the Punjab mission was considered too young for this yet to be a priority. Moreover, without the Protestant vision of future independence for new national Churches, Capuchin calls for local donations perhaps lacked urgency and ideological appeal among converts.

Table 2.6 shows the expenditure of the Capuchin mission, with a relatively high proportion of funds dedicated to the building and maintenance of churches and other mission structures. Although the Capuchins were generally happy to live in basic accommodation—this was part of the charism of their Order and could be made into excellent propaganda at home in Europe—they strongly believed that impressive sites of worship, and the ceremonies held within, were an important way of influencing Punjabi minds. Heavy expenditure upon building work could be contentious, however, and just as Mal and Bomford in the CMS were critical on this point, so the Capuchin Fr. Edouard complained early on in the life of the mission that a new church in Dalhousie was to cost around Rs 21,000 when a simpler one might have been built for as little as Rs 4,000.[85]

The Capuchins sometimes actually went into debt in order to finance new buildings: Belgian Fr. 45,000 were borrowed for the building of the church, house, and school at Sahowala and a convent nearby.[86] Nor could their spending power ever compare to that of the CMS. Just before the First World War the figure for the Capuchin mission income in rupees was similar to the CMS's figure in pounds sterling. At 1914 exchange rates, this meant that the CMS's income in Punjab was around fifteen times that of the Capuchins.[87] Given this discrepancy, and the

[84] Letter from Ladiolas-Michel, Archbishop of Thebes (Apostolic Delegate), to the Bishop of Lahore, 6 Aug. 1893.

[85] Letter from Fr. Edouard to Provincial, 8 Nov. 1892, ABC, L91.

[86] Letter from the Bishop of Lahore to Procuror, 29 Sept. 1897, ABC, L267.

[87] Approximate 1914 exchange rate given by the Revd C. F. Hall (CMS) as Rs 150 = £10; C. F. Hall, 'A Suggested Policy for Mass Movements', *CMR* 65/781 (May 1914), 282.

TABLE 2.6. *Expenditure of the Capuchin mission in Punjab, 1900–1935 (Rs, annas, paise)*

Expenditure	1900	1905	1910	1915	1920	1925	1930	1935
Catechists	n/a	n/a	n/a	3,347/14/0	4,756/10/0	6,443/0/0	n/a	n/a
Maintenance of the missionaries	7,513/12/0	n/a	n/a	n/a	3,173/4/0	4,010/13/0	5,290/1/0	43,692/1/9
$\frac{2}{3}$ quota given to the Bishop	n/a	n/a	n/a	n/a	n/a	10,484/10/8	n/a	n/a
Sanatorium in Dalhousie	n/a	n/a	n/a	1,448/11/0	2,595/9/0	2,306/11/0	n/a	n/a
Alms for mission stations and various apostolic works	n/a	8,406/5/0	11,217/3/6	4,053/6/0	1,750/0/0	2,127/03/0	9,991/0/0	4,088/11/9
St Anthony's College	321/4/0	n/a	n/a	n/a	n/a	n/a	n/a	n/a
New missionaries	n/a	n/a	n/a	n/a	2,299/7/0	1,296/3/0	n/a	335/6/0
Clothes, vestments	n/a	1,377/6/0	1,463/15/0	886/13/0	1,819/10/0	1,289/4/0	6,628/15/0	810/8/8
Annual retreats	n/a	250/0/0	757/0/0	571/0/0	702/11/0	690/0/0		
Travel, transport of goods	776/2/9	1,284/7/0	1,543/3/0	298/2/0	737/14/0	634/12/0	4,540/0/0	1,096/12/0
For the publication of two books	n/a	n/a	n/a	n/a	n/a	556/0/0	n/a	n/a
For the purchase of books	n/a	n/a	636/1/0	134/2/0	n/a	n/a	n/a	n/a
For use of the Regular Superior	n/a	n/a	n/a	407/0/0	444/9/0	424/0/0	1,994/12/0	2,212/4/0
For the sick and dead	n/a	836/11/0	139/2/0	1,136/13/0	805/15/0	365/0/0	918/11/0	1,302/15/0
Other (incl. buildings, maintenance)	5,813/8/3	4,906/15/0	1,363/15/0	n/a	n/a	2,025/0/0	8,330/3/0	11,435/14/0
TOTAL	14,434/11/0	17,261/7/3	17,122/8/0	12,183/13/0	19,081/9/0	32,652/9/8	37,893/10/0	64,974/8/6
Mission surplus	5,556/11/11	7,228/10/6	11,008/3/2	12,770/10/01	25,883/6/0	17,844/0/3	2,115/7/9	23,717/15/11

Note: n/a = not available. The categories used are my own amalgamation of changing categories employed by the Regular Superior. The lack of regular categories or published records for Belgian Capuchin finances in Punjab has resulted in an incomplete table, although the totals and surpluses shown are those given by the Regular Superior. From 1926 onwards, 'Alms for various mission stations and various apostolic works' included the payment of catechists' wages.

Source: *Letters and Reports of the Regular Superior to the Provincial and SCPF.*

Capuchins' wish to extend their mission as far outside their urban and cantonment bases as possible, it is striking that in most years such large amounts of money were kept back by the mission. The sources do not reveal the reasoning behind this, but it is possible that a sum was withheld as a capital endowment for the future of the mission—particularly given the fears of the Apostolic Delegate regarding the political climate in Europe.

CMS and Capuchin financial statistics suggest that the two missions assessed their spending priorities in different ways. The Capuchins enjoyed the same basic economies associated with frugal communal living and an absence of dependants that had allowed religious Orders in Belgium to undercut their rivals in the provision of education and other influential social services. Friars frequently ridiculed what they saw as CMS missionaries' extravagant colonial lifestyles, although they were all too aware of the benefits of social proximity to the Raj. In proportional terms the CMS outspent the Capuchins on medical establishments and bureaucracy, while the Capuchins outspent the CMS in building works (particularly churches) and, crucially, the employment of Indian agents. This is illustrated in Fig. 2.2.

Although the comparison is rendered imperfect by the range of categories utilized by the two missions over time, it is clear that in a period when the mass-movement influx into the CMS and Capuchin missions had peaked, and the manpower resources of both groups were at their most strained, a notably larger proportion of CMS expenditure continued to go towards the employment of European rather than Indian personnel. This could, however, have been because the Belgian Capuchins simply felt they could not spare many more than the 13 or 14 per cent of their number shown in Table 2.3 for mission work in Punjab. In any case, so much larger was the CMS than the Capuchin budget that the number of Indian missionaries and catechists attached to the former mission easily outstripped those of the latter, by 340 to 70 in 1925.[88]

Both missions enjoyed a brief rise in income after the First World War, facilitated partly by generous giving to the Churches in thanksgiving for peace and, in the Capuchins' case, Masses said for the dead. However, the Capuchins later suffered as a result of economic crisis in Belgium (including a drastic devaluation of the Belgian franc in the

[88] Figures taken from *Proceedings of the CMS, 1924–5* (London, 1926), and *Analecta Ordinis Minorum Capuccinorum* (1925).

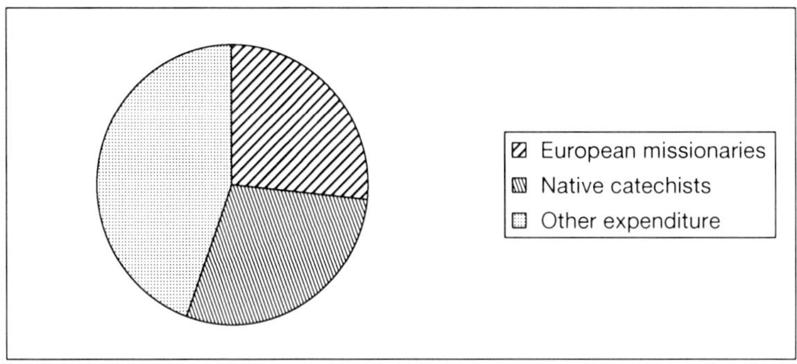

(*a*) Capuchin expenditure, 1920–1925

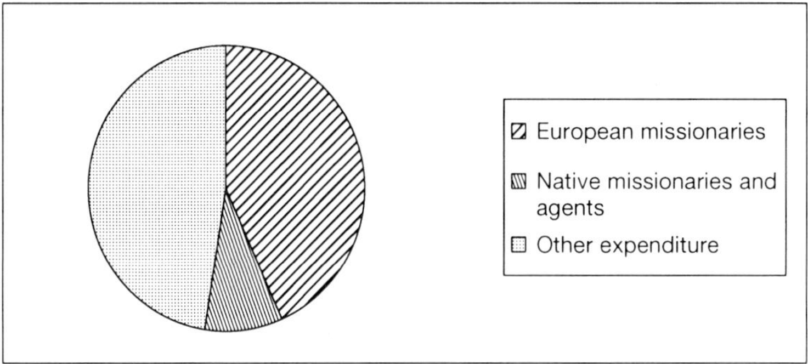

(*b*) CMS expenditure, 1919 and 1924

FIG. 2.2. Capuchin and CMS expenditure on Indian and European personnel. Whereas CMS mission expenditure on personnel was regulated annually, in the Capuchin mission there were no set maintenance grants for European personnel and no standard yearly budget for Indian personnel. Thus, Fig. 2.2(*b*) is based on CMS figures for 1919 and 1924 only, while Fig. 2.2(*a*) uses Capuchin figures for 1920–5 in order to guarantee a fair average. For both figures, 'other expenditure' refers to spending within India only, and excludes money lost on currency exchange, for example. Travel to and from Europe is included in the 'European missionaries' categories. Both keys retain the use of the word 'Native' from Capuchin and CMS source material.

Source: *Letters and Reports of the Regular Superior to the Provincial and CMS Proceedings* (London, various years)

mid-1920s), while the CMS mission continued to be hamstrung by financial retrenchment at home in London.

Internal Tensions

Aside from matters of finance, areas of concern voiced by Punjabi Christian delegates to the PNCC in the 1870s, 1880s, and 1890s included the apparent reproduction of European and American Protestant culture and denominational rivalries in Punjab. 'We are too few to be divided,' insisted Mya Das in 1878, asking that 'Church government and mode of worship . . . be as far as possible Punjabi'.[89] Another delegate, Sher Singh, had accused English missionaries the year before (despite their training) of ignorance where Punjabi 'customs and ideas' were concerned.[90] Imad-ud-din similarly cautioned converts against the affectation of 'English ways' and, while stressing that it would be wrong to object to converts raising their social status through conversion or gaining employment through the mission, he cautioned Christians to remember that the advantages enjoyed by the English came from God and were within the grasp of all nations.[91]

PNCC delegates also expressed concern about the CMS's lack of attention to rural mission work. The 'simple-minded and open-hearted men and women of the villages' represented a more reliable basis for a Punjabi Church than career-minded urbanites, claimed Das, yet European missionaries were not properly equipped for the task.[92] Few of them spoke good Punjabi, and Urdu was virtually useless in the villages, where it was regarded as a dead language; many villagers did not even recognize the sound of it, and assumed that missionaries were speaking English. At the Sixth Meeting of the PNCC, in 1881, the Revd Mian Sadiq gave a scathing account of the efforts of one particular missionary, whom Sadiq had accompanied on a village tour:

The Missionary took his walking stick, and drew two lines on the ground saying: 'This is Mahomed and this can only lead to hell, and this is Christ and

[89] Mya Das, speaking at the Third Meeting of the PNCC; ACMS, *Third Meeting, 1878* (Lahore, 1879), 60–1.

[90] Sher Singh, speaking at the Second Meeting of the PNCC; ACMS, *Second Meeting, 1877*, 75–9.

[91] The Revd Imad-ud-din, speaking at the Second Meeting of the PNCC; ACMS, *Second Meeting, 1877*, 71–3, 85.

[92] Mya Das, speaking at the Sixth Meeting of the PNCC; ACMS, *Sixth Meeting, 1881* (Lahore, 1882), 40–2.

heaven . . . To be a Christian is to go to heaven'. This was all that could be said [because of language difficulties] . . . no wonder, then, that the people would be bewildered. They would ask of the native helpers what was meant by the sahib.[93]

Sadiq went on to argue that only Indians could be effective village evangelists, combining the roles of teacher, 'true friend', and counsel. Delegates recommended a concentration of one Indian catechist for every twenty-five villages, and suggested that catechists reside in one of their appointed villages.

Missionaries were also criticized for sacrificing efficiency to territorial ambition,[94] and for insisting upon the use of English hymns in evangelization work when to Punjabi ears the melodies sounded morose and members of the audience thought that the singers sounded as though they were crying.[95]

The issues raised by the PNCC represented more than mere disagreements over policy; they reflected real frustration at the methods and attitudes of some CMS missionaries. By the late 1880s and 1890s trust between many European missionaries and PNCC delegates had broken down. The Revd H. U. Weitbrecht, staying at the prominent Christian Rullia Ram's house during the meeting of the PNCC in 1888, detected 'a good deal of. . . soreness on the race question' and a belief that mission policy was made by Europeans and merely presented to the PNCC to be rubber-stamped.[96] An article in *The Masihi* in 1898 claimed that Indian pastors were 'slave[s] to the will of [the] Padri Sahib'.[97] Tensions continued in the joint European–Indian Central and District Mission Councils (CMCs and DMCs), which replaced the ailing PNCC and Church Committees in the early twentieth century. On one occasion a vote in the CMC on stipends for Indian clergy split the Council exactly along lines of race.[98] Even the shift from the PNCC to Central

[93] The Revd Mian Sadiq, speaking at the Sixth Meeting of the PNCC; ibid. 48–9.

[94] Ibid. 53–7.

[95] Mr Basu, Headmaster of the Government School in Multan, speaking at the Sixth Meeting of the PNCC; ibid. 58.

[96] Letter from the Revd H. U. Weitbrecht to CMS Secretary, 12 Mar. 1888, ACMS, G2/I4/O 1888, n. 136.

[97] Extract from 'Punjab Native District Church Council', *The Masihi*, Feb. 1898, ACMS, G2/I4/O 1888, n. 121.

[98] H. G. Grey, 'Native Church Organisation in India II: The Punjab', *CMR* 60/724 (Aug. 1909), 481.

and District Councils had only been accomplished after a period of wrangling among CMS personnel over whether Indian and European voices ought to be heard in separate or joint representative bodies.

At the same time, however, the language of urban Punjabi Christians suggested they had imbibed something of the ambiguous popular European attitude towards the countryside as unspoilt and full of potential yet at the same time backward and unrefined. Despite their calls for rural evangelism, some Council delegates looked down their noses at the rural converts who began to enter the Church in the late 1880s and early 1890s—even when the Revd Mian Sadiq warned that the Church should guard against social divisions.[99] Wadhawa Mal, for example, claimed that Christians 'from the lower classes' had 'an extraordinary weakness for following one another like sheep . . . they are also very changeable; secretly they often have worldly objects in view [and] keep their own interests carefully in sight'.[100]

Tensions also arose within the CMS mission-Church between a number of European missionaries and their policy-making superiors in Punjab and in London. The perceived slowness of policy-makers to rise to the challenge of evangelization in the countryside became a major point of contention by the 1890s, as missionaries began to be deluged by rural petitions for teaching and for baptism. The Revd Rowland Bateman accused the CMS of lacking commitment, writing to the CMS Secretary in London, in 1900:

> As far as I know, no male missionary in the Punjab is preparing for [village] itineration, or for Punjabi work properly so-called. Surely if it be the case that . . . the bulk of the Christian community has been won from the villages this ought not to be even approximately true. But so long as it is so, and nobody either protests or laments I have to ask myself almost daily whether as soon as I am gone my 2,000 Christians will be left to the U.P. [United Presbyterian] and R.C. [Roman Catholic] Missionaries, and in that case whether it is worthwhile to leave more than an umbrella behind me as dowry.[101]

Bateman went on to describe the latest CMS appeal for restraint in mission expenditure as 'pathetic'. He agreed with the PNCC, whose proceedings he had on one occasion attended as a guest, that there ought

[99] The Revd Mian Sadiq, speaking at the Fifth Meeting of the PNCC; ACMS, *Fifth Meeting, 1880* (Lahore, 1881), 40–1.

[100] Copy of *Eighteenth Meeting, 1895* (Lahore, *c*.1896), ACMS, G/CCb 4/2c, pt 2.

[101] Letter from the Revd R. Bateman to CMS Secretary, 18 Sept. 1900, ACMS, G2/I4/O 1900, n. 141.

to be greater economy in urban educational institutions—particularly those in Amritsar and Karachi, which had had 'lakhs of rupees spent on them for a generation and a half'. New missionaries ought to be trained by successful rural evangelists such as the Revd Edward Guilford, so that they might 'be taught . . . to enter open doors instead of kicking at closed ones in cities'.[102]

Some missionaries objected to the everyday working methods imposed on them by the CMS. Edward Guilford, who was a comrade-in-arms of Bateman and almost as in awe of him as Maconachie,[103] disliked the heavy bureaucratic responsibilities that came with the job, while the Revd J. Tunbridge viewed the CMS school system as dominated by 'heathen' students and staff, and as successful only in fostering dependency upon the mission and restricting his own freedom to pursue what he regarded as real mission work.[104]

Other fissures between European missionaries related to educational and social background. Graduates of Islington College complained that 'University men' were consulted more frequently on matters of policy and were promoted to positions of responsibility in mission stations faster than 'Islington men'. Bomford warned the CMS Secretary in 1888 that there had been talk in Punjab of Islington men grouping together to 'secure their rights' against those they saw as their university-educated competitors. Bomford believed that the relative social inferiority of these men in England rendered it more difficult for them to establish a rapport with Punjabis because they arrived in the province desperate to be paid 'respect' as 'Masters of the land', lacking courtesy towards Punjabis as a result. In some cases they deliberately kept Indian clergy waiting on their verandas and refused to allow them to sit down in their presence.[105]

The Capuchins tended to be more open than the CMS in expressing disagreements within their mission. Missionary correspondence reveals serious acrimony between the missionaries themselves and successive bishops of Lahore. As with the CMS, the issue of money—where to obtain it and how to spend it—was often a source of division. The

[102] Letter from the Revd R. Bateman to CMS Secretary, 18 Sept. 1900.

[103] Guilford dubbed Bateman the 'prince of missionaries' (quoted in Maconachie, *Rowland Bateman*, 158–60).

[104] Letter from J. Tunbridge to CMS Secretary, 10 Oct. 1896, ACMS, G2/I4/O 1896, n. 119.

[105] Letters from Bomford to CMS Secretary, (undated) 1888, ACMS, G2/I4/O 1888, n. 170; 16 Nov. 1896.

requirement for Capuchin military chaplains to give two-thirds of their income to the diocese caused great resentment, particularly when a given bishop was viewed as greedy, bad with money, or ungenerous in his attitude towards the indigenous mission. Missionaries often accused the bishop of thoughtlessly overspending while mission workers lived frugally and tried to save money for evangelization. Fr. Edouard complained in 1892 that Mgr Van Den Bosch's spending was exceeding his income by between Rs 300 and Rs 400 per month.[106]

Bishops, for their part, could make life difficult for the missions by stretching the generosity of the Catholic laity in the diocese. In 1896 the missionary in charge of procuring funds, Fr. Jean-Baptiste, complained directly to the Bishop about a recent wave of collections which he had ordered:

> May Your Highness excuse my frankness, for it is in the interest of the mission itself that I feel that I must tell you; your Highness is slightly spoiling my job. Everywhere I go I receive complaints that His Excellency is insatiable, that people are bleeding themselves dry. Incessantly repeated demands anger and irritate people. Therefore, Your Highness, if you continue this system of incessant collections I will be forced to retire for my job [is becoming] unbearable.[107]

Tensions arose once again in 1921 when Fr. Marc, the Regular Superior, discovered that the diocese was in debt to the Punjab Government by Rs 170,000. The Bishop at this time, Mgr Eestermans, inflamed the situation further by refusing to discuss the matter. Fr. Marc suggested to the Provincial that the matter be brought immediately to the attention of the SCPF.[108] Little was done, and two years later Fr. Marc found himself having to explain to the missionaries that there was only enough money to pay half the catechists' wages. Privately, he noted that the Bishop claimed to be 'as poor as me', and thus unable to help him, yet was busy building himself a new house in Dalhousie.[109] Only after some of these complaints had been published in a Capuchin journal did Mgr Eestermans respond, in a letter to the Provincial in 1925. Eestermans pointed out that the Regular Superior had taken on new catechists without permission; there was plenty of money available for the others.[110]

[106] Letter from Fr. Edouard to Provincial, 8 Nov. 1892, ABC, L91.
[107] Letter from Fr. Jean-Baptiste to Bishop of Lahore, 3 July 1896, ABC, L223.
[108] Letter from Provincial to General, 13 Apr. 1921, GACO.
[109] Letter from Regular Superior to General, 20 June 1923, GACO.
[110] Letter from the Bishop of Lahore to General, 22 July 1925, GACO.

Such incidents were part of a general sense of dislocation between mission and diocese. The inherently conflicting imperatives of the two organizations were a constant source of trouble for the Capuchins, superseding the bonds of a shared Rule and nationality. The main protagonists here were usually the Regular Superior and the bishop. The former was the leader of the missionaries, directly answerable to the Provincial and responsible for assigning people to posts and tasks, and for liaising with the bishop, the Provincial in Antwerp, and the General of the Order in Rome.

The bishop was part of a supranational hierarchy which went directly upwards to the Pope. His first priority was the existing Catholic community, and together with his Council (which included the Regular Superior) he was responsible for the administration of the diocese and its funds, including the building of schools and churches and the employment of catechists. Missionaries were obliged to make formal requests to the diocese for assistance with expensive projects, while initiatives such as the planning of new buildings and the employment of Indian personnel required the permission of the bishop whether diocesan finances were involved or not. Considerable diplomacy was required of the Provincial, therefore, when missionaries brought their grievances to him; the bishop addressed the Provincial with deference but was under no ecclesiastical obligation to him.

The key post of Regular Superior in this period was occupied as follows:

1891–1903	Fr. Edouard
1903–7	Fr. Gonzalve
1907–26	Fr. Marc
1927–30	Fr. Felix
1930–3	Fr. Matthew
1933–49	Fr. Arsene

That of Bishop of Lahore was as follows:

1886–90	Mgr Mouard	(died)
1890–2	Mgr Van Den Bosch	(appointed Archbishop of Agra)
1893–1904	Mgr Pelckmans	(died)
1905–28	Mgr Eestermans	(retired)
1928–46	Mgr Catry	(retired)

Relations between the two offices reached their nadir in 1933, when Mgr Catry wrote to the General about the forthcoming election among missionaries for the post of Regular Superior. Catry thought the current occupant of the post, Fr. Matthew, untrustworthy and impossible to work with. Yet he appeared wearily expectant that the 'spirit of opposition to ecclesiastical authority' which characterized the 'traditional politics' of the mission would result in the election of yet another confrontational Regular Superior.[111] Catry had heard that Fr. Felix was deemed unsuitable for the position since he was 'too loyal' to the Bishop—a 'strange argument', as far as Catry was concerned. The election of Fr. Arsene to the post later that year appeared to confirm Catry's suspicions; Catry had previously named Arsene as one of the ringleaders of opposition to both bishop and Council.[112]

Catry's difficulties were partly the fault of his predecessors as bishop, particularly Mgr Eestermans. Although Eestermans had been among the first Capuchins to enter Punjab, he was widely perceived as being wasteful of money, lacking interest in evangelization among Punjabis, and presiding over a damaging '*far niente* [Italian: lazy, lit. 'do nothing']' status quo.[113] And when Eestermans *did* act, it was often to do things which upset the missionaries, such as moving the popular evangelist Fr. Felix away from the young colony of Maryabad and into a desk job in Lahore.[114] By 1911 Eestermans had also acquired a reputation for a 'fanciful way . . . [of] arranging facts' and was described by the Provincial as 'a sly peasant, very stingy', who was 'conscious of his own mediocrity'.[115]

The Provincial was generally to be found on the side of the missionaries in these disagreements. Fr. Vital privately accused Eestermans of giving orders which directly contradicted those of the Provincial,[116] while during an earlier 'shameful fight'[117] between the missionaries and Mgr Pelckmans the Provincial had written angrily to the Bishop: 'you impute to me a load of black envies of which no serious person, not even Your Highness, believes a single word . . . You are aware, Mgr, that our Capuchin Missionaries keep complaining to me that they are not sufficiently supported by Your Highness. . . . can I not hear their prayers?'[118]

111 Letter from the Bishop of Lahore to General, 5 Jan. 1933, GACO. 112 Ibid.

113 Letter from Provincial to General, 10 Dec. 1911. GACO, Letter from Regular Superior to Provincial, 9 July 1912, GACO.

114 Letter from Regular Superior to Provincial, 9 July 1912, GACO.

115 Letter from Provincial to General, (date illegible) 1920, GACO.

116 Letter from Fr. Vital to General, 11 Dec. 1911, GACO.

117 Letter from Fr. Deodat to General, 1 Sept. 1904, GACO.

118 Letter from Provincial to Bishop of Lahore, 15 Sept. 1896, ABC, L227.

The Provincial had also criticized Pelckmans for taking little interest in current building works, which were funded from Belgium but overseen by the diocese of Lahore: 'I would have been glad to receive a little word concerning the hospital, the cathedral etc. The benefactors imagine that all of that is already half built. What do you want me to tell them in order to maintain their good dispositions?'[119]

The popularity of ordinary friars often seemed to rest upon perceptions of their enthusiasm for the indigenous mission. Fr. Gonsalve (Regular Superior 1903–7) was criticized for preaching 'sermons of formality' in the European style rather than 'teaching the catechism in full simplicity through lesson and conversation'. Moreover, it did not go unnoticed that 'almost his entire sojourn in India took place in the mountains in Dalhousie, an excellent climatic situation where one does not suffer the heat like in the plains'. The weight of such sentiments in the mission forced Gonsalve's removal from his post after less than three years.[120] In contrast, Fr. Marc served for eighteen years as Regular Superior and was praised as having 'only ever lived among the Hindus . . . an observant and zealous monk, who loves and understands the ministry of the native missions . . . if only he were bishop!'[121]

There was considerably less bureaucracy in the Capuchin than in the CMS mission, primarily because the Capuchins had very little contact with other Christian missions in Punjab and did not seek to involve the Catholic laity in the day-to-day running of the mission-Church. In accordance with the charism and Rule of the Order, the Capuchins adopted a style of evangelization which was the romantic ideal of men like Bateman and Guilford: as much as possible was left to the personality, skills, and spontaneity of the missionary, relatively free of the impediments of meetings and paperwork. As the Provincial put it in 1920, 'Let us not fall into pedantry, which wants to transform everything into administrative rules . . . Who will teach the heart?'[122]

An important consequence of this was that grievances within the Capuchin mission tended to be aired in correspondence whose privacy was protected by conventions of confidentiality, whereas the CMS's troubles were often publicized, albeit less colourfully and comprehensively, at large, formal Church gatherings, and in a range of newspapers

[119] Letter from Provincial to Bishop of Lahore, 15 Sept. 1896. In a later official account of the mission Pelckmans nevertheless described himself as having been 'desirous above all of consolidating this eminently civilising [mission] work' (Pelckmans, *Dix Années*, 85).

[120] Letter from Provincial to General, (date illegible) 1920, GACO.

[121] Ibid. [122] Ibid.

and journals. The theoretical advantage of CMS organization, however, was that it functioned as a system of checks and balances, at the local, district, and provincial levels. Through a range of committees, subcommittees, conferences, councils, boards, visitations, and meetings the progress of the mission could be monitored and the necessary modifications swiftly made. And yet comments by Punjabi Christians and European missionaries like Bateman and Guilford suggested that this system failed to prevent inertia and conservative policies from alienating talented clergy and laity, thereby damaging the prospects of the mission-Church.

THE MISSION STATIONS

The main centres of activity for Christian missions in Punjab were the 'mission stations', as they were known. Much of missionaries' time was spent in and around these compounds, which incorporated lodgings and often a school and dispensary. Evangelization efforts branched out from here, in the form of preaching, meetings, and village visits. If one of these villages showed a significant interest in Christianity, a sub-station might be built there as a place for mission workers to stay overnight and as a base for teaching, catechism, and other mission work.

The CMS mission stations in the small towns of Tarn Taran and Narowal, situated in Amritsar and Sialkot districts respectively, became a centre of rural evangelization from the late nineteenth century onwards. While Tarn Taran made relatively modest progress in terms of conversion numbers, Narowal, along with the Capuchin mission stations in the villages of Adah and Sahowala (both situated in Sialkot district), became centres of dramatic mass-movement activity in the late nineteenth and early twentieth centuries.

What follows is a brief sketch of these four stations, using available *Gazetteer*, census, mission, and other sources to give a sense of their differing conditions, personnel, and institutions, as well as the size of the Christian population of the areas they served.

Tarn Taran

Table 2.7 shows the growth of the CMS Christian community in Punjab and Sindh at the height of the mass movements (1890–1920).

The missionaries working at Tarn Taran and Narowal during almost the same period (1890–1925) were as follows:

	Tarn Taran	Narowal
1890	Revd Edward Guilford	Revd Rowland Bateman Revd Frederic Lawrence Mrs F. Lawrence
1895	Revd Edward Guilford Revd E. Causton	Revd Rowland Bateman Mr H. F. Rowlands Revd Ihsan Ullah
1900	Revd Edward Guilford Mrs E. Guilford Revd Qutb-ud-din	Revd C. M. Gough Mrs C. M. Gough Mr H. F. Rowlands Mrs H. F. Rowlands
1905	Revd Edward Guilford Mrs E. Guilford Revd Qutb-ud-din	Revd C. M. Gough Mrs C. M. Gough
1910	Revd Edward Guilford Mrs E. Guilford Revd Qutb-ud-din Miss F. M. Saunders	Mr A. Dungworth Mrs A. Dungworth Revd W. P. Hares Mrs W. P. Hares Mr J. D. Finlay Revd J. F. Snee Mrs J. F. Snee Revd Parmanand
1915	Revd Edward Guilford Mrs E. Guilford Revd C. L. Richards Mrs C. L. Richards Revd A. P. Das Mr S. Culley	Revd W. P. Hares Mrs W. P. Hares Mr J. D. Finlay Mrs J. D. Finlay Revd Parmanand
1920	Revd Edward Guilford Mrs E. Guilford Revd A. P. Das Revd P. B. Singh	Revd H. E. Clark Mrs H. E. Clark Revd C. L. Richards Mrs C. L. Richards
1925	Revd A. P. Das Revd D. R. Creighton Mrs D. R. Creighton	Revd C. L. Richards Mrs C. L. Richards Revd Barakat Ullah

TABLE 2.7. *The growth of the CMS Christian community in Punjab and Sindh, 1890–1920*

CMS Christian community	1890	1895	1900	1905	1910	1911	1912	1913	1914	1920
Baptised Christians	4,582	5,069	6,232	10,133	13,159	17,869	21,030	21,220	19,148	24,753
Catechumens	314	785	1,872	1,304	4,347	3,337	4,401	3,964	3,964	5,023
TOTAL	4,896	5,854	8,104	11,437	17,506	21,206	25,341	25,184	23,112	29,776

Note: From 1910 onwards, CMS statistics for their Christian communities referred to Punjab without Sindh or North-West Frontier Province. As can be seen here, and in the corresponding statistics for Tarn Taran and Narowal (Tables 2.8 and 2.10), the CMS generally included as 'Christian' those people who were under instruction and had not yet been baptized.

Source: *Proceedings of the CMS* (London, various years).

Although it is through the eyes of these missionaries that much of the activity of the CMS is inevitably seen, this should not obscure the fact that Tarn Taran and Narowal employed a large staff of non-missionary workers, who undertook the bulk of teaching and administration in the missions. These included Punjabi catechists, teachers, Bible-women, and medical personnel, as well as European and Punjabi mission workers from the CEZMS and other mission societies with links to the CMS.

From Amritsar, Tarn Taran was situated almost halfway to Lahore. The town had been founded by the fifth Sikh guru, Arjun (d. 1606), in the late sixteenth century. Arjun built a tank and a temple on the site, claiming that the waters of the tank could cure the leprosy of anyone who swam the length of it. The town thus became known as Tarn Taran, meaning 'aiding [i.e. beneficial] to swim across'. Large numbers of lepers were subsequently drawn to the town, and an asylum was set up which later came under the management of the CMS. By the 1880s Tarn Taran was a major political and economic centre; the principal town of one of Amritsar district's three *tehsils*, with a population of 3,210 which was divided almost equally between Sikhs, Hindus, and Muslims.[123]

Although situated in a very fertile tract of land, Tarn Taran's main source of income was what the British called *octroi*: a municipal tax on certain types of goods entering the town.[124] Much of this income was stimulated by pilgrims and tourists, since a religious festival was held in the town every month, the main two occurring in March and August.[125]

A permanent missionary was first stationed at Tarn Taran in 1885. The Revd Edward Guilford had made occasional visits to the area since 1882, travelling from Amritsar, but settled into a newly built bungalow with his wife at the end of 1885. Over the course of the next ten years new buildings were added as the work and personnel of the mission expanded. A *zenana* house was constructed in 1886 and two mission workers, Miss Hanbury and Miss Grimwood, were transferred there in 1888. A small hospital and dispensary were added to the mission station shortly afterwards, and the mission was given honorary superintendence of the Government Leper Asylum from 1886. Daily evangelism in the asylum apparently resulted in the conversion to Christianity of a quarter

[123] *Gazetteer of the Amritsar District 1883–4*, pp. 76–7 and xxiii.
[124] Ibid. 76–7. [125] Ibid. 21.

of the approximately 180 inmates by 1895.[126] Nine years later the asylum was taken into mission hands and rebuilt.[127]

Guilford had joined the CMS in 1881, at the age of 28. He had received a second-class pass in the Oxford and Cambridge Preliminary Theology Exam and had been ordained deacon in June 1881. He went to Punjab four months later and was ordained a priest in 1882 by the Bishop of Lahore. Well known for translation work into Punjabi (including *The Pilgrim's Progress* and the Book of Common Prayer),[128] Guilford preferred village itineration to deskwork and committees. He shared with self-styled 'grassroots people' such as Frank Brayne serious doubts about the sensitivity of heads of large institutions to the real needs of work on the ground. Guilford thought the CMS particularly out of touch in their sluggish response to requests for workers at the height of the mass movements: 'What has befogged our minds', he asked in 1912, 'that we cannot see where strategic points lie?'[129]

Within just over twenty years the work at Tarn Taran expanded to fifteen separate departments, covering itineration in approximately 300 villages, ministry to eight Punjabi congregations, bazaar preaching, superintendence of the leper asylum, village schooling, classes for readers and schoolmasters, Sunday schools, a book depot and reading room, and preaching at monthly festivals. The station's Punjabi staff consisted of male mission agents (a senior catechist, junior catechist, junior reader, and four other readers[130]) and a range of female workers: Bibi Dorcas (Bibi meaning 'sister' or 'woman') ran a kindergarten class of nineteen children, Bibi Lachhmi taught classes on catechism and St Matthew's Gospel to the women of Bhojian village, Bibi Jhandi ran reading classes for female village readers and the women of the town and compound,[131] and other workers established a Women's Prem Sabha and Working Party.[132] The Revd Guilford's first wife had fallen ill and returned

[126] The Revd E. Guilford, Annual Letter 1895, repr. in Church Missionary Society, *Extracts from the Annual Letters of the Missionaries for the Year 1894–5*, ACMS (hereafter *EAL*) (London, 1895), 100.

[127] *Tarn Taran Mission of the Church Missionary Society, Punjab, India: Report and Accounts* [*TTRA*] *for the Year 1911* (Lahore, 1911), 3, ACMS, G2/I7/1, 2.

[128] *Register of Mission and Native Clergy, 1808–1904*, printed by the CMS for private circulation (London, 1904), ACMS.

[129] *TTRA 1912* (Lahore, 1912), 7, ACMS, G2/I7/1, 2.

[130] *TTRA 1908* (Lahore, 1908), inside cover, ACMS, G2/I7/1, 2. These titles corresponded with varying levels of experience and training.

[131] *TTRA 1912*, 17.

[132] *TTRA 1905* (Lahore, 1905), p. iii, ACMS, G2/I7/1, 2.

to England in 1894, where she later died. His second wife, whom he married in 1896, ran an advanced reading class during the week, another one on Sundays for villagers and 'stray folk', and occasionally itinerated in nearby villages with Bibi Jhandi.[133]

Tables 2.8 and 2.9 show the growth of the Tarn Taran mission's mostly low-caste Christian community over time, and the finances of the mission station for 1905 and 1917. Together they show slow but steady growth in the local mission-Church. Punjabi financial contributions remained slight in this period, usually paid in kind at the biannual harvests and then offset against mission sundries. In 1905 they added up to no more than the equivalent of one-tenth of teachers' salaries at the station.[134]

It was of great significance for notions of authority in the emerging mission-Church that decisions relating to how much each family ought to contribute were made by the village or caste *panchayat* rather than a representative of the mission. These bodies clearly retained an important influence after conversion, and Guilford reported that families rarely gave less than the *panchayat* asked them for.[135] At the same time, there was room for mission initiative in the area of financial self-sufficiency. Guilford made it an article of policy that no church would be built until the local congregation had advanced 'a considerable sum' towards the costs. The mission would then supply wood and, if required,

TABLE 2.8. *The growth of the CMS Christian community in Tarn Taran, 1890–1920*

CMS Christian community	1890	1895	1900	1905	1910	1911	1912	1913	1914	1920
Baptized Christians	103	186	207	394	801	914	1211	1,318	1,405	1,165
Catechumens	0	0	180	30	286	227	349	69	50	247
TOTAL	103	186	387	424	1,087	1,141	1560	1,387	1,455	1,412

Note: From 1910 onwards, CMS statistics for their Christian communities referred to Punjab without Sindh or North-West Frontier Province. Neither the CMS nor the Capuchins enumerated converts and catechumens by caste, so precise statistics for low castes are unavailable.

Source: *Proceedings of the CMS* (London, various years).

[133] *TTRA 1912*, 17. See Ch. 4 for details of Tarn Taran's educational and medical institutions, the latter including St Mary's Hospital, established in 1910 by the CEZMS.
[134] *TTRA 1905*, 4. [135] *TTRA 1912*, 4.

TABLE 2.9. *Earmarked receipts for Tarn Taran from the Parent Committee (London) and expenditure, 1905 and 1917 (Rs, annas paise)*

	Earmarked receipts		Expenditure	
	1905	1917	1905	1917
Balance from 1904	34/3/3	n/a		
Medicines			23/5/0	n/a
Indian clergy	660/0/0	799/15/10	n/a	799/10/0
Catechists and readers	1,435/0/0	1,905/0/0	1,627/15/3	1,905/0/0
Printing, stationery, postage	23/5/6	n/a	24/1/6	n/a
Repairs	50/0/0	n/a	252/7/3	n/a
Mission servants	144/0/0	144/0/0	144/0/0	144/0/0
Itineration	283/4/0	353/0/0	285/8/9	353/0/0
Travel	50/4/0	44/10/9	60/14/0	44/10/9
Rent, taxes	628/2/9	600/0/0	29/14/3	600/0/0
TOTAL	3,308/3/6	3,846/10/7	2,521/1/6	3,846/10/7

Note: n/a = not available. Indian clergy were not paid out of these funds in 1905, hence the surplus for that year.

Source: ACMS, *TTRA, 1905 and 1917.*

skilled labour. The congregation paid the balance over a number of years.[136]

Although the community at Tarn Taran had expanded considerably by 1913, and the work of the mission had diversified, the mission station still appeared steeped in English middle-class methods, routines, and culture. This was evident in the hierarchy of employees and their titles, and in the educational and medical work which they were set. Socialization into a very English brand of Christianity was apparent at the station's Christmas celebrations, which featured a selection of largely English songs, a children's tea party, a trained parrots' show, jugglers, conjurors, and various games.[137] There is little evidence, in the sources, of discussion relating to Punjabi influences upon the mission-Church, although it appears that minor cross-cultural exchanges *were* taking place; for example, the turning of a very English annual singing

[136] *TTRA 1912*, 5.

[137] *TTRA 1913* (Lahore, 1913), 18, ACMS, G2/I7/1, 2. The Christmas programme for the Leper Asylum ended with the judging of inmates' living quarters on points of cleanliness and tidiness, an activity strongly reminiscent of the 'outsider' uplift discussed in Ch. 1; Report of the Revd A. P. Das, repr. ibid.

competition into an issue of local pride among Punjabi Christians, with contestants marching to the competition under the flags of their respective villages.[138]

Narowal

The small trading town of Narowal was located halfway between Amritsar and Sialkot, and was 500 years old when the first CMS missionary, Dr Bruce, arrived in 1858. It was not a wealthy area, with incomes for tenant cultivators standing at just over half that of the average for Punjab, even by the 1930s.[139] A population of 4,558 was dominated by 2,935 Muslims and 1,429 Hindus,[140] and drew most of its income from *octroi*,[141] although agriculture and products in leather (including saddles and shoes), brass, and copper were also economically significant. The 1870s and 1880s were a time of considerable structural change in the town, with the paving of many streets, the building of bridges, and the construction of a modest drainage system.[142] Little village evangelization was undertaken during the first thirty years of the mission, and the town itself was considered hostile to Christianity. In 1888 the station boasted only 176 Christians and the first local convert, a prominent local trader named Mian Hussain Baksh (renamed Mian Paulus after his baptism), had found himself the subject of no less than twenty-one lawsuits, all filed in a single day by townspeople outraged at his conversion. Paulus was forced to buy his own drinking water and to live on a piece of wasteland, even though he owned several houses and shops.[143] Nevertheless, Narowal's period of ascendancy under the Revd Rowland Bateman, a man destined to become something of a legend in CMS circles, had begun.

Bateman was born in 1840 and educated at Brighton College and later Magdalen College, Oxford, where he rowed and played cricket. Like Guilford he was ordained deacon within a year of finishing his BA, applying to the CMS in 1868 and hoping to be sent to northern Canada, to the Arctic Circle. The possibility that a desire for heroic adventure

[138] *TTRA 1915* (Lahore, 1915), 17, ACMS, G2/I7/1, 2.

[139] Lucas and Thakur Das, *The Rural Church in the Punjab*, p. iv.

[140] *Gazetteer of the Sialkot District 1883–4* (Lahore, 1884), p. xxiii.

[141] *Gazetteer of the Sialkot District 1894–5*, 175.

[142] *Gazetteer of the Sialkot District 1883–4*, 110–11.

[143] Clark, *The Missions of the Church Missionary Society and the Church of England Zenana Missionary Society in the Punjab and Sindh*, 101.

influenced Bateman's decision to become a missionary unfortunately appears not to have interested Maconachie, who stated blandly that Bateman had decided upon a career in the Church before leaving university.[144]

Finding himself in Punjab rather than the Arctic Circle, Bateman struggled with the local language but embodied the contemporary ideal of active Christianity in his use of cricket as a way of connecting with village society.[145] Upon transfer to Narowal in 1875 he sought to enhance these bonds by living according to his impression of local life. Distancing himself from the society of other European missionaries, he stayed in a simple mud house and wore a turban and Indian shoes. He was remembered by Guilford as having preached in sandals, pyjamas, and a black clerical hat.[146] On another occasion, in 1901, Bateman himself proudly reported that he had survived an attack by robbers by asserting his credentials as an old fakir and displaying his beard as a sign of age and position. His watch and other belongings were duly returned to him. 'I did not say "Thank you",' Bateman recalled, 'for that is not the custom out here. On the contrary, I acted the correct Punjabi part by at once complaining that he had not given me back my keys.'[147]

The church which was built under Bateman's direction in 1874 reflected his enthusiasm for inculturation as it did for manly labour; he apparently undertook some of the building work himself, training on the job with a group of Punjabi workers and arranging a five-year contract to take the sweepings of the town for brick-making fuel, since local traders refused to sell him bricks.[148] The CMS's official biographer, Eugene Stock, tactfully reserved judgement on the new church, saying only that it was possibly the first to be built 'in the oriental style . . . not unlike a mosque in appearance'.[149] (See Figure 2.3).

Bateman seemed to relish the occasional hostility with which his evangelization efforts were met in Narowal, going to perhaps unnecessary lengths to ensure secrecy for young inquirers. He warned one man, Waris, never to greet him openly in the bazaar; he should instead just touch Bateman's ear as he walked past, to let him know that he was still interested in Christianity. When Waris decided to be baptized, Bateman

[144] Maconachie, *Rowland Bateman*, 8–9. [145] Ibid. 30–1, 45.

[146] Testimony of the Revd E. Guilford, repr. in Maconachie, *Rowland Bateman*, 159.

[147] Report of the Revd R. Bateman, repr. in *Proceedings of the CMS, 1901–2* (London, 1902), 252. [148] Maconachie, *Rowland Bateman*, 77.

[149] Stock, *History of the Church Missionary Society*, iii. 156.

Fig. 2.3. The CMS Church at Narowal, 1874.

Source: Maconachie, *Rowland Bateman*, facing p. 77

made sure that the Superintendent of Police would be present at the public announcement.[150]

Bateman built up an underground network of young, middle-class male inquirers, using a style of evangelization which he called *shikar karna* ('to hunt down'). This involved sending one boy—an inquirer or convert—to seek out other boys whom Bateman had heard were interested in Christianity and to bring them to a meeting. In this way Waris brought Prithu to Bateman, and both were later ordained priests. The account given of Bateman's methods by another young convert, Jalaluddin Ambar, illustrates the sportsman–spy tactics favoured by Bateman:

> He knew his game. He would use appropriate means for reaching men of different stages of society . . . an affectionate well-reasoned discourse would not be kept back by him when coming into contact with literate or a bit educated men. His life in those days was an organised plan for bringing young men to Christ. Youth was his special field, and it is surprising indeed how with a shikari's [huntsman's] eye he could discern in young men raw material to work up for Christ . . . I do not know of any other missionary in the Punjab who has attracted so many youths for Christ.[151]

The language which Bateman used in a letter to Maconachie to describe his role in the conversion of a second cousin of Waris in 1901 shows another dimension to his thinking as a missionary:

> [At the age of 18, Waris] has just come out clear of his mother's and father's entreaties and threats and declared that he will be a Christian. I have been angling for him ever since he was two years old, when his father put him into my arms proudly, and I told him that I should keep the boy and try and make him a Christian. So off and on it has been going on with the father's knowledge all these years, and this hour the bud has burst, and the beauty and sweet perfume of the opening flower almost robs me even of the thought of wishing you and yours the fullest measure of Christmas blessedness.[152]

Bateman sought to remain as close as possible to converts and catechumens in Narowal. Although married, he chose to continue living in a small house in the town rather than the newly constructed mission compound on the outskirts. He encouraged people to knock on his door at any time, day or night, since this gave him the feeling

[150] Testimony of the Revd Waris-ud-din, repr. in Maconachie, *Rowland Bateman*, 78–9.

[151] Testimony of Jalaluddin Ambar, repr. in Maconachie, *Rowland Bateman*, 131–2.

[152] Letter from Bateman to Maconachie, 5 Dec. 1901, repr. in Maconachie, *Rowland Bateman*, 123.

of constant itineration, even though he might actually be ploughing through administrative work. Competition from other mission societies was distinctly unwelcome, and Bateman eagerly negotiated the United Presbyterians' departure from Narowal in 1889.[153]

The congregation transferred from the United Presbyterians boosted CMS Christian numbers to 1,446 by 1890. From here they rose rapidly in the early years of the twentieth century, as Narowal found itself inundated with requests for attention from low-caste families in the area. The vast majority of Narowal's Christians were drawn from the Chuhra caste, the men of the families working as agricultural labourers and the women taking responsibility for the sweeping work with which their caste group remained associated in this area. By 1916 converts and catechumens were spread across 168 villages, and it was reported that in almost every village in the Narowal area Chuhras had enlisted as catechumens.[154] The growth in the CMS Christian community in the Narowal mission is shown in Table 2.10.

The Revd C. M. Gough, who took charge of the mission following Bateman's departure from India in 1897 and saw it through the period of its most rapid expansion, became one of the CMS's leading theorists on the mass-movement phenomenon, alongside the Revd W. P. Hares and the Revd C. F. Hall. Hares noted with anger in 1916 that the mission had lost a number of converts to the 'Romanists', who had

TABLE 2.10. *The growth of the CMS Christian community in Narowal, 1890–1920*

CMS Christian community	1890	1895	1900	1905	1910	1911	1912	1913	1914	1920
Baptized Christians	1,446	1,451	879	1,057	1,908	2,431	3,000	3,784	4,472	5,800
Catechumens	0	310	424	451	2,216	2,025	2,000	1,986	2,167	1,800
TOTAL	1,446	1,761	1,303	1,508	4,124	4,456	5,000	5,770	6,693	7,600

Note: From 1910 onwards, CMS statistics for their Christian communities referred to Punjab without Sindh or North-West Frontier Province.

Source: *Proceedings of the CMS* (London, various years).

153 Maconachie, *Rowland Bateman*, 103–8.

154 W. P. Hares, 'The Narowal Mission: A Ten Years' Retrospect', *CMR* 67/810 (Nov. 1916), 555.

begun to work in Narowal in recent years.[155] The Catholic diocese of Lahore had indeed established a mission station in the town in 1924, attracted—by their own admission—to the mass movement under way in the area and hoping to expand upon their existing evangelistic work around Pasrur.[156] Fr. Roger, sent to Narowal at the end of 1924, described the CMS mission organization as 'very strong', encompassing institutions of which, 'humanly speaking, they can be proud'.[157]

As one of the few mission stations to be administered by the PNCC, Narowal's finances are more difficult to summarize than those of Tarn Taran. There are also fewer financial reports available which deal specifically with Narowal. It clearly attracted considerable investment by 1908, with sums in excess of Rs 20,000 per annum passing through a series of different accounts, and large amounts were spent on the Christian Boys' Boarding School.[158] A sizeable proportion of Narowal's income was collected in England by a Mrs Melvill and earmarked for the Narowal mission in particular.[159]

Adah and Sahowala

The villages of Adah and Sahowala (see Maps 2.2 and 2.3 for their location) were two of four rural centres of evangelism near Sialkot established by the Capuchins in 1889, in response to a surge of interest from around eighty rural communities.[160] It was quickly discovered that this first small movement had been engineered by a number of discontented

[155] W. P. Hares, 'The Narowal Mission: A Ten Years' Retrospect', *CMR*, 557–8.

[156] Letter from Regular Superior to General, 17 Nov. 1925, and Letter from Regular Superior to General, 13 Nov. 1924, both GACO.

[157] Letter from Fr. Roger to General, 27 Jan. 1925, GACO.

[158] *Narowal Mission of the Church Missionary Society, Punjab, India: Report and Accounts for the Year, 1909*, 26, ACMS, G2/14/O 1909, n. 115. Twenty-seven per cent of the sum for the boarding school was drawn from CMS funds, with 34 per cent drawn from fees and the rest taken from various small grants. No government grant for boarding schools was available. See Ch. 4 on government and mission education.

[159] In 1908 these contributions amounted to more than Rs 1,000; ibid. 26. Mrs Melvill was none other than Bateman's mother-in-law, Eliza Johanna Melvill (Robert Maconachie, 'Rowland Bateman: A Fragmentary Tribute', *CMR* 67/805 (May 1916), 286; <www.familysearch.org>). She had married Philip Sandys Melvill, an ICS official serving in Punjab from 1846 until 1882, and later moved to London, at least by 1901 (*The India List and India Office List* (London, 1900), 484; <www.1901census.nationalarchives.gov.uk>, 161).

[160] The other two stations were Seowale and Daoki. The latter station was closed down in the early 1890s, when almost all its converts migrated to the new Catholic village of Maryabad.

Protestant catechists. Interest soon melted away, generating a strong Capuchin invective against 'false converts . . . instruments of Satan who were only showing zeal . . . so as to satisfy their low greed'.[161] Memories of the 'abominable conduct of the [Protestant] catechists'[162] and the 'volatility of Orientals'[163] remained with Capuchin missionaries and coloured apparently long-standing prejudices well after this first bruising experience had passed. Future failings were blamed on Catholicism's unpopular, though virtuous, emphasis on the blessedness of poverty, in contrast to the behaviour of 'sectarian ministers' who 'cunningly exploited to their profit the shortcomings and passions of the natives' where material things were concerned.[164]

Many of the 117 adults baptized in 1889 had been residents of the village of Adah, so despite early disappointments the mission there had to be continued. Adah was one of the larger villages of the Sialkot *tehsil*,[165] 8 miles from the town itself and with more than 90 per cent of its Chuhra population listed as Muslim.[166] Fr. Lievin was the first missionary to be sent there on a full-time basis, living in a small mud hut (see Fig. I.1) until a brick structure was completed in June 1891. His recall to Lahore the next year, and the short stays in Adah of Fr. Engelbert (1892) and Fr. Edmund (1894), resulted in a diminished congregation by 1894, and the station at Adah was almost closed down.[167]

Fr. Vincent arrived at Adah in 1894 and, as with Narowal, it appeared that under the influence of a new missionary the fortunes of a mission station could be reversed. Fr. Vincent re-established Adah's ailing school and celebrated the first Communion of ten children in 1895. He was joined by Br. Constant the same year, whose relatively developed knowledge of the local language made possible the renewal of village itineration. Much of this was among Sikhs, and although little came of it, the Capuchins nevertheless reported cordial relationships with Sikh villagers. Modest progress with other groups in the district was soon made, and was rewarded in 1897 with the replacement of the old mission buildings with larger ones capable of housing three missionaries,

[161] Pelckmans, *Dix Années*, 64. Fr. Clement's failure to 'see through this deceit' upset his colleagues, who had seen Rs 2,000 per month spent on catechists in the short period of the movement. He was quickly transferred elsewhere in the Punjab mission. Ninove, *The Capuchin Mission in the Punjab*, 130–1.

[162] Ibid. 374. [163] Pelckmans, *Dix Années*, 65. [164] Ibid. 65.

[165] *Gazetteer of the Sialkot District 1883–4*, 71.

[166] According to statistics of the 1901 Census, repr. in *Gazetteer of the Sialkot District 1904, Statistical Tables* (Lahore, 1907), p. xxvi.

[167] Ninove, *The Capuchin Mission in the Punjab*, 129–32.

and the consecration of the Capuchins' first indigenous mission church, the Church of Our Lady of Mount Carmel (see Fig. 2.4).[168]

Adah soon became a model for future enterprises, and as interest from surrounding areas increased, the Capuchins hoped that young Christians raised in the village would soon work as catechists in nearby villages.[169] By 1910 a number of Catholic institutions had taken shape in Adah. The original school had split into a primary school for boys and a lower primary school for girls. Seven outstations had been established, five of which had their own lower primary schools, open to both boys and girls.[170]

Sahowala was a large community of 13,000 people that relied upon Hindu and Sikh commerce and Muslim agriculture for its prosperity and was situated about 7 miles from Sialkot. A visit by the Capuchin chaplain at the Sialkot military cantonment excited the interest of a number of local families in the village which were later described by the Capuchins as belonging to the Chuhra caste and occupying 'the lowest rung of the social ladder . . . at the mercy of their [Hindu, Muslim, and Sikh] masters'.[171] Fr. Lievin began to make regular journeys there from Adah in the early 1890s. Such was the level of enthusiasm in the village that a small mission station was established there in 1897, initially just a two-roomed house which functioned as accommodation, school, and chapel.[172]

Fr. Archange and Br. Constant were sent to Sahowala as the station's first permanent missionaries. Br. Constant's linguistic skills, which had served Adah well for a short time, now enabled him to make sufficient progress with the people of Sahowala that attendance at the mission school started to rise.[173] Although the mission suffered a temporary setback when Br. Constant was taken ill with pleurisy and died in October 1897, a church (the Church of the Sacred Hearts of Jesus and Mary) and presbytery were nevertheless established in Sahowala a few months later. The blessing of the new church in 1898 was later recalled in a Capuchin publication: 'By the size, by the ornamentation of the edifice, by the garlands . . . decorating the walls, the ceremony had

168 Cuthbert, *The Capuchins*, ii. 121.

169 The catechists' training school set up in Adah for this purpose is looked at in Ch. 3.

170 Ninove, *The Capuchin Mission in the Punjab*, 191.

171 Pelckmans, *Dix Années*, 93.

172 Ibid. 96.

173 Soon around 100 boys and girls were receiving catechism classes and being taught to read and write Urdu; ibid. 101.

Fig. 2.4. The Church of Our Lady of Mount Carmel at Adah.
Source: ABC, *Panjabmissie De Bestaande Posten in Beeld*

to be extraordinary. It attracted an enormous crowd whose respectful attitude was very pleasing.'[174] A village dispensary was soon set up which brought Punjabis from surrounding villages to Sahowala and led to the establishment of a number of outstations in the Sahowala mission.[175]

As two of the earliest Capuchin mission stations in Punjab, Adah and Sahowala became the basis for much of the Capuchins' understanding of rural low-caste society, as well as major test sites for mission strategies and for the dialogue between mission and converts through which early Catholic communities emerged. Missionary personnel at the two mission stations varied from year to year, so it is not possible to give a detailed list as in the case of Tarn Taran and Narowal. The names of Frs Vincent, Lievin, Deodat, Edmund, and Quirin ought to be noted, however, as prominent and long-serving missionaries in Adah and Sahowala.

Table 2.11 shows statistics for the growth of the Capuchins' Punjab mission. The period of most rapid growth was between 1910 and 1915, approximately a decade after the most intense mass-movement period for the CMS. This ten-year delay was often used by the CMS—along with the fact that they had been in Punjab almost forty years longer than the Capuchins—to claim that the latter deliberately set out to evangelize among Protestant converts rather than work in areas where no Christian mission had yet established itself. The Capuchins admitted this—in the case of Adah, it was conceded that other missions had been at work there for fifteen years by the time the Capuchins won their first converts in 1889[176]—but their private correspondence suggests that their reason for frequently concentrating on Protestant areas was not the ease with which rural Punjabis might be won from Protestant to Catholic Christianity, as the CMS claimed. The Capuchins thought that winning converts from Protestantism was more difficult than winning them from older, non-Christian attachments, primarily because Protestant missionaries allegedly held out material rewards to converts. Instead, the Capuchins acted as they did because they saw Protestantism as their biggest immediate enemy in Punjab. Accounts of Protestant activity featured regularly in Capuchin correspondence, far more so than mentions of Catholicism in CMS writing, and it was clearly the Capuchins' aim—in a distinct echo of Catholic–liberal rivalries in Belgium—to force their opponents out of parts of Punjab by displacing Protestant institutions.

[174] Pelckmans, *Dix Années*, 102. [175] See Ch. 4 on medical mission.

[176] Letter from Fr. Deodat to General, 1 Sept. 1904.

TABLE 2.11. *The growth of the Catholic community in Punjab and Sindh, 1905–1934*

Catholic community	1905	1910	1912	1915	1918	1921	1925	1928	1931	1934
Indian	n/a	n/a	n/a	17,468	21,712	23,314	30,307	33,165	35,855	41,187
European, Eurasian	n/a	n/a	n/a	1,892	2,293	3,277	2,919	3,218	3,120	3,962
TOTAL	5,142	7,591	11,896	19,355	24,005	26,591	33,226	36,383	38,975	45,149

Source: Order of Friars Minor Capuchin, *Analecta Ordinis Minorum Capuccinorum*, various years; GACO, Reports from Regular Superior to General.

Fr. Deodat informed the General in 1908 that two new schools in the Sahowala mission would soon expose Protestantism as 'the work of the demon', and would compel American and Scottish Presbyterian missions to leave the area.[177]

In this crusade against European and American Protestantism, Capuchin missionaries sought to portray themselves as poor and embattled, the natural allies of downtrodden and resourceless low-castes. Protestant missionaries were depicted as preoccupied with social position and family—in addition to their suspiciously close relationship with the colonial state. For their part, Protestant missions seem to have been well aware of the fight which they had on their hands. Fr. Lievin informed the Provincial in 1890 that 'the presbyterians have posed us a strong battle these last few days':

> They are shouting from the rooftops that they would chase the papists from the Punjab, and I think they were really in good faith because never before have they applied to it so much rage. But thanks to God they did not hurt us . . . the people, as ignorant as they may be, know how to distinguish the charity of the Gospel from the violent and calumnious language of the sectarians.[178]

CONCLUSION

By the end of the 1880s two missions were at work in Punjab that drew on a common heritage but deployed it in dramatically differing ways. Both the CMS and the Capuchins conceived of mission work as bringing to Punjabis a religious message that would be their reformation and their salvation. Both groups were relatively fresh in purpose and commitment, the CMS representing a zealous revival of religion, broadly conceived, and the Capuchins fighting to win territory for Catholicism as part of the Church's battle to save mankind from itself, in a hostile and corrupt modern age. The importance of establishing institutions that would represent and engender sympathy with Christianity was recognized no less by Catholics than by Evangelicals. Similarly, both groups viewed their mission stations along the old monastic lines of a healthy, spiritual centre radiating positive influence and forging connections with the surrounding community which, over time, would be intellectually and culturally transforming.

[177] Letter from Fr. Deodat to General, 26 Apr. 1908, GACO.
[178] Letter from Fr. Lievin to Provincial, 20 Dec. 1890, ABC, L64.

And yet the two missions would have been easily distinguishable in the field. The Capuchins were uniform in their monastic habits—all male, and without wives or families. This combined with their relative dislocation from secular authorities to render an image suggestive of a socially active Indian *sannyasi*. Their message emphasized a sacramental community that transcended national boundaries, and whose mediators they were, dispensing supernatural and material gifts to their Punjabi audience. As individuals, Belgian Capuchins had been raised in a culture in which the Church fought hard to secure public affection and loyalty. The battle for Punjab was similar in both object and nature, with schools, orphanages, and relief work helping to represent Catholicism as at once gently paternal and omnipresent. Protestant missions were vilified, meanwhile, as representing the worldliness and the individualistic convenience of modern Europe's schismatics and secularists. Finally, Capuchins brought with them a tradition of governing local societies more than listening to them or encouraging them to articulate and develop their own aspirations as Christians. The equality implied by getting their hands dirty with agricultural labourers in Belgium and Punjab remained an abstraction for much of the time, far from cancelling the superior claims of priestly status, education, and culture.

CMS missionaries would often be difficult to tell apart from British officials and memsahibs. All shared a sense of broad mission, a style of dress and behaviour, and a similar prioritization of morality and conduct as indicative of a healthy state of mind and soul. The Capuchins were regarded as grumbling, insular relics, bringing the malign influence of the 'Church of Rome' to India, and acting with none of the respect—particularly with regard to sharing mission territory—that characterized the work of Protestant mission societies in Punjab. CMS missionaries believed that the Capuchins threatened to take Punjabis backwards, whereas their gospel was one of progress, of individual salvation through true Evangelical conversion, and of spiritual and ecclesiastical independence. Literacy and a grasp of the basic tenets of the faith were deemed essential for this kind of salvation, where for Catholics an appropriately timed progress through the Church's sacraments was paramount, and education was valuable more for its Catholic socialization than for concrete literary gains.

While both missions preached self-sufficiency therefore, it was not an article of faith for Capuchins as it was for Protestants. The Catholic salvation of Punjabis could be catered for admirably by foreign priests acting with a minimum of administrative and lay support, notwithstanding the papacy's wishes for an indigenous clergy at some point in the future. India looked like a safe, though not ideal, situation for Catholic evangelization, and there appeared no need to hurry Indians into seminaries. The CMS, on the other hand, were keen to re-create the lay bureaucracy of British Low Church Anglicanism, as a training ground for future leaders of Punjabi Christianity who could take over the reins and free CMS missionaries for new adventures.

Despite these oft-stated aspirations, the thrust of CMS strategy and structure remained, as with the Capuchins, predominantly male and European. It is not simply that female and Indian agency was deliberately obscured by male authors of major letters and reports, although there was undoubtedly an element of this, as writers like Jeffrey Cox have pointed out;[179] there is a sense also that the full extent and utility of female and Indian agency was not yet realized or admitted by enough people on the ground.

There was clearly a social and racial element here, with Indians—especially poor and uneducated ones—not thought to possess sufficient 'character', trustworthiness, or genuine commitment to the cause. Just as the derogatory and essentializing end of colonial psychiatry tended to see Indians as suffering related, but more severe, forms of psychological frailty when compared with Europeans, so CMS and Capuchin missionaries saw rural Punjabis as afflicted similarly yet more intensely than the rural poor of Europe by a range of shortcomings.[180] As suggested in Chapter 1, the solutions were not thought to differ substantially, but the amount of time required for them to take effect in India was measured in generations rather than years. Another factor in the apparent sidelining of women and Indians was, somewhat ironically, the sheer idealism of many missionaries new to Punjab. Just as they vilified those who tied their hands, whether CMS urbanites or Catholic bishops of Lahore, they worried about anything that might dilute the element of personal achievement, or cloud authorship of the new chapter in Christian history that they were busy writing. The picture is more complex still: while for some foreign missionaries this idealism made for cynicism where the worthiness of Indian catechists and teachers was concerned, for others like Bateman it led to a radical and urgent conviction *in favour* of Indian agency.

179 See Cox, *Imperial Fault Lines*.

180 The psychoanalytical writings of Owen Berkeley-Hill are particularly revealing in this regard. See Christiane Hartnack, *Psychoanalysis in Colonial India* (Oxford, 2001).

What is striking in the case of the CMS mission is that, despite a strong undercurrent of racial tension, major divisions in the mission-Church did not come down solely to nationality or race. Two broad views of mission were apparent within the CMS. The first, associated with the likes of Robert Clark, Thomas Valpy French, and possibly Wadhawa Mal, was of a highly structured and stratified mission-Church, imperialist in idiom, territorial ambition, prioritization of cultural influence, and the desire to co-opt society's elites.[181] The 'quality' of converts was more important than the quantity, and the life of the Church revolved to a great extent around the diocese and urban colonial society. Accusations of racial chauvinism made by ambitious Punjabi Christians might not always imply opposition to elitist mission-Church structures and policies—more a desire to take the reins.[182]

Another kind of evangelistic vision was embodied in Rowland Bateman, Edward Guilford, Mian Sadiq, Mya Das, and T. Bomford, caught up with the romance of itineration and the forging of personal connections with 'real' Punjabis. Although British missionaries like Bomford were probably no less convinced of European superiority than those whose personalities or behaviour made their prejudices painfully obvious, there was nevertheless a qualitative difference in this second group's attitude towards the CMS and colonial society. A dislike of conferences and paperwork, and a suspicion of urban Christianity's apparently Anglophile trajectory, indicated a resentment of cumbersome social and organizational ties, and pessimism about Punjabi Christianity's flimsy culture.

Issues like these intersected with general questions about mission-Church authority and internal mission politics. The extent to which missionary energies were expended in arguing with one another is somewhat surprising, and reminds us that, where questions of transcultural evangelism and conversion are concerned, we ought not to forget about the universal culture of the institution, to which many in both the CMS and Capuchin missions appeared to have fallen victim. The fact that it took the CMS almost half a century to realize the crucial source of intelligence on Punjabi opinion (albeit from a narrow social

[181] Jeffrey Cox has suggested that an imperialist mindset dominated the CMS mission in Punjab, and that Robert Clark led a group of missionaries who were institution builders first and evangelists second; Cox, *Imperial Fault Lines*, 27.

[182] This ambition extended to the attempt by prominent urban Christians such as Rullia Ram to enter the political arena in the early twentieth century, as socially and culturally well-placed mediators between the British Government and Indian nationalists.

spectrum) that the PNCC offered, and to act properly on its advice about rural evangelism, speaks volumes about the impeding effect of institutionalization upon mission.

Time and again CMS and Capuchin missionaries wrote wearily about another suggestion they had made that would probably be ignored, or about a problem they had warned about years ago that was only now being taken seriously. More importantly perhaps, CMS sources suggest that this kind of wrangling dented Punjabi respect for European personnel, whether it was through a perception of vested European interests and racism, or weariness at a constant succession of bureaucratic initiatives that had little to do with real life among Punjabi Christians. When Bomford asked one Punjabi Christian what he thought of the new CMC and DMC system, which had replaced the old PNCC, he received the reply that it was merely a European idea, which would be substituted for a new one as soon as the Europeans became bored with it.[183]

[183] Bomford, 'The Development of the Church in India', 18.

3

The Communication of Christianity

THE vast majority of rural Punjabis who became interested in Christianity did not first hear about it from the lips of a foreign missionary. Nor were their subsequent years as catechumens and converts marked by extensive direct contact with such people. Instead the day-to-day communication of Christianity was largely the business of Punjabis themselves. Acting for local interests or as paid agents of Christian missions, they mediated the relationships between Punjabis and foreign missionaries that helped to shape both the mass movements and the new mission-Churches to which they gave birth.

The first part of this chapter looks at the role of 'informal' agents in rural evangelization in general and in the mass movements in particular. These were people who operated independently of the direction and interests of the missions. Traders, travellers, ex-army personnel, migrants, and village and caste elders, often operating through long-standing inter-village social networks, spread information about Christianity and about the social and educational activities of foreign missionaries. They played key roles in individual, family, and group decisions to send delegations to the missions to request attention, teaching, and baptism. The apparent lack of interest on the part of the Capuchins and CMS in exploring or recording these people's contributions in any detail renders precise identities and activities difficult to trace. Efforts will nevertheless be made to uncover as much as possible about the presentation of Christianity which was made by these agents, and their role in giving the mass movements the direction and character which so baffled missionaries in this period.

Following on from this is an examination of the 'formal' agency of those Punjabis who were employed by the missions as catechists: their selection, training, payment, and standing in the missions. Such issues are highly revealing of the changing dynamics of rural mission in this period, particularly the effect that early village itineration had upon

CMS and Capuchin mission strategies and the looming challenge of the mass movements.

A note on terminology should be offered at the outset. Catholic missions generally used the term 'catechist' to describe all agents with roles as religious teachers. The CMS as well as the Society for the Propagation of the Gospel (SPG, whose archives are drawn upon here) differentiated between 'readers' and 'catechists'. Readers usually stayed in one village, whereas catechists generally had a higher level of training and experience, and were given responsibility for education and welfare in twenty or thirty villages. These distinctions will be elaborated over the course of the chapter, but for simplicity's sake the term 'catechist' will be used to include readers except where there is specific need for a distinction to be made.

EARLY ENCOUNTERS

The Joys of Village Itineration

Despite criticisms levelled at the CMS by its European missionaries and the Punjab Native Church Council regarding the inadequacy of village evangelization, as early as the 1880s and 1890s a modest amount of village itineration was taking place around Tarn Taran and Narowal. The CMS also expanded upon the pioneering rural mission work of Church of England Zenana Mission Society (CEZMS) missionaries around Jandiala and Ajnala (*c.*1881), while Capuchin village evangelization grew outwards from Sialkot after 1889.

For most CMS and Capuchin missionaries, direct contact with interested Punjabis was highly prized. The long distances involved—sometimes travelled in a caravan of bullock carts and assistants and at other times on horseback or simply on foot—made this an arduous task, particularly given the extremes of weather on the plains. Protestant and Catholic propagandists were quick to highlight the exertions of missionaries, juxtaposing the heroism and endurance of these women and men with the childlike inadequacies of the Punjabi public for whom they toiled. The following example, from a Capuchin history of their mission, was typical:

> Under a burning sun [the missionaries] had to go . . . During the rainy season, when the dirt paths were flooded, they were forced to take off their clothing

and to cross one or several miles plunged in water up to the belt. In the evening, exhausted by hunger and fatigue they had to satisfy themselves with a meagre meal, a little bit of rice cooked in water . . . And for rest an indigenous bed, under a big tree, around which the indigenous people, attracted by curiosity, came crowding around, noisy and dirty.[1]

Bateman was one of the CMS's favourite itinerant heroes, his biographer praising his 'obviously capable manliness' and 'unobtrusive spirituality' and making clear that stagecoach travel was a rare and 'unusual luxury', which Bateman might accept as a gift but would never arrange for himself.[2]

Propaganda aside, the distances involved in making village visits were formidable, and motorized transport remained a luxury in the Christian community right up until the end of the Raj. CMS missionaries tried to impress upon their superiors in London the increasing unmanageability of the situation in rural Punjab, which could extend to two missionaries and their wives ministering to 1,000 Christians across 100 villages. Both CMS and Capuchin correspondence towards the end of this early period was full of requests for more personnel to be sent from Britain and Belgium respectively. The idea was rarely questioned that the personal involvement of European missionaries represented the supreme form of evangelization.

Missionaries usually spent between two and four days in each village, engaging in informal resthouse or home discussions with leading villagers. The Revd A. Haig of the SPG described this as an 'Eastern custom', which he found preferable to more formal European styles of presentation.[3] Public talks and magic lantern shows were also a regular feature of rural evangelization, with evenings generally found to be the most effective time owing to the pressures of the working day. Bomford suggested that after sunset, 'if the [magic lantern] pictures are good, and the preaching in [the] local dialect, [villagers] will come and sit on the cold ground and listen for one or two hours'. As many as 250 people might gather at such meetings, especially if there were the promise of seeing photographs of nearby towns, villages, and local leaders.[4] The drama of some of the Bible stories also proved popular, not least among the young. Following a magic lantern presentation on Lazarus, Miss Gorham of the SPG was asked by a small boy whether she would

[1] Pelckmans, *Dix Années*, 63–4.
[2] Maconachie, *Rowland Bateman*, 130.
[3] The Revd A. Haig [of the SPG], 'Village Work in the Karnal District', *DMN* 1/11 (July 1897), 7.
[4] Letter from Bomford to CMS Secretary, 16 Nov. 1896.

sell him a book in which he could read for himself 'about the man who was raised after he had been dead four days'.[5]

For some, however, this kind of interest was no more than passing curiosity, and Mian Sadiq noted in 1881 that villagers had been known to use tracts and Bible excerpts as fuel.[6] Miss Gorham recorded, in a slightly surreal account, a similar lack of enthusiasm when she sat down with a Brahman woman to show her a set of Bible picture cards: '[She] requested me not to open the portfolio for fear of displeasing the Cow. And when I began to sing she made me desist from that also, as that sacred creature, who shared her apartment, showed some sign of disapproval.'[7]

Other missionary tactics included forceful claims of the superiority of European power and knowledge. The Revd T. Williams of the SPG used a small globe to impress upon villagers the smallness of India when compared with Russia (many people having heard of Russia). He comforted his awestruck listeners by assuring them that the British empire was bigger than the Russian empire, but pointed out that it was the rejection of idolatry and the embrace of Christianity that had enabled both nations to become great. Williams also showed the oceans of the world, which he said were made of salt water and not sugar-cane juice, beer, melted butter, or milk, as he believed the Shastras (Hindu scriptures) literally claimed.[8]

The CMS furthered their efforts at reaching adults by turning their small village school complexes into hives of activity, where parents could come to listen to their children's answers in the classroom or to visit the attached dispensary, post office, and lending library, the last holding titles such as *The Pilgrim's Progress* and books on the 'Hindu–Muslim controversy'. In this way they hoped to attract the attentions of Punjabi adults, who, they noted, 'are never in a hurry'.[9]

Informal Agency and Rural Interest in Christianity

Missionaries quickly found that much in their work depended upon the active goodwill of village or caste headmen. Guilford was informed by a messenger on his approach to a village that the chief men of the

[5] The boy's words were quoted by Miss Gorham in 'More Camping Notes', *DMN* 7/6 (Apr. 1914), 72.

[6] The Revd Mian Sadiq, speaking at the Sixth Meeting of the PNCC; ACMS, *Sixth Meeting, 1881*, 49.

[7] Gorham, 'More Camping Notes', 72.

[8] The Revd T. Williams, Quarterly Letter, Dec. 1885, ASPG.

[9] *Proceedings of the CMS, 1898–9*, 220.

village had already been 'discussing your religion and saying that it is the true one'.[10] On a previous occasion he had received assurances directly from village headmen themselves that they possessed great influence over their fellows, but would only make the 'public confession of Christ' for which Guilford asked them when they felt the moment to be right. In the meantime, they asked Guilford to have patience. Guilford was enthusiastic about the power of headmen, and petitioned the CMS in London to send out a band of 'Associated Evangelists' (yet more Europeans) to establish regular contact with influential rural leaders.[11]

The first outstation of the Tarn Taran mission was set up in 1890 in Zunnardar village, principally through the agency of the (unnamed) headman of the village. He had been the first to convert and soon brought many other villagers with him. By 1906 there were forty-three Christians in the village and the headman had started to act as pastor of the congregation. Bomford, taking over from Guilford for a short time at this point, hoped that the man could be trained as a teacher, thereby making the new outstation simpler and cheaper to maintain. The only problem was that the headman had so many other duties that he was unable to spend time away from the village to receive training.[12] Perhaps if the CMS had succeeded in turning local leaders like these into catechists, mission–convert relations might have been closer and less marked by conflict than they were in many areas of Punjab.

Similar themes were emerging in the SPG mission. Writing in *Delhi Mission News* in 1917, the Revd G. Hibbert-Ware of the SPG recounted the role of a Chamar headman, Tota, in stimulating a movement at Khanpur and in a number of surrounding villages. Tota appeared to hold sway over Chamars in these nearby villages. On one occasion he introduced to Hibbert-Ware a young man—referred to by Tota as 'brother', a term often used to signify distant relatives—who had come to request a Christian teacher on behalf of the Chamars of his village. Not long afterwards the man visited Hibbert-Ware again, this time bringing with him five or six of the leading men of his village. Hibbert-Ware apparently took some persuading, however, and it was

[10] Quoted in *Proceedings of the CMS, 1896–7*, 225. When the Revd T. Williams of the SPG offered leaflets to his listeners, the headman spoke up, saying that the leaflets had already been read to the villagers and that no more were required. A number of villagers who had approached Williams for a leaflet sat back down again and could not be persuaded to take anything; the Revd T. Williams, Quarterly Letter, Dec. 1885, ASPG.

[11] The Revd E. Guilford, Annual Letter 1892, repr. in *EAL 1891–2* (London, 1892), 230.

[12] *TTRA 1906* (Lahore, 1906), 5, ACMS, G2/I7/1, 2.

only after a third journey that he was finally impressed with the urgency of the situation. Lacking sufficient resources to accede to the request, he sent a letter to the CMS to ask for assistance.[13]

Based on his experiences around Khanpur, Hibbert-Ware expounded a theory of rural conversion in which a leader—not always a head-man—emerged from among the people, became the first to convert, and then brought the community with him. This leadership extended to the persuasion of individuals who resisted conversion, as well as arranging a house in the village which could be used as a chapel and classroom.[14] Hibbert-Ware did not describe the means of persuasion employed by such leaders, but in an environment of interdependence there were many sanctions, social and economic, which could be brought to bear by local leaders, in addition to their acknowledged status as chiefs or elders.

Where dominant castes in the village disapproved of low-castes' relations with mission societies, it was often these same local leaders who suffered most. Tota's house was broken into by local landowners, threats were made to his wife, and Rs 16—almost a month's earnings—was taken from her.[15]

Hibbert-Ware believed that his theory explained the seemingly random development of the conversion movements, and he was clear about the proper missionary response: 'Our business is to follow it; for we cannot limit it to one direction, else it simply eludes us; nor can we bid it wait for us till we gather up adequate forces, for then we risk its dying out altogether.'[16]

The Capuchins took a similar view in responding to interest from low-caste people around Adah in the early twentieth century. In the case of a group of Chuhras from Jamki village, an outstation of the Adah mission which lay about 7 miles from Adah itself, a catechist was swiftly appointed and large numbers prepared for baptism, only for almost all the villagers to fall victim to plague.[17]

Travel and migration were powerful forces in the spread of Christianity. Williams recorded in his Annual Report of 1886 that the brother of

[13] The Revd G. Hibbert-Ware, 'Baptisms in the Villages', pt 2, *DMN* 8/6 (Apr. 1917), 69. [14] Ibid., pt 1, *DMN* 8/5 (Jan. 1917), 55.

[15] Ibid. 56. See Ch. 4 on village reactions to low-caste Christian conversions.

[16] Hibbert-Ware, 'Baptisms in the Villages', pt 2, 70.

[17] Ninove, *The Capuchin Mission in the Punjab*, 143. The account is undated, but these events occurred around 1903–4.

a village headman had travelled widely as a non-commissioned officer in the army. On his return to Punjab the man's greatly diminished regard for village deities became a fresh creative force among his brother's people.[18] Seasonal or permanent urban migrants played a similar role in communicating fresh perspectives and aspirations to their village relatives. While some low-caste migrants responded to poor working conditions, spatial segregation, and the replacement of interdependence with wage labour by developing their own *bhakti*-inspired religious associations,[19] others became interested in Christianity as a means of expressing and complementing their new status. An SPG missionary reported in 1914 that a Chamar Christian convert from Delhi had asked him to visit some relations in the village of Shahabad, saying that they would welcome Christian teaching. The entire Chamar community of the village soon began to attend classes, and many became catechumens.[20]

The influence of family was also apparent in a request received by the Revd J. J. Hughes in 1915, from a man whose two sons were engaged to Christian girls and who therefore wanted to know more about the religion.[21] When such girls moved into their new villages after marriage, they had the potential to function as informal catechists: three instances were recorded in villages in Kartarpur district of a Catholic girl joining a family of non-Catholics in the mid-twentieth century, through marriage, and the entire family becoming Catholics within a short space of time.[22] (This was still common in Punjab at the beginning of the twenty-first century.) Girls were able to 'withstand all the cultural and social humiliations' of conversion and in doing so they opened the door for missionaries to visit the rest of the family and the village.[23] Conversely, there was a fear in the Capuchin mission at the turn of the twentieth century that when girls left their village to go and live with

[18] The Revd T. Williams, Annual Report, 1886, ASPG.

[19] Nandini Gooptu, 'Caste, Deprivation, and Politics', Peter Robb (ed.), *Dalit Movements and the Meaning of Labour in India* (Delhi, 1996), 277–9, and id., *The Politics of the Urban Poor in Early Twentieth-Century India*, 145–66.

[20] The Revd Noel Marsh, 'Village Work', *DMN* 7/10 (Apr. 1915), 118.

[21] The Revd J. J. Hughes, 'Growth of Christianity in the Villages', *DMN* 8/1 (Jan. 1916), 8.

[22] Two of the families had previously been Protestant and one had been Sikh. The three cases were all either one or two generations back, in the twenty-year period after Independence. Punjab–UK interviews, various interviewees in Kalmar, Sarekhas, and Sayekar villages, 30 and 31 Jan. 2003.

[23] Punjab–UK interviews, Fr. Michael Ani, 31 Jan. 2003; Letter from Fr. Vincent to General, 20 Jan. 1897, GACO.

their new husband's family, they would effectively be lost to the mission if there was no mission station in the new area, and all the time spent catechizing them would have been wasted.[24]

In villages where there had not yet been any conversions to Christianity, the role of female missionaries in making contact with women at home, while husbands were working in the fields, was vital to evangelistic efforts. The CMS worked with the CEZMS for such purposes, while also employing increasing numbers of women directly.[25]

Catholic and Protestant missionaries alike seemed to believe women especially resistant to religious change. Haig described Punjabi women as the most 'zealous upholders of orthodox Hinduism in its popular and grossly idolatrous form . . . [offering] the most determined and bitter opposition to any proposal on the part of any of the men of the family to leave the faith of their fathers'.[26] Similarly, the Revd C. F. Hall claimed that women were the 'drag [in] every batch of new inquirers', and usually the force behind any convert lapses back into old forms of worship.[27] The Catholic Bishop of Lahore claimed that it was women in particular who were affected by 'the insurmountable prejudices of caste', and he urged the SCPF to find a female religious organization in Europe which could send women to help in the religious education of Punjabi girls and women.[28] This was achieved a few years later when both the Sisters of Jesus and Mary (Lyon) and the Sisters of Charity (Ghent) were at work in Punjab.

It is debatable whether many male European missionaries understood very much about Punjabi women. Their impressions were quite possibly informed by the intense devotionalism which sometimes characterized female religious worship in Europe, as well as by the role of women in policing the observances and morals of the home in both European and Punjabi society. An illustration of this in Punjab was provided by Prakash Tandon in his family biography, with an account of the domestic religious ceremony which his mother performed upon his recovery from chicken-pox.[29]

[24] Letter from Fr. Vincent to General, 20 Jan. 1897, GACO.

[25] By 1910 this had risen to twenty-nine single women and forty-three wives of missionaries in Punjab, compared with fifty-eight male clergy and lay missionaries; *Proceedings of the CMS, 1910–11*, 138.

[26] Haig, 'Village Work in the Karnal District', 7.

[27] Hall, 'A Suggested Policy for Mass Movements', 286–7.

[28] Report of the Bishop of Lahore to the SCPF, 2 May 1895, ABC, L200.

[29] Tandon, *Punjabi Century*, 32.

Domestic gatherings of non-Christian Punjabi women, at which *bhajans* (religious songs) were often sung, represented ideal opportunities for evangelization. Where female missionaries were able to engineer invitations to such gatherings, they attempted to introduce Christian songs to the proceedings, using Indian melodies and taking care to explain the meaning of the words.[30] Deaconess Maud Favell of the SPG reported that hymns were also a means by which Chamar men who attended Christian services sometimes passed on elements of Christianity to sceptical wives.[31]

The cultural environment of the village and of low-caste communities in particular also presented a major obstacle for missionaries, although this became more apparent after conversion, during the process of community-building and socialization into new ways of life. The challenges posed by low-castes at the evangelization stage, as missionaries saw them, included the sheer strength of their demands and a potential receptivity to any group from outside village society that would afford them a respectful hearing. Missions thus found themselves competing among themselves, with education—and the implied prospects for social and economic advancement—a major factor from the outset. Missionaries were aware that this was rather close to bribery, and at times they accused each other of establishing schools solely as a way of enticing young people into the fold, arguing that their *own* schools, on the other hand, were educational institutions worthy of respect.

Mass-Movement Dilemmas

By 1921 Punjabi Catholic numbers were approaching 25,000, with converts and catechumens—almost all from the Chuhra caste[32]—spread across 894 villages.[33] Resources were stretched to the point of crisis, and the 'rapid decay' of the mission loomed.[34] Still bruised by the

[30] Gorham, 'More Camping Notes', 72.

[31] [Deaconess] Maud Favell, 'Hopeful Work among the Chamars', *DMN* 8/2 (Apr. 1916), 23–4. A deaconess was a female worker in the Anglican Church, theologically trained, able to conduct services, and parallel with male deacons in all but her potential to proceed to the priesthood. The office of deaconess was established in 1862. Bebbington, *Evangelicalism in Modern Britain*, 129.

[32] Fr. Macaire, 'Les Conversions en masse au Punjab', *Analecta Ordinis Minorum Capuccinorum* (1925), 148–56.

[33] The mission at Adah employed four catechists to serve seventy-one villages, while the mission at Sahowala employed five catechists to serve sixty villages; Letter from Regular Superior to General, 16 Nov. 1921, GACO.

[34] Letter from Provincial to General, 13 Apr. 1921, GACO.

early disappointments of their mission, the Capuchins were highly sensitive to any suspected material dimension to Punjabi requests. Such misgivings tended to remain private, however. In public, a material dimension was declared natural, and missionaries likened the Chuhras to the Jews of Jesus' time, whose understanding of 'salvation' and a 'new Kingdom' had not been entirely spiritual. This analogy allowed the Capuchins to portray their acceptance of the Chuhras into the Catholic fold as an emulation of Jesus himself, who had chosen not to rebuke his Jewish audience but instead to give them 'an over-abundance of material bread in order to attract their hearts to celestial things'. In time the Chuhras, noticing that 'the life of the Catholic missionary is poor, chaste and selfless [would] become attached to him, give him their trust, call him their "guru"...and become his disciples'.[35]

The Capuchins' strategy here was bolstered by what they discovered of Chuhra religious beliefs, in particular the conviction that salvation would come from without and that the 'hour of their rehabilitation' was at hand.[36] Nevertheless, there was a tension in the Capuchin vision of mission work among low-caste Punjabis. On the one hand, they thought that a combination of Chuhras' clear material needs and the guru–disciple paradigm through which they appeared to understand religion would lead to a broad dependence upon the missionaries, a positive first step towards the formation of a Catholic community. This process was aided by the role of the 'caste group'—seen by the Capuchins as 'strongly preoccupied with unity'—in transferring an individual's interest in Christianity 'to [the] whole social organism'.[37] On the other hand, many Capuchin missionaries worried that the convert generation would always view Catholic conversion as the *modification* of the group's identity rather than its displacement in favour of a new, Catholic, identity. As a result, these first converts would only ever be 'imperfect' Christians, their material and social aspirations capable of limited manipulation but never fully controllable. Instead, the real prize would be '[the] children and all the future generations', who would grow up with their Catholic identity at the fore. The shortcomings of the present generation seemed confined to low-castes, in Capuchin eyes.[38]

[35] Letter from Regular Superior to Provincial, 6 Aug. 1912, ABC, L781.

[36] Ibid.

[37] Blondeel, *In Het Land Der Vijf Rivieren*, 288.

[38] Letter from Regular Superior to Provincial, 6 Aug. 1912.

Friars working with 'higher-class' people in areas like Dalwal claimed that converts there would all be 'solid'.[39]

Pessimism over this state of affairs came to a head when resources were stretched. Fr. Edouard had warned the Provincial in 1892 that the mission was on the verge of bankruptcy and that it was only the financial aid supplied to converts that persuaded them to attend Church and catechism:

> [They are] only Christians for money . . . [and] we are noticing it more every day. They do not have faith, do not pray. If it was not for the baptised children who have died, and there are quite a few, and a few adults who we were able to help . . . to die well, we would regret having opened this mission.[40]

The effect on morale is clear from frustrated descents into contemporary stereotypes. Edouard complained that 'to make Christians out of them, it would be necessary to make men out of them . . . but that is the difficulty'. Whereas if higher-castes had been persuaded into the Catholic fold the Chuhras would have followed, Edouard worried that Chuhra conversions at this early stage dramatically reduced the chances of higher-castes being attracted towards Catholicism.[41] A year later Fr. Edmund, despondent about his failure to galvanize the Christians of Adah, told the Provincial that the people of the village were 'too savage' to show him any gratitude, differing 'only very little from reason-less beings in their way of life'.[42]

In the CMS mission by 1920 there were 29,776 catechumens and baptized Christians, compared with 4,896 just thirty years earlier. A CMS publication had claimed in 1911 that there was now 'practically no limit to the number of people who may be influenced and instructed . . . Depressed classes are so desirous of embracing Christianity that they are willing to contribute to the support of teachers, and in their anxiety to be enrolled in the Christian Church they are prepared to pay for being baptised.'[43]

The Revd W. P. Hares and the Revd C. F. Hall both noted a distinct social aspect to the movements by the time of the First World War. Hares pointed to the 'indignity' suffered by non-Christian Chuhras when they visited Christian relatives, of 'having to eat from separate dishes and [being excluded] from the smoking of the *huqqa* [pipe]'. Such

[39] Letter from Frs Edouard, Fabian, and Felix to Provincial, 7 Oct. 1900, ABC, L315.

[40] Letter from Fr. Edouard to Provincial, 8 Nov. 1892, ABC, L92.

[41] Ibid.

[42] Letter from Fr. Edmund to Provincial, 18 Dec. 1893, ABC, L131.

[43] *Proceedings of the CMS, 1911–12* (London, 1912), 94–5.

keenly felt social stigmatism, combined with the difficulties of making good marriage alliances within a decreasing non-Christian Chuhra population, amounted to a strong compulsion for many Chuhras to convert.[44] Hall corroborated this, having traced many enquiries from low-caste villagers back to a desire to make a particular marriage alliance with a Christian family.[45]

Missionary views of informal agents such as Tota appeared to fall within this paradigm of a social movement. The accounts given by Hibbert-Ware, Guilford, and others emphasized the role of these agents as community leaders rather than men of intense spirituality or personal conviction. Some of them were later valued as paid agents of the mission, but for their stature and influence rather than their qualities as Evangelical preachers.

Perhaps this explains the comparative lack of interest shown by CMS and Capuchin missionaries in inquiring into the dynamics of the rural communication of Christianity. The stirring of interest among rural Punjabis by informal agents was only the first half of a two-part process. The second part, in the eyes of missionaries, was the more significant: the turning of a social movement into a spiritual one, through the genuine conversion and comprehensive socialization of people who so far had only the dimmest awareness of the meaning of Christianity. This was the task for which the CMS and Capuchins, in their differing ways, urgently required Punjabi catechists and teachers.

Although CMS missionaries shared Capuchin misgivings with regard to the apparent prominence, in low-caste decisions to seek teaching and baptism, of aspirations for education, employment, and land—the last due in part to the spread of rumours among non-Christian Chuhras that the Punjab Government had given land to members of their caste who had become Christian—they readily admitted the difficulty of making accurate and definitive statements regarding motivation. It is generally fair to say that missionaries moved from a negative to a positive understanding of 'mixed motivations'; from seeing this as undesirable to seeing it as entirely natural, both in human terms and particularly given the context in rural Punjab. The Revd C. L. Richards pointed out that it was possible for individuals to be actuated both by material concerns *and* by the expectation of spiritual betterment for themselves and their families. He gave the example of a well-respected low-caste

[44] Hares, 'Mass Movements and their Consequences', 29.
[45] Hall, 'A Suggested Policy for Mass Movements', 280.

convert in Narowal: 'He desires baptism for himself and his family, in the first instance for the freedom and new position which are gained by it, but at the same time he has some idea of, and desire for, the spiritual blessings which Christianity confers.'[46]

Similar sentiments were expressed by Hares, who used the Bible message that 'godliness is profitable unto all things' to suggest that Chuhras were right to seek better terms of social interaction through conversion. Hindus and Muslims would naturally be more ready to accept 'a clean respectable Christian than a dirty, uncouth and ignorant Chuhra'. And converts seemed to be prepared to endure much to achieve this, including the sneers of other villagers when they put on clean clothes for church, as well as beatings and wage reductions at the hands of their employers for not asking for permission to go. Hares went on to point out that *higher*-caste Indians' reasons for converting to Christianity were possibly not 'always of the highest'.[47] This line of thinking was revealing of the way in which British missionaries' culturally subjective notions of good character, behaviour, appearance, and personal hygiene increasingly obscured spiritual matters in the CMS's language of evangelization, as their rural mission expanded.

CMS missionaries seemed to agree by the end of this early period that, just as with their own decisions to apply for mission work, good motivations might be distinguished from bad ones but this was not the same as differentiating between spiritual and material ones. Although both the CMS and the Capuchins clearly had their own reasons for making arguments like these, in historiographical terms too the available evidence suggests that the epithet of 'rice Christian' applied to converts at this time was inaccurate and suggestive of a mindset that was out of touch with, and quite possibly lacking in sympathy for, the reality of low-caste lives. It allowed to Punjabi labourers only the capacity to think about their stomachs, and not the power to understand the roots of their exploitation, or to plan and to push for change. In fact, a complex weave of aspirations and ideas was at work in Punjabi individuals, families, and communities which renders questions about categories of motivation contextually inappropriate.[48]

[46] *Proceedings of the CMS, 1912–13* (London, 1913), 107–8.

[47] Hares, 'Mass Movements and their Consequences', 30–2.

[48] See Susan Billington Harper, *In the Shadow of the Mahatma: Bishop V. S. Azariah and the Travails of Christianity in British India* (Richmond, 2000), esp. pp. 284–5.

The employment of Punjabi catechists would not solve missionaries' dilemmas. The Capuchins and, to a lesser extent, their CMS counterparts shared a belief that only communities in which Christianity had had long years in which to embed itself could be truly Christian. The Belgian Provincial warned the General of the Order in 1921 that the social environment in Punjab was such that real virtue would not be attained until communities could claim 'several generations of Christian ancestors'.[49] CMS commentators regularly compared converts to the 'Primitive Christians of Apostolic times', whose vices had been documented by St Paul in his epistles.[50]

Yet the employment of catechists was clearly a sensible response to many of the immediate practical needs of the missions. The mainstream view in both the CMS and Capuchin camps was that the mass movements represented a kind of two-stage model of conversion. The first stage was the desire of low-caste Punjabis themselves for some kind of association with Christianity, born of a range of motivations. The second stage would consist of missionaries and their agents distilling these motivations, and properly channelling the desire for Christian association into something that more satisfactorily resembled a Christian conversion and religious life.

Punjabi catechists were seen as firmly second-best to the army of European missionaries that would ideally effect this second stage, but, as the situation stood, they represented the most realistic hope for the mission–convert relationship—mostly on missionary terms—that was essential for the work of conversion to be completed. This general recognition of the importance of catechists was clear from the controversies that arose in the Capuchin and CMS missions over their recruitment, training, and working life.

THE CATECHISTS

Catholic Catechists: Selection and Formation

Young men were the favoured candidates for training as catechists since, in the eyes of the Capuchins, the CMS, and Punjabi society,

[49] Letter from Provincial to General, 13 Apr. 1921, GACO.

[50] *Report of Special Committee of CMS Punjab and Sindh Conference for Enquiring into the Shortcomings of the Native Church of Punjab, May 1885* (hereafter *Shortcomings*), 5, ACMS, G2/I4/O 1885, n. 123.

the largely public role of the catechist—which incorporated pastoral duties approaching those of a priest and involved independent work and travel—rendered women unsuitable. Women frequently worked instead in schools, dispensaries, hospitals, and a variety of other roles; this was particularly so in the case of female Catholic religious Orders that focused upon evangelization among women.

In the early days of the Capuchin mission the friars relied upon orphanages and schools to supply catechist recruits, since there were not yet enough Catholic families to produce boys of what was deemed reliable character. An alternative option was for the local missionary to scour the area for a suitable candidate. Among the sought-after traits were good manners and reputation, and agreeability to the leading men of the community, so as to ensure trust.[51]

Age was also critical; the Capuchins thought that the older the candidate, the greater the danger that he would simply sit under a tree and smoke, gathering news from passers-by and then presenting it to the missionary as if he had discovered it all at first hand. This had been the experience of the past, and the friars were determined not to repeat their mistakes. And yet a candidate should be mature, and married; an official Capuchin publication noted that while 'a *fakir*, unmarried, is allowed . . . a boy from the world, who should marry still . . . is mistrusted'.[52] Moreover, there was the moral danger to consider of impressionable young catechists being thrust into 'an environment of infidel Hindus . . . contaminated by continuous conversations about sexual things and immoral practices'.[53]

Missionaries would usually try to keep their search for a catechist secret for as long as possible; otherwise they found themselves deluged with offers. Existing catechists might recommend relations for the job, and even Protestant catechists offered their services when they came to hear that a position was available. Missionaries preferred colleagues to recommend someone, but since availability was constantly a problem they found themselves having to wade through numerous unsolicited applications.

A visit to Punjab by the Provincial in 1894–5 exposed the great need, particularly in the Adah mission, for an institution dedicated to the training of catechists. In 1897 the Provincial supplied Rs 3,000 for the cause and Mgr Pelckmans sent six orphan boys from St Francis's

[51] Blondeel, *In Het Land Der Vijf Rivieren*, 277–8. [52] Ibid. 278.

[53] Letter from Provincial to General, 13 Apr. 1921, GACO.

Fig. 3.1. Catechists at Maryabad village.
Source: ABC, Photographic Archive

Orphanage in Lahore to Fr. Vincent in Adah for training. However, the school was closed down after just two years owing to what was perceived to be more pressing needs for limited resources. In the years before the onset of the mass movements, Capuchin policy-makers thought that three good catechists were all that the mission required.[54]

In 1903 Fr. Vincent was joined in Adah by Fr. Deodat, a French Capuchin who hoped, with the aid of wealthy French patrons, to reopen the catechist school as soon as possible. A deal was struck between the mission and the diocese whereby the former would cover the costs of the building and furniture while the latter would pay the living costs of the students. The new building was capable of holding twenty students, although only five candidates were initially available. Subjects at the school included religious doctrine and principles, Church history, and an introduction to the tenets of Hinduism, Islam, and Sikhism. An Indian teacher was employed to teach linguistics and 'other useful secular subjects'.[55] The boys took it in turns to look after the sacristy and chapel and were taken on village visits with missionaries, during which the most senior of the catechists would give a lesson to local children as the missionary looked on.

Vincent adopted a paternal role, not unlike that of a senior friar helping to form new arrivals to the Order. He shared the boys' leisure time, hoping to guide their conversations around to a discussion of theology and the practicalities of catechist work. The image of formation in a friary or junior seminary was also invoked by the ongoing training and formation of catechists, long after they started work. A monthly conference was held on the first Friday of the month, at which catechists gathered to receive new teaching on a particular point of doctrine. The aim was for catechists to meet each other, share experiences, and develop a sense of solidarity. A magazine, *Catholic Naqib*, was published in Urdu, partly written by the catechists themselves. It usually included 'a polemical essay that refutes protestant problems and complaints'.[56]

The Adah training school became the focus of controversy in the early 1920s. Despite its success it had been closed down by the Bishop of Lahore in 1918, on the basis that there were too few suitable candidates. It was to be replaced by a new training institution and seminary attached to an ordinary day school at Dalwal. This outraged Fr. Sigismond, since it had been done at the busiest period in the

[54] Blondeel, *In Het Land Der Vijf Rivieren*, 274–5. [55] Ibid. 275.
[56] Ibid. 275–81.

history of the Punjab mission, and with neither the Bishop's Council nor experienced missionaries consulted.[57] Sigismond suggested to the Bishop in December 1918 that rather than suppress the school because there were too few candidates who met the conditions of entry (a problem experienced by the CMS thirty years earlier), some of the less appropriate conditions ought to have been altered.[58]

These conditions included the requirement for candidates to be between the ages of 14 and 16. Sigismond pointed out that by this age most of the Christians in the area, belonging as they did to the 'servile class', were engaged in agricultural work and were trying to make ends meet for their families. Students ought therefore to be selected for the school earlier, between the ages of 7 and 11. This would have the added benefit of allowing them more time to receive 'a profoundly Christian education'. Another condition was that candidates should be born of Catholic parents. Sigismond thought this a tall order in a mission which was only a generation old, and suggested that the children of catechumens ought to be acceptable. He was happy, however, that a line continued to be drawn at those 'educated in protestant establishments and imbued with their errors'.[59]

Sigismond went on to point out that in the vicinity of Adah there were currently only thirteen priests and two or three catechists, serving a widely dispersed indigenous Catholic community of 19,493 catechumens and at least 21,000 baptized Catholics. If something were not done soon, they would have to 'bid farewell to future conversions [while] the mission entered a state of complete stagnation'. He stressed that he was not demanding large sums of money or any kind of 'innovation' (clearly a dirty word in episcopal circles), but rather the reopening of the 'humble school' established by Fr. Vincent: 'As your Highness is aware, your missionaries sacrifice their comfort, their health, even their lives, to the spread of the gospel in your Diocese. A great number have fallen and others will fall victim to their duty. Without catechists, useless sacrifices!'[60]

[57] Letter from Provincial to General, 13 Apr. 1921, GACO.

[58] Letter from Fr. Sigismond to Bishop of Lahore, 1 Dec. 1918, GACO.

[59] Ibid. Although in Punjab the evidence suggests that the CMS was equally unwilling to employ former Catholics as catechists, in Tranquebar the Danish Lutheran Mission found Catholic families who converted to Protestant Christianity to be a useful source of candidates for training as catechists; Liebau, 'Country Priests, Catechists and Schoolmasters as Cultural, Religious, and Social Middlemen in the Context of the Tranquebar Mission', 74–5.

[60] Letter from Fr. Sigismond to Bishop of Lahore, 1 Dec. 1918, GACO.

Sigismond sent a copy of the letter to the Regular Superior and to all the members of the Bishop's Council. The Provincial also became involved, prompting a swift reply from the Bishop, who professed support for the school and insisted that he was merely 'waiting for the opportune moment' to reopen it.[61] Members of the Bishop's Council were more forthcoming, revealing to Sigismond their impotence in the face of the Bishop's stubborn unilateralism. Fr. Leopold put the position in the following terms:

> His Highness never listens to his advisors and once he has made a decision there is nothing left to do. One day, I had formed the project of a great indigenous Christian school for the formation of catechists, priests, etc. I talked about it to Mgr, and . . . abandoned my project . . . Prospects are not brilliant for this diocese.[62]

Sigismond also received despondent replies from fellow missionaries, comparing the good old days of the early twentieth century to the current state of affairs, in which one missionary had been forced to readmit catechists he had previously fired[63] and another said of his work, '[it] disgusts me because it is useless'.[64]

By 1921 the situation was still at a stalemate, and Sigismond's pointed insistence to the Bishop that Punjabi converts' imperfections were due to 'exterior causes' rather than 'internal dispositions' suggested a suspicion on Sigismond's part that in spite of thousands of conversions the diocese still did not think the indigenous mission worthwhile.[65] Such was the level of discontent among missionaries by this point that the Provincial wondered whether the SCPF ought to be informed of the problems in the diocese as a matter of urgency.[66]

The training school at Adah was never reopened, despite the obvious shortcomings of the Dalwal school. Instead, catechists were trained at local stations by the missionaries when time could be found. This was far from ideal, and Fr. Macaire was convinced that, once all the catechists trained at Adah had gone, there would no longer be anyone left who was capable of 'teaching religion'. The mission would then 'face an obstacle which it will never survive'.[67] The establishment of a

61 Letter from the Bishop of Lahore to General, 10 Dec. 1918, GACO.

62 Letter from Fr. Leopold, Member of the Bishop of Lahore's Council, to Fr. Sigismond, 5 Dec. 1918, GACO.

63 Letter from Fr. Arsene to Fr. Sigismond, 17 Oct. 1920, GACO.

64 Letter from Fr. Capistran to Fr. Sigismond, 28 Oct. 1920, GACO.

65 Letter from Fr. Sigismond to Bishop of Lahore, 24 Dec. 1921, GACO.

66 Letter from Provincial to General, 13 Apr. 1921, GACO.

67 Letter from Fr. Macaire to Fr. Sigismond, 30 Nov. 1920, GACO.

new training school for catechists in Jalandhar in the 1930s suggests a belated realization on the Capuchins' part that a dedicated institution like the Adah school was indispensable.

Regardless of their level of training, Catholic catechists were required to attend an annual retreat in fulfilment of a requirement set out by the Synod of Lahore that the depth of knowledge and working methods of teachers of religion should be checked once every year. A description of the 1912 retreat, written by a Capuchin biographer of the mission, Fr. August, emphasized the guiding hand of European missionaries and the supposedly innate weaknesses of the thirty Punjabi agents who attended the retreat:

> [They] squatted around the priest, eager to display their wisdom to him. At each issue put up for discussion by the priest twenty or more would venture to give advice. They would all voice their opinions at the same time, such that they would drown each other out, no one knowing what his neighbour had yelled. When they had wandered away from the question for hours . . . the Father would bring them back to the proposed subject, about which he would give a vivid exposition. This brought gratitude from the catechists, clarifying . . . the dark sides of the Eastern soul.[68]

From 1931 onwards these retreats were formalized as a 'Refresher Course', devised by the Bishop of Lahore himself. It was held each year after Easter and lasted two weeks, five days of which were spent in spiritual seclusion, to be broken only by three sermons a day. The remainder of the fortnight was spent in education, the days divided into a course on religion given by a missionary and then a course on practical catechists' work given by a selected catechist. At the end of the retreat there was a written exam, with a medal for the highest mark and a prize of Rs 5 for the best score from each mission centre. All the costs of the course were paid by the diocese, except accommodation and a Rs 2 charge, both of which were the responsibility of the catechists.[69]

The main fear among the Capuchins, and one of the driving forces behind these 'Refresher' initiatives, was that catechists might become bored or lazy in their work, or fall into teaching in the 'Protestant fashion', whereby the catechist 'created his own catechism', claiming to have been moved by the Holy Spirit. The hope was instead that catechists would eventually develop levels of commitment and religiosity equalling 'the most excellent Catholics of Europe'. Many catechists

[68] Blondeel, *In Het Land Der Vijf Rivieren*, 283. [69] Ibid. 283–4.

were even encouraged to join the Third Order, the lay branch of the Franciscans.[70]

CMS Catechists: Problems of Independence and Respect

The CMS's Evangelical focus upon an individual's transforming response to the Word of God arguably put them in greater need of effective catechists and religious teachers than the Capuchins, for whom entry to the sacramental community of the Church at baptism was the key event in conversion. Yet many CMS missionaries regarded the paying of Punjabis to work as catechists as less than ideal since it raised the prospect of a culture of dependency upon 'foreign money'.[71]

Particularly damaging was the tendency for CMS catechists to be drawn from among converts rendered unemployed or homeless owing to the reaction of the local community to their conversion. Bomford thought it not unreasonable that the mission should wish to do all it could for such people, including providing them with employment as catechists, yet this had the negative effect of making catechists the paid assistants of particular missionaries rather than independent agents of the Church. Bomford argued that the situation was exacerbated by missionaries—particularly those from the south of England (though this was an issue of class rather than geography)—who expected a certain amount of 'deference' from Indians on account of their position, and found it distasteful to work with men of differing opinions from their own.[72] An equally negative effect of this state of affairs was the lack of respect accorded to catechists by villagers, who assumed that they had been given the job on account of their inability to do any other kind of work.[73] Catechists could also be ridiculed because of their association with low-castes—there are cases of mission personnel, including missionaries, being dubbed *Chuhra ka guru* ('teachers of Chuhras').[74]

Bomford hoped that, in time, members of new Christian communities would be sufficient in motivation and in number for the work of the

[70] Ibid. 284.

[71] Bomford suggested in 1896 that the payment of agents by a foreign mission society 'retard[ed] the development of the Church' (Letter from Bomford to CMS Secretary, 16 Nov. 1896).

[72] Ibid. [73] *Shortcomings*, 9.

[74] Webster, 'Dalits and Christianity in Colonial Punjab', 102.

catechist to be undertaken by a collection of unpaid, independent volunteers.[75] Bomford's reading of first-century Christian history, differing from that of some of his highly placed colleagues including Robert Clark, suggested to him that any new congregation that advanced to the stage of meriting its own pastor ought to be left to select that pastor for itself. It should then ally itself with other congregations in the area—and across India—rather than with the mission. Until that stage was reached, however, the CMS should continue to minister to these congregations and should not rush to appoint unsuitable people as pastors[76]—even though this tended to be looked upon back at headquarters in London as a test of a mission's progress.[77]

The CMS institution that most nearly equated to the Capuchins' training school at Adah was St John's Divinity School, Lahore. The school was the brainchild of the Revd Thomas Valpy French, an Oxford graduate who had already established—and served as Principal of—a similar Divinity School in Agra in the early 1850s, and who became the first Anglican Bishop of Lahore in 1877. French hoped that a Divinity School in Punjab would give clergy, catechists, and readers in the region 'the finest polish possible', through a direct and intensive master–disciple teaching relationship. Made in the intellectual and theological image of the missionaries, these 'choicest minds' would guarantee the safe future of the Church once the CMS left India.[78] They would also enable Christian theology to cross cultural and linguistic divisions, which French believed would always remain unsatisfactorily understood by European missionaries.[79]

French won a battle to have the school situated in Lahore rather than Banaras—despite the fact that socio-religious and political tensions there rendered public speaking in the bazaars rather an alarming prospect for trainee preachers[80]—and the first eleven students were enrolled in November 1870. They were admitted on the basis of recommendations from missionaries or 'leading Christians' of the CMS and also the SPG.

[75] Letter from Bomford to CMS Secretary, 16 Nov. 1896. At the same time Bomford acknowledged that it would be a while before rural Christian communities developed to this stage.

[76] Bomford, 'The Development of the Church in India', 9–10.

[77] *Shortcomings*, 10.

[78] The Revd T. V. French, quoted in Clark, *The Missions of the Church Missionary Society and the Church of England Zenana Missionary Society*, 131–2.

[79] The Revd T. V. French, quoted in Stock, *History of the Church Missionary Society*, ii. 577–8.

[80] *St John's Divinity School Report, October 1880 to March 1882*, ACMS, G2/I4/O 1882, n. 114.

Particular care was urged to ensure that candidates were not actuated by financial motives in seeking to attend the school. There followed the equivalent of an entrance examination, testing knowledge of Urdu (in which much of the teaching at the school was conducted), as well as maths, geography, and Indian history.[81]

The standard course lasted for nine terms, spread over three years. Students might remain in the school for the two short vacations but would be required to return to their mission stations during the summer.[82] The curriculum included Scripture studies in Hebrew and Greek, the Book of Common Prayer, Church history, dogmatic theology, 'Christian Evidence and Analogy', pastoral and natural theology, and 'Hindu and Mahomedan Controversy'.[83] As with the Adah school, training at St John's included experience of village itineration with missionaries.[84] Scholarships of Rs 8 and Rs 12 were given by the school to unmarried and married students respectively,[85] with support also provided by European benefactors.[86]

The curriculum was challenging, and various missionary teachers at St John's appeared to relish the opportunity to exchange simple village preaching for lecturing on Anselm, Augustine, and Paley. The heavily intellectual atmosphere at the school, and the gratification with which its successful first few years were greeted by missionaries, suggested that it occupied a special place in the CMS's battle for cultural sway in north India: the Principal wrote, in 1875, of his pleasure at seeing the school 'sought after . . . by men of great intellectual power and great social importance . . . we begin now to raise the standard of admission, so that eventually we may have only those of higher power and influence'.[87]

The CMS was proud of the achievements of one early student, Dina Nath, who finished his course in 1881, was ordained deacon in December of that year, and went on in 1882 to lecture at the school,

[81] The Revd H. U. Weitbrecht (Acting Principal), *St John's Divinity School, Lahore: Rules, August 1883*, ACMS, G2/I4/O 1883, n. 227.

[82] *Proceedings of the CMS, 1874–5* (London, 1875), 103.

[83] The school also received students for shorter periods of training. The Headmaster of the CMS School in Narowal took three months off from his job in 1874–5 to study at St John's. Ibid. 100.

[84] Clark, *The Missions of the Church Missionary Society and the Church of England Zenana Missionary Society*, 131.

[85] *Proceedings of the CMS, 1874–5*, 103. These scholarships were by far the largest items of spending for the school, amounting in 1880–2 to almost half its total expenditure; *St John's Divinity School Report, October 1880 to March 1882.*

[86] *Proceedings of the CMS, 1877–8* (London, 1878), 120.

[87] *Proceedings of the CMS, 1874–5*, 107.

in Greek, Hebrew, and theology.[88] But not all graduates of the school proved satisfactory. High expectations and notions of superiority were difficult to avoid among students, and alumni rarely seemed to do justice to the CMS rallying cry of 'spiritual men for spiritual work'.[89]

By 1884 numbers at the school had dropped from a high of nineteen in 1876 to just seven, a fact which the Revd H. U. Weitbrecht candidly attributed to the near-exhaustion of the supply of suitable candidates.[90] Serious concerns began to be expressed about the school. Bomford claimed that the Revd Fath Masih's time at the school had transformed him from a truly Evangelical preacher into one whose esoteric theological references so baffled and bored his congregations that they supposed the Bible by itself to be of little use in understanding their religion, and thus became inclined to stop reading it.[91] Bomford blamed the heavy theological standards imposed by successive bishops of Lahore, some of them 'not in sympathy with the CMS'. He pointed to the dangers of confusing the needs of the diocese with those of the mission, and suggested that the bishop bear responsibility for training clergy, and the mission confine itself to training 'evangelists'.[92] The CMS otherwise risked compromising the Evangelical character of their mission, should an 'ultra-Ritualistic' or 'sacramentarian' bishop be appointed to Lahore in the future.[93]

Catechists who did not attend a divinity school such as St John's were educated in ordinary CMS schools and then given specialized training in the field. In addition, the CMS organized a summer school for its catechists from mid-April to mid-May every year. These were run by local missionaries with occasional help from other Protestant missions in the area. A range of general subjects were reviewed, alongside daily devotional meetings and specialized Bible topics such as the 'Call of Isaiah'.[94] Individual mission districts organized their own short courses at other

[88] *Proceedings of the CMS, 1881–2* (London, 1882), 100–1, and *1882–3* (London, 1883), 113. Nath resigned from the CMS, however, in 1888, condemning its 'despotic principles of administration' (quoted in Cox, *Imperial Fault Lines*, 101).

[89] This comment was made by the Revd F. A. P. Shirreff in his Annual Letter for 1894, repr. in *EAL 1893–4* (London, 1894), 352.

[90] *St John's Divinity School and Lahore Church Mission Report, 1st March 1882 to 31st December 1883*, ACMS, G2/I4/O 1884, n. 122. An additional factor was the establishment at this time of a new CMS Divinity School in north India, at Allahabad, which drew many potential students away from St John's.

[91] Letter from Bomford to the Revd Robert Clark, 16 June 1887, ACMS, G2/I4/O 1887, n. 224.

[92] Ibid.

[93] Letter from Bomford to Clark, 25 July 1887, ACMS, G2/I4/O 1887, n. 227.

[94] The Revd C. L. Richards, Annual Letter 1918, ACMS.

times of the year. A four-week course was run at Tarn Taran in June and July 1895 by a new temporary missionary, Mr Storrs, with morning classes on the Old Testament and afternoon classes on Moule's *Outlines of Christian Doctrine.*[95] A monthly 'agents' meeting' was also held, consisting of two days of devotion and instruction. The Revd Weitbrecht in Batala attributed much of the progress of his district to these meetings.[96]

The Reality of the Job

Remuneration for Catholic catechists was given monthly and was the approximate equivalent of a fourth-rank office clerk in Punjab (about Rs 20 a month by the 1930s), with a slightly higher rate for catechists who worked in the cities. Catechists also received gratuities for marriage or baptismal services, and their relative prosperity was said to be obvious in the villages from their clothes. No pension was provided, however. Once they reached the stage where they were unable to fulfil their strenuous task, they were left to fend for themselves.[97] Pay for CMS catechists varied according to location and seniority, but since it generally approximated to that of Catholic catechists, the potential drift of agents from one mission to the other was always a serious worry for missionaries.

Neither the CMS nor the Capuchins appeared to believe that their agents were worth the money. The continuous mission efforts described above, to ensure conformity and loyalty in catechists, was a sign of the power of catechists' contact with villagers. The missions could not afford to let error creep in, because it might be months before they themselves visited the area and got to hear about it. Catholic catechists were quizzed weekly on their work, their weaknesses pointed out and efforts made to instil in them the 'true spirit' of the gospel.[98] Capuchin missionaries were required to keep notebooks, in which they recorded the villages which catechists claimed to have visited, including the places where they

[95] The Revd A. H. Storrs, Annual Letter 1899, repr. in *EAL 1898–9* (London, 1899), 211. The Revd H. C. G. Moule was a well-known Evangelical theologian and former principal of an Evangelical theological college at Cambridge. He was appointed Bishop of Durham in 1902. His *Outlines of Christian Doctrine* (London, 1899) reflected the trends of the day in Evangelical theology, laying emphasis upon 'the Holy Scriptures as Divine Revelation and the ultimate Spiritual Authority' (John Battersby Harford and Frederick Charles McDonald, *Handley Carr Glyn Moule, Bishop of Durham: A Biography* (London, 1922), 168–71).

[96] The Revd H. U. Weitbrecht, Annual Letter 1891, repr. in *EAL 1891–2*, 232.

[97] Blondeel, *In Het Land Der Vijf Rivieren*, 299.

[98] Ibid. 280–1.

had slept each night. Once the hot season was over, missionaries visited these villages for themselves and checked up on the catechists, who faced awards or fines according to the perceived standards of their work.[99]

By 1921 the closure of the Adah school seemed to have reduced the Capuchin mission to a new low. Fr. Marc complained to the General of the Order that only one catechist in the mission was now truly satisfactory:

> The greatest number of them are not worth the salt that they eat. Two are blind; another is paralyzed; a fourth is a madman who has already served quite a long term at the madhouse in Lahore; and finally, worse still, several are former Protestants, and when it comes to doctrine they are more familiar with the Protestant independence than the Catholic submission to the laws of the Church. How can the work be serious under these conditions?[100]

The CMS were almost as harsh:

> [Catechists] may come to Bible classes by order, but they take no interest in them. They will often commit to memory a few verses useful for bazaar preaching . . . but the Bible is not read or studied as a light on their paths.[101]

The Revd C. M. Gough complained that, far from being fit guides for low-caste converts, many of his village readers required 'constant shepherding' themselves.[102] Despite desperate personnel shortages, Guilford preferred to withdraw two of his three catechists from service in 1892, rather than have harm done to a promising new Christian community.[103] Tentative missionary voices suggested that the poor state of affairs was partly the fault of the CMS itself. An anonymous Delhi missionary (either CMS or SPG) was quoted in 1885 as saying that the training given to catechists 'denationalized' them, proof of which could be found in the lack of naturalness in their work, their preference for European styles of dress, and their desire to educate their children into English habits. The resulting cultural distance from their audience rendered them ineffective and without respect.[104]

Catechists seemed to remain unpopular in the villages even when they progressed to ordination as deacons or priests. They were viewed as the 'missionary's hack': trained in foreign institutions and elevated to

[99] Blondeel, *In Het Land Der Vijf Rivieren*, 298.
[100] Letter from Regular Superior to General, 16 Nov. 1921, GACO.
[101] *Proceedings of the CMS, 1906–7* (London, 1907), 200.
[102] The Revd C. M. Gough, Annual Letter 1899, repr. in *EAL 1898–9*, 210.
[103] The Revd E. Guilford, Annual Letter 1892, repr. in *EAL 1891–2*, 230.
[104] *Shortcomings*, 11.

the level of pastor as a result of proven loyalty and subservience to the mission. Neither wanted nor respected by their flock, these agents found themselves with too much time on their hands and eventually became involved in activities which upset their missionary employers.[105]

One must be wary of this view, however. Studies from other parts of the world—sometimes where reliable first-hand accounts by catechists and other indigenous evangelists are available—suggest that relations between local agents and the people to whom they preached and ministered was far from simple. The status of catechists in the eyes of local communities could fluctuate, depending upon factors such as the quality of their preaching. In some cases, far from their reputation suffering because of links with the missions, evangelists who could *not* claim sufficient closeness to British or other foreign missionaries were looked down upon by disappointed communities. Elsewhere the personal styles and religious natures of catechists—which varied from hellfire preaching to the softer sides of Christianity—influenced their reception to a great extent.[106]

The Capuchin ideal was for one catechist to be placed in a single village and to remain there for between twelve and eighteen months, until catechumens were ready for baptism and communion. In practice, however, catechists had to be assigned to twenty or thirty villages, there being neither the money nor the personnel for a smaller ratio. The village duties of Catholic catechists included teaching, leading services, distributing Catholic songs—thought to be an effective method of reaching the 'mind of the choohras'—and notifying missionaries of births, deaths, and illnesses. They did all the work of a missionary, short of saying Masses, hearing confessions, administering Holy Oils, and performing marriages:[107]

When the *baboo*[108] arrives at the village at dawn, he will usually go straight to the head of the Christians or to another trustee. There he will rest a bit over the *hooka* and fish for news of the village. Afterwards he himself, or a helper, goes from house to house to inform all the Catholics of his arrival. In the meantime he has arranged a drum and a singer and starts to sing one song after another. Soon some Christians gather around him, and others will draw up as well and

[105] Letter from Bomford to CMS Secretary, 16 Nov. 1896. Propriety seems to have got the better of Bomford, who refused to elaborate on certain 'scandals' (ibid.).

[106] See Brock, 'New Christians as Evangelists', 132–52.

[107] Blondeel, *In Het Land Der Vijf Rivieren*, 289.

[108] Catechists were often referred to as 'babu', a term denoting a clerk or an official of similar rank.

soon they all hum or sing along with the *baboo*. A new song is greeted with great satisfaction and they will repeat it until they know it. His word bristles with bible texts and quotes from the catechism. Sometimes it is difficult to find much coherence or theology in it, sometimes it is alive with . . . inconsistencies or dogmatic inaccuracies, but still the use of such a sermon . . . cannot be underestimated, since his moral evocations are usually correct and the people like religious orations very much.[109]

The catechist would then invite questions about the sacraments, but frequently received requests for help with local difficulties instead. These related to disagreements with employers (generally farmers), with whom the catechist was asked to speak as soon as possible. Once these points had been settled, the catechist could embark upon the question-and-answer method of teaching which he had been trained to use, including repetitions of up to twenty times and a 'peppered complement of Indian curses' or a 'physical reprimand' for erroneous answers given by men and children, respectively. Catholic women were reportedly not keen to attend these occasions.[110]

As spokesman for the community, 'guardian' of the local chapel, 'superintendent of public morality', director of the local school, middle-man in disputes and financial transactions, and general servant of the community, both Protestant and Catholic catechists often found their village visits extremely hectic.[111] The Revd C. L. Richards estimated in 1927 that 75 per cent of his agents' time was taken up in arranging marriages, settling arguments, recovering 'run-away wives' or kidnapped girls, and protecting the community from 'the deserved or undeserved attentions of the police'.[112]

The catechist was at constant risk of incurring the displeasure of both his people and the missionaries. The danger in the former case was that, if people did not receive the help for which they asked, they might leave the Church. A frustrated Catholic catechist told his missionary that people were upset by his insistence in making First Communion

[109] Blondeel, *In Het Land Der Vijf Rivieren*, 291–2. This programme had hardly changed in 2003, when the author accompanied a Catholic catechist, Babu-ji Younis, in making his rounds in Dugri village (near Jalandhar City), before a Mass was held. Younis was on very relaxed terms with the villagers. He drank tea in the house of the village headman and had to resist vigorously numerous subsequent offers of tea and food from other Catholic families.

[110] Blondeel, *In Het Land Der Vijf Rivieren*, 291–2.

[111] Capuchin Mission Unit, *India and its Missions*, 227; Letter from Fr. Vincent to General, 4 Jan. 1905, GACO.

[112] The Revd C. L. Richards, Annual Letter 1927, ACMS.

preparations instead of helping them deal with the police or write letters for them. 'I have heard that the protestant *baboo* has been in their village already,' he added nervously.[113]

The situation was made more complex by the desire among Capuchin missionaries to give the help for which they were asked, as a way of breaking low-castes' allegiances to their old community (direct attacks on caste were believed to do 'more harm than good'[114]):

> Further aid may be proffered the low castes by shielding them from their tyrannical masters; by defending them in their just rights before the civil authority; by not segregating the caste from the non-caste people in the churches. Such kindly acts are powerful factors for the uplift of the lower castes. They strike a responsive chord in the heart of the downtrodden.[115]

As Catholic and Protestant missionaries discovered that times of crisis represented an important opportunity to impress low-caste villagers with 'kindly acts', catechists found that their workload became heavier and considerably more dangerous. When plague hit Punjab in 1924, and Narowal was one of the worst affected areas, CMS catechists were forced to carry on their work as usual while conducting three or four funerals per day. Sometimes there was no time to complete these ceremonies with the full Christian rites, and catechists later found themselves blamed by Richards for allowing converts to lapse back into 'superstitious practices'. Catechists worked at extremely high risk to their own health, since there had been no time to inoculate many of them; the fact that Richards saw this as beneficial to the mission (local Christians were in awe of what they assumed was the independent heroism of the catechists[116]) suggests a rather callous view of individual catechists as expendable and perhaps more effective as martyrs than as teachers or preachers.

The propaganda stakes were particularly high during these periods of plague. An outbreak in Sialkot district in the 1890s was later remembered by a Capuchin historian as a tale of Catholic bravery and Protestant spinelessness: 'Whilst our missionaries were destroying the horrors of plague and smiling into the spectral face of death itself . . . the Protestant missionary remained at Sialkot and his catechist absconded home for fear of infection.'[117] Richards was sufficiently worried by the

113 Blondeel, *In Het Land Der Vijf Rivieren*, 297.

114 Capuchin Mission Unit, *India and its Missions*, 279.

115 Blondeel, *In Het Land Der Vijf Rivieren*, 279–80.

116 The Revd C. L. Richards, Annual Letter 1924, ACMS.

117 Ninove, *The Capuchin Mission in the Punjab*, 150.

Fig. 3.2. Unnamed catechist receiving the 'Purple Distinction, Benemerentis [well deserved]' from Mgr Catry, for twenty-five years' unbroken service.
Source: ABC, Photographic Archive

poor performance of one of his catechists during the 1924 outbreak of plague that he visited the area in person, accompanied by the unfortunate catechist and a United Presbyterian missionary. The three of them used the Presbyterian's new Ford car to reach the elders of the offended community as soon as possible. The catechist was induced to confess his failings and beg the elders for forgiveness. Richards then suggested that, if the elders still wanted to break with the CMS, they would be better off going to the Presbyterians rather than to the 'Romans', since the latter would 'deprive them of their Scriptures'.[118]

Even more serious difficulties could occur for the missions if the catechist himself apostatized, since he might have enough influence to take a number of his catechumens or Christians with him to another mission. Fr. Vincent complained to the General of the Order in 1905 that he had lost half a dozen children as a result of an apostate catechist. The parents had 'sold their children to the Protestants for a few rupees a month'. Fr. Vincent could only hope that the 'little ones', who were surely there 'against their will', would some day return to the Catholic fold.[119]

CONCLUSION

By 1920 informal agency had made a profound impact upon the CMS and Capuchin missions, setting challenges that formal agency struggled to meet. The communication of information about Christianity and decisions made to seek the attention of missionaries were governed by a range of influences, which frequently acted in combination. Caste leaders and low-caste village headmen, occasionally wielding power across more than one village, played a decisive role in giving direction and urgency to the rapidly multiplying requests for teaching and baptism which, by the early twentieth century, missionaries came to call 'mass movements'. Such was the power of these leaders that missionaries like Guilford and Bomford, who regarded themselves as rural specialists, hoped to co-opt them in the running of strong, cohesive Christian communities.

These leaders' notions regarding Christianity did not appear out of thin air, however. Migrant workers and members of extended families who moved between villages, particularly at times of marriage, furnished these leaders with second-hand accounts of Christian teaching, the work

118 The Revd C. L. Richards, Annual Letter 1924.
119 Letter from Fr. Vincent to General, 4 Jan. 1905, GACO.

of the missions, and the altered lives of low-caste Christian converts. In some cases, local leaders appear to have had little at all to do with processes of communication and inquiry. Instead, decisions were made at the individual and family level, with the role of women and girls seeming often to have been crucial. The potential of newly-wed Christian girls to become either emissaries for their religion or the cul-de-sac of the Christian lineages on which future Punjabi Churches depended put them in a position of extraordinary influence.

The exact substance of what was communicated among rural Punjabis depended upon the channels of agency involved. Whereas local caste leaders prioritized the unity and security of the group, it was within individuals that perceptions of material and social benefit had the capacity to develop into religious belief and commitment, and possibly to displace older forms of belief. The available archival material affords little insight into any such personal processes as may have occurred during the early stages of the mass movements. Instead, Chapter 4 attempts to trace related themes through the development of the new Christian communities which emerged from the movements.

For the missionaries' part, the evidence of early itineration suggests a missionary mindset of unequal relationships in which Punjabis were always at a disadvantage. This was rooted in Christianity's European experience, from perennial evangelistic concepts of 'givers' versus 'receivers' of the Word to more modern notions of uplift: physical and intellectual advancement, and civic-minded individualism versus indolence, squalor, primitive superstition, and slavishness to caste. Although recent historiography has done much to recover the autonomy and rationality of a social group often depicted as passively responding to mission initiative,[120] the effect of the mass movements upon missionaries themselves was to reinforce the crude stereotypes to which many of them already adhered. This carried over into the employment and training of catechists. Such was the strength of missionary opinion regarding the degraded social and moral condition of the low-caste rural Punjabis from among whose ranks most catechists were drawn that they were not considered to have made the leap from one side to the other.

More important than missionary perceptions of catechists was the latter's standing among villagers. The evidence offered in Chapter 1 suggested that real access to low-caste Punjabi society and culture

[120] See e.g. Webster, *A History of the Dalit Christians in India*; Cox, *Imperial Fault Lines*.

depended upon the establishment of a connection with low-caste socio-economic perspectives. If this were to happen, CMS and Catholic catechists, as the main points of contact between villagers and a small cadre of European missionaries, would play a pivotal role in presenting Christianity as the salvation alluded to in Chuhra eschatology. Catechists would also have to communicate low-caste perspectives back to the missions, so that mission strategies for building new communities could take them into account; for example, in details of worship, structures of authority, and prospects for education and socio-economic advance.

Although the CMS and Capuchins noted woefully little detail about the lives and accomplishments of their catechists—there was nothing which equated to the eagerness with which the CMS recorded discussions in the PNCC, for example—it seems clear that in general catechists were not highly rated by villagers. The reason for this was that catechists were the point of contact for two groups with strong ideas about how the other ought to behave. Both the CMS and the Capuchins had brought with them to Punjab fairly concrete models and expectations for rural evangelization. Theological conformity and logistics might be debated, but the dynamics of low-caste interest in Christianity were of little interest. Most missionaries' views of the basically unequal relationships they entered into in Punjab—influenced both by similarly unbalanced pastoral relationships in Europe and by their limited contact with the rural Punjabi poor—gave them such a simplistic view of low-caste society that inquirers' interest in social and material opportunities was not taken as an indication of more complex perspectives but rather as an inevitable poverty-induced desperation which ought to be seized upon and transformed into spiritual inquiry, with no further questions asked.

The result was that missionaries appear to have sought little information from their catechists except that which pertained to the progress of missionary plans. Even the insights of Hares or Macaire into Chuhra culture were purely anthropological, and implicitly dismissive. The enhanced linguistic and cultural access that men like French hoped that catechists would bring to the missions was a prelude to convert re-formation rather than the basis for serious engagement. Catechists were thus carefully trained for roles that were important and varied but highly specific. Almost all methods, materials, and spiritual and intellectual reference points were European. Even those that were ostensibly Indian—techniques of 'controversy', bazaar preaching, and information on Indian religions—were European interpretations. In such circumstances it was unsurprising that catechists appeared to show little initiative, waiting instead for 'an order for every little thing they do'.[121]

As the anxious debate among PNCC delegates suggested, as long as Punjabi mission-Churches still depended upon European money and personnel, their future direction would be discussed and planned on European terms. With any creative potential of catechists apparently squandered by the missions, it appeared that the 'Punjabi' character of the new Churches would emerge only slowly, through the development of new Christian communities themselves. These communities are the focus of the next chapter.

[121] *Shortcomings*, 18. It should be noted that while missionary accusations of inertia were frequently reserved for low-castes in particular, at other times it was claimed that lack of spontaneity was a '*national* failing' (ibid. 18). Heike Liebau has pointed out that although missionaries relied upon Indian agents for information about local societies, the former's domination of this process was rarely challenged; Liebau, 'Country Priests, Catechists and Schoolmasters as Cultural, Religious, and Social Middlemen in the Context of the Tranquebar Mission', 84–5.

4

Living in New Traditions

Waves of large-scale conversion crashed over the CMS and Capuchin missions at different times from the 1890s onwards. Only once these had subsided did the real drama begin, as missions and converts surveyed the landscape left behind and began to build up a body of real knowledge about each other.

As had been the case from the very beginning, the substance of communication in the mission–convert relationship was shaped profoundly by the routes through which it passed. In the early days, information about Christianity had been filtered through the ideals of local leaders, through family networks, and through the activities of catechists—in the last case the results determined by personality and training as well as by the limits of what critical village audiences were prepared to listen to. Now, the brute logistical fact of new convert groups tucked away as minority citizens in hundreds of scattered villages meant that contact would be sparse and sporadic. In these circumstances even the smallest gestures that passed between mission personnel and converts—whether of initiative, creativity, defiance, or hostility—might well be crucial to the impressions formed about one another.

This restrictive physical and cultural context suited no one. For CMS and Capuchin missionaries the hope that the mass movements might herald a broader Indian interest in Christianity was one of very few consolations in a situation that many of them would otherwise have described as disastrous. As they saw it, they were now responsible for huge numbers of people who had been baptized but for whom 'conversion', in the senses intended by the two missions, remained a distant and perhaps unachievable prospect. Most converts were entirely without education, were living in villages bereft of Christian influence, and relied for their livelihoods upon people either indifferent or hostile towards their recent conversion. On top of this, converts had come to Christianity—as missionaries were well aware—largely through the very bonds of extended family and *biraderi* (community) that a true Christian identity sought to trump. This was hardly a level playing field for the confrontation missionaries expected between converts' old lives and their new ones.

Punjabi converts appear not to have shared quite this level of gloom, perhaps not least because they were less preoccupied than the missions with the need for deep and thoroughgoing lifestyle changes as part of new Christian communities. Isolation in often hostile villages of course worried people, but in the sense of heightened socio-economic and physical vulnerability rather than a shortage of Christian culture and contact. Converts wanted to be able to call on the missions when they needed them, but *too much* interaction with missionaries or local agents could quickly become unwelcome, viewed even as intrusive.

This chapter looks at life in these new Christian communities: the ways in which mission personnel and converts sought to exercise control, the sites of conflict that emerged as a result, and what these early years of contested community-building suggest about the original inclinations that drove the movements. 'Community', in the sense used here, refers to a group of people from one village or a cluster of villages who received instruction from the same mission agents and attended the same church services and special events. These communities were the constituent parts of the broader CMS and Capuchin mission-Churches.

Attention turns first to the contours of these new communities and the impact of attempts by local villagers, converts, and missionaries to influence their development. CMS and Capuchin variations on popular mission themes of education and medical care should be looked at as a response to these early dilemmas. Their closeness to European evangelistic and social-work models is, in part, a sign of the extent to which missionaries failed to see how or why they should engage with the specificities of the Punjabi context. Was this a failure of communication or the triumph on all sides of enduringly independent views about what the mission–convert relationship should be? Did the new Christian communities represent a necessary attenuation of incompatible ideals, or did mission personnel and converts alike imagine they had a battle on their hands which they might yet win?

CONTOURS OF THE NEW COMMUNITIES

Village Interests and Influences

The number of converts and catechumens in the Catholic mission stood at well over 26,000 by the beginning of the 1920s, nearly 90 per cent of them rural low-castes. The same figures for the CMS mission were closer to 30,000, and the numbers in both communities were set to grow rapidly over the next twenty years.[1] Despite these numbers, however, a fundamental fact of life for the new communities was that after conversion rural Christians remained socio-economically embedded in their villages, comparatively isolated from other Christians and from the infrastructure of the mission-Church. They were usually heavily outnumbered by non-Christian villagers, who viewed their conversion as a serious blow to existing systems of interdependence and authority, and to the availability of cheap or unpaid labour. Catechumen and convert relations with these villagers, and in particular with their *sepidari* employers, represent an important general area of inquiry since they are revealing of the dynamics of local society in a way that the opinions of foreign missionaries are not.

As an example of this, in Shahabad village the presence of Christianity dated back to the visit of a single Chamar representative to a missionary of the SPG, one of the organizations with which the CMS had considerable contact in Punjab, persuading him to send personnel to the village. Evidence suggests that local landowners interpreted this low-caste interest in Christianity as a major switch in social loyalties, dating not from the moment of baptism but from the very first audiences that low-caste groups gave to mission personnel. This raises a question. If one set of local villagers, i.e. landowners, understood the nature and timing of contacts with the missions in this way, is it possible that another set of villagers—low-castes themselves—did too? CMS and Capuchin sources support the impression of an early and fundamental disjuncture between convert and missionary thinking on this point. Where missionaries envisaged a religious transformation at baptism, deepening over subsequent months and years, converts clearly thought in terms of a broader social as well as religious event that included a

[1] See Ch. 2.

change in public allegiance.[2] Where, then, missions agonized over how quickly and under what circumstances they should give access, through baptism, to their Churches, rural catechumens may well have considered one of the most important events in their relationship with Christianity to have already passed, weeks and possibly months before.

Convert thinking here is not easy to trace, but the evidence suggests that conversion was seen in part at least as something of a tactical affiliation with a locally powerful group—experimental in nature, and by no means permanent—with the important dimension that converts did not necessarily appreciate or support the full theological claims of the missions. In Shahabad village it had been the singing of Christian *bhajans* (religious songs) by low-caste villagers, long before their baptism, that had catalysed landlord anger. Given the prominence of songs, controversially worded, in low-caste religious traditions, it is reasonable to speculate that the singing of these Christian *bhajans* might have been infused with social meaning even at this early stage. If so, landlords were not precipitous in their anger; instead, they recognized here a level of significance that eluded the missionaries. Some of the low-caste villagers involved soon found themselves arrested on false charges.[3] Nor was Shahabad a unique case: echoes can be found in the experiences of CMS and Capuchin converts, as well as in the treatment of low-castes, whose association with the Arya Samaj angered local landowners.

The willingness of low-castes to endure the harsh repercussions of their apparent repudiation (or at least dilution) of old patron–client relationships—from the stopping of their wells and the stealing of their cattle to neighbours' encouragement of their own cattle to eat low-castes' crops and the refusal of landlords to allow schools to be opened in their villages[4]—demonstrates the importance that many attached to their new identity. Even where landowners in Tarn Taran offered low-castes material inducements to renounce their new ties, the Revd Guilford noted that such offers tended to be ignored.[5]

It is unclear exactly how far converts expected the missions to protect them in these circumstances, in the absence of a sympathetic local community or police force. The demands made of local catechists suggest

[2] On this point, see also Webster, *A History of the Dalit Christians*; Bugge, *Mission and Tamil Society*.

[3] Marsh, 'Village Work', 118.

[4] Landowners had the legal power to prevent buildings from being used for purposes of which they disapproved; Hibbert-Ware, 'Baptisms in the Villages', pt 1, 55.

[5] The Revd E. Guilford, Annual Letter 1892, repr. in *EAL 1891–2*, 230.

that catechumens and converts did not expect drastic socio-economic change as a result of their new affiliations, but simply more favourable resolutions to perennial arguments over labour and reward. Missions would gladly have recorded more extravagant demands had they been made, since these would further have illustrated the preoccupation with material and social concerns which they believed lay at the heart of many of the inadequacies of the rural Church. Instead, mission personnel encountered little opposition from within convert communities when they reassured landowners of their broad support for the existing social fabric of the villages. As an SPG catechist told a disgruntled landowner, if converts 'did not carry out their duties they should tell the Mission agent, and he would charge them to be faithful'.[6]

The missions were well placed to help catechumens and converts where demands were modest. The opening-up of local politics to scrutiny by outsiders represented a real constraint upon the coercive potential of village elites, and if missions urged fair play and cooperation upon catechumens and converts, they looked for no less from village employers. Where secular authorities might lack the manpower or the inclination to see that local law and custom were upheld, the missions possessed both a ready-made information network, in the form of peripatetic and reasonably well-connected catechists, and good knowledge of, and access to, the legal system.

This new dynamic in village life—troublesome as well as insulting for landowners—was in evidence in both Protestant and Catholic missions. An SPG missionary, the Revd Hibbert-Ware, went to great lengths to ensure that Chamar converts were paid for their field labour according to government provisions.[7] In the Capuchin mission a Catholic man named Hakim Ali, from Sheikhpura district, asked for help with a legal case which was being brought against him by local landowners. Fr. Felix sought to make Hakim's a test case which would highlight what he saw as landowners' vindictive treatment of the poor. With the help of a Christian lawyer from Lyallpur, Fr. Felix fought and won.[8]

More common in the missionary sources than this kind of activism, however, was Hibbert-Ware's response to the situation in Tota's troubled village of Khanpur: 'we bade them be patient and

[6] The words are those of Hibbert-Ware, reproducing the comment of a catechist in his mission; Hibbert-Ware, 'Baptisms in the Villages', pt 1, 55. [7] Ibid. 55.

[8] Rooney, *Into Deserts*, 69. The Salvation Army went as far as supporting a strike by Christian sweepers in Dera Baba Nanak district, only to see it defeated when villagers cleaned their own toilets; Cox, *Imperial Fault Lines*, 126.

pray . . . patiently to endure persecution is a hard thing, but undoubtedly it is . . . for these depressed people, the shortest way out'.[9] Despite the fact that a tougher line against oppressive village politics would be a popular and, in many ways, positive dimension of community-building, there were a number of reasons why missions did not come to people's aid more often.

Firstly, they worried that it would detract from mission personnel's primary responsibilities of evangelization and teaching, draining precious resources and distracting converts and catechumens with an excessively militant impression of Christianity. Secondly, missionaries sought to avoid upsetting the social order in such a politically sensitive province. The Punjab Government was already nervous about the mission presence in the countryside. Any major incidents which threatened security or aggravated landed elites might well lead to their expulsion.

Thirdly, Protestant and Catholic missions tended to be at one in believing that encouraging the new community to deal with its own problems was healthy for the development of self-sufficiency. As Hibbert-Ware put it, this required a great deal of self-restraint on the part of the missions, but it was the only way to ensure that converts 'grow up'.[10] If Christian communities were based from the outset upon such obvious patronage as legal representation, both their religious dimension and their general standing within a sceptical Indian society—many Europeans included—would be seriously compromised.

Finally, both the CMS and the Capuchin missions were firmly rooted in the concept of submission to legitimate government.[11] Neither represented sections of European society which were given to social rebellion, and the enduring hope that higher-castes in the Punjab countryside might eventually be drawn to Christianity acted as a retarding force upon any challenges to existing customary arrangements in the villages. Whether or not these higher-caste conversions were achieved,

[9] Hibbert-Ware, 'Baptisms in the Villages', pt 1, 56. See Ch. 3.

[10] Ibid., pt 2, 71.

[11] 'Let every person be subject to the governing authorities. For there is no authority except from God, and those that exist have been instituted by God. Therefore he who resists the authorities resists what God has appointed, and those who resist will incur judgment . . . Pay all of them their dues, taxes to whom taxes are due, revenue to whom revenue is due, respect to whom respect is due, honour to whom honour is due' (Rom. 13: 1–7).

true self-sufficiency and self-extension in rural Punjabi Churches in any case required the building of good relations with powerful elements in the countryside, which the CMS and Capuchin missions could no more afford to alienate than could other social reformers—even those within the Punjab administration like Brayne and Darling.

Sources of Authority: Mission, *Panchayat*, and Church Council

The Capuchins made limited provision for lay cooperation or communication among new converts. In the absence of any tradition in Catholicism of lay government in Church affairs, Catholic Punjab was held together by the mission's personnel and few institutions. Relations with village or caste leaders were rarely mentioned, and the Capuchins seemed keen to become involved in local matters of order or discipline only where they felt that a particular point—for example, regarding Christian marriage or proper burial rites—needed to be illustrated. Only in the case of Catholic colonies such as Maryabad did missionaries take on general responsibilities among Christians, and even here there appeared little scope for lay leadership. Punjabis seeking that kind of influence would have to work as catechists or apply for the priesthood.

For a lay Evangelical society such as the CMS, the co-option of devout and powerful laypeople into a hierarchy of responsibility within the Church was a priority. Caste or village *panchayat*s—local institutions of leadership and customary arbitration[12]—were a natural building block here, appealing to many missionaries as a distinctly Indian germ of self-government and self-sufficiency. CMS missionaries appeared to take their lead here from the government, which introduced several pieces of legislation in the early twentieth century with the intention of reviving the *panchayat* system (which the imposition of a centralized legal framework after 1857 had all but destroyed) and reducing the frequency with which Punjabis took each other to court.[13]

Missionary experiments with *panchayat*s encountered difficulties, however, with experiences in south India suggesting complications in grafting a mission-sponsored power structure onto an existing Indian one: *panchayat* justice of temporary self-exclusion from the community by the wrongdoer was alien to European missionaries, who were equally

[12] See Jagdish Pal Singh, 'The Panchayats in Punjab, 1849–1947', *Punjab Past and Present*, 13/1 (Apr. 2001), 116.

[13] Ibid. 116–23.

unprepared for the breadth of responsibility in low-caste society to which their innovations appeared to commit them.[14]

Nevertheless, in Punjab the CMS tried hard to bring all matters of behaviour under the mission's control and then to delegate responsibility downwards to newly formed special *panchayat*s or 'Church Committees' (depending upon how local people opted to refer to them). In 1922 Guilford laid out the basic duties of these local bodies:

1. To look after the place of worship and encourage attendance at divine services.
2. To investigate any cases of wrongdoing in the congregation and to report their findings to the Pastorate Committee of the Mother Church at Tarn Taran, which meets monthly.
3. To assess the amount of the congregation's contribution to the Mission funds for the upkeep of the work in their own congregation . . . and to collect the amount when due.[15]

Guilford saw this as a way of making people feel they were 'part of the show'. In general he hoped that the 1920s would be a 'time of training [for Punjabis] for future responsibility as Elders of the Church', these positions held in the short-term at least by village or caste headmen trained for new roles through personal tutelage under European missionaries. To emphasize their closeness to the mission Guilford invited these local leaders to monthly meetings held for mission workers and hosted a New Year dinner for them.[16]

It was hoped that the use of an Indian system of order would give a sense of continuity and legitimacy to the new communities, perhaps also rendering Christian principles more intelligible through the interpretative function of the *panchayat*. And yet this was only a superficial blending of authority structures. In practice, *panchayat*s ignored missionary advice where they did not agree with it—the Revd C. L. Richards's calls for moderation were laid aside at a *panchayat* meeting in his Narowal mission where leaders decided that Christians should be barred from attending the wedding of the daughter of an adulterous member of the community[17]—and retained their old punishment of

[14] Bugge, *Mission and Tamil Society*, 116–19.

[15] The Revd E. Guilford, Annual Letters 1922 and 1917, ACMS.

[16] Ibid.

[17] The Revd C. L. Richards, Annual Letter 1918. The Revd Hall wrote of similar experiences in one of his mass-movement articles; Hall, 'A Suggested Policy for Mass Movements', 284.

excommunication even though its meaning was fundamentally different in a Christian community.

Nor did the use of Indian authority structures and methods represent any meaningful concession to Punjabi power in the mission-Church. The limits of local responsibility were clearly set out, and real power remained in the hands of the CMS in London and senior missionaries in Punjab. Suggestions in the Punjab Native Church Council (PNCC) that European missionaries sought to hand over their workload rather than their power appeared vindicated by the minute book system used by Church Committees and *panchayats*.[18] In dealing with minor issues these bodies were asked to keep a record of the punishments which they handed down to offenders, so that visiting mission agents could retain the final say—by extending or rescinding penalties—without having to waste time actually dealing with the matter in the first place. In other cases the *panchayat* or Committee would not even be entitled to consider an issue, passing it directly to the local clergyman or the Bishop instead.[19]

The late nineteenth century saw a shift in CMS organization in Punjab from what eventually came to be regarded as the undesirable European–Indian segregation of the PNCC to a system where all mission personnel would work together.[20] The planning stages for the new system revealed serious tensions in the CMS. The Revd Robert Clark wrote of the thousand-year experience of the English Church and the danger that inexperienced Punjabis might be liable to cast a 'wrong vote' in any future institution.[21] Concerns were also raised over issues of equal pay. The Revd Imad-ud-din worried that Punjabi representatives might suffer 'subjection' and 'bondage' at the hands of Europeans.[22] The Revd A. E. Day echoed concerns

[18] Guilford admitted in 1892 that he hoped Punjabi agents would 'set the foreign missionary free for more direct evangelistic labours' (the Revd E. Guilford, Annual Letter 1892, repr. in *EAL 1891–2*, 231).

[19] Hall, 'A Suggested Policy for Mass Movements', 285.

[20] See Cox, *Imperial Fault Lines*, for suggestions about a range of other factors which may have been involved in the PNCC's demise.

[21] Robert Clark, *Indian Christian Workers in CMS Missions, With Special Reference to the CMS Native Church Council in the Punjab and Sindh* (Simla, 1888), 9–12, ACMS, G2/I4/O 1888, n. 271. Clark's subsequent claims that clerical offices should be given to whoever was most 'suitable', regardless of race (ibid. 22), ought to be interpreted in this light.

[22] The Revd Imad-ud-din, quoted in ACMS, Letter (11 Jan. 1897) and Papers from Clark to the Revd C. H. Gill (Secretary, CMS Conference, North-West Frontier Province), ACMS, G2/I4/O 1897, n. 209.

back in England when he suggested that distinct roles should be maintained in the mission-Church: Europeans as evangelists, meeting in the Missionary Conference, and Punjabis as teacher–pastors, meeting in the PNCC.[23]

There were further anxieties over the liturgy, with European clerical correspondents repeating the platitude of the need for an 'indigenous Church' yet fretting at the same time that Anglican theology might be compromised.[24] Just as Church Committees represented a brand of 'self-government' which was alien in form and extremely limited in scope, so the larger structures to which such bodies were connected represented a European straitjacket designed to ensure that spontaneity in the 'Punjabi' Church would not get out of hand. Crossing cultures seemed to entail far greater risks and uncertainty for Evangelical Protestant than for Catholic Christianity: whereas an Evangelical response to the gospel in a highly regulated Christian society was in some senses predictable, non-Christian societies presented an unnerving range of variables.

By the early twentieth century those in favour of joint European–Punjabi structures (including Clark, who changed his mind on the subject) got their way. At the top of the new system was the CMS Parent Committee in London, which retained the right to veto decisions taken at a lower level. The next rung down was the Central Mission Council (CMC), led by the Bishop of Lahore as President. This consisted for the most part of European and Punjabi appointees by the Parent Committee (CMS donor interests were undoubtedly a factor in establishing these rather conservative foundations), and took on the work of the old Missionary Conference and Corresponding Committees.[25]

Below the CMC were six District Mission Councils (DMCs): Lahore, Amritsar, Himalaya, Kashmir, Frontier, and Sindh and Baluchistan. All, it was hoped, would be dioceses in the future, and all were entitled to send delegates to CMC meetings.[26] DMC functions also included setting and paying all Punjabi clergy and agents' salaries, and receiving their reports, funding schools, selecting candidates for Orders, and managing

[23] Copy of the Revd A. E. Day, 'The Proposed Amalgamation of the CMS Conference of Missionaries and the Native Church Council', 27 Mar. 1897, 4–5, ACMS, G2/I4/O 1897, n. 209.

[24] Bishop Harold Browne of Winchester, quoted in Letter (11 Jan. 1897) and Papers from Clark to the Revd C. H. Gill, ACMS, G2/I4/O 1897.

[25] *Punjab, North-West Frontier and Sindh: Final Draft Constitution, 6th and 7th April 1904*, ACMS, G2/I4/O 1904, n. 192. The Punjab Corresponding Committee was finally abolished in 1936; Hewitt, *The Problems of Success*, ii. 70–1.

[26] *Punjab, North-West Frontier and Sindh: Final Draft Constitution.*

and inspecting schools.[27] All CMS clergy (Indian and European), English lay missionaries, Punjabi teacher–pastors, and at least two lay delegates from each pastorate had seats on the DMC, although real power was concentrated in the hands of the Chairman, an appointee of the Parent Committee. At the next level down were the Pastorate Committees, chaired by the local pastor and drawing representatives from the grassroots: the *panchayats* or Church Committees in the local area. The Pastorate Committees were responsible for taking care of the upkeep of buildings belonging to the Church and generally overseeing the life and conduct of its congregation(s).[28]

The collection and distribution of funds illustrated the upward flow of responsibility and downward flow of control that characterized CMS organization in the decades during and immediately following the mass movements, before the more genuine and widespread devolutionary mood of the 1930s set in. Money was collected by the Pastorate, but a proportion of it had to be given to the DMC and then requested back for specific purposes. The DMC operated in the same way in relation to the CMC. Immovable property across the mission remained in the hands of the CMC, which in its early days was still 'swamped' by a 'mass of Europeans', according to one observer.[29]

Few village Christians were chosen as delegates to either the DMCs or the CMC, while the role of women was also restricted, with many mission personnel seeking to exclude the latter altogether from certain sessions of the CMC and the DMCs.[30] Well might these bodies have been described as 'merely a European idea' (see Chapter 2). They were worlds away from the ordinary experience of most CMS converts, and yet they threatened to draw village communities into broad—provincial and national—structures of authority and responsibility of which it is far from clear that rural Punjabis had ever sought membership. In the short term these might be staffed by old caste or village leaders,

[27] *Minutes of a Joint Committee of Members of the CMS Conference and Native Church Council, 16th and 17th April, 1903*, ACMS, G2/I4/O 1903, n. 152.

[28] In some cases a pastorate would consist of more than one congregation; *Punjab, North-West Frontier and Sindh: Final Draft Constitution, 6th and 7th April 1904*.

[29] Grey, 'Native Church Organisation in India II', 480.

[30] The Revd H. G. Grey blamed the conservatism of male Punjabi clergy for this, but from the limited available source material it is impossible to gain an accurate sense of the actual roots of this policy towards women. It is likely that reference to European models—themselves still limited in the roles afforded to women—was made. Grey, 'Native Church Organization in India, II', 479. On village Christians here, see Hares, 'Mass Movements and their Consequences', 34.

but in the long term there was potential for legitimacy and leadership privileges to pass from those qualified by custom and birth to those perceived as fitting social and religious ideals laid down by outsiders.

The attempt by CMS personnel to order, through bureaucratic structures, the socio-religious task they saw as facing them in rural Punjab is revealing of the rather rigid and formulaic approach to mission that characterized the upper echelons of the organization both in Britain and in Punjab. The CMS tended to create their own dilemmas, around policy, income, and missionary personality, rather than attend with any great interest or sensitivity to what was driving events on the ground. Hence perhaps a disjuncture—a feature also of the Capuchin mission—between bureaucratic and ecclesiastical attempts to 'form' Christian communities and the sites of conflict and change that were genuinely influencing the substance of Punjabi Christianity: direct exchanges between converts and mission personnel. On the issue of authority, converts, by refusing to make a decisive move away from the *biraderi*, sounded a decisive note of independence from Christian mission-Churches that soon found echoes in other areas of everyday life.

Everyday Life and 'Attachments to Ancient Customs'

From the relatively little that is reliably known about ceremonial aspects of low-caste life it is clear that rites of life such as birth, marriage, and death were attended by rituals no less complex than those of other social groups in Punjab. The stage was thus effectively set for conflict, with Christian marriage and family in particular representing fundamental ideals for the Capuchins and the CMS, and both groups seeing little room for compromise with converts here. In Europe, Pope Leo XIII's encyclical *Arcanum* (1880) had denounced recent liberal attacks on the 'unity' and 'perpetuity' of Christian marriage, and bishops across the world were urged to fight to preserve its sanctity and inviolability.[31] Pope Pius XI's encyclical fifty years later referred to marriage as the 'principle and foundation of domestic society', placing it at the centre of a range of major social questions: individual consent in contracting marriage, power relations between husband and wife, polygamy, extramarital sex, divorce, prostitution, parental responsibility with regard to children's

[31] Leo XIII, *Arcanum*, 10 Feb. 1880 (Vatican, 1880).

upbringing, and the proliferation of books and films with questionable subject matter.[32]

In Punjab, CMS and Capuchin mission correspondence suggests that the most pressing objection among mission personnel was converts' continuation in old modes where the contracting of marriage was concerned. For converts, marriage remained just that: a contract—between two families, sealed with the bridegroom's payment of a 'bride price' to the bride's family. For missionaries like Richards, this amounted to no more than the 'absolutely shameless' selling of girls, which he claimed could extend to multiple engagements secretly being made for the same girl, later to be broken; the father, meanwhile, would spend months in idleness, 'living on the proceeds'.[33] Richards described other 'thoroughly depressing' incidents which led him to believe it a 'common trait among the depressed classes' that girls be seen by their fathers as financial assets once they passed a certain age.[34]

The year 1923 was a particularly bad one for the Narowal mission in this respect, and Richards wearily recounted what seemed to be recurrent problems:

> [Christian] Brides running away from newly married husbands, husbands discarding wives, girls being kidnapped and sold . . . there was the case of a girl being kidnapped by two Christian servants out of my own compound, to be sold very likely to some non-Christians . . . Not the least sad point of this was that the father of the girl seemed more affected by the loss of her value as a marriageable article than by any natural affection.[35]

A major factor in the disappointment expressed by Richards and mission personnel who shared his views was an inability fully to understand the complexities of low-caste betrothal and marriage (see Chapter 1) and a disturbingly telling failure to exercise any kind of guidance or impact upon converts at this key moment in their lives.

[32] Pius XI, *Casti Connubii*, 31 Dec. 1930 (Vatican, 1930). The Anglican Church's opposition to polygamy was set out at the First Lambeth Conference (1867), after which the CMS in India admitted polygamists only as catechumens. Both the Capuchins and the CMS saw it as a virtue of their missions that polygamy was not tolerated. In central India low-caste converts had been known to flout mission-Church proclamations on adultery, in order to fulfil a pre-existing practice of *churi*, secondary marriage. Saurabh Dube, *Untouchable Pasts: Religion, Identity, and Power among a Central Indian Community, 1780–1950* (New York, 1998).

[33] The Revd C. L. Richards, Annual Letter 1930, ACMS.

[34] Richards noted that before this age children were treated with great affection; the Revd C. L. Richards, Annual Letter 1923, ACMS.

[35] Ibid.

This seemed to be as true after marriage as it was beforehand. On one occasion in 1923 Richards was called to resolve a dispute in which a new Christian bride had gone home to visit her family and had refused to return to her husband. The situation deteriorated to the point where the husband, on Richards's advice, tried physically to pull his wife away from the front of her family home. He dragged her 400 yards while she screamed at him to leave her alone. A crowd gathered, and Richards advised the husband to let her go. The girl never went back to the husband, who was forced to consider risking excommunication by taking a new wife during the lifetime of the first.[36]

It seemed that, for converts, both missionaries and very possibly the information-gathering catechists remained at the periphery of the everyday social world. There was no reason to alter their way of life in the ways that mission personnel requested—if indeed the mission vision of proper social behaviour was even clear to them. Mission personnel were seen instead as a source of support to be drawn on when required but who otherwise could be kept at arm's length.

The Capuchins recorded similar experiences of what they called 'an ignoble traffic' in young women, but appeared no more able than the CMS to access the dynamics of local culture that produced these arrangements.[37] They were more interested in the fact that 'immorality' was the result,[38] and it is far from clear whether they actually knew of instances of 'immoral' behaviour or whether these were general assumptions, an extension of a default negative view of converts' lifestyles and culture.

As will be shown shortly in the context of their medical work, the friars were fond of the direct approach in their mission. In the late 1890s Fr. Vincent, in Adah, had married a couple who he knew had failed to gain parental permission. For five months he had sought this permission on their behalf but, having no more success than Richards in establishing his influence in such matters, decided to go ahead with the ceremony in secret. When the marriage was discovered, it 'nearly caused a revolt' in the area, but in the end it was allowed to stand. Fr. Vincent believed that an important victory had been won through

[36] Revd C. L. Richards, Annual Letter 1923. [37] Pelckmans, *Dix Années*, 11.
[38] Ninove, *The Capuchin Mission in the Punjab*, 140–2.

simple demonstration: 'our people understood that whether they like it or not, if they want to be Christians they have to abandon their anti-Christian customs'.[39]

Vincent went on to claim that since this incident a number of engagements of which he had publicly disapproved had been refused or cancelled, and that many Christians had promised not to marry off their children without the approval or 'counsel' of the missionary. A theme beginning to emerge in the Capuchin mission was that it would be for the boys and girls of the mission to 'establish' comprehensively such 'reform[s]' in the future.[40] A few years later, Fr. Bernardin, also in Adah, described his visit to a nearby village, where he had heard there was a child close to death. He had visited the family and, after talking casually with them for a while, had steered the conversation around to the health of the children. Upon receiving the reply that one of them was dying, he had told the parents that he would baptize him. 'Before they had time to reply, the little one was Catholic . . . three hours later he was an angel in the sky.'

A further success, in Fr. Bernardin's eyes, lay in persuading the family to have the child buried in the Catholic cemetery at Adah, rather than in what he described as the 'communal cemetery of the Chuhras'.[41] It appears that this battle, like the others described above, was one of wills rather than reasoned persuasion. An official Capuchin account later attributed their seven-year delay in achieving the first full Catholic funeral in Adah to 'ridiculous [Chuhra] beliefs regarding death'. Low-caste burial customs, which included washing and laying out the body in a manner understandable to the Capuchins but also elements of singing and gesturing around the body that were

[39] Letter from Fr. Vincent to General, 16 Jan. 1899, GACO. The work of Bishop Azariah in Dornakal diocese epitomized what Catholic and Protestant Churches saw as this constant fight to protect the institution of marriage. Azariah vehemently opposed child marriage, divorce, and remarriage, on the basis of 'natural' and Jewish as well as Christian law. He struggled to prevent mixed marriages from being contracted (this was frequently a problem since converts preferred to marry non-Christians within their own *jati* rather than Christians of another *jati*), to promote marriage ceremonies in the church rather than the home, and to modify converts' sexual behaviour according to what the Anglican Church regarded as proper. See Billington Harper, *In the Shadow of the Mahatma*, 266–9.

[40] Letter from Fr. Vincent to General, 16 Jan. 1899, GACO.

[41] Letter from Fr. Bernadin to Provincial, 27 Sept. 1911, ABC, L690.

clearly less so, were described in one Capuchin publication as 'play-acting'.[42]

Such incidents confirm that adherence by new converts to mission ideals—and possibly even basic knowledge about them—was patchy at best, with the missions viewing failures to adopt their ways of thinking and acting as the norm, and picking out successes as rare victories. One final dimension to these local contests, which were helping by increments to define rural Punjabi Christianity in its early years, was the continuance of converts in pre-Christian beliefs and acts of worship. The available evidence suggests that converts generally saw no inconsistency in retaining old religious customs and practices as a complement to their new faith. This accretive approach to devotion was not unnatural in a rural Indian setting, where people often took part in forms of worship that originated in other religious traditions. From the evidence looked at in Chapter 1, this appears to have been a particular feature of low-caste religious culture. It nevertheless caused considerable consternation among mission personnel, who had doubted the 'solidity' of low-caste conversions from the outset and who were increasingly pessimistic about the extent of converts' receptivity to their authority—and to their vision of Christianity.[43]

The enduring popularity of old forms of worship—a maximization of supernatural and social defences against life's various ills that the missions decried as 'attachments to ancient customs'[44]—is significant because it represents clear input to a nascent Punjabi Christian culture by ordinary converts. The persistence of Christians at Narowal in wearing charms around their necks and worshipping at old shrines[45] appears to have been just such an independent religious observance. These were made far more frequently at times of plague, despite the attempts of mission personnel to persuade villagers that it was their very idolatry that brought such horrors upon them in the first place.[46] The Capuchin Br. Guerin complained that adults who were baptized when they were ill with the plague made 'the most beautiful promises', but once recovered they failed to keep them. In some cases

[42] Pelckmans, *Dix Années*, 69–70. See also Blondeel, *In Het Land Der Vijf Rivieren*, 157–60.

[43] For Capuchin doubts about convert 'solidity', see the comments of Frs Edouard, Fabian, and Felix in Ch. 3.

[44] Letter from Fr. Vincent to General, 17 Jan. 1906, GACO.

[45] The Revd C. M. Gough, quoted in *Proceedings of the CMS, 1900–1* (London, 1901), 285–6.

[46] The Revd C. L. Richards, Annual Letter 1924. See below.

they no longer even extended to missionaries the 'banal courtesy' of a salute, usually made to any holy man upon arrival at someone's home.[47]

It is impossible to say for certain whether the continuation of pre-conversion religious observances was simply natural to converts, or was the result of a deliberate decision at the individual, family, or local caste level, but it may be significant that Richards and the Revd C. M. Gough chose to appeal directly to the people themselves—publicly destroying their charms in church, or tearing down 'mud pillar' shrines (to Bala Shah)[48]—rather than to negotiate quietly on these points with local leaders (no accounts of such conversations have been found). Despite their awareness that such leadership had been crucial in many cases to the original decision in favour of Christianity, missionaries preferred to direct violent acts of 'moral persuasion' at individuals.[49] Gough's likening of convert behaviour in Narowal to that exhibited by the 'degraded' at home in rural England[50] was just one of a long list of unflattering missionary remarks that revealed frustration and fear at the inscrutability of low-caste society. 'Inertia', 'low culture', and 'darkness' were among the most common other themes. 'Darkness' was particularly telling, since it was suggestive of both the social and spiritual imperfections of converts and the practical limitations of missionaries, in terms of what they knew about rural converts and what they could ever expect to understand.

Perhaps this explained the reluctance of CMS and Capuchin missionaries to make the cultural accommodation that their superiors in London and Rome frequently urged upon them even into the 1920s and 1930s. Only minor successes were achieved, one being Capuchin attempts to reconcile low-caste ancestor worship with the Catholic veneration of saints. This incurred the disdain of Protestant missionaries, who viewed both forms of devotion as popular, pre-Christian bunkum. An example of this sort of acculturation has been the lasting appeal in rural Punjab of the Virgin Mary, a popular focus for devotion even in the early twenty-first century. Just as with Catholicism in other cultural

[47] Letter from Br. Guerin to General, 25 Jan. 1903, GACO. There is no record of a Br. Guerin among the Capuchin missionaries in this period. He may have been visiting the mission of Adah from another Order.

[48] The Revd C. M. Gough, quoted in *Proceedings of the CMS, 1900–1*, 285–6.

[49] The Revd C. L. Richards, Annual Letter 1924.

[50] The Revd C. M. Gough, Annual Letter 1902, repr. in *EAL 1901–2* (London, 1902), 384.

contexts, this kind of devotion has led to a blurring of the distinction between Catholic saints and the ancestors of local people. In addition, cases have been reported of Catholics, Protestants, and non-Christians in Punjab worshipping individual statues of Mary as gods, in and of themselves.[51] Fig. 4.1 shows a statue of Mary sculpted by a Capuchin around 1960, designed to fit with Indian imagery of female deities.

The Endurance of Tradition

Converts do not appear to have considered themselves close enough to the missions for any process of accommodation to be necessary or appropriate. They had made a significant socio-religious commitment capable of withstanding harassment and abuse at the hands of influential villagers (mission failings were more likely to prompt a switch in allegiances than was this kind of provocation). Yet this commitment was not one that treated mission ideas about authority and the Christian life as inviolable. Converts seemed to view their new status as Christians as part of a broader set of aspirations. Some sought jobs with the mission, but most hoped instead for higher status and fairer relations in the village, as illustrated in appeals to catechists and missionaries over local disputes. Few expected socio-economic revolution or saw it as lying within missionaries' power to achieve.

Missionaries were left feeling alienated and excluded, not only from certain aspects of low-caste culture but, crucially, from the internal lives of individuals and from the dynamics of low-caste society which produced and perpetuated that culture. Readers of missionary correspondence will find out far more about what missionaries thought about this religious culture than what they actually knew. Missionaries could not get over the conditions in which their converts lived, Fr. Edouard claiming that they did not respect themselves and that religion had 'no leverage' on them because they had never had proper access to scriptural religions like Hinduism.[52] In such circumstances concessions made to local practices would represent a surrender to meaninglessness.

A fitting point of comparison would be the first Bishop of Mexico, whose proud boast was that he 'personally had smashed over 500 [Aztec] temples and 20,000 idols'.[53] As the actions of missionaries like

[51] Punjab–UK interviews, Fr. Michael Ani, 31 Jan. 2003.

[52] Letter from Fr. Edouard to Provincial, 8 Nov. 1892, ABC, L92.

[53] Quoted in Johnson, *A History of Christianity*, 402.

FIG. 4.1. 'Statue of Our Lady', by Fr. Diego van Schuylenbergh, in preparation, *c.*1960.

Source: ABC, Photographic Archive

Gough suggested, this was one of the few ways of appealing to people seen as no more than 'half-weaned from idolatry'. Longer-term (and more subtle) options included the missionary staples of education and medical care. Genuine expressions of Christianity and of the missionary impulse in their own right, they also promised missionaries a deeper access to individuals' thinking and a more profound impact upon the surrounding culture than the casual, everyday interactions that had so disappointed them.

EDUCATION

Even the most informal of educational initiatives—there are accounts of CMS missionaries giving classes in cowsheds[54]—were seen by Protestant and Catholic missionaries as crucial to the success of new Christian communities. Education in Europe traditionally functioned as part of a nexus of Christian influence upon the individual, alongside parental formation and participation in the services and observances of the Church calendar. The high priority given to education was attested to in missionary letters and reports urgently requesting more resources for their schools or anxiously reporting the multiplication of schools in rival missions. Education was also a site of conflict with non-Christian socio-religious movements such as the Arya Samaj, and between low-caste converts and their village employers, who regarded with horror the prospect of their servants enjoying higher levels of literacy than they themselves possessed. Landowners were concerned that once low-castes were educated they would no longer be willing or economically compelled to work the land on the old terms.[55]

This section looks at the role which CMS and Capuchin missionaries envisaged for education within the new Christian communities, from the educational context of colonial Punjab to the intellectual, cultural, and psychological hurdles that the CMS and Capuchins hoped rural Punjabi converts would successfully jump in the course of their development as Christians. Capuchin education is looked at in greater detail than CMS education, since the lack of Catholic lay authority structures

[54] *Proceedings of the CMS, 1906–7*, 200.

[55] John C. B. Webster, *The Christian Community and Change in Nineteenth Century North India* (Delhi, 1976), 147; Hibbert-Ware, 'Baptisms in the Villages', pt 1, 55.

renders education proportionally more significant in any analysis of their mission strategies.

The Government of India's own education policy was an echo of contemporary thinking in England: private institutions would provide the bulk of education, funded and inspected by government, whose role it was to provide the original stimulus and school models.[56] To this end the Wood Dispatch of 1854 effectively standardized education in India, established government inspection and examining bodies (run by local universities), and introduced a new grants-in-aid system. It was viewed by mission societies as a 'generous invitation' from government to establish systems of schooling, from primary to university level.[57]

This policy was limited in its success in Punjab, primarily because for much of the nineteenth century the only private institutions which provided an increasingly sought-after Western education were Christian missions—in particular, the American Presbyterians and the CMS. Fearful of upsetting religious and political sensibilities here—stoked by a local press increasingly interested towards the end of the nineteenth century in highlighting the political connections of various Christian mission societies—the Government was forced to open more of its own schools.[58] But Christian institutions frequently undercut state-run schools, as they did in Europe, while proving their adequacy—and in some cases superiority—in published examination tables, to which Punjabi parents paid great attention. Fee competition was used by a range of private institutions to try to win students from the government-run sector.[59]

Government education was in any case a safe bet in comparative rather than absolute terms. An analysis of Reports on Public Instruction

[56] John C. B. Webster, 'Competing Systems of Western Education in the Punjab, 1858–1882', *Indian Church History Review*, I (June 1967), 60.

[57] *The Dispatch of Lord Halifax, No. 49, 19 July 1854* (London), repr. in J. P. Haythornthwaite, 'The Scope and Policy of Educational Work in Relation to the Indian Government', *CMR* 62/747 (July 1911), 412.

[58] An example of this was the opening of a government secondary school in Jalandhar in 1892, forcing the local Presbyterian school to the verge of bankruptcy by 1908; Webster, *The Christian Community and Change in Nineteenth Century North India*, 174–5.

[59] Fee competition was a tactic employed to great effect by institutions like the Arya Samaj Dayanand Anglo-Vedic College in Lahore, against the Christian Forman College in the last two decades of the twentieth century. In 1898 the fees for Government, Christian, Arya Samaj, and Muslim colleges in Lahore, per student, were Rs 81.88, Rs 62.09, Rs 32.89 and Rs 21.77 respectively. Ibid. 174 and 157.

in the Punjab shows the Government struggling with the apparent contradictions of a policy of religious neutrality and an educational philosophy built upon moralistic notions of 'character' that were firmly rooted in English Christian culture. The Director of Public Instruction for Punjab openly acknowledged in 1898 that the lack of an appeal to religious sanction was a 'disability' in character formation.[60] A Moral Reader had been introduced in 1891, achieving limited results with a euphemistic-sounding basis in 'principles of natural religion'.[61] English public-school methods were taken up, including the use of teachers as role models—'living illustrations of the way in which high ideals and pure motives influence life and conduct'[62]—and the promotion of 'manly sports'.[63] Classroom study of the 'structure, habits [and] utility' of various animals was used to promote ideals of 'love of parents, loyalty to Government, charity, punctuality, industry [and] honesty'.[64]

Punjabi parents were generally aware that no matter who provided it—the Government, or Hindu, Sikh, Muslim, or Christian institutions—full-time education would have the effect of socializing children into particular attitudes and values, as much through contact with peers and the social and professional spheres into which education propelled them as through the content of learning. At best, this was seen as an advantage in itself; at worst, simply part of the price to be paid for securing a successful future.[65]

A number of barriers prevented children from rural low-caste families from receiving government education. Tuition fees were not waived for them, as they were in the case of children of designated 'agricultural castes'. And the distance from many villages to the nearest government school was made more of a problem by strong family pressures upon children to engage in paid work for much of the day. A third factor was caste. A Report on Public Instruction in Punjab acknowledged in 1892 that low-caste pupils were frequently made to 'sit outside the class

[60] *Report on Public Instruction in the Punjab* [*RPIP*] *1897–8* (Lahore, 1898), 92. Another 'disability' was students' home life, leading one school inspector to express the hope that the boarding school system might soon expand; ibid. 92–4.

[61] *Recommendations of the Education Commission, 1882*, repr. in Haythornthwaite, 'The Scope and Policy of Educational Work in Relation to the Indian Government', 417.

[62] *RPIP 1897–8*, 92.

[63] *RPIP 1903–4* (Lahore, 1904), 35.

[64] *RPIP 1909–10* (Lahore, 1910), 23.

[65] The experiences in the late nineteenth-century of Prakash Tandon's father, at a government school in Gujarat and then at the Arya Samaj Dayanand Anglo-Vedic College in Lahore, are interesting to note on this point, for the defining effect that they had upon the man, his wife, and their family. See Tandon, *Punjabi Century*, 25–35.

line, frequently in the doorway'—a 'school-boy social ostracism' that jeopardized low-caste educational progress. The Government's response was to accept the necessity of segregation, opening 'low castes' schools', which received grants under the rules for elementary indigenous schools and which were often run by mission societies.[66]

By the 1920s an increasing demand from low-caste families for education combined with a slight easing of caste antagonisms and new policies on the waiving of fees and supply of school books[67] to produce a rise in low-caste attendance at the ordinary vernacular primary schools at the expense of the old low castes' schools. Measures were also taken to encourage young people from low-caste backgrounds to enter teacher-training institutions,[68] although they still rarely progressed into the middle and higher classes of government schools. Of 9,261 low-caste boys in ordinary schools in 1924–5, only 552 were in the middle classes and under twenty in the higher classes.[69] By 1936 there were 28,598 boys and 1,912 girls from low castes in education in Punjab, and evidence was detected both in the classroom and on the sports field that caste prejudice continued to decrease among children.[70]

CMS and Capuchin Education

The educational philosophies of the Capuchin and CMS missions converged in the concept of character formation. 'Character' and even 'manliness' is culturally defined, of course, and CMS education's blend of Victorian notions of class, comportment, and civic responsibility distinguished it clearly from its Capuchin counterpart. The resulting anxiety over the 'Anglicizing' effects of CMS education was clear in the case of the Alexandra High School for Girls in Amritsar, which, named after Princess Alexandra, daughter of Queen Victoria, was well known for high standards of English and low standards of Urdu. An anonymous

[66] *RPIP 1891–2* (Lahore, 1892), 95. [67] *RPIP 1925–6* (Lahore, 1926), 104.

[68] *RPIP 1929–30* (Lahore, 1930), 141.

[69] *RPIP 1924–5* (Lahore, 1925), 71. These figures do not include low-castes enrolled as 'Native Christians'.

[70] *RPIP 1935–6* (Lahore, 1936), 89. Literacy rates among low castes were slow to rise, however. In 1891 the figure stood at 0.14 per cent for Punjabi Chamars and 0.2 per cent for Punjabi Chuhras, rising by 1921 to just 0.4 and 0.5 per cent, respectively. Ten years later the figures for males had risen to 1.1 per cent among Punjabi Chamars and 1 per cent among Punjabi Chuhras but remained low for women, at 0.1 and 0.2 per cent, respectively. *Census of India 1891, 1921 and 1931, Punjab Report, Part II (Statistical Tables).*

Delhi missionary (either CMS or SPG) described the school as 'wholly pernicious' in its Anglicizing tendencies, and one Punjabi father was apparently incensed to find his 8-year-old daughter diligently trying to follow an Indian church service using an English Bible.[71]

And yet there was no easy solution for the CMS. Parents sought for their children an education that would equip them to succeed in contemporary society such as it was. It might well be regrettable to some parents, and to a number of CMS missionaries, that the English language and certain incongruous norms of behaviour were part of this society, but neither group could do much to change the fact. The CMS therefore risked losing ground to government or rival private institutions if they attempted to remove these aspects of education. Such had been the CMS's experience in Japan, and they were keen not to repeat the mistake in India.[72]

In Tarn Taran, Guilford lent his support to a brand of village schooling strongly reminiscent of rural English 'uplift' education, which sought to equip and encourage villagers to sort out their own problems through thrift and good hygiene, and in the case of boys to follow and be proud of the professions of their fathers rather than hanker after urban careers.[73] Tarn Taran's schools therefore focused on providing a basic religious education and the literacy required to read and understand the Bible. This was supplemented with practical work skills and lessons on health, hygiene, use of precious resources, and the proper treatment of women and girls.[74] This was very much in line with the assessment of a village education commission appointed by the National Missionary Council of India in 1919, which envisaged most rural children's schooling beginning and ending with a 'vocational middle school'.[75] In Narowal's schools a playful competitive element reminiscent of Victorian Sunday schools was apparent in the awarding of prizes—of cloth, sweets, pictures, or copies of the gospel—for students who excelled in 'religious knowledge' examinations.[76]

By 1920 there were eighteen village primary schools in the Narowal mission and fourteen in the Tarn Taran mission. They were run at no cost to the CMS, since government grants, modest tuition fees, and direct contributions from donors in India and Britain covered all

[71] *Shortcomings*, 11–12.
[72] *Centenary Committee Report, Section II*, ACMS, G/CCb 4/2a, 5.
[73] The Revd E. Guilford, Annual Letter 1895, ACMS. [74] Ibid.
[75] Hewitt, *The Problems of Success*, ii. 132–4.
[76] The Revd C. L. Richards, Annual Letter 1918.

expenses.[77] However, the restrictive terms of government grants when it came to the teaching of religious subjects were felt by many in the CMS to compromise the efficacy of the school's work of Christian formation, as did the employment of non-Christian schoolmasters and the high proportions of non-Christian students.[78] Bomford wondered whether policy-makers in London and Punjab were in fact more interested in competing with government schools than providing the most important dimension of education: religious teaching.[79]

CMS industrial schools, which reflected the Society's interest in the 'moral and educational force' of manual labour, and in providing new communities with the basic skills of self-sufficiency, are looked at in Chapter 5 in the context of the Christian village experiment.

The Catholic view of school education was that it ought to play a 'subsidiary and complementary' role to that of the family and the Church in the proper formation of the individual. *Divini Illius Magistri* (1929) sought to remind Catholics that the natural and historical roots of education lay with the family and the Church, and that, if state-school systems were structured accordingly, the result would be men and women who were acceptable as both true Christians and responsible citizens. Together, school, family, and Church should 'form . . . a perfect moral union, constituting one sanctuary of education'.[80]

The late nineteenth century had been a difficult period for this holistic vision of Christian formation. Pope Leo XIII had called attention, in 1878, to the deterioration of the family as a model of Christian virtue, echoing an earlier papal attack on state-sponsored education as advocating relativism in religious matters and imperilling young people's loyalty to the Church.[81] Leo believed it imperative that Catholic students be taught by Catholic masters in *all* subjects (since 'every discipline has its own dangers'[82]), using materials approved by local

[77] *TTRA 1906*, 5. Government grants were variable, depending upon the examination performance of pupils; *TTRA 1910* (Lahore, 1910), 8, ACMS, G2/I7/1, 2.

[78] Religious education was usually limited to the visit of a 'Christian inspector', who checked general standards and gave lessons on the Ten Commandments and the Bible. The Anglo-Vernacular School at Narowal had just thirty-five Christian pupils in 1909, compared with sixty-six Muslim and fifty-four Hindu pupils; *Narowal Mission Report, 1909*, 5 and 18.

[79] Letter from Bomford to Clark, 21 May 1883, ACMS, G2/I4/O 1883, n. 166ii.

[80] Pius XI, *Divini Illius Magistri*, 31 Dec. 1929 (Vatican, 1929).

[81] Leo XIII, *Inscrutabili Dei Consilio*, 21 Apr. 1878 (Vatican, 1878); *Cum Non Sine*, Epistle from Pope Pius IX to the Archbishop of Freiburg (Vatican, 1864).

[82] Leo XIII, *Militantis Ecclesiae*, 1 Aug. 1897 (Vatican, 1897).

bishops.[83] Concerns over the cultural safety of education were a regular feature of late nineteenth- and early twentieth-century encyclicals addressed to all parts of the world, as were warnings regarding the proliferation of unsuitable reading material. The problem of Catholic formation in an unsafe environment was therefore one with which European Catholic missionaries were entirely familiar from their home countries.

The bedrock of Catholic mission education was the humble village primary school, declared by the Apostolic Delegate to be 'almost the only way to make real and solid Christians'.[84] Time was of the essence. The Capuchins feared the waning of British colonial power less than the CMS, but they had their own pressing concerns in the form of well-funded Protestant schools that looked set to engulf them. Even those children who benefited from one of the Capuchins' few village primary schools—there were just three in 1891[85]—subsequently 'escaped' into the clutches of Protestant secondary schools, since the Capuchin mission did not yet provide secondary education for Punjabis.[86]

The fact that there was still no Capuchin secondary school by 1909 can be attributed as much to extreme caution in the mission regarding finding suitable teaching staff as to financial shortages. Belgian educational philosophy operated on a 'voluntary principle',[87] which had the advantage for the Catholic Church of ensuring the religious and cultural safety of education by emphasizing local control and parental opt-out. The state was left with the limited role of funding and inspecting schools, and certificating teachers. Belgian education thus reflected and sustained local culture (the teaching staff of many schools was made up of ex-pupils), and was criticized across Europe for its low standards and poor results in terms of literacy.[88]

Catholic religious Orders supplied thousands of primary-school teachers in Belgium at this time, and their exemption from the state-set minimum wage allowed Catholic schools to undercut—and in some cases force out of business—many of their competitors.[89] In Punjab the Capuchins hoped to staff their schools with male and female religious,

[83] Leo XIII, *Affari Vos*, 18 Dec. 1897 (Vatican, 1897).

[84] Letter from Archbishop of Thebes (Apostolic Delegate) to Bishop of Lahore, 6 Aug. 1893, ABC, L121.

[85] This figure excludes institutions established for Europeans and Eurasians.

[86] Letter from Regular Superior to Provincial, 22 Dec. 1909, ABC, L575.

[87] This was viewed by Belgium's first modern nationalist writer, Edmond Picard, as the particular genius of the Belgian people; Blom and Lamberts (eds), *History of the Low Countries*, 346.

[88] Crook, *Belgium*, 79–80.

[89] Rowntree, *Land and Labour*, 271–3.

but in practice they were forced to rely upon unqualified Punjabi teachers, whose lack of expertise was redeemed, as in the Belgian context, by their cultural acceptability as reasonably good Catholics. Even thirty years into the Capuchin mission only the new Dalwal High School (see below) and the (high-caste) Girls' School in Lahore employed qualified teachers for Punjabi pupils.[90]

With one eye on the activities of Methodist and Anglican missions, the Belgian Provincial, on a visit to Punjab in 1910–11, recommended that the Capuchin mission make it a priority to establish a complete system of schooling as soon as possible: primary schools, middle schools, and a high school in Lahore. Ten years later, however, the middle schools remained a work in progress, with buildings yet to be bought or built. Missionaries suspected that diocesan authorities were still not sufficiently enthused about their Punjabi mission. Fr. Marc complained in 1921 that the Bishop had bought a hotel in Dalhousie in order to open a high school that would churn out '5 or 6 European or Eurasian mademoiselles per year', while leaving 'no money to build schools for the Indians'.[91]

At Adah there had long been a small school attached to the church, in which boys and girls sat at opposite ends of the classroom and learned the basics of the Catholic faith, along with the reading and writing of Urdu.[92] Fig. 4.2 shows students of the school, together with Fr. Vincent. In the late 1890s the school was attended by around fifty children, rising to around eighty by the turn of the century.[93]

Despite the success of small schools such as those at Adah and Sahowala the Capuchin education infrastructure was ill-prepared for the mass influx of catechumens and converts in the early years of the twentieth century. By 1921 there were still only twelve schools for Punjabis across the whole mission;[94] the CMS had three times as many schools around Tarn Taran and Narowal alone. Fr. Deodat had expressed the fears of many missionaries in 1906 when he warned the General of the Order that the Capuchins were virtually surrounded by Protestant institutions: 'the Protestants have established schools everywhere . . . where they have 50 schools we just have one. I am planning to send you a detailed report of the works of the Protestants

[90] Letter from Regular Superior to Definitor, 1 Feb. 1921, GACO.

[91] Ibid. [92] Pelckmans, *Dix Années*, 73–4.

[93] Letter from Fr. Vincent to General, 20 Jan. 1897; Letter from Fr. Vincent to General, 20 Jan. 1900, both GACO.

[94] Letter from Regular Superior to Definitor, 1 Feb. 1921, GACO.

FIG. 4.2. The school at Adah, *c.*1897, with Fr. Vincent.

Source: ABC, Photographic Archive; also in G. Pelckmans, *Dix Années d'Apostolat au Pundjab* (Bruges, 1900), 67

in the Punjab, so that you may see the enormous disproportion which exists between their works, their schools and the works of the Capuchin fathers.'[95] For Fr. Sigismond, by 1920 the situation was simply 'heart-breaking': 'it is pointless to talk about schools [since] we do not have any'.[96]

Capuchin education finally began to develop in the 1920s. Four schools were upgraded to the status of high schools, with 905 students between them and classes that ranged from kindergarten through to what was called the 'Rhetorique' in Europe at the time—the highest class before university.[97] The basis of religious teaching in all Capuchin schools was the old Hindustani catechism and New Testament produced by Bishop Hartman, a Capuchin.[98] In addition, the Capuchins in Punjab quickly began to generate their own teaching materials. Fr. Vital produced the first catechism in Urdu in 1892, which went through three editions. Fr. Deodat wrote a 'Bible History' in 1906, while Fr. Victor produced manuals for missionaries in the field, including a *Manuale Missionariorum* and a *Handbook for Catholic Chaplains and Missionaries*. In 1910 Vital produced the first known Catholic text in Punjabi: a catechism of thirty-six pages, of which 2,000 copies were printed and sold at the equivalent of 10 Belgian centimes each. The simplicity of the Punjabi was matched by the simplicity of the book's three-part layout, as Vital explained to the General of his Order:

First Part: Everything we must believe to go to heaven.
Second Part: Everything we must do and avoid in order to go to heaven.
Third Part: Everything that helps us to go to heaven.[99]

Vital offered no further insights into the exact content of the book. It would be interesting to know whether the Punjabi version echoed contemporary catechisms in Belgium, which featured the weaving together of political and religious subjects in the usual question–answer catechetical formula with no apparent sense of disjuncture:

Q. Then it is wrong to support [liberalism]?
A. Yes, and those who vote for Liberal candidates, knowing them to be unfavourably disposed towards religion . . . do wrong. Their fault may be

[95] Letter from Fr. Deodat to General, 26 Oct. 1906, GACO.
[96] Letter from Fr. Sigismond to Provincial, 8 Aug. 1920, GACO.
[97] Letter from Regular Superior to General, 13 Nov. 1924, GACO.
[98] *Report of the Mission of Lahore for the Year 1891.*
[99] Letter from Fr. Vital to General, 31 May 1910, GACO.

compared to that of a child who helps someone to injure his mother . . . [It is] a sign of sin if one runs the risk unnecessarily of losing one's faith, especially . . . by frequenting schools condemned by the Church . . . by reading habitually and subscribing to newspapers and magazines hostile to the Church, [or] by becoming a member of Liberal or Free Mason Associations.[100]

The likelihood that Vital's catechism would have included minor points on Punjabi social and religious politics is strengthened by evidence that from 1910 onwards Punjabi Catholics were recruited by the Capuchins to produce translations of highly politicized and vociferously anti-Protestant pamphlets from the Catholic Truth Society (CTS).[101] Francis Hadiri, of Adah, and Dr M. B. Utarid gained particular prominence in the mission for their translation work, and their publications became indispensable for Punjabi catechists.[102]

The Capuchins were less than satisfied with the results of their educational initiatives, however. They welcomed non-Catholics into their schools in the hope of gaining influence and eventually making conversions, but found that a critical mass of non-Catholics almost always resulted in a less Catholic atmosphere and created a bar to conversions. An added problem was the need to follow the government curriculum in order to attract funding and pupils. The Dalwal school, opened in January 1900 as a primary and secondary school for Punjabi boys and a training centre for future catechists and clergy, became a symbol of these problems. By 1924 the school's roll of 500 students included only twenty-five Catholics (for whom places were reserved), while not a single catechist had been

[100] From a catechism used in the Diocese of Namur (in the south of Belgium), repr. in Rowntree, *Land and Labour*, 276–7.

[101] Rooney, *Into Deserts*, 38–9. The CTS was founded in England in 1868 and re-established in 1884. Politics aside, the popularity among Capuchins of CTS publications was an indication of the mission's attempt to find a level of education suitable for rural Punjab. One of the earliest CTS publications had been the 'Simple Prayer Book', designed with working-class Catholics in mind and aimed at evangelization as well as instruction—Catholics were encouraged to leave copies of it on trains, for example. *CTS History*, <www.cts-online.org.uk/CTS_history.htm>. It also perhaps reflected the slight novelty for the Capuchins of working in an environment where Protestantism was a strong adversary. There were only around 10,000 Protestants in the whole of Belgium at the turn of the twentieth century, whereas the English Catholic founders of the CTS had a long history of struggle against the strong demographic, political, and cultural influence of Protestantism. An Indian Catholic Truth Society was set up in 1921. Capuchin Mission Unit, *India and its Missions*, 243.

[102] Rooney, *Into Deserts*, 38.

produced. Fr. Marc referred to it as 'sterile', and attributed its failure to an inescapably secular academic focus and the lack of any moral training:

> That school will form educated young people, good mathematicians etc; they will know the history of the British Empire presented from the point of view of the Protestants. In the years spent in these schools, they will have studied from morning to evening, day in day out, to pass the exams, without having had time to seriously take on the study of religion.[103]

Missionaries such as Fr. Marc and Fr. Sigismond, who fought most spiritedly for the rights of the indigenous mission, instead defended the more modest and appropriately focused Adah catechists' school. They also supported the idea of industrial schools and orphanages as the genesis of a truly Catholic community. Such missionaries' championing of simple, grassroots Catholicism did not necessarily equate to an interest in accommodation with Punjabi culture, however. *Dix Années*, a Capuchin publication celebrating the first ten years of the mission in Punjab, showed in the imagery it associated with Adah the extent to which rural Belgium was an important model for so much of what the Capuchins did: Adah became a 'real parish' once a church was built there, the 'joyful notes' of the church bell calling Catholics to worship. In addition, 'the persevering efforts of Fr. Vincent [have] triumphed over the difficulties which afflict the hearing of the indigenous people in getting used to the harmony of our music . . . after much patience he managed to teach the children the songs of the Holy Mass'.[104]

One important thing that the early twentieth-century Belgian educational context taught the Capuchins was the usefulness of industrial schools (known as 'St Luke's schools', the apostle Luke being the patron saint of a number of manual trades, including bookbinding, brewing, and lacemaking). These schools provided a vocational education for the

[103] Letter from Regular Superior to General, 16 Apr. 1924, GACO. An unnamed Capuchin missionary echoed these sentiments when interviewed by Sir Malcolm Darling at Dalwal in 1930–1. Darling was told that, just as in Belgium, high school education risked rendering boys dismissive of agricultural pursuits. In Punjab it was largely a question of *izzat*. By 1930 the school was still going strong, however, with around 400 pupils; 500 'old boys' had served in the First World War, and the Capuchins were proud of the school's record in contributing recruits to the Indian Army. Darling, *Wisdom and Waste in the Punjab Village*, 56–7.

[104] Pelckmans, *Dix Années*, 73. Although this account was written for Belgian consumption, the attitudes reflected in the extract found strong echo in private correspondence. The only difference was that private letters revealed missionaries' frustrations at how far Punjabi Catholic communities had yet to go before realizing this ideal.

children of lower classes (particularly the loyally Catholic rural labourers of Flanders), in contrast to the literary education which was generally the preserve of wealthy Francophone elites.[105] The Capuchins in Punjab hoped that industrial schools would raise up a generation of Catholics able to support themselves through carpentry, telegraphy, bookbinding, weaving, new farming methods, banking, and railway-building.[106]

Most of these institutions were attached to orphanages, to which, as the financial assessment in Chapter 2 suggested, the Capuchins devoted a considerable proportion of their available funds. Charitable motivations were an important factor here, since high rates of mortality from disease and famine in rural Punjab orphaned large numbers of young children.[107] Catholic orphanages increased in size and status (even gaining official recognition from the Punjab Government) as monsoon failures in 1896, 1897, and 1898 brought severe famines across India. Where they had previously been little more than a corner of a basic mission building, by 1895 there were two dedicated orphanage buildings in the Lahore diocese: St Francis's Orphanage for boys and St Joseph's Native Girls' Orphanage. These expanded as Punjab was hit, in the first two decades of the twentieth century, by outbreaks of cholera, bubonic plague, and Asian flu.

In the absence of reliable and detailed information it is difficult to comment upon the conditions inside such institutions. In Belgium they had been criticized for breeding such an intense dependence in orphans that the latter had been known to stay inside orphanages well past the age of majority. Such was the discouragement of contact with the outside world that by the age of 21 some believed themselves incapable of surviving outside the institution.[108]

Whether or not this was the case in Punjab, the Capuchins clearly believed that they had the right to plan the futures of their orphans:

> The most serious and intelligent are chosen to prepare for seminary, for serious studies and to form one day, if possible, an indigenous clergy. The other orphans, after two or three years of religious instruction and after being admitted to

[105] Boulger, *Belgian Life in Town and Country*, 119–20. Even access to secondary school was restricted: in 1902, 800,000 children attended primary schools in Belgium but only 23,000 progressed to secondary school. Ibid. 120.

[106] Capuchin Mission Unit, *India and its Missions*, 240.

[107] Mgr Pelckmans claimed that many orphans became the 'victim[s] and slave[s]' of higher-caste families unless they were helped by charitable organizations; Report of the Bishop of Lahore to the SCPF, 2 May 1895.

[108] Rowntree, *Land and Labour*, 485–7.

baptism, confirmation and first communion will be sent to Maryabad to work the earth and hence form the seed of a Christian colony full of future. When the time comes they will marry one of our orphan girls and found Christian families.[109]

This was no mere idle romantic fancy. In the midst of major financial troubles in 1897 the Capuchins accepted fifty orphan girls into St Joseph's so that there would be enough wives for the inmates of St Francis's Orphanage when the time came for marriage. The influx brought the numbers to an almost perfectly matched 103 male orphans and 96 female orphans.[110] New Catholic colonies such as Maryabad, Khushpur, and Franciscabad were the principal recipients of orphan couples. Fig. 4.3 shows recently married couples from one of these institutions. Franciscabad even acquired the nickname of Yatimabad, meaning 'Orphan Town'.[111] A number of Christian families in Pakistan at the beginning of the twenty-first century remembered with apparent fondness the way in which mission workers matched orphans for marriage, lining up girls on one side and boys on the other, and then walking down the lines and pairing the orphans off with each other.[112]

It was not unknown for the orphanages to help young men from the broader Catholic community find suitable spouses. A Punjabi schoolmaster, Patrick, was brought by Fr. Philippe to St Joseph's Orphanage in Lahore in 1902 to find a wife. One of the girls, Clementine, was offered by the Sisters as a good match:

Indians are generally quite picky when it comes to beauty and Clementine does not shine in that aspect; but she can read and write and she possesses other qualities which the Father and his protégé appreciated; hence the engagement was concluded at the very first meeting.[113]

The wedding followed within a matter of weeks, and the couple left to begin their married life:

Our big girl left happy as a queen, with her husband and her treasures, namely: a crucifix, a few new clothes, a pot to cook rice, a box of salt and pepper, a

[109] Report of the Bishop of Lahore to the SCPF, 2 May 1895. See also Ch. 5 on Maryabad.

[110] Letter from the Bishop of Lahore to Procuror, 29 Sept. 1897, ABC, L267.

[111] Rooney, *Into Deserts*, 47–8.

[112] Linda S. Walbridge, *The Christians of Pakistan: The Passion of Bishop John Joseph* (Richmond, 2003), 30.

[113] Letter from Sr Vernardine (of the Sisters of Charity) to the General Mother Superior, 10 Apr. 1902, ABC, L331.

Fig. 4.3. Recently married couples from a Capuchin canal colony orphanage, Maryabad or Khushpur.

Source: ABC, Photographic Archive

catechism and a holy history, thread and needles! Hardly arrived in Khushpur, she started to catechise the little girls, and she's not doing badly at all, Father Philippe writes to us. As a housewife, she is marvellous; the good Patrick is delighted to have a wife who knows how to make him shirts and who is not scared of doing the laundry or sweeping the house.[114]

That good Catholic families with good Catholic names (Clementine's previous name was Kegilas[115]) should be the aim of Capuchin education and charity demonstrates the enduring influence of centuries of Catholic thinking on the ideal society, reinforced by modern SCPF policy and Belgian culture.

The Fate of Educational Strategies

Religious education was frequently a less than inspiring experience for many young Punjabi Christians, as it was for their European counterparts. 'What is one to say of the lack of the desire to learn?' asked an exasperated Richards in his 1917 mission report, 'or . . . of the extraordinary difficulty of getting the simplest truths of the gospel into minds and hearts?' Richards had asked a group of children what they thought was good about Christianity. Twice receiving only the answer that they thought it better than other religions, he had proceeded to explain at length, and in every way he could think of, John 3: 16: 'For God loved the world so much that he gave his only Son, so that everyone who believes in him may not die but have eternal life.' He put his question for a third time. The answer once again, according to Richards, was simply: 'We like this religion.'[116]

Children could often not even be persuaded to attend school at all. In Adah, Fr. Philippe complained that people failed to see the value of education 'unless we promise them either a job, or money, or food, or some kind of support . . . they refuse to understand that it is impossible for us to give a job to everyone, or to continually give food or clothes'.[117] In Rewari the Revd T. Williams of the SPG had to pay a local boy Rs 2 a month to round up Chamar boys for the low-caste school. Attendance continued to be poor, however, and even the collector himself was

[114] Letter from Sr Vernardine to the General Mother Superior, 10 Apr. 1902, ABC, L331.

[115] Ibid. It is not clear whether Patrick was born a Catholic or whether he too had been given a new name.

[116] The Revd C. L. Richards, Annual Letter 1917.

[117] Letter from Fr. Philippe to General, 13 Dec. 1897, GACO.

occasionally absent. When Williams put a stop to his Rs 2, no one turned up at all and the school had to be closed.[118] The CMS and Capuchins endured similar basic problems of non-attendance, finding that Christian parents often preferred to use their children in the fields rather than send them on a long trek to school.

Elsewhere, however, minor breakthroughs were made in finding popular ways of inspiring interest in religious education. Hibbert-Ware found that by accommodating Indian religious traditions of storytelling and hymn-singing the attention of both children and adults could successfully be engaged. The talents of some catechumens in 'preserv[ing] the flow of descriptive language' proved highly effective in gripping a mixed audience of other catechumens and village onlookers. 'It was like an evangelistic meeting,' declared Hibbert-Ware in 1916, 'but the speakers were themselves unbaptised Chamars.'[119]

Hymn-singing went hand in hand with storytelling as an effective means of religious education, passing from Punjabi agent to convert or between converts within a village or household. New Punjabi *bhajans* represented a contribution to a canon of rural Christian devotional works which was emerging at this time—at the expense of urban literature, which had often been produced under the aegis of European missionaries and which was inaccessible to a rural world with almost no tradition of literacy whatsoever.[120] Yet, despite recognizing the contribution of rural converts in composing *bhajans* for use in church services, neither the CMS nor the Capuchins seem to have encouraged this kind of creativity in any organized way.[121] By contrast the United Presbyterians and other missions in Punjab compiled collections of *bhajans* written by rural Punjabis. Jeffery Cox has suggested that these represent the 'fullest expression of indigenous Punjabi Christianity', particularly effective in tapping into female piety.[122]

Hymnody certainly played a major role in church services I witnessed in the village of Dugri, near Kartarpur. The local catechist, Babu-ji

[118] The Revd T. Williams, Quarterly Letter, Dec. 1884, ASPG.

[119] Hibbert-Ware, 'Baptisms in the Villages', pt 2, 69.

[120] Avril Powell has pointed out that Imad Ud-din's celebrated works of Christian literature and anti-Islamic polemic had a limited impact on rural Punjabi Christianity; Avril A. Powell, '"Pillar of a New Faith": Christianity in Late-Nineteenth-Century Punjab from the Perspective of a Convert from Islam', in Frykenberg (ed.), *Christians and Missionaries in India*, 231–3.

[121] *Proceedings of the CMS, 1894–5* (London, 1895), 124.

[122] See Cox, *Imperial Fault Lines*, 147–52.

Younis, played a *tabla*, and led the congregation in a succession of short *bhajans*. Later, in the house of Dayal Masih (Sayekar village), an impromptu performance of Christian *bhajans* was given, featuring a harmonium, *tabla*, and several vocalists.

Village theatre was another medium by which Christian messages might be transmitted, just as it was used by political groups and others to spread their message in the Indian countryside; K. Damodaran's play *Arrears in Rent* is one of the better-known examples. The Capuchins, concerned by what they viewed as the 'immorality' of rural drama, organized their own vernacular plays to coincide with religious festivals (especially Christmas) and store 'the impressionable mind of the Hindu . . . with representations of the pure and beautiful'. At the same time 'the catchy refrains' sung by the chorus were useful in evangelization and would help 'to supplant . . . filthy songs'.[123] The problem with this approach was that converts would be more likely to see these as an addition to the usual round of village festivals and entertainment than as a replacement. There is little evidence that they were successfully persuaded to avoid non-Christian village events.

In contrast to this vibrant rural culture of storytelling, hymn-singing, and theatre, CMS church services—particularly in urban Punjab—seem to have been rather dreary affairs. CMS missionaries noted that parts of the liturgy did 'more to disgust people than anything else', and one urban Christian dismissed the Sunday service as 'the same old thing always'.[124] Church attendance was noticeably higher among converts who owed their livelihoods to the mission than among those who did not.[125]

The impression given in Capuchin sources is of a mission-Church still so much in its infancy that it was thought too early to comment at length upon the educational and other shortcomings of the Catholic community. In logistical terms, the problems of Punjabi Catholicism remained immense. In 1921, out of a Catholic population of more than 20,000 spread across 894 villages, not more than 250 people regularly attended Sunday Mass. Capuchin correspondents blamed their own shortages of resources and staff, conceding that Catholics could not go

123 Capuchin Mission Unit, *India and its Missions*, 219. 124 *Shortcomings*, 5.

125 'It is to be feared that they look upon church attendance as part of the work they are paid to do,' a CMS report concluded; ibid. 1. This is an interesting echo of labourer attitudes towards Anglican services in some parts of rural England in the same period.

to Masses if none were being said,[126] nor could they attend schools which had not been established.

MEDICAL CARE

Pope Pius XI declared in 1926 that 'missionaries who preach to the heathen know only too well how much good will and real affection is gained for the Church by those who look after the health of the natives and care for their sick, or who show a true love for their infants and children'.[127] By following the actions and commandments of Jesus—'into what city so ever you enter . . . heal the sick that are therein, and say to them: The Kingdom of God is come nigh unto you'[128]—mission personnel demonstrated 'how readily the human heart responds to charity and to kindness'.[129] Pius' words held for both the Capuchin and CMS missions, for whom tending the sick was at once a response to biblical injunction and an extremely effective way of gaining access to new village communities.[130]

The CMS Punjab Medical Mission became well known throughout India, established by Dr Henry Martyn Clark in Amritsar in 1882 with the hope that frontier areas around Afghanistan, virtually inaccessible by other means of evangelization, could be reached through the establishment of medical outposts.[131] In the more distant future Dr Clark hoped to establish a branch dispensary in the working sphere of each and every catechist and Punjabi clergyman.[132] By 1913 the Punjab mission incorporated hospitals at Amritsar, Multan, Srinagar, Islamabad, Peshawar,

[126] Letter from Regular Superior to General, 16 Nov. 1921, GACO.

[127] Pius XI, *Rerum Ecclesiae*, 28 Feb. 1926 (Vatican, 1926).

[128] Luke 10: 8–9, quoted ibid.

[129] Pius XI, *Rerum Ecclesiae*.

[130] Robert Clark made a very similar point to Pius', regarding the biblical basis for medical mission, in his account of the CMS mission in Punjab. Clark, *The Missions of the Church Missionary Society and the Church of England Zenana Missionary Society*, 69.

[131] Hewitt, *The Problems of Success*, ii. 145–6.

[132] The Revd Robert Clark, *The Medical Mission, Umritsur* (Lahore, 1883), ACMS, G2/I4/O 1883, n. 24, 7. The Punjab Corresponding Committee resolved the same year that the Parent Committee should be asked to make grants-in-aid for medical establishments similar to those which were provided for mission schools; *Minutes of a Meeting of the Punjab and Sindh Corresponding Committee*, ACMS, G2/I4/O 1883, n. 102.

Bannu, Dera Ismail Khan, and Quetta, 750 beds in all, with 10,700 in-patients receiving treatment in just one year (1913). Across India there were 204 mission hospitals, most of them run and staffed by the Church of England Zenana Mission Society (CEZMS). Many of the larger hospitals were funded through private practice by mission doctors, although by the mid-1930s even the largest hospitals were beginning to fall badly behind government services in terms of the quality of equipment.[133]

The CMS envisaged medical mission having a particular attraction within rural communities, and sought to locate large medical institutions in centres that gave easy access to villages. 'None who come to us for healing [should] leave us without having the Gospel put before them in some way,' declared Dr Clark in 1891. This could take a number of forms, from preaching to outpatients to religious conversations held in the hospital (where only Christians were to be employed) and a range of lectures intended to lead people from Nature (in terms of medicine and the body) to Nature's God.[134]

In order to expand its numbers of trained medical missionaries, the CMS began, in the 1890s, to offer financial assistance to medical students who enrolled as missionary candidates. This assistance amounted to the total cost of the students' fees, the students being asked to pay only for their own maintenance. Meanwhile, ordinary missionary candidates continued to receive basic medical training at Islington, since they were often required to perform 'small operations' and dispense basic medicines in the course of their everyday work.[135]

St Mary's hospital at Tarn Taran, established in 1910 by CEZMS missionaries, was a flagship institution for the CMS, employing (by 1912) four female European staff, two Punjabi Bible-women, one Punjabi staff nurse, and six Punjabi nurses on three-year training courses. Miss Cox was in charge, urging the staff not only to tend the sick but also to deal with the incurable by encouraging them 'to turn [their] thoughts to the world to come'. While this was reported as being stressful for the staff, it was quite possibly far more unpleasant for some of the patients. Miss Cox reported the case of one woman who lay in

[133] Hewitt, *The Problems of Success*, ii. 148–50.

[134] Dr Martyn Clark of the Amritsar Medical Mission, quoted in Clark, *The Missions of the Church Missionary Society and the Church of England Zenana Missionary Society*, 72.

[135] Stock, *History of the Church Missionary Society*, iii. 703.

the hospital for two months pleading 'Give me health' while members of staff took turns to bombard her with Bible stories, daily and often twice daily.[136] Bandages, clothes, and dolls were sent from Britain to St Mary's, for which Miss Cox thanked readers of the mission reports.[137]

Missionaries rarely lost sight of the need to use every available circumstance to enhance their influence in rural communities, which, in their eyes, frequently seemed criminally indifferent to the Christian message. Richards reported a shortage of food in 1918 (due to poor rainfall) as being a positive thing in the sense that it 'gave a spur to recruiting for the Christian regiment'.[138] The Revd S. Ghose said of Chamars near Delhi that famine had 'enhanced their willingness to listen' to missionaries.[139]

The greatest significance of all was that placed upon medical work conducted at times of plague, which allowed the missions to stake their claim as the real guardians of the community. During the plague outbreak in the Narowal mission in 1923–4, not only were CMS catechists' duties supplemented by the conduct of large numbers of funerals,[140] they were also charged with the task of inoculating local people, supplying iodine kits (both as prevention and treatment), and coordinating the evacuation of some of the worst-affected villages.[141]

Regular medical care was offered by the Capuchins in the form of small pharmacies and dispensaries. These, it was hoped, would be particularly useful in helping missionaries to establish contacts with Punjabi women, whom early experiences had shown to be a powerful yet inaccessible force in Punjabi society. The Capuchin dispensary at Sahowala (Fig. 4.4) was established in November 1897 and run by Br. Martin from one of the rooms of the new church building. It proved highly successful in attracting the women and children of Sahowala and its surrounding villages.

Dispensaries like these challenged village communities on one of their most sensitive points: the ability to heal. This challenge had the

[136] *TTRA 1912*, 25. Susan Billington Harper has found that in Dornakal diocese vaccinations were accompanied by the gift of gospel tracts or the presentation of magic lantern shows; Billington Harper, *In the Shadow of the Mahatma*, 265.

[137] *TTRA 1912*, 25.

[138] The Revd C. L. Richards, Annual Letter 1918.

[139] The Revd S. Ghose, 'Work amongst Chamars', pt 1, *DMN* 2/3 (July 1898), 35.

[140] See Ch. 3.

[141] These evacuations were only partially successful. On a number of occasions people returned to their villages in order to collect more belongings. They became infected, and plague quickly spread to other evacuees. The Revd C. L. Richards, Annual Letter 1924.

FIG. 4.4. St Margaret's dispensary, Sahowala, *c*.1897. The Capuchin pictured is most probably Br. Martin.

Source: ABC, Photographic Archive

initial effect of heightening and focusing sentiments of hostility towards the mission presence, resulting in angry demonstrations by local holy men, who forbade mission agents to approach private family houses. Occasionally such people were won over, and although it is difficult to say how far villagers' confidence shifted in favour of the mission, St Margaret's dispensary at Sahowala certainly bloomed. By the end of the nineteenth century 100 people a day were being treated by a missionary or agent armed only with salt, castor oil, and camphor.[142]

While the aim of CMS medical mission was first and foremost to acquire a sympathetic audience for the gospel, with the means seen as justified by the ends, the Capuchins' deployment of their comparatively modest medical infrastructure went much further, suggesting more limited expectations regarding converts' abilities to understand and respond to evangelization. Fr. Deodat, for example, tried to wean converts in the village of Sedinkala (in the Adah mission) off their old forms of worship by telling them that their devotion to a 'vile idol' had brought a recent plague upon them. Deodat's words had the desired effect, and two villagers later helped him demolish the idol, the 'pious dispositions' exhibited in doing so only slightly tarnished by a subsequent request for payment for their labour.[143]

More drastic was the engagement, at St Margaret's dispensary, of Capuchin friars in the surreptitious baptism of sick infants for whom there was no hope of recovery:

> Under the pretext of administering lotions to the little unfortunate who was dying in the arms of his mother he [the Capuchin brother] made him pass from the darkness of original sin to the divine light of grace under the eyes of the parents and other infidels who assisted, stupid and unconscious, in the hidden mystery of regeneration.[144]

Three hundred and seventy-six children were secretly baptized in this way between 1 November 1897 and 30 September 1899,[145] potentially a scandal in some eyes, but for the missionaries one of the consolations of a sacramental concept of religious community. The Capuchins were overjoyed when the head female doctor at one of the two Protestant hospitals in Lahore converted from Protestantism to Catholicism in the early 1890s. Her five nurses followed her into her new faith—a rather

[142] Pelckmans, *Dix Années*, 99. From 1 Oct. 1898 to 30 Sept. 1899, 13,739 people received assistance; ibid. 99.

[143] Letter from Fr. Deodat to General, 24 Aug. 1905, GACO.

[144] Ibid. 99–100.

[145] Ibid. 100.

interesting form of informal agency in its own right—and with their help Capuchin missionaries were able to baptize dying children at the hospital.[146]

Policy on medical relief was refined in 1909, almost at the same time as education policy was reassessed. Provision of medical care at local level became the main priority, since the Capuchins felt unable to compete with the large urban hospitals of mission societies like the CMS. The number of dispensaries rose to a peak of fourteen in the mid-1920s, and in 1930 it was recommended that Capuchin missionaries be trained in the basics of tropical medicine before they went to the Punjab.[147]

CONCLUSION

Continued Capuchin and CMS interest in the kind of hermetically sealed Christian village environments looked at in Chapter 5 attests to a sense of failure in both missions by the late 1930s where their dealings with rural converts were concerned. Although the scope of our comparative Protestant–Catholic analysis has been limited by what missionaries themselves were able to discover of convert lives, it is clear that across a number of aspects of life in the new communities there was a significant disjuncture between the socio-religious endgames envisaged by the Capuchins, the CMS, and groups of rural Punjabi converts.

Many of these were tied to the nature of 'community' itself. The evidence of Chapter 1 suggested that rural-labourer religion and society in Punjab and in England was, in its very essence, the closed affair of the rural labouring community. There might be a modicum of outward socio-religious conformity, depending upon labourers' perceptions of obligations owed to the people who paid their wages or upon whom they relied in other ways. But labourers retained a private sphere whose inviolability was part of its function and meaning.

Nothing in the nature of the mass movements suggested that converts envisaged a revolution in these local social relationships. Instead, references by Capuchin and CMS missionaries—frequently sarcastic—to attempts by converts to curry simple favour with them support the idea that most converts understood their relationship with the missions in

[146] Report of the Bishop of Lahore to the SCPF, 2 May 1895.

[147] Rooney, *Into Deserts*, 24.

similarly limited and distanced terms. Br. Guerin bemoaned 'beautiful promises' that were quickly broken. Fr. Philippe's observation on rural converts was that Christianity had yet to 'penetrate their hearts' and that instead they thought they needed only 'to be liked by the priest' or by the 'Protestant minister', nothing more.[148] Richards's catechism classes seemed more successful in eliciting general assurances of support for Christianity than any desire to engage with it.

The minor skirmishes that occurred with mission personnel over marriage and funeral arrangements, modes of worship, and other areas of everyday life fit this same pattern of fairly rigidly defined terms where the mission–convert relationship was concerned. Were converts likely to become more flexible on these points as time went on? There is simply not enough evidence to answer questions like these. Converts most likely expected their association with the missions to proceed as other unequal local relationships had: the details worked out over time, gradually taking on customary form. If so, some of the early problems that arose in the new communities were likely to have been viewed as part of this process: disagreements over attendance at church services and schools, for example. Other areas of conflict with the missions, however, were clearly seen as representing an unacceptable level of scrutiny and meddling in convert lives. These were unprecedented demands on their conduct, on their social relations, and on their time, especially given the fact that people seeking to join the Christian movement—the 'masihi quam'—did not see why knowledge of Christian doctrine ought to be a condition.[149] Moreover, Christianity appeared to want to devour all other forms of worship. The crude demonstration effect to which mission personnel seemed to resort, where the wearing of charms or the contracting of marriages was concerned, suggests a fairly blunt back-and-forth process that was not helped by inadequate language skills among missionaries and a lack of frequent contact with converts.

Strikingly similar language used in the CMS and Capuchin missions indicates a high rate of failure among mission personnel in contests of will and legitimacy where these dimensions of the new communities were concerned. This was regularly attributed by both groups to the generations of poverty, material and spiritual, from which converts were only just emerging. The Capuchins in particular saw the efforts of this

[148] Letter from Fr. Philippe to General, 13 Dec. 1897, GACO.
[149] See O'Brien, *The Construction of Pakistani Christian Identity*, 582.

generation of missionaries as simply softening things up for a future generation of Catholics and priests: 'there is so much goodwill [among the Catholics in the Adah mission], but we cannot visit or educate them regularly . . . the most we can do is go there from time to time to keep them attached to our religion, so that later a father can go to live among them and he will be well received'.[150]

The serious disagreements that flared up between mission personnel and converts during these early years often elicited similar reactions from the Capuchins and the CMS. Both groups seem to have failed to make the kind of engagement with rural low-caste culture that Chapters 1 and 2 suggested would be crucial to forming a mission–convert relationship based on genuine mutual identification rather than relatively shallow social and material reciprocity. This did not mean, however, that the two missions had anything like the same socio-religious goals in mind. Strategies of education, intervention in everyday life, and provision of basic medical care, as well as a clear lengthening of the timescale for true 'conversion' in rural Punjab, mask what were in fact distinct and ambitious blueprints for Punjabi Christianity.

The Capuchins worked to instil in converts a sense of being part of a far wider Catholic community, both in the sacramental sense and in the global sense, centred upon Rome and the Mother Church. Punjabi Catholics were to be drawn away from their immediate village environment and into contact with a hierarchy of Church representatives—teachers, catechists, priests, friars, nuns, the bishop—who managed converts' progression through the sacraments and at the same time provided a focal point for Catholics' humility and aspirations. The high status of the Bishop in this Catholic community was demonstrated to converts on a visit to Adah in May 1897, when he was welcomed with the ringing of bells, a magic lantern show, and a firework display.[151] Limited resources were similarly marshalled to offer converts a hint of the mystical aspect of their religious community: special midnight Masses, illuminations of the chapel,[152] and days of 'perpetual Adoration'.[153] Ordinary friars saw themselves well equipped, through their formation in the Capuchin tradition, for the all-important personal relationship that they sought to establish with Punjabi Catholics. The success of converts' development

150 Letter from Fr. Philippe to General, 13 Dec. 1897.
151 Ninove, *The Capuchin Mission in the Punjab*, 135–6.
152 Letter from Fr. Vincent to General, 19 Jan. 1898, GACO.
153 Ibid., 20 Jan. 1900.

was more frequently measured in missionary letters by their attachment to mission workers than by their understanding of the Catholic faith.

In fact these personal relationships and this sense of a Catholic community was part of understanding the Catholic faith, as far as the Capuchins were concerned. Carefully managed schooling played a key role in making this clear to converts in the first generation. It was envisaged that this key task of the mission school would gradually shrink over time, as the baton of Catholic formation was passed to the family: 'When our children, whom we educate, start little families we will have the joy of having a few real Christian parents.'[154] Commitment to this task by Patrick and Clementine might earn their children an education with a more literary focus, once Catholicism had safely struck social roots in Punjab. In the meantime, friars took comfort in being able to open the gates of the Catholic community to dying babies through baptism.

Where it would have been natural for Capuchins to talk about 'the Church in Punjab', the CMS looked forward to a self-governing 'Punjabi Church', and sought to put in place lay as well as ecclesiastical arrangements to this end. However, although basic mission schools seemed to function well (problems of attendance notwithstanding), organizational bodies like the PNCC, and later the CMC and DMC, floundered. Even the few urban Christians who were aware of them and participated worried that they were almost an irrelevance at this early stage, distracting missionary attention and resources from the deep rural engagement that was urgently required.

This incongruity of such institutions in the rural Punjabi context perhaps overshadowed the creativity and realism of missionaries like Guilford and Bomford. Nevertheless, the language used by CMS mission personnel was generally more upbeat than that of the Capuchins. Where the Capuchins had a relatively fixed idea of the kind of community they sought, and were prepared to wait generations for it to evolve, many in the CMS reacted to difficulties in this early period by gently shifting their expectations. They still sought a genuine personal response to the gospel in their converts, but, given the conditions in which low-caste Punjabis lived, they were prepared for this to take a more modest form, grounded in people's clear social needs.

[154] Letter from Fr. Philippe to General, 13 Dec. 1897.

The conciliatory language in which these modified Evangelical expectations were expressed must partly have been for the benefit of colleagues and mission donors, but missionary correspondents like Hares showed unmistakable signs of being forced by the situation in Punjab slightly to adapt their social and religious ideas. This approach to defining and building a religious community, which distinguished CMS from Capuchin thinking in this first generation, was clearly expressed in their management of the Christian village of Clarkabad, looked at in the next chapter.

A degree of generalization is inevitable in bringing out these themes in community-building by the CMS and the Capuchins. Missionaries from the same organizations disagreed more than ever during this phase of their work, and the thoughts of mission agents—if they had been sought and recorded by missionaries—would doubtless have added to this spectrum of opinion. However, one theme that linked almost all European personnel in the CMS and Capuchin missions was regular recourse to models from home in attempting to construct new Christian communities. Missionary strategies were put together with almost no reference whatsoever to Punjabi converts, and on the basis of scant knowledge about their lives. 'Christian community' appeared to be a European template, whose intrinsic validity depended upon neither culture nor context, except where Europeans decided that minor adaptation was warranted. This missionary notion that rural Punjabi society and culture were essentially phenomena to be overcome rather than taken into serious account supports the suggestion in Chapter 3 that, in the view of the Capuchins and the CMS, the social processes that rendered Punjabis receptive to the missions in the first place were essentially unimportant since all catechumens and converts were ultimately to be moulded into the same shape.

And yet there was little evidence that these strategies worked in rural Punjab. Aside from the clear social distance that converts sought to put between themselves and the missions, even the most optimistic among the missionaries detected no trend towards the development of new religious or spiritual convictions among converts. Missionaries observed convert behaviour carefully at times of trauma, such as the onset of plague, as a way of taking crude measure of Christianity's internal impact. Ideally, converts ought to turn for solace only to Christian worship, to the catechist, or to the missionary: real faith would render all other devotional sources of comfort obsolete, even offensive. No such profound transfer of trust was apparent in either mission by the 1930s.

What then did the future hold for the new communities? Might either side opt out of this less than perfect relationship? By the 1930s a combination of reluctant admission of failure on the ground and shifting political and ecclesiastical dynamics at the international level, looked at in the next chapter, were starting to push mission policy in the direction that the more far-sighted among Punjabi and European mission personnel had been urging for decades. However, this would take time to percolate through to the mission stations at Narowal, Tarn Taran, Adah, and Sahowala.

In the meantime, the strategies and conflicts that had characterized community-building thus far looked set to continue. It was far from clear whether existing low-caste beliefs about the supernatural world would evolve under the influence of Christianity or whether the missions could persuade converts to alter aspects of their social life. The CMS and the Capuchins were not prepared to give up, and crucially Punjabi converts too, having led the pace in first requesting mission attention, appeared similarly unwilling to go back on their decisions. The mass movements towards Christianity were not followed by mass movements away again.

Yet just as the limitations of the village environment suited no one in the mission–convert relationship, so the state of affairs in this first generation did not represent the fulfilment of anyone's aspirations. Missionaries may have been resigned to a rather depressing war of attrition with pre-conversion habits and attachments, perhaps even seeing this as the inevitable pace of real change under the circumstances. And yet there was no guarantee that Christianity would not just remain the adjunct to low-caste socio-economic and spiritual well-being that to many it currently appeared.

Many CMS and Capuchin missionaries clearly hoped for some kind of indication, within their own lifetimes, that their efforts were not entirely in vain. But, as missionaries frequently confided to one another, the only way to counter the retarding effect of a hostile village environment and intermittent contact with converts was by recourse to institutions like the orphanage and boarding school. These offered a chance to form Christians, undisturbed, in the CMS or Capuchin mould and to set an unmistakable example of what real conversion ought to mean. The problem was that, for this kind of environment to be re-created on a sufficient scale, entire villages would have to be taken over or constructed from scratch. Yet the province was already crowded, with population pressure on the land rising steeply and Christians usually a small minority in their villages. When the Punjab Government decided to increase agricultural productivity in the province by opening up vast new tracts of land through irrigation, both CMS and Capuchin missionaries considered their prayers to have been answered.

5

Visions of the Future

[In the Christian villages] there will spring up a new communal life, morally and spiritually in advance of the old, [escaping] many of the evils of Western civilisation with its rush and hurry and materialism. They will be living examples, peculiarly Eastern, of some sides of the Gospel which are not seen markedly on a large scale in the West . . . 'Be not anxious for tomorrow; consider the lilies of the field, how they grow' [Matt. 6: 28]. Such words as these will gather fresh emphasis if seen in the lives of villagers, whose cheerful contentment [will be] a standing rebuke to the heart-weariness that follows the modern worship of success and material gain.

(The Revd C. F. Andrews, *Delhi Mission News*)

THE concept of 'Village India', like Ruskin's rural England, was immensely attractive to those Europeans and Indians who were disturbed by the spiritual poverty of industrial, 'civilized' society. Romantic notions about the regenerative potential of a simple, healthy environment, where people's needs were modest and their sense of interdependence and mutual respect well attuned, influenced the vision of thinkers from Sir Malcolm Darling to Mahatma Gandhi. For Christian missions in Punjab, the fresh land being opened up by canal irrigation in the late nineteenth and early twentieth centuries—11 million new acres by 1947[1]—represented an opportunity to go far beyond simply escaping the consequences of Western-style development: entirely new village communities could be created, based on the fundamentals of the gospel.

[1] Imran Ali, *The Punjab under Imperialism, 1885–1947* (Princeton, 1988), 10. See also id., 'Malign Growth? Agricultural Colonization and the Roots of Backwardness in the Punjab', *Past and Present*, 114 (Feb. 1987).

Missionaries may have shown themselves relatively uninterested in the details of rural low-caste culture, but they were deeply impressed by the formative power of the village environment both in Europe and in Punjab—particularly upon those with limited experience of education or travel beyond the locale. In Punjab, converts' villages contained every one of their socio-economic, cultural, and supernatural points of reference, making it doubtful whether catechesis alone could effect the necessary cognitive revolution of placing the Christian God at the very centre of converts' understanding of the world.

In the past, missionaries had been able to isolate Christian converts in geographically distinct communities. Spanish and Portuguese missions had done it in Latin America in the sixteenth and seventeenth centuries, hoping to insulate fragile converts from the equally malign influences of pagan 'Indios' and ill-living Iberian adventurers. Such an approach would be ideal in the Punjabi context, not least in the light of the continuing logistical nightmare of arranging solid pastoral care for hundreds of widely scattered villages. New, Christian villages would allow for a more effective concentration of limited manpower and resources, while helping inculcate the sense of membership of a global Christian Church which both the Capuchins and the CMS, in their different ways, desired. The experience of an environment of village interdependence where every role was filled by Christians would be a step in the right direction, simultaneously re-forming converts' senses of cosmology, self, and community. Geography, caste, and culture might satisfactorily be subordinated to Christianity. In short, if rural Punjabi minds were formed by their environment, then a wholly Christian environment must inevitably produce Christian minds.

This final chapter looks at visions of the future for this book's three main protagonists: Punjabi low-caste converts, the CMS, and the Capuchins. The primary focus is upon the Christian village experiment, set in the context of Indian and international themes that affected the CMS and Capuchin mission-Churches in Punjab throughout the 1920s, 1930s, and beyond. The question 'What does it mean to be a Christian?' was contested daily in the villages of Punjab, but it was also considered afresh in Europe and across India, spurred by waves of socio-political change sweeping the two continents in the aftermath of the First World War. These broad cross-currents are examined under the heading of 'three post-war worlds': firstly, India, and Punjab in particular, and then the Catholic Church, and an increasingly unified Protestant missionary movement. The focus then shifts to the CMS village of Clarkabad and the Capuchin village of Maryabad. Both were established while mission experience of the mass movements and the attendant dilemmas of community-building was still limited. Over time, as missionaries became more and more anxious to point to somewhere in Punjab where their ideals were being realized and their expenditure upon rural evangelization vindicated, villages like these began to be hailed as flagship Christian communities. Offering as they did unprecedented control of the natural and social environment, they represent insights into the real extent and intensity of CMS and Capuchin aspirations in Punjab. They also provide a new angle on rural Punjabi convert aspirations. What did the journey away from an old life and towards a new one mean for the people who undertook it? What were their expectations of life in a Christian village, and what can this tell us about the broader dynamics which drove people towards the missions in the first place? Was this genuinely a new start for all concerned, or were old contests simply relocated to a new setting, with the outcome once again unpredictable?

THREE POST-WAR WORLDS

From the 1920s onwards the rhetoric and accomplishments of the Indian nationalist movement and the increasing politicization of religious community and caste put Punjabi Christians in an ambiguous and potentially dangerous position. At the same time, European missionaries were forced into a reappraisal of their purpose on the subcontinent. Rioting in Punjab in April 1919, sparked initially by the passing of intensely controversial government legislation, highlighted the precarious position of new Christian communities in India. The CMS church at Amritsar joined various banks and post offices on the list of symbolic 'colonial' targets, and was destroyed. Troops were called in to protect the CMS Girls' School. Elsewhere there were reports of Indian and European mission-Church personnel being attacked and having their houses burned down.[2]

Amid what was a new and disturbing level of violence on all sides, rural Christians seem to have escaped serious harm, but the long-term future

[2] Committee on Disturbances in Bombay, Delhi, and the Punjab, *New Light on the Punjab Disturbances in 1919: Volumes VI and VII of Disorders Inquiry Committee Evidence* (Simla, 1975) [*NLPD*], 248 and 275.

of Christianity in Punjab looked uncertain. Its social and professional heterogeneity was already emerging as a powerful determining factor in interactions with Indian nationalism. While prominent urban Punjabi Christians tried to assume the role of political intermediaries between the Government and nationalists—with limited success—rural Christians remained comparatively isolated.[3] They were generally neither targets nor aggressors in 1919, nor were they enthusiastically for or against non-cooperation in 1920–2. Gandhian rhetoric about Hindu–Muslim unity (which crowds could be heard chanting in Amritsar in April 1919[4]) quite possibly seemed irrelevant to them, not only as Christians but also as members of a disadvantaged section of rural society that was largely sidelined by elite political leaders.

From the available information, the majority of rural low-caste converts appear to have understood their association with Christianity in strictly local terms well into the 1930s, bound up with the immediate village environment that the missions feared as so debilitating to their efforts at Christian formation. If any wider sense of community based in caste or political affiliation of some kind existed, then not only CMS but also Capuchin missionaries—the latter with no particular affection for the British—either failed to discover any evidence of it, or otherwise chose not to refer to it even in private correspondence.

For the CMS and other Protestant missions in the province and further afield the politicization of urban Punjab came at a time when they were just beginning to step back from the frenzy of the mass movements and develop their experiences into a systematic analysis of modern mission. The Edinburgh World Missionary Conference in 1910 had marked the beginning of this at an ecumenical level. The first conference of its kind, featuring around 1,400 delegates from across 260 Protestant denominations (the Catholic and Orthodox Churches were not represented), it came to be seen as 'the birthplace of . . . international and inter-denominational Christian co-operation'.[5]

An emphasis at the Conference upon the initiative and achievements of Western mission personnel was reflected both in attendance ratios—only seventeen of the 1,400 delegates came from the new

[3] See Webster, 'Punjabi Christians and the Indian Nationalist Movement', particularly pp. 128–9.

[4] *NLPD*, 273.

[5] Ellen A. Hankinson Cox, *The Story of the World Missionary Conference at Edinburgh* (London, 1912), 11; A. Lehmann, *Mission zwischen Gestern und Morgen* (Stuttgart, 1952), 8, repr. in Wilhelm Andersen, *Towards a Theology of Mission: A Study of the Encounter between the Missionary Enterprise and the Church and its Theology* (London, 1955), 16.

mission-Churches themselves—and in the language of the chairman, John Mott: 'We have a larger knowledge of the purposes and designs of God . . . Therefore with rich talents like these which we bear forth, surely our best days are ahead of every one of us, even the most distinguished person in our great company.'[6]

Among the important new initiatives that flowed from Edinburgh were the International Review of Missions, first published in 1912, and the National Missionary Council of India, which was established in 1914 and was renamed the National Christian Council of India, Burma, and Ceylon in 1923.[7] The latter became an important forum for Indian Christian opinion: Indian participation was set at a minimum of 50 per cent, and the Council worked towards the erosion of the denominationalism that delegates of the Punjab Native Church Council had condemned more than forty years earlier. The National Council frequently discussed the mass movements, commissioning the survey by J. Waskom Pickett that was eventually published as *Christian Mass Movements in India: A Study with Recommendations.*[8]

The fact that some of the most comprehensive missionary planning took place in the 1920s and 1930s, at a time when the early optimism of the 1910 Edinburgh Conference began to be trampled by social turmoil in Europe, falling financial contributions to the missions, and a decline in churchgoing, might seem paradoxical. In fact it was precisely these trends, signalling the end of what had been the most energetic period of Christian evangelization in modern times, which pushed missionary societies into finally taking the devolutionary decisions urged by radicals since long before the turn of the century. One clear sign of this was CMS policy-makers' talk of 'diocesanization': the long-term solution of cultural, racial, and mission–diocese tensions through the gradual transfer of power from foreign missions to dioceses whose personnel would increasingly be drawn from the ranks of local Christians.

As ever, mission policy was hampered by the myriad interests and fissures within the organizations themselves. Despite the request by a CMS delegation to India in 1921–2 that missionaries now consider themselves agents of the diocese rather than the mission, there remained strong pressure from donors in England for their money to be spent accountably and according to the original evangelistic ideals of the CMS—in other words helping British missionaries to make fresh,

[6] Quoted in Andersen, *Towards a Theology of Mission*, 17.
[7] New York, 1933.
[8] Hewitt, *The Problems of Success*, ii. 51.

bold gains rather than simply subsidizing foreign congregations. These pressures were compounded both by old Evangelical suspicions of ecclesiastical hierarchy and by the conviction among urban Christians in Punjab that their struggle for authority could be more effectively waged within the familiar CMS mission-Church framework than through the institutions and personalities of a wider diocese awash with European power and interests. Unsurprising, then, that progress was slow and the Bishop of Lahore complained as late as 1938 that the Parent Committee in London continued to exert strong influence in the diocese.[9]

Where rural Christianity was concerned, the prevailing missionary view was that expressed by the Revd C. F. Hall: 'Haste will give us an ignorant, ill-taught Church, unable to read the Bible, only half-weaned from idolatry, a prey to superstition, and a real stumbling block to future progress among the caste people . . . [but] delay is even more dangerous for it means not ill-taught but untaught, and merely self-styled Christians.'[10]

The hope was for a rural Church comprising simple village communities looked after by a 'peasant priesthood' of teacher–pastors, in which literacy rates were high enough that someone besides the teacher–pastor was always available to lead church services. Hall insisted that schools could be built cheaply (for around £10 each) and situated in converts' section of the village, with the congregation initially paying a contribution towards—and eventually covering entirely—an annual upkeep of £4 or £5 (the remainder to be covered by government grants). The teacher–pastor would then teach for four hours a day, in addition to conducting services and itinerating in nearby villages.[11]

Strategies such as these featured heavily in mass-movement fundraising campaigns established by the CMS after the First World War. One such campaign was launched in London in 1918, covering large-scale conversion movements in India, Nigeria, and Uganda and focusing upon the provision of teachers and schools. Leadership in India was provided by Bishop Azariah of Dornakal and Bishop Whitehead of Madras, the former using the CMS Annual Sermon in London in 1920 to underline the social aspect of the movements and to urge the Indian Church to 'throw her whole available strength into the work

[9] Hewitt, ii. 71.

[10] Summary of the Revd C. F. Hall's article 'A Suggested Policy for Mass Movements', *Proceedings of the CMS, 1913–14*, 110.

[11] Hall, 'A Suggested Policy for Mass Movements', 281–3.

of receiving and raising these people that the Spirit of God is driving into the Church'.[12] Whitehead lent his support, claiming to have long believed that Christianity in India would progress in the same way as it had in the Roman empire: as a movement from below which succeeded by undermining the foundations of existing religious structures.[13]

A Mass Movement Commission established ten years later and also presided over by Bishop Azariah noted the need for more mission agents in north India in particular, where logistical difficulties were at their most acute. The Commission made special appeals to the Church of England Zenana Mission Society and the Zenana Bible and Medical Mission for much-needed extra female help, and highlighted the need for greater cooperation from educated Christians and for the more extensive provision of Christian literature. Punjab was singled out as the most promising area in a challenging region.

In the Catholic Church pessimists saw the First World War as a victory for Anglo-Saxon Calvinist and capitalist liberal power (not to mention the rise of communism in Russia[14]) and as indicative of the continued undermining of the concept of 'Christendom' by that of 'nation'. As the diplomatic influence of the papacy continued on its long downward trajectory, Pope Pius XI (1922–39) set out to promote a global, catholic vision of Christianity that took European nations to task for cultural chauvinism in the colonial world. The apostolic letter *Maximum Illud* (30 November 1919) called for the de-politicization of the missions, and for those missionaries who 'think more of the worldly than of the heavenly fatherland' to curb their nationalism and show respect for the cultures in which they operated. The 'salvation of all people' was to be effected through an emphasis upon the training of indigenous clergy and the establishment of indigenous hierarchies.[15]

Rome's renewed desire to promote its catholicity and universalism—particularly in light of what was regarded as the dangerous Protestant ecumenism of the Edinburgh Conference—was evident in the use of the plural 'ecclesiae' (Churches) in papal documents from this period onwards. As with the CMS, however, calls for the missionary surrender of ecclesiastical power in newly evangelized territories were nothing new, and little had so far been achieved. The first Indian

[12] Bishop Azariah, CMS Annual Sermon 1920, quoted in Hewitt, *The Problems of Success*, ii. 107.

[13] Stephen Neill, quoted in Hewitt, *The Problems of Success*, ii. 111.

[14] Karl Von Aretin, *The Papacy and the Modern World* (London, 1970), 176–7.

[15] Benedict XV, *Maximum Illud*, 30 Nov. 1919 (Vatican, 1919).

Catholic bishop was not consecrated until 1923, and Punjabi Catholics had to wait until 1945 for their first non-European priest. Instead, policy made in the Vatican tended to be invoked on the ground in Punjab mainly where it helped the Capuchins to secure more resources for the mission or enabled them to challenge the diocese's apparent prioritization of the European–Eurasian community. The notion that rural Catholic converts would soon rise up to run their own Church was viewed as far-fetched, to put it mildly, among Capuchins working in the province in the 1920s and 1930s.

Most friars instead continued to see a network of rural Catholic schools as their priority and as a far more feasible prospect in the short term than an indigenous priesthood. Such schools were the key to ensuring that girls and boys brought into the fold through the mass movements were given an appreciation of what their new faith ought to mean to them. The general Capuchin strategy was to focus upon the future potential of these children, accepting that adults were mostly lost to the 'apathy, uncleanliness and disorder' that surrounded them.[16] This was a huge challenge at the beginning of the 1920s, given the financial hardship faced by the mission (a post-war Belgian national debt of almost 22 billion francs put the long-term future of the mission in jeopardy) and the loss of experienced missionaries through the deaths of Frs Marc, Lievin, Sigismond, and Vincent.[17]

CLARKABAD

The Canal Colony Project in Punjab

The canal irrigation begun by the British in 1885 and shown in Map 5.1 represented a level of social and economic intervention by an imperial power never before seen in India.[18] Whereas in the United

[16] Pelckmans, *Dix Années*, 85–6. Some Capuchin missionaries retained a degree of faith in adult converts, however. Fr. Vincent suggested the opening of catechetical night schools, to fit around adults' working commitments. There was rarely a great deal of urgency expressed with regard to such plans, however. They appeared in mission correspondence as mere footnotes to far longer accounts of progress in children's education. Letter from Fr. Vincent to General, 6 Jan. 1903, GACO.

[17] The Capuchin mission gained more missionaries than it lost in this period, however. Between 1919 and 1930 twenty-nine missionaries began work in the mission and only fourteen either left or died. See Appendix.

[18] Ali, *The Punjab under Imperialism*, p. viii.

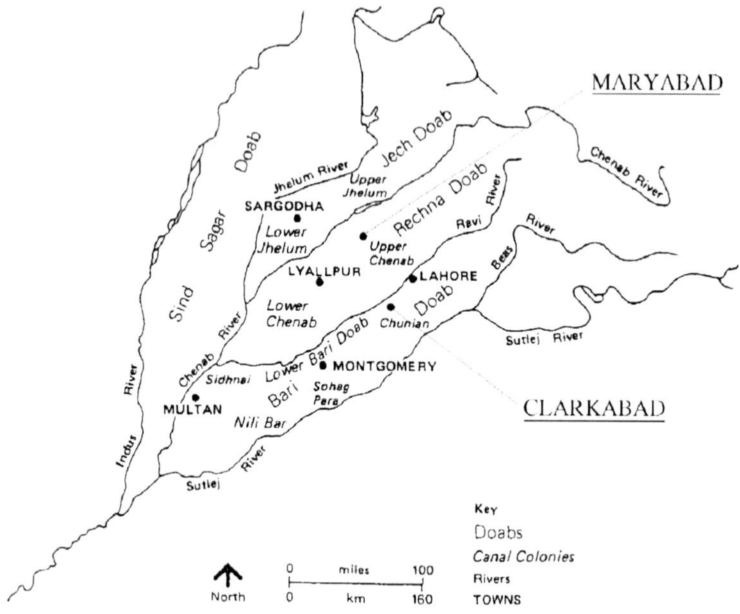

MAP 5.1. Maryabad, Clarkabad, and the canal colonies. The approximate locations of Maryabad and Clarkabad have been added to the original.
Source: Imran Ali, *The Punjab under Imperialism* (Princeton, 1988)

Provinces canals served tracts that were already settled, in Punjab the condition of the land in question was such that only small numbers of semi-nomadic groups inhabited it prior to canal irrigation, and these groups relied upon underground sources of water. This meant that canal irrigation effectively established brand new 'hydraulic' societies, through migration, over which the Punjab administration assumed an unprecedented degree of control.[19]

The opportunity to exercise this power was not wasted. The British were determined to settle only certain Punjabi cultivators on the high-quality land that irrigation produced. Relying on detailed studies of rural Punjabi society made in previous decades, the British embarked upon an ambitious programme of social engineering. They aimed to

[19] Ali, *The Punjab under Imperialism*, p. viii.

colonize the new land with 'well-to-do yeomen of the best class of agriculturalists, who will cultivate their own holdings with the aid of their families and of the usual menials . . . and will constitute healthy agricultural communities of the best Punjab type'.[20]

The 'best type' was the most loyal type. Grants of land were made strictly according to caste and family, and the vast majority of the grants (amounting to 78.3 per cent of the land in the case of Chenab Colony) were for occupancy tenancies rather than proprietary rights, and were available only to designated 'agriculturalist' castes. In this way the British could legally remove a colonist as they wished, by showing them to be in breach of the terms of their tenancy. These terms were first introduced in 1887 and typically included having to live on the land, cut wood from specified areas, maintain a clean compound, and make arrangements for the sanitary disposal of night soil.[21]

Moderately well-off peasant families from central Punjab—Lahore, Amritsar, Gurdaspur, Hoshiarpur, Jalandhar, and Ferozepur—applied for land via colonization officers, who were based in the districts in which applicants currently resided. Knowing applicants personally, these officers believed themselves to be in a competent position to judge people's potential as colonists.[22] Successful applicants then made the journey to the colonies, braving the early lack of railway access, the imperfect (sometimes unbuilt) watercourses, and the anger of pre-irrigation inhabitants, who occasionally became violent. The 1904 *Chenab Gazetteer* cheerfully reported that 'those who persevered, and were not carried off by a severe epidemic of cholera, were rewarded by an excellent crop'.[23]

Low-caste Punjabis were effectively excluded. In a process designed as an extension of the Punjab administration's existing rural policy, these 'menials' were left simply to follow their *sepidari* patrons to the canal tracts. Yet even the favoured 'well-to-do yeomen' did not enjoy complete freedom. They discovered the Government to be an overbearing landlord, and soon found themselves forced into open revolt against a heavy-handed and interfering administration. The final straw was the 1906 Bill for the Colonization of Government Lands, under which government officials were to be given the power to evict tenants

[20] *Gazetteer of the Chenab Colony 1904* (Lahore, 1905), 29.

[21] N. Gerald Barrier, 'The Punjab Disturbances of 1907: The Response of the British Government in India to Agrarian Unrest', *Modern Asian Studies*, 1/2 (1967), 357.

[22] Paul W. Paustian, *Canal Irrigation in the Punjab* (New York, 1930), 65.

[23] *Gazetteer of the Chenab Colony 1904*, 30.

without having to go through the civil courts. Strict primogeniture was to replace customary division of land among male heirs, a measure designed to curb fragmentation of holdings.

Arriving close on the heels of colonist complaints about corruption and bribe-taking among lower-level officials, as well as the destruction of the 1905–6 cotton crop by bollworm,[24] the Bill succeeded in uniting in anger two separate and powerful groups that the administration had long sought to keep apart: rural elites and urban middle classes, the latter with strong investment interests in the canal colonies. The so-called Disturbances of 1907 were the most serious instances of unrest in Punjab since it had come under British rule. The Government in Delhi was forced to veto the proposed legislation, an embarrassing result for an administration which prided itself on the sheer beneficence of the irrigation project.[25]

If the Colonization of Government Lands Act (Punjab) of 1912 represented the adoption by a rattled administration of a more laissez-faire attitude in the colonies (peasant tenants were now allowed to buy their land ten years after occupancy rights were received, or fifteen years after settlement, at rates well below market level[26]), it was also, as Imran Ali has implied, a retreat from the old strategy of engineering socio-economic development from above.[27] There seemed to have been a point at which external pressure and intervention began to produce negative results.

It is against this backdrop of grand plans and compromises that similarly ambitious schemes initiated by Christian missions must be considered. Those in control of the new environments had socio-religious rather than socio-economic re-formation in mind, but the potential clearly existed for similar problems to arise between landlords and tenants with differing visions of life in the colonies.

The Birth and Development of Clarkabad

The village of Clarkabad was founded by, and later named after, the Revd Robert Clark in 1869. It was built on the right bank of the Bari Doab canal, 56 miles south-west of Amritsar,[28] with good rail links on

[24] Barrier, 'The Punjab Disturbances of 1907', 357–61.

[25] Fox, 'Urban Class and Communal Consciousness in Colonial Punjab', 479–80.

[26] Penal codes were also lightened and appeals against revenue decisions were permitted in the local courts; Barrier, 'The Punjab Disturbances of 1907', 380.

[27] Ali, *The Punjab under Imperialism*, 70.

[28] See Map 5.1.

the Lahore–Multan line. The nearest train station, Kote Radha Kishan, was just 3 miles away. According to the Revd T. Holden, a missionary stationed at Clarkabad, this was an ideal distance. It was conveniently close, yet far enough that Clarkabad could 'escape . . . the contamination resulting from contact with the residents of large towns'.[29]

Following their request for land to house new Christian converts currently suffering hostility in their own villages as a result of their conversion, 1,935 acres of land were leased by the Government to the CMS. Special legislation was required for the granting of the land to a Christian group,[30] and Punjabis who were suspicious of the administration's attitude towards Christian missions did not fail to notice this significant departure in policy. The lease was granted for ten years, and was renewed in 1879. At the end of the 1880s the lease was renewed for the rest of the life of the settlement and from 1881 the CMS paid Rs 500 a year to the Government.[31] Three-quarters of the land had been brought under cultivation by 1882.[32]

Clarkabad's early years were unpromising. The land was apparently slow to improve in quality, even under irrigation, and few of the early migrants (mostly Christian converts from among the Chuhra caste[33]) knew much about cultivation. Even those men and women who had taken on temporary fieldwork in their old villages had an incomplete knowledge of the overall farming process, having been directed in every aspect of the work by their employers. I. C. Singha, a delegate to the PNCC in 1899, called for converts to be given agricultural training as a matter of priority.[34]

Clarkabad initially relied heavily upon the contribution of Hindu, Sikh, and particularly Muslim farmers, and although the village's 700 inhabitants (in 1882) included a number of carpenters, weavers, blacksmiths, and shopkeepers, there was as yet no sign of the purely Christian interdependence of which missionaries dreamt.[35] A Christian

[29] Letter from the Revd T. Holden to Clark, 22 Sept. 1890, ACMS, G2/I4/O 1890, n. 464.

[30] Lucas and Thakur Das, *The Rural Church in the Punjab*, 3.

[31] *Gazetteer of the Lahore District, 1893–4* (Lahore, 1894), 98.

[32] Ibid., *1882–3* (London, 1883), 112–13.

[33] The Revd C. M. Gough, Annual Letter 1909, repr. in *EAL 1909–10* (London, 1910), 501.

[34] *Proceedings of the Twenty-Second Meeting of the PNDCC, 1899* (Lahore?, 1899?), 18–19, ACMS.

[35] Even by 1893 Muslim farmers still outnumbered Christians in the village, by 600 to 423; Letter from Miss Ellwanger to Clark, Jan. 1893, ACMS, G2/I4/O 1893, n. 34; *Proceedings of the CMS, 1882–3*, 112–13.

population of one-third was comparatively high for a Punjab village, but a much higher ratio was sought by the Revd Rowland Bateman when he arrived in Clarkabad in 1879 to begin an energetic three years of transforming the village, beginning with the building of a new church.

It was a nervous time in Clarkabad. One of the conditions of the Government's original ten-year lease of the land to the CMS had been that, if a large proportion of the land was not brought under cultivation by Indian Christian managers, the entire colony would revert to Government. If this, and other conditions, were fulfilled, however, the Christian villagers would acquire proprietary rights. By 1879 it was clear that Clarkabad would not meet the necessary target. A deal had to be made, with Bateman accepting personal responsibility for the settlement for a period of five years.[36] His was to prove a radical vision of Punjabi Christianity's future.

Bateman began work by intensifying the CMS's evangelistic efforts in Clarkabad, managing to baptize thirty-five people in a single day, following public examination.[37] Work on the new church was completed in 1881, along with a mission house and boys' school. The Amritsar Boys' Orphanage was soon moved to Clarkabad and attached to the boys' school.[38] A girls' school followed.[39] Houses were built by the mission and rent of Rs 1 a month charged to the inhabitants. New roads were constructed and more than 2,000 trees and shrubs planted. A new wall enclosed the village, and a large tank and new watercourses were dug.[40] A dispensary was set up, run by a Punjabi Christian doctor, Abdul Rahim Khan.[41]

All the institutions of a CMS mission station were effectively put in place alongside the practical necessities of a canal colony. A new well dug in the shadow of the church symbolized a successful transformation that was described by Clarkabad's pastor, the Revd Daud Singh (the first Anglican convert from Sikhism), as one of desert scrubland into a modern, Christian village.[42] Clarkabad retained this structure well into the twentieth century. Lawrence Benjamin, who lived and studied there as a child in the 1940s and 1950s, was struck by 'all the beautiful

[36] *Proceedings of the CMS, 1879–80* (London, 1880), 61. [37] Ibid. 61.

[38] Inmates numbered twenty-six by 1893; Miss Ellwanger, Annual Letter 1893, repr. in *EAL 1893–4*, 41. [39] *Proceedings of the CMS, 1883–4* (London, 1884), 115.

[40] Ibid., *1882–3*, 112–13. [41] Ibid.,*1883–4*, 115.

[42] Ibid., *1880–1* (London, 1881), 86.

streets . . . [with] so many trees planted, and [the] church right in the middle'.[43]

One of the major remaining disappointments to the CMS after this initial period of construction, however, was villagers' slowness to develop a sense of self-sufficiency. Missionaries saw this as typified by requests, after a poor harvest in 1885, for help from the mission in paying the *mamla* (water-due).[44] To help things along a number of small independent industries were established in the village. Modest successes were soon scored with the cultivation and sale of fruit, vegetables, roses, and plants by the boys' school and orphanage. Not only was a small net income gained by the village boys, but they were 'usefully employed' at the same time. Brick-baking and silkworming were also tried as possible industries, and by the early 1890s shoemaking and carpentry were proving moderately successful.[45] It was later suggested that, with Lahore relatively easily accessible by train, a dairy industry might be a profitable prospect for six months of the year.[46] Another avenue tried by CMS personnel in seeking to encourage self-sufficiency was the Revd Fath Masih's forgoing of his CMS salary in 1903, living instead upon the charity of his congregation.[47]

There was more at stake here than lessons in self-sufficiency and interdependence. Holden noted in 1890 that, with canal land rapidly being snapped up, there would soon come a time when Christian migrants would be forced to take up non-agricultural forms of employment. Clarkabad was to be a testing ground for industrial alternatives and a beacon to future colonies.[48]

Within just six years Clarkabad's annual income increased threefold, from Rs 3,000 in 1882 to Rs 9,000 in 1888. It was claimed that Clarkabad was the only CMS mission station in Punjab which, with the exception of the missionary's allowance and institutions such as the schools, effectively paid its own way.[49] This included its local dispensary,

[43] Punjab–UK interviews, Lawrence Benjamin, 21 May 2007.

[44] *Proceedings of the CMS, 1885–6* (London, 1886), 109.

[45] Ibid.; the Revd T. Holden, Annual Letter 1891, repr. in *EAL 1890–1* (London, 1891), 358.

[46] Letter from the Revd T. Holden to the CMS Secretary, 19 Dec. 1902, ACMS, G2/I4/O 1903, 57.

[47] *Proceedings of the CMS, 1902–3* (London, 1903), 238.

[48] Letter from the Revd T. Holden to Clark, 22 Sept. 1890, ACMS, G2/I4/O 1890, n. 464.

[49] Letter from Mr Beutel (responsible for running the boys' school and orphanage, and overseeing the life of the village in general) to Clark, 14 June 1888, ACMS, G2/I4/O 1888, n. 263.

doctor, and Punjabi pastor. Rs 20,000 had been invested in government securities by 1899 (at the Agra Bank), to be used in times of emergency such as famine or plague.[50] A system of accounts was now set up, with the aim of separating village from CMS funds—a vital step on the road towards true self-sufficiency. Future surpluses were to be spent locally: on drainage, sanitation, roads, and other projects.[51]

Clarkabad also seemed to score successes with its social life. The CMS missionary Miss Ellwanger reported in 1893 that converts from a range of caste backgrounds were increasingly willing to sit together in church, while alcohol-related problems had almost disappeared.[52] Evangelization in the villages surrounding Clarkabad was gathering pace, and large numbers of low-caste groups were beginning to show an interest in receiving catechism. Ellwanger thought that much of this interest was due to land hunger but was confident that the solidity of Christian life at Clarkabad would soon turn such desires into a genuine receptivity to the gospel.[53] Punjabi Bible-women were having a major impact among low-caste women in one particular village near Clarkabad, taking them to one side and giving them instruction in the Bible, the Lord's Prayer, and the Ten Commandments.[54] A small school was built for the girls of the village in 1895, with a female agent visiting from Clarkabad to teach reading and writing Punjabi script (Gurumukhi) and verses of Scripture.[55]

In Clarkabad itself the ongoing evangelization effort included the opening of a night school for local landowners and ex-students of the orphanage. In addition to reading lessons (using the Bible), classes on agricultural techniques were given, based on government textbooks. Part of the aim of the night school was to prevent conversion to Islam, which had recently been a notable trend among orphans once they left the school.[56] The pastoral care of the village, overseen by the PNCC, met with little interference from the CMS. The spiritual aspect of the work in Clarkabad appeared to be one of its strongest points, and its pastor was allowed significant creative room for manoeuvre by the CMS.

[50] Memo by Colonel Hutchinson, dated 17 Jan. 1900, ACMS, G2/I4/O 1899, n. 51.

[51] Ibid.

[52] Letter from Miss Ellwanger to Clark, Jan. 1893, ACMS, G2/I4/O 1893, n. 34.

[53] Miss Ellwanger, Annual Letter 1890, repr. in *EAL 1890–1*, 40.

[54] Ibid., Annual Letter 1893, repr. in *EAL 1893–4*, 41.

[55] Misses M. E. and M. J. Farthing, (joint) Annual Letter 1895, repr. in *EAL 1895–6* (London, 1896), 205.

[56] The Revd T. J. L. Mayer, Annual Letter 1892, repr. in *EAL 1892–3* (London, 1893), 420.

Figs 5.1 and 5.2 are photographs of Clarkabad and its villagers, taken by CMS personnel for journal publication. Fig. 5.1 shows Clarkabad's church, the regulation-width streets, recently planted trees and shrubs, and a number of villagers. Government engineers had set a minimum road width of 50 feet for canal colonies, and this appeared to be binding upon mission societies such as the CMS to whom leases of land were made. It was likewise compulsory for large compounds to be attached to every house,[57] as shown in Fig. 5.2: a village house and compound, with the church in the background.[58]

Clarkabad under CMS Control

Clarkabad's legal status changed in the late 1880s, with the CMS acquiring full proprietary control. The mission now took the opportunity to bring the village into closer conformity with their ideal, to which end Bateman and his future biographer James Maconachie put together detailed proposals in 1892 under four main headings: rights of tenants; village government and discipline; income, expenditure, salaries, and accounts; and relations of local auxiliary institutions to the local executive and management.[59]

At the core of the new proposals was the withholding of full tenancy rights from villagers, in order that the mission might retain the 'power of alienation' as the basis of their social and economic influence. Five grades of tenant were suggested, ranging from those on yearly leases to those with tenancy for life and even tenancy capable of devolving to male children. All tenancies, except yearly leases, were to be granted only to Christians, and would rest upon tenants' exhibition of 'good character'. Only adult males were eligible to take on tenancies, although temporary leases could pass to widows as long as they were able to provide for cultivation. Such leases would not, however, be renewable.

Offences punishable by withdrawal of tenancy rights fell into categories of secular and religious. The former were based upon government models and included neglect of duties of cultivation, failure to pay rent, indebtedness against the wishes of the Executive Authority (see below),

[57] H. Whitehead, 'Bishop Whitehead in the Punjab: Extracts from his Journal', *CMR* 64/772 (Aug. 1913), 488.

[58] The photographs appeared together in a CMS file for 1883, with no details attached; ACMS, G2/I4/O 1883, n. 134.

[59] Memo on Clarkabad Arrangements by R. Bateman and R. Maconachie, 1 May 1892, ACMS, G2/I4/O 1892, n. 217.

Fig. 5.1. Clarkabad village, 1883. Clarkabad's church can be seen in the background, with groups of villagers and a missionary in the foreground.
Source: ACMS, G2/I4/O 1883, n. 134

Fig. 5.2. Clarkabad house and compound, 1883. A small group of villagers can be seen in the foreground.

Source: ACMS, G2/I4/O 1883, n. 134

interference with the flow of water, alienation of the land with the intention of personal (i.e. non-taxable) profit, and the trespass of cattle on neighbouring land. Religious offences included 'breach of the Ten Commandments', 'habitual non-attendance at public worship', failure to send children to school, fraud, 'stirring up strife', inciting litigation, gambling, drunkenness, gross violation of Christian decency, and 'conduct involving public scandal'.[60]

Charges of religious offences could be brought only by the local pastor or European missionary, and would be heard in the first instance by the Church Committee. Secular offences were to be heard by the Village Committee. Both Committees were elected bodies but the Executive Authority had the final say in both religious and secular offences. This Authority consisted of the local European missionary and pastor, and the head of the Village Committee. Ultimate authority rested with the CMS, since the missionary had the power to override the other two members of the Authority and was bound only to record their disagreement. The names of those found guilty of religious offences were posted at the west end of the church, along with details of the offence and the punishment. Only in extreme cases were offenders forced out of the village.[61]

The CMS seemed to be falling into the same trap as the Punjab administration: given huge new potential for social and economic interference, they could not resist making maximum and potentially reckless use of it. According to Bateman and Maconachie's suggestions a cash economy (which had caused considerable damage elsewhere in Punjab) was to be encouraged in Clarkabad, by charging tenants who paid their rent in cash just one-eighth of their harvest income, as opposed to one-sixth charged to those paying in kind. To ensure that this cash economy would rest as far as possible in the hands of Christians, non-Christian cultivators were to be charged one-*quarter* of their produce as rent, even if they paid in cash (value was to be determined according to prevailing market price).[62] So 'moderate' did Bateman and Maconachie consider this arrangement that they suggested a revision after five years, with a view to increasing rent charges. To add to the sense of a mini-theocracy already created by the new tenancy

60 Memo on Clarkabad Arrangements by R. Bateman and R. Maconachie, 1 May 1892.

61 Statement of the Revd T. R. Wade to the Centenary Committee, answering questions in section IV, ACMS, G/CCb 4/2a.

62 Memo on Clarkabad Arrangements by R. Bateman and R. Maconachie.

conditions, 'religious' offences, and differential rates of rent, the village's non-Christian manager was now to be sacked and replaced with a Christian. Clarkabad was henceforth required to submit an annual budget to the Corresponding Committee, for its approval.[63]

Although it is not possible to say with certainty whether Bateman and Maconachie's suggestions received amendment before they were implemented, CMS policy in Clarkabad in subsequent years clearly matched that seen in the document. A similar tone underlay CMS dealings with the PNCC and the later revision of the Punjab mission-Church constitution. CMS policy-makers in all three areas appeared to see no inherent contradiction in promoting financial and administrative self-sufficiency through rigid, externally imposed structures.

At times these detailed measures made it seem as though Clarkabad were being run as a large boarding school. CMS personnel thought 'discipline' so low in the village that it was 'necessary to have regular rules in regard to even such elementary things as Sabbath observance, attendance at church, and the education of children'.[64] Miss Ellwanger described the people of Clarkabad as 'stupid folk, mostly, [who] do not think of consequences'. When two girls received a beating from their new husbands for refusing to bring them food while they were working in the fields, Ellwanger appeared distinctly unsympathetic. She gave the girls a lecture on their behaviour, and later noted with pride that 'it has not happened again'.[65]

Clashes in the Canal Colonies

By the turn of the century Clarkabad was entering CMS mythology as the model Christian village, with visiting missionaries writing of their surprise at the 'clean, straight, wide, airy streets' of Clarkabad, so unlike the 'filthy, crooked, narrow lanes of the average Punjabi village'.[66] The virtues of villagers' simple lives were extolled: healthy, functional employment, with a minimum of worldly goods; village trades limited to those essential for self-sufficiency—weaving, blacksmithing, carpentry, and shopkeeping. A vogue had emerged among missionaries for using biblical metaphors to express what they imagined the full theological

[63] Memo on Clarkabad Arrangements.

[64] The Revd C. M. Gough, Annual Letter 1909, repr. in *EAL 1909–10*, 501.

[65] Letter from Miss Ellwanger to Clark, Jan. 1893, ACMS, G2/I4/O 1893, n. 34.

[66] Report of the Revd J. A. Wood, repr. in *Proceedings of the CMS, 1900–1*, 288–9.

and socio-religious scope of the Christian village achievement might prove to be. Robert Clark was one of the first, drawing on the Old Testament book of Isaiah in a comment on Clarkabad: 'The desert now rejoices, with the joy and laughing of the thick standing corn, and blossoms abundantly as the rose; while the seeds of Life from the Word of God are sown bountifully every day in the hearts of the people.'[67]

The government seal of approval was given in 1901 when the Lieutenant Governor of Punjab, Sir William Mackworth Young, laid a memorial stone to the Christian worker Miss Tucker, and gave a short speech:

> Clarkabad is a signal instance of what a Christian village can be, with its finances sound; its institutions of a church, school, and dispensary, all self-supporting; and its agriculture flourishing. In these respects it affords a valuable example for the Native Christian community, whose principal need is self-help and self-support. It is in this aspect that the history of Clarkabad possesses such a deep interest for Government . . . The number of Native Christians is rapidly increasing, and, as we firmly believe, is bound to increase and prevail; and one thoroughly successful instance of self-support at the early stage of Christian development is of incalculable value. Such progress on the part of a section of the community is of supreme importance to Government . . . Speaking purely as Lieutenant-Governor, I should conclude by wishing Clarkabad nothing more than it should fulfil the mission of a pioneer village, and show Native Christians how to be self-reliant, thrifty and successful. But I am speaking also as a Christian man to Christian men, and as such I cannot refrain from pointing out to you what a splendid opportunity is offered to this community of showing by their conduct the beauty of the religion they profess.[68]

It is not difficult to see how Mackworth Young's words found their way into a CMS journal. His testimony, replete with references to what was best for the 'Native Christian community', picked out many of the ideals, familiar from English uplift initiatives, that lay closest to the hearts of CMS strategists in Punjab. Letters and reports from this time suggest, however, that missionary plans had already begun to unravel.

Industrial work at the boys' school and orphanage, noticeably absent from Mackworth Young's remarks, had been halted in the spring of

[67] Report of the Revd R. Clark, 25 Nov. 1887, ACMS, G2/I4O 1887, n. 365. See Isa. 35: 1: 'The wilderness and the solitary place shall be glad for them; and the desert shall rejoice, and blossom as the rose.'

[68] Address of Lieutenant-Governor Sir W. Mackworth Young to the inhabitants of Clarkabad, spring 1901, repr. in *Proceedings of the CMS, 1900–1*, 289–90. Young had previously been a member of the CMS Punjab Corresponding Committee; *Proceedings of the CMS, 1896–7*, 219.

1901. The lack of a 'qualified European' to supervise the work—despite a request by Holden ten years previously—was blamed for the fact that boys were 'virtually learning nothing' at the school. Holden now blamed the (Hindu) teacher there, accusing him of 'drawing his liberal pay for teaching nothing'. Clients for the goods produced at the orphanage had started to complain that the quality did not reflect the price. Orders were being withdrawn.[69]

Attendance at the school was on a similarly dangerous trajectory, despite the threat of a fine imposed on Christian parents for failing to send their children to school.[70] This was a far cry from the 'good moral tone' and 'happy', energetic boys described by Miss Ellwanger ten years earlier. At that time there had been a different housemaster, perhaps indicating the importance of personnel to the success of the school.[71] All had clearly not been well even then, however, with Ellwanger reporting secretly to Clark that the American Presbyterians judged Clarkabad a 'failure'.[72]

Boarding students too were less than perfect. Holden believed that, in their 'absurd straining after . . . English manners and customs', they were forgetting their own, with the result that many people were commenting on their rudeness, particularly towards the elderly. There was a danger, thought Holden, that the experience of boarding school would alienate boys from the reality of existence in the outside world and render them unfit for normal public life, particularly where recognition of the 'dignity of honest manual labour' was concerned. The practice of providing tea for the boys every morning was put forward as a relatively trivial yet telling example of the unhelpful socialization taking place in the school.[73] Holden had issued similar warnings ten years previously, claiming that it could end 'only one way; by the girls desiring to adopt hats, bonnets and parasols, and the boys broadcloth and dress shoes'.[74]

Many of the orphans were developing the dangerous conviction that they were guaranteed well-paid, safe employment in the future, simply by virtue of their place in the orphanage. More generally—and very much in line with uplift ideals expressed in England and elsewhere in Punjab—Holden believed that the community in Clarkabad did

[69] Letter from the Revd T. Holden to the Secretaries of the CMS (London), 19 Dec. 1902, ACMS, G2/I4/O 1903, n. 57.

[70] Ibid.

[71] Miss Ellwanger, Annual Letter 1893, repr. in *EAL 1893–4*, 41.

[72] Letter from Miss Ellwanger to Clark, Jan. 1893, ACMS, G2/I4/O 1893, n. 34.

[73] Letter from the Revd T. Holden to the Secretaries of the CMS (London), 19 Dec. 1902.

[74] The Revd T. Holden, Annual Letter 1893, repr. in *EAL 1893–4*, 348.

not understand the dangers of debt and the need for self-reliance. The 'immorality' of debt had to be drummed into boys at the school as much as possible.[75]

The CMS were finally worried. Having apparently ignored the early warnings of personnel like Holden (as on other issues the voices of Mian Sadiq, Bateman, and Bomford tended to be heard only belatedly), senior CMS missionaries in 1902 at last appointed a subcommittee to investigate what was going wrong in Clarkabad. The subcommittee found that 'the general state of the school is most deplorable, there being an absence of order, discipline and method, and apparently little interest taken in the welfare of the boys'. The school was drawing on its reserves and was very close to bankruptcy. This was particularly galling given the amount of money that the CMS were pumping into various institutions in the village: CMS expenditure had amounted to Rs 13,322 in 1901, much of it (Rs 6,851) spent on the boarding school, along with Rs 1,898 and Rs 2,724 spent respectively on industrial work and a 'New Industrial Scheme'.[76]

Bateman had recently suspended the headmaster of the school (who had also been occupying the post of housemaster, drawing both salaries) for inefficiency.[77] The headmaster now resigned before the subcommittee had the chance to fire him. The dormitories were found to be dirty and the room for sick boys 'cheerless'. The income from working the land was markedly lower than that for the girls' school. The subcommittee suggested that, if the land could not be made to turn a greater profit, it might as well be leased out to someone else.[78]

The school's workshops were being used more by outside workmen than by the boys. This too had to change. The subcommittee suggested that the school's potential as an industrial centre be exploited by the construction of useful Indian products rather than 'articles of a more or less fancy nature' like tennis racquets—a market in which the school could not hope to compete in terms of quality or price. Moreover,

[75] Letter from the Revd T. Holden to the Secretaries of the CMS (London), 19 Dec. 1902.

[76] Report of a Sub-Committee appointed by the Punjab CMS Conference to visit the Boys School at Clarkabad, ACMS, G2/I4/O 1902, n. 190.

[77] Copy of the Remarks Entered by the Revd. R. Bateman in a Clarkabad Record Book, 17 Jan. 1902, ACMS, G2/I4/O 1902, n. 190.

[78] Report of a Sub-Committee appointed by the Punjab CMS Conference to visit the Boys School at Clarkabad.

the school should not be used as an employment site 'for Christians who find it difficult to get work elsewhere'. Only schoolboys should be trained there, and they should then move on to placements in workshops in Lahore, where they could further their skills while staying at the hostel attached to St John's Divinity School.[79] (Christian villagers were not permitted to stay long in Lahore, however, since town life was thought unhealthy for them—spiritually, morally, and physically.[80]) It was further recommended by the subcommittee that an English missionary take full charge of the school, although it was thought that the headmaster should be Punjabi. All non-Christian employees at the school should be dismissed as soon as possible and housework should be done by the boys themselves.

No sooner had conditions in the boys' school started to improve—partly thanks to a new village superintendent and school carpentry instructor (ploughs apparently replaced tennis racquets[81])—than Clarkabad was hit by a genuine crisis. The village was hit first by plague and then by serious unrest as inhabitants demanded proprietary land rights.

In April 1906 the majority of tenants refused to pay any rent, on the basis that having tilled the land for so long they had a right to its ownership. They seemed to be aware, through various contacts, that in other colonies proprietary rights were already available. Attendance at church, seemingly a reliable indicator of converts' satisfaction with the mission–convert relationship, now fell drastically.[82] A number of tenants converted to Islam and took up offers of land at Lyallpur. The CMS wasted no time in initiating legal proceedings, successfully evicting most of the main protesters within a few months. Those who had left for Lyallpur were denounced as being of a 'class' that was easily baited with offers of land.[83] Some of those evicted were allowed to return a couple of years later. Those identified as 'ringleaders' and 'bad characters' were kept out.[84]

Clarkabad's fortunes improved after 1909, with rising Christian numbers, improved harvests and school attendance (the latter still

[79] Report of a Sub-Committee.

[80] The Revd C. M. Gough, Annual Letter 1909, repr. in *EAL 1909–10*, 502.

[81] Ibid. 501–2.

[82] Report of Miss E. M. Hall, quoted in *Proceedings of the CMS, 1905–6* (London, 1906), 193.

[83] Mr H. E. Clark, Annual Letter 1906, repr. in *EAL 1906–7* (London, 1907), 523.

[84] Ibid., Annual Letter 1908, repr. in *EAL 1908–9* (London, 1909), 339.

requiring back-up from village regulations however[85]), and the opening of Bishop Lefroy Training School in 1914 to train a basic class of village readers who would be able to run small Christian schools for boys while their wives taught the girls.[86] However, Clarkabad was not the only instance of the Christian village experiment inspiring heightened expectations of the mission–convert relationship.

The CMS village of Montgomerywala, established in the Jhang Bar (Chenab Colony) in 1898, had the trappings of a Christian penal colony, with many of its villagers sent there by missionaries for causing trouble in their old villages.[87] It represented an interesting test case for future Christian settlements since villagers' rights as tenants were granted directly by the Government,[88] meaning that Christian cultivators could—in the words of the CMS themselves—'renounce [their faith] and yet suffer no worldly loss'.[89] As early as 1902 villagers became unhappy with the local administration, furious that a European missionary rather than a local man had been appointed headman of the village (the familiar reason given by the CMS had been the 'unfitness of the people for the office').[90] Bateman was subjected to a barrage of insults on a visit to the village, while the life of the pastor Waris-ud-din (one of Bateman's early urban converts) was apparently in such danger that steps had to be taken to provide him with physical protection.

Religious services were boycotted and threats were made of conversion to Islam and Catholicism. The CMS response was once again a hail of indignant abuse. Holden sarcastically praised the villagers for their 'ingenuity and originality' in obstructing the normal life of the place, saying that the 'oft-repeated allegation that Chuhras are a dull-witted race' had been effectively dispelled.[91] Home was once again a reference point. Miss E. F. Fox described her work in Montgomerywala as 'much like slum-work in England transferred to Arcadian surroundings . . . there is the same dense ignorance, the same oppressing temptation to the indulgence of animal passions'.[92]

85 Mr H. E. Clark, Annual Letter 1910, repr. in *EAL 1909–10*, 502–3.

86 E. F. E. Wigram, 'The Christian Campaign in the Punjab', *CMR* 66/795 (July 1915), 415.

87 Whitehead, 'Bishop Whitehead in the Punjab', 479–80.

88 *Gazetteer of the Chenab Colony 1904*, 59.

89 *Proceedings of the CMS, 1898–9*, 217.

90 Report of the Revd T. Holden, repr. in *Proceedings of the CMS, 1902–3*, 238–9.

91 Ibid.

92 Miss E. F. Fox, Annual Letter 1909, repr. in *EAL 1909–10*, 504–5.

News of the upheaval in Montgomerywala even reached the Government, where it was attributed to the absence in the CMS's armoury this time round of the penalty of ejection from the village. The *Gazetteer* for 1912 wondered whether it was perhaps 'not altogether good for converts drawn usually from the lowest classes of society to be promoted to sudden affluence'.[93] It had certainly never been the Government's policy to risk such promotion. Holden too suggested that the new freedoms provided by the colonies were too much of an intoxicating experience for certain 'classes' of Christian, with unruly behaviour and few real loyalties the result.[94]

The news for the CMS was no better where socio-religious conformity was concerned. Although the social and ritual framework of the old villages had been removed, the drastic changes in lifestyle expected as a result had not materialized. In 1907 Holden discovered that 50 per cent of marriages among Christians in the Jhang Bar colonies were still being conducted according to non-Christian rites.[95] Miss A. W. Gross described her efforts to change converts' behaviour as a 'hand to hand fight with Satan'.[96] Village schools still struggled to attract interested pupils, and Holden reported in 1905 that a number of them had been forced to close owing to poor attendance.[97]

Even by 1913 Montgomerywala continued to have a bad reputation. At the time of a visit by the mass-movement expert and Bishop of Madras Henry Whitehead, the village was known for its high level of litigation among inhabitants. It was also under police surveillance and had only narrowly escaped 'punitive measures' in recent months. Whitehead, nevertheless, took a rather more optimistic view than most CMS missionaries of this unexpected and revealing dimension to the Christian village experiment, expressing admiration for the 'vigour' and the spirit of independence which he saw at Montgomerywala.[98]

[93] *Gazetteer of the Chenab Colony 1912* (Lahore, 1913), 60; the Revd T. Holden, Annual Letter 1905, repr. in *EAL 1905–6* (London, 1906), 211.

[94] The Revd T. Holden, Annual Letter 1905, 211.

[95] Ibid., Annual Letter 1908, repr. in *EAL 1907–8* (London, 1908), 442–3.

[96] Miss A. W. Gross, Annual Letter 1912, repr. in *EAL 1911–12* (London, 1912), 170.

[97] The Revd T. Holden, Annual Letter 1905, 211.

[98] Whitehead, 'Bishop Whitehead in the Punjab', 479–80.

MARYABAD

> It has its own presbytery, its little church and its priest . . . The entire population lives in the shadow of the church; the priest can take care of his school and the education of his students.
>
> (Fr. Marc, on the Catholic village of Franciscabad, 1925)

> Here too we find a presbytery and a chapel and a missionary-priest, but . . . we have to look for the Catholics in 181 villages, spread here and there over a distance of 2,000 miles. Hence the Father, instead of busying himself in a school, is continually on his bicycle and manages to visit his dispersed subjects two or three times per year. Needless to say, the education does not add up to much.
>
> (Fr. Marc, on the mission of Sargodha, near Franciscabad, 1925)

The Establishment of Maryabad

The official Capuchin version of the establishment of Maryabad was one of an oppressed people being set free from 'ruthless Muslim landlords', through the sacrifices of missionaries and the practical aid of the episcopate.[99] The village was planned with the example in mind of Chuhari village, in Bettiah (Bihar). Chuhari had been granted to the Capuchins in the 1760s as part of an indemnity settlement, following a war in the area, and had subsequently become what the Capuchins regarded as the model Christian village.[100]

In terms of territory, Maryabad was a comparatively modest undertaking. Early in 1892, at the first auction of land on the Rakh branch of Chenab Colony, the Bishop of Lahore (Mgr Van Den Bosch) had bought 645 acres in Mauza No. 3,[101] near the planned Jhang–Multan railway line.[102] This compared with nearly 2,000 acres for Clarkabad. It appears that the Capuchins preferred to buy the land rather than lease it, and regarded the price they paid as fair.[103] Nevertheless, a Government Colonization Officer had specifically recommended to the CMS *not* to

[99] Pelckmans, *Dix Années*, 77. [100] Rooney, *Into Deserts*, 59.

[101] *Gazetteer of the Chenab Colony 1904*, 59.

[102] Letter from Fr. Edouard to Provincial, 9 Mar. 1892, ABC, L91. [103] Ibid.

purchase canal colony land: 'I think you would be rather ill advised to buy what you have already got without payment, there being no further advantages to be secured by acquiry [*sic*] of proprietary rights in the land.'[104]

Maryabad's land was to remain in the hands of the diocese, with the village's Christians given the status of tenants of the Church. It lay in the recently colonized Hafizabad *tehsil* (Gujranwala district), around 40 miles north-west of Lahore, and was fed by the Lower Chenab Canal. The 1890s and 1900s were a period of large-scale migration to this area, particularly from Sialkot and Gujarat. Many migrants were from low-caste backgrounds, and although very large numbers of Chuhras in the district had converted to Christianity by 1935, those that did not live in Christian villages remained in the service of landowners. The *Gazetteer* for 1935 placed them in the '*sepi* Chuhra' category (see Chapter 1).[105] Gujranwala soon developed a comparatively high population density for Punjab (237 people per square mile by 1911, rising to 319 by 1935), but, as the last *tehsil* to be irrigated, Hafizabad's was relatively low (209 in 1911, rising to just 233 in 1935).[106]

Whereas the CMS preferred to emphasize the institutions, developments, and general progress in civility in their colonies, the Capuchins gave considerable space in their accounts of Maryabad to the bravery and sacrifices of both Christians and missionaries during the early years of the village. The Capuchins' description of the journey to Maryabad in January 1893 (see Introduction) featured the 'courageous pioneers' Frs Lievin and Engelbert and three Catholic families from Niki Daoki.

After six days of hard walking Fr. Lievin and company had arrived at the newly purchased land. Lievin and Engelbert stayed long enough only to share out the land among the three families, and then left. Two new missionaries, Fr. Felix and Fr. Desiree, were sent to the area three months later to begin actual construction of the village. Fr. Felix oversaw the establishment of a reliable water supply, to tackle the sickness that was already appearing among villagers.[107] Fig. 5.3 is a Capuchin plan of the village in its early years, showing a yard (A) and stables (B) for farm animals, the post office (C), a gate (D), some village housing (E), a police station (F), and a second village gate (G).

104 Copy of letter 1044 from the Colonization Officer to H. W. Weitbrecht, dated 18 Apr. 1901, ACMS, G2/I4/O 1901, n. 206.

105 *Gazetteer of Gujranwala District 1935* (Lahore, 1936), 160.

106 *Gazetteer of Gujranwala District 1912, Statistical Tables* (Lahore, 1913), p. vii; *Gazetteer of Gujranwala District 1935*, 43–4.

107 Rooney, *Into Deserts*, 61.

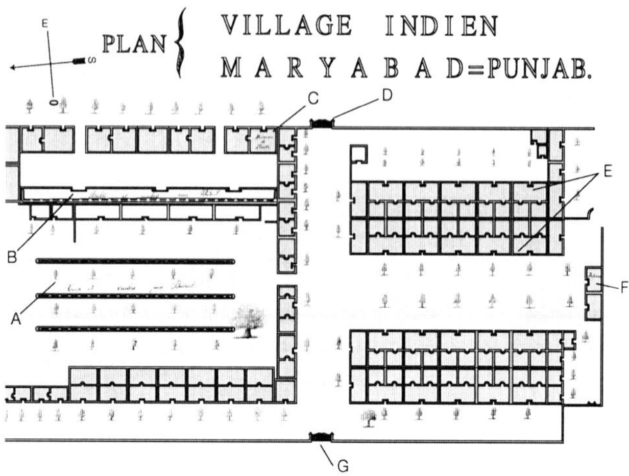

Fig. 5.3. Capuchin plan of Maryabad, *c.*1905. The letters A–G have been added for the purposes of this volume.

Source: ABC, 'Les Colonies Chrétiennes de Maryabad et Khushpur, fondées par les RR.PP. Capuchins de Belgique au Punjab', scrapbook

For a while the two missionaries had to stay in another village, several miles away. Vivid official accounts have them sleeping in a 'warehouse', obliged to use the same table for eating breakfast, for saying Mass, and for sleeping. They eventually had a small 'shack' built for them in Maryabad, but lived there for only a few weeks before being forced to return to Lahore in order to recover their health. Apart from its respectable Franciscan roots, this style of leadership had the further benefit of helping to underline the Capuchins' cherished distinction from Protestant missionaries, who, they claimed, would have been too busy with their families and with colonial hobnobbing to get their hands dirty with the villagers:

> Becoming everything to everyone [the Capuchin missionary] did not hesitate to go down into the ditch and guide the uncertain paths of his colonists. He took the axe in the same hand which served to manipulate the compass. And in turn [he became] farmer, artisan, engineer, doctor of the soul and of the body. Because his zeal extended to all these needs, he created a village full of activity where there had reigned for long years the silence of the deserts.[108]

108 Pelckmans, *Dix Années*, 90.

Although Maryabad undoubtedly represented a new direction for the Belgian Capuchin mission in Punjab, the missionaries themselves had ample experience in rural Belgium on which to draw. The Belgian countryside in this period saw a decisive shift away from wage labour and towards the ownership, by the rural poor, of small pieces of land. By the turn of the twentieth century only 35 per cent of agricultural workers were dependent wage labourers, a dramatic change that was eased (and controlled) via an interventionist role played by labourers' former employers and new educational institutions, helping them learn to manage their own land. Local governmental authorities even sponsored *agronomes* (expert lecturers) and mobile schools, supplying advice on agriculture, dairying, and domestic economy. While the schools stayed for an average of three months in a given area before moving on, the aim was for *agronomes* to be local to the area and well acquainted with the people.[109] Just as idealized rural Belgian parishes inspired missionaries like Fr. Marc, so the carefully managed progress of Belgium's rural poor offered a template for tutoring Catholic converts in Maryabad. A number of early infrastructural innovations in Maryabad bear this out, including the almost immediate establishment of cooperative storage houses.[110]

Life and Work in the Village

Non-Christian migrants soon joined Maryabad's first villagers, and together with Br. Constant (Fr. Felix's health still not having recovered), they began to prepare the land for cultivation. Br. Constant spent most of his time in the fields, directing villagers' work. He then brought Catholic colonists together every day in a chapel, 10 feet square, for catechism and recitation of the rosary. Nowhere in the sources is there any mention of assistance from Punjabi mission personnel at this early stage. Maryabad was considered blessed with a continual European presence, and Punjabi agency was a matter of pragmatism rather than policy in the mission.

Unfortunately, the land on which the village was built was bordered by marshes, and Constant quickly succumbed to malaria and severe dysentery. He was taken away to recover[111] and Fr. Felix returned to take over, carrying on Br. Constant's early work and superintending the construction of thirty-five small houses, each with three small rooms

[109] Rowntree, *Land and Labour*, 202–3, 219–22.

[110] Rooney, *Into Deserts*, 64.

[111] Br. Constant died a few years later in Sahowala.

(see Fig. 5.3, marked 'E').[112] The material for the houses—timber and baked brick—was produced in Maryabad, part of a conscientious drive for self-sufficiency that mirrored CMS efforts in Clarkabad.

The duties of superintendence were many, and the Capuchin vision of missionary example and leadership would have been tough for friars who genuinely aspired to it:

[The missionary] has to allot the land according to the needs and capacities of individual families; to distribute the water for irrigation; to watch that the land be properly tilled, and sown at the proper time; to determine the rotation of crops; to collect and store that part of the produce wherewith to pay the rent, rates and taxes [to the diocese]; to see that nothing be smuggled away or sold clandestinely; to watch the fluctuations of the market to enable the farmers to sell their crops when prices are high. Further, he has to deal with the Government officials of the different departments, and to protect his Christians against vexation, interference, or exaction on the part of pagan officials and others.[113]

Capuchin missionaries also took it upon themselves to guard against the range of 'problems' among converts with which they were already wearily familiar. These included falling victim to moneylenders, contracting debt for what the Capuchins described as 'vain demonstrations and luxurious entertainments on the occasions of weddings'. Friars also looked after the spending of village money on public works, including an infrastructure for sanitation. The locus of general authority lay (as it did less obviously but no less certainly in the case of the CMS) with the friars, who enjoyed 'magisterial powers'.[114]

The exact use to which these powers might be put is unclear, since no comparable document exists in the Capuchin archives to Bateman and Maconachie's Christian village manifesto. Capuchin sources refer only to the desire to replace old ways of 'theft and vice' (a popular and misleading blanket assessment of low-caste converts' previous sources of income and entertainment) with good, productive farming. Unsurprisingly, there were no moves towards self-government by converts.

Maryabad soon came to resemble other Catholic mission stations in Punjab, with a convent, dispensary, and school. The village was self-supporting by the end of the century, a feat achieved in half the time taken by Clarkabad and which included the upkeep of European missionaries and the maintenance of the school. This was thanks, in

[112] Pelckmans, *Dix Années*, 84.

[113] Ninove, *The Capuchin Mission in the Punjab*, 169.

[114] Ibid.

part, to the cultivation and export of cotton, whose crop in 1895 was said to be 'very beautiful' and worth around Rs 1,000.[115] (Cotton was a popular crop in Gujranwala district: by 1935, 42,195 acres of the district were under cotton cultivation.[116])

Although cotton brought cash into the village, Maryabad's economy continued to be based largely upon barter. In later years the Capuchins came to see this as having been a disadvantage, and new colonies were run on a cash basis where possible.[117] Following a famine in 1900, which filled all the orphanages of Lahore, fifty-one boys and fifteen girls were sent to Maryabad to help build up the future Catholic community. Orphanages for both boys and girls were established and put under the direction of Fr. Felix. Fifty-two more boys followed shortly afterwards, thirty-four of whom were baptized in December 1901.[118]

Aside from the practicalities of tending to the land and promoting economic self-sufficiency, the Capuchins were anxious that an exemplary sense of religious community should develop in Maryabad. To this end the village witnessed more than its fair share of episcopal visits and solemn ceremonies. The Bishop's visit in October 1896, during which he administered several baptisms and laid the foundation stone for the new church, was particularly significant for the new community. The ceremonies conducted during the visit were said to have 'succeeded marvellously in the eyes of our moved Christians and catechumens'.[119]

Maryabad's church, the 'jewel of the indigenous mission', was finally finished in 1898 (see Fig. 5.4). It had taken two years to build and was a major part of the drive to generate this sense of religious community and to 'stimulate a sense of the supernatural'.[120] It had cost Rs 10,500—three times that of the church at Montgomerywala, which housed twice as many people.[121] The building of the church, the purchase of an additional 500 acres of land in 1894 for Rs 25,000, and the 'regular relief' given to colonists in support of their farming efforts completely exhausted the funds of the mission.[122] Self-sufficiency had been purchased at an astonishingly high price.

[115] Letter from Fr. Edouard to Provincial, 9 Oct. 1895, ABC, L203.

[116] *Gazetteer of Gujranwala District 1935*, 133.

[117] Rooney, *Into Deserts*, 63.

[118] *Les Colonies Chrétiennes*, ABC.

[119] Pelckmans, *Dix Années*, 87. Only seven months later the Bishop appeared in Adah, to conduct a very similar ceremony.

[120] Ninove, *The Capuchin Mission in the Punjab*, 170. When Fr. Felix died, in 1932, he was buried in the grounds of the church.

[121] 'Church Building at Montgomerywalla, Jhang Bar, Lahore', 31 May 1901, ACMS, G2/I4/O 1901, n. 206.

[122] Ninove, *The Capuchin Mission in the Punjab*, 160.

Fig. 5.4. Interior of Maryabad church, 26 December 1923.

Source: ABC, Photographic Archive

Maryabad in the Twentieth Century

By the end of the nineteenth century Maryabad's population had risen to more than 500, and although it is not clear what proportion of new migrants during the 1890s were non-Christians (in 1895 the ratio of Christians to non-Christians in Maryabad was approximately 2:3[123]), the Capuchins clearly felt the need to enlist the help of other Catholic Orders. Early in the twentieth century Franciscan Sisters from Lyon arrived in the village, taking on the work of the girls' orphanage and school and giving catechism classes to the women of the village. The boys' orphanage was entrusted to a small group of German Franciscans, and was given the name of St Roch's Orphanage. The orphanage became a site for small industrial operations, the first of which was a carpet factory. A farm was established not long afterwards.[124] It is unclear why St Roch was chosen for the name of the orphanage. Roch was French, rather than German, did not lose his parents until he was around 20 years old, and, among a list of rather unglamorous patronages, including diseased cattle, skin rashes, cholera, and falsely accused people, there is nothing that would naturally link him to an orphanage.

The village survived a plague epidemic in 1904. While nearby villages were virtually wiped out, in Maryabad only eight people lost their lives: four Christians and four Muslims. By 1910 the village was thriving, with thirty-three families farming between 10 and 20 acres of land each. Wheat, sugar cane, and cotton were the main produce, and while the Capuchins shook their heads at the farmers' continued preference for the Indian over the European plough, they did not always interfere.[125]

Aside from the farmers there were various craftsmen in the village: carpenters, blacksmiths, tailors, cobblers, weavers, barbers, and washermen. Everyone took part in gathering the harvest when it was time to do so. Out of the harvest farmers had to pay two taxes to the Government—Land Tax (Rs 1/14/0 per acre in 1914) and Water Tax—as well as rent to the mission. Of the remaining produce farmers kept approximately 60 per cent for themselves and their families.[126]

Like Clarkabad, Maryabad became a model for new colonies in the early decades of the twentieth century. The Capuchins' thinking was similar to that of the Punjab administration: small groups of

123 Report of the Bishop of Lahore to the SCPF, 2 May 1895.

124 Rooney, *Into Deserts*, 78–9, 164–5.

125 Ibid. 166.

126 Ibid. 168.

dependable, capable farmers were the best guarantee of success in new lands. To this end veteran families from Maryabad were sent out to new colonies like Khushpur, Franciscabad, and Anthonyabad—all established by the time of the First World War. As had been the case with Montgomerywala, these new Catholic colonies were established on the basis of land mortgaged directly by Christian tenants from the Government. The same appeared to be true of most, if not all, grants of land made to mission groups after 1898, American and Scottish Presbyterians included.[127]

For new Catholic villages the diocese of Lahore mediated the arrangements, effectively acting as the Government's agent and tax collector. This offered a level of independence highly sought-after by colonists, and the inhabitants of Maryabad soon demanded equal treatment on the issue. The decision was eventually made, in the 1950s, that Maryabad should become a cooperative farm (the simple sale of land to tenants was ruled out because it was feared that only the good land would be bought and the diocese would be left with the rest).[128] Available sources offer no hint as to the level of anger in Maryabad over this decision, and the time taken to reach it—possibly because Maryabad had fewer missionary residents and visitors than a village like Clarkabad. The Capuchins may of course have wished to play down conflict in their prize colony, but this would be at odds with their sometimes painful candour where other difficulties in the mission were concerned.[129]

Documented problems in Catholic villages included a perilous consanguinity in marriages, since colonists had far fewer connections with surrounding villages than they had in their previous districts. The Capuchins' relatively liberal approach to economic self-sufficiency also began to backfire as richer families attempted to compete with, and acquire land from, smaller-scale farmers.[130] Finally, the First World War was extremely disruptive for the village. The Capuchins were cut off from their financial sources in Antwerp when Germany invaded Belgium, while two of their mission workers in Maryabad were interned by the British because of their German origin.[131]

The fact that both the CMS and the Capuchins went on to establish a number of other villages in the wake of Clarkabad and Maryabad,

[127] *Gazetteer of the Chenab Colony 1904*, 59.

[128] Rooney, *Into Deserts*, 113–14.

[129] The archives of the auxiliary French and German missions mentioned above fall outside the scope of this book, but would merit future investigation.

[130] Ibid. 67.

[131] Ibid. 78–9.

despite the heavy initial costs and with the apparently willing participation of new 'pioneer' villagers, suggests early success in the colonies and a degree of optimism among CMS and Capuchin missionaries. Major logistical problems (principally of convert dispersal across wide areas) could effectively be solved in this way, and large numbers of low-caste Punjabis who had previously been locked into exploitative socio-economic relationships were acquiring new skills as labourers and as industrial workers in a variety of potentially lucrative trades and professions.

And yet the Christian village experiment was, in social terms, far less ambitious than it might have been—particularly in the lack of autonomy granted to Punjabi Christian farmers. Missions seemed unable to divest themselves of notions of paternal responsibility, or to move beyond the formation of their approach to mission in the domestic British and Belgian contexts. For the CMS in particular, at times of crisis in their Christian villages the socio-religious critique and inculturative efforts which they were developing elsewhere in India faded into the background and this domestic formation moved to the fore, providing familiar ideological support and a practical template for action.

With large amounts of European money being spent and a low initial base of education and vocational skills among converts, it was inevitable that a certain amount of leadership would rest with the missions. Yet the European vision for the ideal Christian community was comprehensive to the point of suffocation, both in its detail and in its implementation: only semi-democratic CMS bodies, heroic and all-powerful Capuchin missionaries, and a variety of economic, social, moral, and psychological sanctions employed by both missions. Many of the sources of Punjabi input into rural Christianity seen in Chapter 4 were suppressed, with no new avenues for creative contribution opening up in their place. Villagers who raised objections to this state of affairs, or who continued in their 'old ways', were subject to attacks from mission personnel more severe than those aimed at smaller Christian communities across the province. Such was the missions' view of colonists—which they shared with the Punjab Government—as a highly privileged group who ought to know better. The broad implications for the mission–convert relationship of this Christian village experiment are explored in the concluding chapter.

Conclusion

THE modest six-day migration made across Punjab in 1893 by a small company of local families and Capuchin friars was dwarfed half a century later by the millions of people forced to pass through similar terrain at Partition, on longer and very much more dangerous journeys. As endless convoys of Hindu and Sikh families worked their way east and their Muslim former compatriots travelled west, some in the village of Clarkabad—situated just over the new border in Pakistan—helped to feed and shelter migrants passing through while others were driven into the church and onto their knees by the sight of dead bodies floating down the Upper Bari Doab canal.[1]

Many rural Christians in Pakistan were soon packed up and on the move again themselves. The replacement of 4 million emigrant Hindus and Sikhs with 6 million incoming Muslims, many of them poor and in search of work, led to a fall in demand for casual agricultural labour and an unprecedented pressure on land, forcing large numbers of Christians out of their villages and into the towns. The grassroots Punjabi Christian communities which had been born in pre-Partition Punjab and were yet to take a shape that either converts or missions could call stable or satisfactory were now, many of them, broken up. Small improvised urban communities (*bastis*) developed instead, only to be dispersed yet again when homes were demolished to make way for new buildings.[2]

These shifting urban groupings in Pakistan were a long way from the first missionary blueprints for future Christian communities, but

[1] Punjab–UK interviews, Lawrence Benjamin, 21 May 2007. 'I saw that myself,' recalls Lawrence Benjamin. 'I was eight years of age. It was a horrible time, I remember it very well. People used to spend a lot of time in the church, worrying about what might happen. But thank God Clarkabad was safe' (ibid.). John Webster has noted the extent to which a certain communal neutrality in this period allowed Christians to play a role as mediators and sources of support for refugees. See Webster, *A Social History of Christianity*, 275–8.

[2] Rooney, *Into Deserts*, 99; Bishop of Lahore (Anglican), 'The Rural Church in West Pakistan', *East and West*, 19 (Jan. 1953), 22–3.

now perhaps more than ever converts drew close to Punjabi and (what remained of) European mission-Church personnel for security and a sense of continuity. Where forced migration pushed Protestants out of the reach of their old denominations, there were conversions to Catholicism. Vulnerable Sikhs too became Christians or Muslims amid the uncertain religious politics of the new nation.

At the same time, contributions from Protestant congregations in Europe and America were falling, even as optimistic moves gathered pace towards the formation of multi-denominational Churches of south India (1947), north India (1970), and Pakistan (1970). A series of earthquakes and floods further added to the uncertainty already created by dislocation from old jobs and communities and a deterioration in financial support. The peasant priesthood envisaged by missionaries like Hall, and the industrial skills promoted by both Capuchin and CMS missions as economic back-up in times of trial, failed to materialize on the necessary scale. A report by the Anglican Bishop of Lahore in the early 1950s suggested that only in the Christian villages had anything like a 'settled Christian life' been established: in six Anglican villages 10,000 people were housed and 2,000 children were receiving a regular education in day or boarding schools. New catechists and pastors were in training.[3]

Yet even these Christian villages were vulnerable. Maryabad—situated, like Clarkabad, inside Pakistani territory (see Fig. C.1)—recovered from the floods of the early 1950s only to find the developed world's preference for man-made fibres over cotton starting to jeopardize one of her main export staples,[4] while those able to take advantage of the basic education which they had received to find employment as domestic staff or factory workers were in the minority.[5]

The manner in which so many rural Christians were buffeted by the aspirations of others in the late 1940s—from Indian, Pakistani, and British political leaders and officials to the millions of ordinary people forced to compete for jobs, land, and other scarce resources—serves as a reminder that ambitions are rarely pursued in a vacuum. This was particularly true of the pivotal local relationships which developed in Punjab between oppressed rural Punjabis and foreign Christian missions, and which have been the focus of this book. Here, the aspirations of

[3] Ibid. 22–5. [4] Rooney, *Into Deserts*, 108.

[5] Report of the Belgian Capuchin Mission at Lahore, Pakistan, 1952–1953, GACO. See O'Brien, *The Construction of Pakistani Christian Identity*, 586–9.

Fig. C.1. The grotto at Maryabad, *c.*1950.
Source: ABC, Photographic Archive

both sides necessitated the making of extensive demands upon the other. As this became clearer over time, what all concerned had first hoped would be a relationship of mutual cooperation and benefit became instead a tug-of-war over deeply rooted and barely compatible visions of the future.

Popular unrest in Clarkabad and Montgomerywala in the first decade of the twentieth century and the fury that lay behind CMS personnel's language in response—of a different order from that usually deployed either in private or in public—revealed the precipice to which the Christian village experiment in particular pushed the mission–convert relationship. Powerful latent anger in the CMS, at the failure of early rural converts across the mission to appreciate the opportunities being laid before them, was finally released as what missionaries regarded as their extraordinary generosity in their Christian villages was thrown back at them. Referring to Montgomerywala's troubles in 1902–3, Holden complained that 'the whole affair has rudely shaken one's faith in the sincerity of even the best—for these are considered the cream—of this class of Christian'.[6] Given that the CMS had set out hoping to inculcate a sense of close Christian interdependence and partnership in their Clarkabad villagers—as a demonstration of the kind of relationships Christian conversion implied—it is hard to imagine them taking a more retrograde step than launching legal action to expel people from their midst. Events like these support the suggestion made in Chapter 4 that convert expectations of their association with Christian missions were flexible rather than uniform: as with other village relationships, the terms would evolve over time and gradually take on an agreed form. Whereas in most parts of central Punjab converts did not press mission personnel for land but instead lobbied occasionally for work, food, legal representation, or letter-writing, some converts in Clarkabad clearly saw the potential for the mission–convert relationship to stretch much further.

From the evidence presented in this volume, two dimensions to convert aspirations for religious transformation can be suggested. Firstly, conversion movements across the province were driven by a general anticipation, based in rural low-caste groups' understanding of themselves as a distinct local community, of a relative enhancement in their independence and status, in ways that defy attempts to separate the

[6] Report of the Revd T. Holden, repr. in *Proceedings of the CMS, 1902–3*, 238–9.

social from the supernal. This was shaped by a paradigm of village interdependence and intra-village relationships which withstood mission efforts to implant an alternative sense of Christian community and international connectedness. The insights provided by radical low-caste subaltern religious culture, comments recorded by the likes of Sir Malcolm Darling ('God has saved us from [landlord] power') and the contests which characterized post-conversion community-building all point to the desire for a reconfiguration of local intra-village relationships rather than an escape from them, or fundamental remaking of them. Converts sought continued participation in the village community once their relationship with Christianity had been established, but now on terms sufficiently altered that it pushed dominant villagers to violence, vandalism, and legal action. This combination of self-determination and the expectation of 'salvation' from without represented a challenge and a potential source of confusion for the Christian missions, as it did also for all those—Indian and non-Indian alike—interested in social uplift among low-caste communities and the rural poor in general.

Secondly, there appeared to be concrete and detailed aspirations among certain groups of converts, which varied at the local level—a combined function of circumstances, the promises of influential individuals, and the experiences of Christian conversion which were communicated by ordinary converts to non-converts through family networks. These latter two key processes of 'informal agency', as I have referred to them, were recognized in both the CMS and the Capuchin missions. In Tarn Taran and elsewhere, local leaders of the sort found in other missions in Punjab by scholars like John Webster were gratefully embraced by missionaries for their advocacy of Christianity.[7] Tota of Khanpur was an example of a leader capable of urging changes of custom or behaviour upon people throughout extended kin networks, spanning several villages.

As the CMS and Capuchins quickly learned, however, this local leadership was a dynamic not easily manipulated or harnessed. Missionaries in both camps went through the distressing experience of seeing their efforts unravel as groups of converts disappeared into the arms of another mission. Elsewhere these local leaders were vilified for raising and distorting expectations among converts; such appear to have been the 'bad characters' in Clarkabad who had encouraged social rebellion and whom missionaries were anxious to remove.

[7] See e.g. Webster, *A History of the Dalit Christians in India*.

The attitude taken to these leaders by local landlords reasonably well placed to understand the dynamics of low-caste decision-making, despite their clear lack of sympathy, underlines the significance of this kind of leadership. Where landlords sought to demonstrate their opposition to Christian conversion, local leaders were among the targets that they chose. Tota himself was robbed, his wife threatened, and his house broken into. The timing of villager reactions suggests that converts may well have dated their commitment to the missions from early contacts—perhaps even from the very first meeting—rather than from a point, such as approval for baptism or baptism itself, that missionaries might more readily have recognized.

There are important details missing here, of course, which even the closest comparative reading of missionary sources cannot provide and for which there is little in the way of alternative source material. Firstly, the tiny ratio of documented descriptions of informal agency to actual conversions invites caution. How common were the forms of informal agency discovered in this book, and how many others went unrecorded by missionaries, is impossible to say. Secondly, as is most likely, did these leaders embody or pander to aspirations that already existed among ordinary people when it came to spreading information about Christianity and persuading people to convert? Or were they perhaps more isolated and creative in their thinking, in which case what were the thought processes through which they went on their way to advocating Christian conversion?

The difference made by personality among Punjabi leaders and other informal agents of Christianity is also difficult to assess. This is all the more frustrating since evidence from African, Pacific, and other mission contexts—as well as the experience of Lawrence Benjamin's paternal grandfather Milad Masih, who worked independently and unpaid as a Christian preacher—suggests that personal and idiomatically sound testimony regarding the transformative effect of Christian conversion was absolutely key to the efficacy of informal agency.[8]

Everyday family interactions were another crucial aspect of informal agency in the spread of interest in Christianity. A humbling experience at the hands of a newly supercilious Christian relative might provide an inducement to inquiry, as might a desire to marry into a Christian family—in some areas because non-Christian marriage partners were increasingly hard to find as the conversion movements gathered pace.

[8] Punjab–UK interviews, Lawrence Benjamin, 21 May 2007.

Marriages between Christians and non-Christians could also be a catalyst for change, with a daughter-in-law acting as an evangelist in her new home.

Where does this leave questions of individual versus group meaning in conversion? Evidence gathered for this book from CMS and Capuchin experiences, together with anecdotal evidence gathered from interviews conducted in Indian Punjab and in the United Kingdom, suggests a balance of the two. Converts perceived a step up, in social terms, for those who converted, partly at the expense of extended-family members who did not. As an individual, too, the brightening of future prospects carried clear meaning. A pattern which emerged during conversations with rural converts and descendants of mass-movement converts in Indian Punjab was of a gradual evolution in individuals' impressions about where the ultimate source of improved conditions of life might lie. Dayal Masih, of Sayekar village near Jalandhar, remembered that his father, a low-caste convert from Sikhism, had been struck by the concern shown for him and his community by an American missionary who called village labourers together, distributed bread and milk powder, and gave a religious talk. The revolutionary experience of receiving consideration at the hands of an outside power under the noses of higher-caste villagers was the first part of a consciousness of Christianity that later turned to private questions about what Jesus might be doing for him.[9] These are informal findings, and a systematic approach to the use of oral history in this area might well yield new and useful hypotheses.

European Christian mission had always been concerned with the export of an entire system of life, carrying as its message not merely the life-changing news implicit in the gospel but also an explicit blueprint of how a changed life should be led. CMS and Capuchin missionaries in Punjab, cognizant of their position as heirs to this long tradition, pursued modern, updated forms of this blueprint with the aid of new technologies of public influence—from mass education to various forms of media—which were already being deployed in the context of ideological struggles in their home countries. In England, Church and state skirmished for control of institutional education, while Evangelicals and concerned citizens took to urban slums and rural backwaters in an uplift drive that marked a fresh stage in their struggle for self-definition,

[9] Punjab–UK interviews, Dayal Masih, 31 Jan. 2003.

both as socio-economic leaders and as Christians. In Belgium the 'great war' that was supposedly being waged against the Catholic Church[10] galvanized members of religious Orders into fighting liberal and socialist influence in trade unions, primary schools, and orphanages.

It would be wrong to suggest that charitable work was taken up in a more cynical manner in this period than in any other, yet such was the recognized power of arenas like education and health care that, once one group entered them, others were forced to follow suit. Combative self-definition via these modern channels, whether religious, cultural, or political, soon became a fact of life in urban and rural Punjab as it had in Europe. The Ninth Principle of the Arya Samaj—'the welfare of the individual should be regarded as contained within the welfare of all'—epitomized the same spirit of rival ideological groups contesting alternative futures which characterized the Europe of CMS and Capuchin missionaries' birth and the Punjab of their evangelistic aspirations.

However, no methodological concord between CMS and Capuchin missionaries could ever have obscured the fundamentally differing conceptions of Christianity and mission work revealed in this book, from Catholic culture's emphasis upon filial loyalty to the institution of 'Mother' Church and the sacramental saving of souls to British Evangelicalism's concentration upon an individual's transforming response to the Word of God, in which the agency of an established Church was far less direct. Catholicism presented itself as solemnly ritualistic, with an image of awe-inspiring churches and simple, single friars and nuns: uniformed, disciplined, and dominant. The renunciation of the world and disdain for its standards that lent aspects of Catholicism a certain gravitas and counter-cultural mystique in nineteenth-century Belgium carried over to Punjab: in architecture, music, and ceremony. In contrast, the CMS's embrace of a particularly conducive colonial context was exemplified by the joint rural tours undertaken by the missionary and the ICS officer: Rowland Bateman and his future biographer James Maconachie.

It was in the details of the precise journey which these missions hoped to see converts make, away from their old lives and towards membership of a genuinely Christian society, that the distinct systems of Christian life embodied in the CMS and the Capuchin missions were brought most clearly to the fore. In particular, the

[10] *Syllabus of Errors*, attached to Pius IX, *Quanta Cura*, 8 Dec. 1864 (Vatican, 1864).

post-conversion community-building process highlighted contrasting expectations between missions and converts, between the CMS and the Capuchins, and also a variety of fissures within the CMS and Capuchin missions, over matters of authority, control, and strategic emphasis within the mission-Churches. The CMS was made up of three European components: the Society in London, the episcopate in Punjab, and the missionaries themselves. All operated under differing sets of pressures and rarely assessed their priorities in the same way. The Society Headquarters in London was committed to Venn's three 'self's—sufficiency, government, and extension—yet was required to reassure British donors that their money was being responsibly and accountably spent. It also retained a certain pride in its history and achievements, and was slow to cede influence to indigenous episcopates, whether or not they were run by Europeans.

In addition, both the CMS and its missionaries harboured long-standing Low Church suspicions of the episcopate, which most frequently surfaced where a Bishop of Lahore was perceived to take greater interest in Eurasian congregations and the institutions of the established Church than in rural Punjabis, who were of little socio-economic or intellectual interest. The Capuchin mission was characterized by similar fissures between the bishop and Council on the one hand and a self-ascribed 'indigenous mission' on the other. The latter group viewed the Regular Superior as their hero, while the Provincial could also usually be relied upon to support 'my missionaries', as he referred to them.

In both missions, scarce resources rendered gradations of commitment so crucial that personality and policy differences were often magnified. In the CMS mission Mian Sadiq, Bateman, and Guilford struggled to make the case for rural evangelization, over and above the urban middle-class missions preferred by French and Clark. Among the Capuchins the perception clearly existed that not everyone who had been sent to Punjab was suited to the work; Fr. Gonsalve was ostracized during his short tenure as Regular Superior, in contrast to Fr. Marc, who was almost idolized. Fr. Sigismond emerged as the champion of Punjabi agency when it appeared that many other friars shared his objections to the closure of the Adah catechists' school but had been afraid to speak out.

Traditions endured on all sides of the convert–mission encounter. Convert aspirations continued to evolve via the language and logic of village mutuality, with progress pegged against the socio-religious status of other local groups rather than against any missionary blueprint. In the

CMS and Capuchin missions, two particular sets of pressures emerged in the twentieth century: shifting cultural and ecclesiastical attitudes in Europe, and the emerging shape of rural Punjabi Christianity.

In the 1920s and 1930s, with European chauvinism having taken a knock from both the carnage of a four-year civil war and the ebbing of empire in some areas of the world, policy-makers in Europe were keen to establish a greater balance in relationships between European missionaries and Indian mission-Church personnel and converts. The Protestant missionary movement and the Catholic Church showed signs of sharing in the surge of conscience, idealism, and attention to the aspirations of all peoples that marked the early 1920s—most powerfully expressed by the US President Woodrow Wilson. CMS and Capuchin leaders too experienced something of a 'Wilsonian moment',[11] centred upon recognizing the moral as well as the pragmatic case for urgently promoting local leadership of new Churches.

This was not intended as a boost for nationalism, anti-colonial or otherwise. The CMS was at pains to emphasize an international Christian community, above nations as it was above denominations. Under Popes Benedict XV and Pius XI the Catholic Church, too, openly sought to subvert the secular hierarchies that drew people into a language of race and nation, in favour of a single, divinely instituted system of authority next to which all others were either tributaries or temporary aberrations. The pursuit of this grand, apostolic status in Asia, Africa, and South America—regions that the Catholic Church hoped might escape the weary cynicism of Europe—was a hallmark of many of the pontificates of the twentieth century, not least that of John Paul II.

On the ground in rural Punjab, however, the only sense in which the changing world around them seemed to influence their work was in intensifying missionaries' sense of urgency—almost a last-minute rush to install 'genuine' forms of Christianity while they still had time. The gloomy words of India's Viceroy in 1946 expressed not just the Government's anxieties but also those of men and women hoping to plant two very different forms of European Christianity in the soil of Punjab: 'Our time . . . is limited and our power to control events almost gone.' Theology and international politics were not pitting time against the Capuchins in quite the way that they were for the CMS (a global Catholic

[11] See Erez Manela, *The Wilsonian Moment: Self-Determination and the International Origins of Anti-Colonial Nationalism* (Oxford, 2007). Due apologies to Manela for the slightly altered sense in which 'moment' is used here.

hierarchy ensured that foreign stewardship of Punjabi Catholicism in the next generation would be no more a contradiction than it was in the present one) but future prospects for all were highly uncertain.

This failure of many CMS and Capuchin missionaries in the province to be moved by new policies coming out of Europe in part echoed a dynamic at work in the Indian Civil Service: people serving for long years in India lost touch with shifting attitudes at home in Europe. It also reflected a general notion among CMS and Capuchin missionaries that in the people they encountered in Punjab and the relationships they formed there was essentially nothing new—nothing they had not seen already among the rural poor of Europe. When, for instance, Bateman complained that CMS missionaries were 'kicking at closed doors' in Punjab, he was hinting at a misdirection of scarce resources—towards urban instead of rural areas—rather than a more fundamental problem with the CMS approach. The CMS, like the Capuchins, saw themselves as armed appropriately for their struggle in India and so thought that their strategies did not require significant modification beyond concessions to local forms of entertainment, music, and storytelling. These latter were all devices for transmitting a message rather than facilitating the interested, reciprocal engagement with their general predicament which converts sought. Missionaries' failure here meant that they were seen only in fairly distanced terms as local allies, forfeiting the intimacy and legitimacy among converts which the fulfilment of missionary ambitions required.

Missionaries were able to spend no more than a few short hours every few months with any one group of converts. Given the ideological significance of active itineration for missionaries and the pivotal importance of presentation and perception in the mission–convert relationship, it remains the supreme irony of the conversion movements that there was so little direct, effective communication between European missionaries and rural Punjabis. Yet even these few encounters were used solely to push home an evangelistic message—often with little success in achieving an understanding even of the basics of the gospel message, let alone how these basics related to all the innovations in village life which missionaries sought to promote. Genuine concern for people during periods of extreme difficulty, including times of famine, is evident in private missionary correspondence, but few missionaries saw it as a legitimate use of their time to look critically at converts' position in the village economy or to plead their cause with those government officials whom some missionaries counted among their friends.

This same attitude was revealed in the way that the formal agents of mission, such as catechists, were trained carefully to be the mouthpiece of the missions—instruments of policy rather than information-gatherers or a genuinely flexible cultural and religious conduit. In the CMS and Capuchin missions at least, the result seems to have been a fatal blow to the legitimacy of catechists. Missionaries did not hold the social backgrounds from which rural catechists came in particularly high esteem; they insisted on strict theological conformity—not least because of the danger of contamination in a province suffering denominational overcrowding—and they offered little autonomy. Yet they complained at the same time that catechists lacked initiative and had constantly to be 'shepherded'. Except where local community leaders went on to become catechists, villagers too appear to have looked down their noses at catechists as men whose employment prospects were sufficiently poor that they had surrendered themselves to become the 'missionary's hack'. In any case, many converts saw catechists less as teachers than as advocates for them in the local community, capable of manipulation.

Here, as elsewhere, however, the sheer diversity of the missionary approach in Punjab revealed itself. Within the CMS, attitudes towards catechists and clergy varied from French's desire that his Divinity School give 'the choicest minds' the 'finest polish possible' to Bomford's concern that catechists trained in this way would lack Evangelical fire. In the Capuchin mission Fr. Sigismond saw a key role for catechists in the Punjab countryside, but some of his senior colleagues could not see the point, while others were insufficiently interested or courageous to support him.

The picture of the catechist which emerges in this book is therefore not the pivotal and creative socio-religious interpreter that might have been, but instead someone whose first priority was to hold on to his employment—a job rather than a vocation—in an environment where missionaries demanded a tireless, conformist slog and a love of the work, and where converts might court the catechists of other denominations if their concerns and wishes were not addressed. If personality counted for much in the missions, and there was always a significant range of opinion, then there is no reason why the same might not have been true for catechists. This is another area where further research might clarify the situation—if a sound methodological approach can be devised—perhaps contributing to the sketching out of a true spectrum of thought and identity among catechists.

Confidence in imported European ways of working, and the rather limited role envisaged for catechists (not to mention the small amount of information recorded about them), fit together, in both the Capuchin and the CMS missions, with a language of 'resistance' and 'intransigence' used to describe rural converts. This kind of vocabulary betrayed a strong tendency among European missionaries as well as some Punjabi members of the PNCC towards discussing rural Punjabi converts in collective terms, complete with talk of 'types' and other similarly crude general characterizations. This contrasted sharply with the attention lavished by CMS missionaries like Bateman upon the few educated urbanites such as Waris-ud-din and Jalaluddin Ambar who showed signs of interest in Christianity.[12]

Belgian Capuchins too showed signs of making this general distinction, not of 'rural' versus 'urban' but along lines of class and education. Such considerations seem to have been uppermost in missionary minds both because they marked converts out from many other villagers and because they were a natural dimension of the analogies with the European rural poor which underlay missionary thinking in Punjab. Only where missionaries felt themselves to be dealing with Punjabis closer to their own social and educational status did race instead quickly come to play a more central role in their thinking and rhetoric, as an ultimate guarantee of European superiority in mission-Church leadership. The fact that some Capuchin friars scorned and lamented the Bishop of Lahore's focus upon elite schools was not a reflection of a socially egalitarian sensibility but stemmed rather from the feeling that winning a handful of middle-class souls would be less of a heroic achievement than ushering thousands of lower-class ones into the Catholic fold. When an Anglo-vernacular school was opened in Dalwal—'primarily to make conversions among higher classes than our current Christians, and to get through more to the educated classes'—few doubted that Catholic conversions made there would be more 'solid' than those made among village labourers.[13]

From the tone of friars' letters it seemed that the demands made by the Capuchin charism, successive modern popes, and early Christianity itself to 'go among the poor' weighed all the more heavily because of the sheer loneliness of lacking educated company. So too for the missionaries of the CMS: for all his urgency in advocating a rural mission, Bateman

[12] See Ch. 2.

[13] Letter from Frs Edouard, Fabian, and Felix to Provincial, 7 Oct. 1900, ABC, L315.

clearly found himself able to relate to individuals like Waris-ud-din in a way that was not possible among rural converts in Clarkabad. In the latter context Bateman appeared less the cultured and subtle father figure to the spiritually curious, and more the boarding-school master resorting to the blunt and indirect pedagogy appropriate for the as yet unreflective.

The Capuchins and the CMS shared a concern that the phenomenon of caste might mean slow evangelistic progress if Christianity came to be seen as a religion for those of low birth. But missionaries in both camps were good modern Europeans at heart, and they believed in education and the possibility of improvement above almost everything else. They expected no more in the way of meaningful connections with individual rural converts in Punjab than they did in the course of pastoral work with the rural poor in Europe; even less so, in fact, given the barrier created by language. Such circumstances, combined with the sheer scale of conversions and the missionary focus upon the present and future rather than converts' pasts, go some way to explaining why missionaries were occasionally reduced to demonstrations of brute force, including the physical destruction of charms and shrines. Nor should it be surprising that CMS and Capuchin missionary observers mistook for 'ignorance' and 'ridiculous customs' what has been shown over the course of this book to have been a great openness to new ideas among rural peoples in Punjab—albeit not one that implied the kind of abandonment to Christian spirituality and values for which the CMS and Capuchins hoped.

The Capuchins and the CMS eventually formulated separate routes out of their difficulties in Punjab. The CMS's strategy was clearly discernible in the writing of personnel such as Richards, Hall, Guilford, and Hares: convert impulses that related to bettering their social and physical conditions ought to be seen as a positive sign of a desire for self-improvement, the highest stage of which would inevitably be the leading of a Christian life. The CMS should commit itself to programmes of rural uplift, based upon a simple religious, literary, and vocational education and facilitated by an expanded cadre of Indian agents and a period of tutelage in Church self-government.

This emphasis upon education and participation, for converts and catechumens of all ages, stemmed in part from the theological difficulty for the CMS in accepting a generational argument like the one put forward by the Capuchins. The transforming Word of God, once it was made linguistically and conceptually intelligible, should work its way into the heart of its hearer and, albeit perhaps gradually, effect a clear change in that individual. This was why CMS missionaries always seemed to be trying to offload pastoral and bureaucratic responsibilities: to render them free as itinerating instruments of this transformation, whether in the intellectual style of Thomas Valpy French, the grassroots *shikar karna* of Rowland Bateman, or the simple, down-to-earth idiom endorsed by Edward Guilford.[14]

The Capuchins generally tended towards an acceptance that the convert generation would never become more than 'imperfect Christians', and put most of their available resources into forming converts' children as the responsible Christian parents of the next generation. Immediate individual responses to the gospel were of comparatively little concern, while the Catholic doctrine of purgatory allowed missionaries to delay adult baptism until the moments before death, thereby lessening converts' suffering in the afterlife as far as possible. Nor was there the need to train converts as lay functionaries of a self-governing Church, or to worry in the short term about raising Punjabis to the priesthood. The mission was considered so young and so lacking in resources that few suitable candidates were thought likely to emerge from a struggling Catholic primary-education system in the foreseeable future.

Instead, the Capuchins looked forward, in future decades, to a 'perfect moral union' of school, family, and Church. They struggled against government restrictions, Protestant competition, and episcopal reticence to expand their network of culturally safe primary and secondary schools, while investing relatively large sums of money in orphanages as the surrogate family environments for the super-Catholics of tomorrow. Belgian experience was very much in evidence in all of these endeavours, as it was in the establishment of industrial schools to help ensure socio-economic independence as the bedrock of the future Catholic community.

In the end, however, neither mission managed to solve the deeper contradictions upon which the local relationships which drove the mass conversion movements were based. Neither mission tapped successfully into the low-caste socio-economic perspectives which the evidence of Chapters 1 and 2 suggested would be crucial to their success. This

[14] The belief was expressed by Bomford that missionaries should be freed of the task even of *training* people for these mundane responsibilities. 'Let the Bishop do it' was his view. See Ch. 5.

was due not to an inherent conservatism among missionaries—despite their upbringing in an environment of all-encompassing ideological competition—but rather to a basic conviction that the people who forced themselves upon the missions in this period were cultureless as well as helpless. Where, among converts, there was subtlety in social and spiritual awareness, an understandable taste for independence and economic security, and a great deal of courage and socio-religious creativity, the missions too often saw only poverty, physical and spiritual. The result was that except where events took the revealingly confrontational turn that they did in Clarkabad or Montgomerywala, the early years of post-conversion community-building were characterized by a slow and painful war of cultural attrition, with few concessions made by either side but instead a low-level, enduring, general optimism—expressed most clearly by the Capuchins in terms of 'future generations'.

The accomplishments of the Christian villages should not be downplayed. But if villagers failed, in CMS and Capuchin eyes, to grasp the concept of self-sufficiency or to develop self-respect, then it is worth asking why imported mission ideas were not fundamentally rethought when the context of Christian colonies presented a unique opportunity for doing so. The chance was missed. Far from being the 'peculiarly Eastern' affair to which C. F. Andrews referred, the CMS and Capuchin Christian village experiment might instead be described as peculiarly European.

From early mission–convert encounters, through the difficult and uneven creation of Punjabi Christian communities, to the unique highs and lows of the Christian village experiment, a very great deal had clearly been governed by the internal complexities of three broad systems of life: the rural Punjabi, the British Evangelical, and the Belgian Catholic. This, then, was 'religious transformation' in rural Punjab around the turn of the twentieth century: the coming together of entire models of individual being and of corporate society, communicated and contested in idioms of opportunity, security, conversion, religious commitment, and behaviour. From the constituent parts of two mission Christianities never torn from their European roots, converts refashioned their socio-religious identity. It was not yet everything to which they aspired, but it was to remain distinctively theirs through many more years of migration and hardship to come.

APPENDIX

Capuchin Missionaries Arriving in and Leaving Punjab, 1889–1930[1]

French- and Flemish-language sources render Belgian Capuchin names slightly differently, in terms of both spelling and the use of accents. In places, Latin versions of Capuchin names are also given. For the sake of simplicity this book uses the Flemish versions where possible.

ARRIVED IN 1889

Fr. Symphorien (Mouard) (b. 1828; o. ?; d. 1890)
Fr. Emmanuel (Van Den Bosch) (b. 1854; o. 1879)
Fr. Godefride (Pelckmans) (b. 1854; o. 1878)
Fr. Fabian (Eestermans) (b. 1858; o. 1883)
Fr. Lievin (b. 1851; o. 1886)
Fr. Engelbert (b. 1859; o. 1886)
Br. Felix (b. 1868; o. 1891)
Br. Leo[2] (b. 1862; o. 1890)
Br. Arsene (b. 1864; o. 1890)
Br. Edmund (b. 1865; o. 1891)
Br. Leopold (b. 1866; o. 1891)
Fr. Desiree (b. 1861; o. 1885)
Fr. Antoine (b. 1863; o. 1837)
Br. Theodore (b. 1866; o. 1891)
Br. Constant (b. 1859)

[1] Stan Teuns, *Historische Ledenlijst Minderbroeders-Kapucijnen, 1802–1995* (Sint-Truiden, 1996); Blondeel, *In Het Land Der Vijf Rivieren.* No figures are given for 1890 since there were no changes in mission personnel during that year. The Latin version of each person's name is used (as is common in official Capuchin documents) except where private correspondence has provided an alternative.

o. = ordained to the priesthood; j. = left Antwerp to join the Punjab mission; r. = returned to Belgium; a. = appointed Archbishop of Agra. The names given in parentheses are the surnames of those friars who at some point became Bishop of Lahore, since bishops were frequently referred to in the form Monsignor [surname].

[2] Br. Leo was Leo van Ninove, the author of *The Capuchin Mission in the Punjab: With Notes on the History, Geography, Ethnology and Religions of the Country* (Mangalore, 1910).

Br. Paul (b. 1851)
Br. Ivo (b. 1861)
Br. Martin (b. 1862)
Br. Ferdinand (b. 1860)

ARRIVED IN 1891–1900

Fr. Rochus (b. 1869; o. ?; j. 1891)
Fr. Edouard (b. 1850; o. 1874; j. 1891)
Br. Joachim (b. 1865; j. 1891)
Fr. Peter (b. 1864; j. 1891; o. 1892)
Fr. Daniel (b. 1863; j. 1891; o. 1892)
Fr. Vincent (b. 1870; j. 1891; o. 1893)
Br. Maurus (b. 1869; j. 1894)
Fr. Archange (b. 1870; o. 1893; j. 1895)
Fr. Marc (b. 1868; o. June 1895; j. Nov. 1895)
Fr. Theodule (b. 1873; o. Sept. 1895; j. Nov. 1895)
Fr. Philippe (b. 1869; j. 1895)
Fr. Bernardin (b. 1872; j. 1898; o. 1899)
Fr. Matthieu (b. 1874; j. 1898; o. 1899)
Fr. Quirin (b. 1876; j. 1898; o. 1899)
Br. Idesbaldus (b. 1864; j. 1898)
Br. Florentinus (b. 1872; j. 1898)
Fr. Aemilianus (b. 1872; j. 1898)
Fr. Rochus van Wenduine (b. 1873; o. Nov. 1898; j. Dec. 1898)
Fr. Vital (b. 1874; o. 1897; j. 1898)
Fr. Bonaventure (b. 1845; o. 1870; j. 1900)

LEFT IN 1891–1900

Fr. Rochus (d. 1891)
Fr. Emmanuel (a. 1892)
Br. Paul (r. 1893)
Fr. Engelbert (r. 1894)
Fr. Edmund (r. 1895)
Fr. Theodore (r. 1895)
Br. Constant (d. 1897)
Fr. Daniel (r. 1897)

ARRIVED IN 1901–10

Fr. Deodat (b. 1858; o. ?; j. 1903)
Fr. Gonsalve (b. 1855; o. 1880; j. 1903)
Fr. Ubaldus (b. 1873; o. 1900; j. 1903)
Fr. Macaire (b. 1876; o. 1901; j. 1903)
Fr. Albanus (b. 1876; o. 1901; j. 1903)
Fr. Floribertus (b. 1877; o. 1902; j. 1903)
Fr. Cajetanus (b. 1878; o. June 1903; j. Oct. 1903)
Fr. Victorius (b. 1848; o. 1871; j. 1903)
Fr. Emmanuel (b. 1875; o. 1901; j. 1903)
Fr. Honoratus (b. 1880; o. 1904; j. 1906)
Fr. Constantius (b. 1879; o. 1904; j. 1906)
Fr. Marcianus (b. 1879; o. 1903; j. 1908)
Fr. Romualdus (b. 1880; o. 1904; j. 1908)
Fr. Herman (b. 1881; o. 1906; j. 1908)
Fr. Jean Capistran (b. 1880; o. Aug. 1908; j. Nov. 1908)
Fr. Arnold (b. 1884; o. Aug. 1908; j. Nov. 1908)
Fr. Sigismond (b. 1883; o. 1900; j. 1910)
Fr. Stanislaus (b. 1885; o. 1909; j. 1910)

LEFT IN 1901–10

Fr. Edouard (d. 1903)
Fr. Peter (r. 1903)
Fr. Godefride (Pelckmans) (d. 1904)
Fr. Arsene (d. 1904)
Br. Idesbaldus (r. 1904)
Br. Maurus (d. 1906)
Fr. Rochus van Wenduine (r. 1907)

ARRIVED IN 1911–20

Fr. Rupert (b. 1885; o. 1911; j. 1912)
Fr. Arthur (b. 1885; o. 1911; j. 1913)
Fr. Arsene (b. 1886; o. 1911; j. 1913)
Fr. Fabian (b. 1885; o. 1912; j. 1913)
Fr. Gulie (b. 1885; o. 1912; j. 1913)
Fr. Theodorus (b. 1886; o. 1912; j. 1913)
Fr. Anastasius (b. 1888; o. 1912; j. 1913)
Fr. Simon (b. 1887; o. 1910; j. 1913)
Fr. Hector (Catry) (b. 1889; o. 1914; j. 1919)

Fr. Theophanes (b. 1887; o. 1915; j. 1919)
Fr. Guido (b. 1890; o. 1915; j. 1919)
Fr. Gothardus (b. 1890; o. 1916; j. 1919)
Fr. Calasanctius (b. 1883; o. 1918; j. 1919)

LEFT IN 1911–20

Br. Ferdinand (r. 1911)
Fr. Victorianus (r. 1911)
Fr. Floribertus (r. 1911)
Fr. Antoine (r. 1912)
Fr. Deodat (d. 1913)
Fr. Bernardin (d. 1914)
Fr. Quirin (r. 1914)
Fr. Cajetanus (d. 1914)
Fr. Leo (r. 1914)
Fr. Constantius (d. 1916)
Fr. Rupert (d. 1918)
Fr. Theodorus (d. 1918)
Fr. Vital (r. 1919)
Fr. Simon (r. 1919)
Fr. Honoratus (r. 1920)
Fr. Romualdus (d. 1920)
Fr. Herman (d. 1920)

ARRIVED IN 1921–30

Fr. Sylvanus (b. 1892; o. 1916; j. 1921)
Fr. Rufinus (b. 1892; o. 1920; j. 1921)
Fr. Walterus (b. 1876; o. 1900; j. 1921)
Fr. Hugolinus (b. 1890; o. 1916; j. 1921)
Fr. Sylvester (b. 1893; o. Feb. 1921; j. Nov. 1921)
Br. Angelicus (b. 1884; j. 1921)
Br. Raphael (b. 1889; j. 1921)
Fr. Anscharius (b. 1887; o. 1911; j. 1922)
Fr. Gaspar (b. 1888; o. 1915; j. 1922)
Fr. Roger (b. 1892; o. 1917; j. 1922)
Fr. Innocentius (b. 1892; o. Feb. 1922; j. Oct. 1922)
Fr. Florianus (b. 1894; o. Feb. 1922; j. Oct. 1922)
Fr. Masseo (b. 1893; o. 1922; j. 1924)
Fr. Prudens (b. 1898; o. Jan. 1924; j. Sept. 1924)
Br. Evaristus (b. 1897; j. 1924; o. 1925)
Fr. Balduinus (b. 1891; o. 1915; j. 1925)

Fr. Michael (b. 1892; o. 1916; j. 1925)
Fr. Damianus (b. 1892; o. 1915; j. 1926)
Fr. Ludolphus (b. 1902; o. 1928; j. 1929)
Fr. Thomas (b. 1898; o. 1925; j. 1930)
Fr. Eugenius (b. 1900; o. 1926; j. 1930)
Fr. Agnello (b. 1903; o. 1928; j. 1930)
Fr. Xaverius (b. 1902; o. 1929; j. 1930)
Fr. Hermes (b. 1905; o. 1929); j. 1930)

LEFT IN 1921–30

Fr. Fabian (Eestermans) (r. 1928)
Fr. Lievin (d. 1922)
Fr. Marc (d. 1926)
Fr. Bonaventure (d. 1925)
Fr. Gonsalve (d. 1929)
Fr. Emmanuel (r. 1925)
Fr. Sigismond (r. 1928)
Fr. Vincent (r. 1923)
Br. Angelicus (r. 1928)

Glossary

Ad Dharm Low-caste socio-religious and political group

agronome Expert lecturer in rural economics, Belgium

Arya Samaj Reformist movement within Hinduism

baboo Clerk, lower-level government official

basti Living area segregated by caste, usually in towns and cities

be-izzati Loss or compromise of *izzat*

bétail Farm animals

bhajan Religious song

bhakti Religious devotion

bibi 'Sister', or 'woman' more generally if used in a rural context

biraderi Brotherhood (community)

churi Secondary marriage

crore 10,000,000 (Rupees, e.g.)

Dalit 'Oppressed' or 'broken'; self-ascribed term, often with political connotations, denoting some of India's lowest social and ritual groups

dharm (Religious or social) duty

dharmik Of, or relating to, *dharm*

doab Tract of land which lies between two confluent rivers

fakir Mendicant holy man

far niente (lit. 'do nothing') Lazy

gharib nawaz 'protectors of the poor'

gurdwara Sikh temple

Gurumukhi The Punjabi script

huqqa, hooka Pipe, hookah

ilaqah District, region

izzat Honour, status in the eyes of one's neighbours

jati (lit. 'birth group') Basic unit of endogamous caste system

kursi (lit. 'chair') Seat at the durbar of the collector, commissioner, governor, or viceroy

lakh 100,000 (e.g. Rupees)

lathi Long wooden stick used as a weapon, as well as to measure the depth of rivers or to fend off animals

mamla Water-due (tax)

mandir Temple

masih(i) Christ; 'Messiah' (sometimes used as a Christian surname)

maund Approximately 82 lb

memsahib Term of respect used for white female Europeans in India

Mohammedan Muslim

moulvi, maulvi Muslim theologian, preacher, and teacher

namaste 'Hello' or 'goodbye' (greeting, salutation)

octroi Municipal tax on certain types of goods entering a given town or city

panchayat Ruling 'council of five' caste or village elders, sometimes acting as a court of customary arbitration

panth (lit. 'path') Socio-religious way or community

panthik Of, or relating to, *panth*

pir Muslim religious leader

Puranas Set of eighteen sacred poems in Hinduism

purdah System of seclusion for women

quam Social or religious 'community' or 'people'

quamik Of, or relating to, *quam*

sabha Association

sahib Term of respect for white male Europeans in India

samaj Branch, or local association

samaji Of, or related to, the Arya Samaj, or a particular local branch of the Arya Samaj

sannyasi Mendicant holy man, religious ascetic

sati, suttee The self-immolation of a widow on her husband's funeral pyre

sepi Contraction of *sepidari*, sometimes used adjectivally, for example, '*sepi* Chuhra'

sepidar Individual provider of labour within the *sepidari* system

sepidari Village labour system in which an individual or family provides services directly to another family, in return for a percentage share of the harvest and certain customary rights

Shastras Hindu scriptures

shikar karna To hunt

shuddhi Purification

suttee See *sati*

tabla Indian drum

tehsil Administrative unit for land revenue collection and local government; generally one-third or one-quarter of a district

updeshak Missionary (in the context of the Arya Samaj or Ad Dharm)

varna Theoretical division of four castes (*varnas*) in Hinduism

Vedas Collection of ancient Hindu scriptures

Vedic Pertaining to the Vedas

wajib-ul-'arz North Indian village administration document

zail Group of villages taken together as a single administrative unit

zaildar Individual with legal responsibility for a *zail*

zamindar Landowner

zenana Secluded quarters reserved for women

Bibliography

MANUSCRIPT AND ARCHIVAL SOURCES

Bodleian Library of Commonwealth and African Studies at Rhodes House

Archives of the Society for the Propagation of the Gospel in Foreign Parts (ASPG), Lahore

ASPG, Delhi: Annual Letters of the Missionaries, various years.

Delhi Mission News (*DMN*)

British Library

Oriental and India Office Collections (OIOC)

Brayne Papers, MSS Eur. F. 152, Papers of Lieutenant Frank Lugard Brayne (1882–1953), Various personal papers and cuttings, 1900–52.

Capuchin Historical Institute, Rome

General Archives of the Capuchin Order (GACO)

H59 Lahore, Papers relating to the Punjab mission of the Belgian Capuchins, various years.

University of Birmingham, Special Collections

Archives of the Church Missionary Society (ACMS), Punjab and Sindh Mission

G/AM1: *Instructions of the Committee to Missionaries Proceeding to Various Missions in the Autumn of 1904.*

G/AP2: E. Stock, *An Historical Survey of Women's Work in the CMS at Home and Abroad: A Lecture to a Conference of Ladies at the Church Missionary House, January 1907; Representation of Women on Committees*, Reports I and II, Feb. 1914; *Proceedings of the Committee of Correspondence of February 6, 1912, to be presented for confirmation to the General Committee of February 13, 1912.*

G/C/CC2 and G/CCb: CMS Centenary Committee Papers.

G2/I4/O: Original Papers, various years, incl. *Report of Special Committee of CMS Punjab and Sindh Conference for Enquiring into the Shortcomings of the Native Church of Punjab, May 1885* (*Shortcomings*); R. Clark, *Indian Christian Workers in CMS Missions, With Special Reference to the CMS Native Church Council in the Punjab and Sindh* (Simla, 1888).

G2/I7/1 and 2: *Tarn Taran Mission of the Church Missionary Society, Punjab, India: Report and Accounts* (Lahore, various years). (*TTRA*)

Extracts from the Annual Letters of the Missionaries (London, various years). (*EAL*)

Proceedings of the Church Missionary Society for Africa and the East (London, various years).
Proceedings of the Punjab Native (District) Church Council (Lahore, various years).
Register of Mission and Native Clergy, 1808–1904 (London, 1904).

University of Cambridge, Centre for South Asian Studies

Darling Papers, Papers of Sir Malcolm Lyall Darling (1880–1969).

Headquarters of the Belgian Province of the Capuchins, Antwerp

Archives of the Belgian Capuchins (ABC), Archief van de Punjab Missie

Papers relating to the Punjab mission, various years.

Blondeel, E., *In Het Land Der Vijf Rivieren* (Antwerp, 1938).
Pelckmans, G., *Dix Années d'apostolat au Pundjab* (Bruges, 1900).

OTHER PRINTED SOURCES

Primary

Series

Government of India

Census of India 1881, Punjab Report, Appendix B: Extracts from Mr. Ibbetson's Report on the Punjab Census, noting peculiarities of the Hindoo and Mohammedan religions, as practised in that Province (Lahore, 1883).
Census of India 1891, Punjab Report (Calcutta, 1892).
Census of India 1901, Punjab Report (Simla, 1902).
Census of India 1911, Punjab Report (Lahore, 1912).
Census of India 1921, India Report (Calcutta, 1924).
Census of India 1921, Punjab Report (Lahore, 1923).
Census of India 1931, Punjab Report (Lahore, 1933).
Census of India 1941, Punjab Report (Simla, 1941).

Government of Punjab

Gazetteer of the Amritsar District 1883–4 (Calcutta, 1884).
Gazetteer of the Chenab Colony 1904 (Lahore, 1905).
Gazetteer of the Chenab Colony 1912 (Lahore, 1913).
Gazetteer of the Gujranwala District 1912, Statistical Tables (Lahore, 1913).
Gazetteer of the Gujranwala District 1935 (Lahore, 1936).
Gazetteer of the Lahore District, 1893–4 (Lahore, 1894).
Gazetteer of the Sialkot District 1883–4 (Lahore, 1884).
Gazetteer of the Sialkot District 1894–5 (Lahore, 1895).
Gazetteer of the Sialkot District 1904, Statistical Tables (Lahore, 1907).
Gazetteer of the Sialkot District 1920 (Lahore, 1921).
Gazetteer of the Sialkot District 1931 (Lahore, 1932).
Report on Public Instruction in the Punjab (Lahore, various years). (*RPIP*)

Holy See

Papal Bulls

Leo XIII, *Humanae Salutis Auctor*, 1 Sept. 1886 (Vatican, 1886).

Encyclicals

Pius IX, *Qui Pluribus*, 9 Nov. 1846 (Vatican, 1846).
—— *Quanta Cura*, 8 Dec. 1864 (Vatican, 1864).
—— *Cum Non Sine*, Epistle to the Archbishop of Freiburg (Vatican, 1864).
Leo XIII, *Inscrutabili Dei Consilio*, 21 Apr. 1878 (Vatican, 1878).
—— *Arcanum*, 10 Feb. 1880 (Vatican, 1880).
—— *Auspicato Concessum*, 17 Sept. 1882 (Vatican, 1882).
—— *Immortale Dei*, 1 Nov. 1885 (Vatican, 1885).
—— *Rerum Novarum*, 15 May 1891 (Vatican, 1891).
—— *Ad Extremas*, 24 June 1893 (Vatican, 1893).
—— *Satis Cognitum*, 29 June 1896 (Vatican, 1896).
—— *Militantis Ecclesiae*, 1 Aug. 1897 (Vatican, 1897).
—— *Affari Vos*, 18 Dec. 1897 (Vatican, 1897).
—— *Depuis Le Jour*, 8 Sept. 1899 (Vatican, 1899).
—— *Paternae*, 18 Sept. 1899 (Vatican, 1899).
Benedict XV, *Maximum Illud*, 30 Nov. 1919 (Vatican, 1919).
Pius XI, *Rerum Ecclesiae*, 28 Feb. 1926 (Vatican, 1926).
—— *Divini Illius Magistri*, 31 Dec. 1929 (Vatican, 1929).
—— *Casti Connubii*, 31 Dec. 1930 (Vatican, 1930).

Other Communications

Pius IX, *Syllabus of Errors*, 8 Dec. 1864 (Vatican, 1864).
Leo XIII, *Instructions to the Missions*, 19 Mar. 1893 (Vatican, 1893).

Order of Friars Minor Capuchin

Analecta Ordinis Minorum Capuccinorum (Rome, various years).

Other

Anand, M. R., *Untouchable: A Novel* (London, 1935).
Andrews, C. F., 'Indian Character: An Appreciation', *DMN* 4/8 (Oct. 1905).
[Archdiocese of Agra], *Catholic Calendar and Directory for the Archdiocese of Agra and its Suffragan Dioceses of Allahabad and Lahore and of the Prefectures Apostolic of Rajputana and Bettiah* (Simla, 1907).
Basu, B. D., *Rise of the Christian Power in India* (Calcutta, 1931).
Baverstock, A. H., *The Failure of the Church in the Villages* (London, 1913).
Bishop of Lahore (Anglican), 'The Rural Church in West Pakistan', *East and West*, 19 (Jan. 1953).
Bomford, T., 'The Development of the Church in India', *CMR* 71/829 (Mar. 1920).

Boulger, D. C., *Belgian Life in Town and Country* (London, 1904).
Brayne, F., *Village Uplift in India* (Allahabad, 1927).
—— *Socrates in an Indian Village* (Oxford, 1931).
—— *The Indian and the English Village* (Oxford, 1933).
—— *Better Villages* (Oxford, 1937).
Campbell, G., *Memoirs of my Indian Career* (London, 1893).
Capuchin Mission Unit, *India and its Missions* (New York, 1923).
[Church Missionary Society], 'In Memoriam: Mian Sadiq', *CMR* 67/806 (June 1916).
—— 'In Memoriam: Robert Maconachie', *CMR* 73/840 (Dec. 1922).
Clark, R., *The Punjab and Sindh Mission of the Church Missionary Society* (London, 1885).
—— *The Missions of the Church Missionary Society and the Church of England Zenana Missionary Society in the Punjab and Sindh* (London, 1904); first pub. as *The Punjab and Sindh Mission of the Church Missionary Society* (London, 1885).
Committee on Disturbances in Bombay, Delhi, and the Punjab, *New Light on the Punjab Disturbances in 1919: Volumes VI and VII of Disorders Inquiry Committee Evidence* (Simla, 1975). (*NLPD*)
Cuthbert, *The Capuchins: A Contribution to the History of the Counter-Reformation*, 2 vols (London, 1928).
Darling, M., *The Punjab Peasant in Prosperity and Debt* (London, 1925).
—— *Rusticus Loquitur, or, The Old Light and the New in the Punjab Village* (London, 1930).
—— *Wisdom and Waste in the Punjab Village* (London, 1934).
Deshraj, L., 'Is it Village Uplift?', *Young India*, 17 Oct. 1929.
Disraeli, B., *Sybil* (London, 1845).
Farquhar, J. N., *The Crown of Hinduism* (Oxford, 1913).
Favell, M., 'Hopeful Work among the Chamars', *DMN* 8/2 (Apr. 1916).
Gandhi, M. K., 'Village Improvement', *Young India*, 14 Nov. 1929.
Ghose, S., 'Work amongst Chamars', pt I, *DMN* 2/3 (July 1898).
—— 'Work amongst Chamars', pt II, *DMN* 2/4 (Oct. 1898).
Gorham, Miss, 'More Camping Notes', *DMN* 7/6 (Apr. 1914).
Grey, H. G., 'Native Church Organisation in India II: The Punjab', *CMR* 60/724 (Aug. 1909).
Griffin, L., *Panjab Chiefs* (Lahore, 1865).
Haig, A., 'Village Work in the Karnal District', *DMN* 1/11 (July 1897).
Hall, C. F., 'A Suggested Policy for Mass Movements', *CMR* 65/781 (May 1914).
Hankinson Cox, E. A., *The Story of the World Missionary Conference at Edinburgh* (London, 1912).
Hares, W. P., 'Mass Movements and their Consequences', *CMR* 64/765 (Jan. 1913).

____ 'The Narowal Mission: A Ten Years' Retrospect', *CMR* 67/810 (Nov. 1916).

____ 'Mass Movement Work in Central Punjab: Some Difficulties and Encouragements', *CMR* 69/823 (Sept. 1918).

Haythornthwaite, J. P., 'The Scope and Policy of Educational Work in Relation to the Indian Government', *CMR* 62/747 (July 1911).

Hibbert-Ware, G., 'Baptisms in the Villages', pt 1, *DMN* 8/5 (Jan. 1917).

____ 'Baptisms in the Villages', pt 2, *DMN* 8/6 (Apr. 1917).

Hughes, J. J., 'Growth of Christianity in the Villages', *DMN* 8/1 (Jan. 1916).

Ibbetson, D. C. J., *Outlines of Panjab Ethnography* (Calcutta, 1883).

____ *Tribes and Castes* (Lahore, 1916).

The India List and India Office List (London, 1900).

Las Casas, B. de, *A Short Account of the Destruction of the Indies* (London, 1992).

Macaire, Fr., 'Les Conversions en masse au Punjab', *Analecta Ordinis Minorum Capuccinorum* (Rome, 1925).

Mackworth-Young, W., 'Missions and Governments: Commentary on Resolutions Proposed with Reference to Report of Commission VII of the World Missionary Conference', *CMR* 62/744 (Apr. 1911).

Maconachie, R., 'Rowland Bateman: A Fragmentary Tribute', *CMR* 67/805 (May 1916).

____ *Rowland Bateman: Nineteenth Century Apostle* (London, 1917).

____ 'Nationalism and Christianity in India', *CMR* 68/814 (Mar. 1917).

Marsh, N., 'Village Work', *DMN* 7/10 (Apr. 1915).

Montalembert, Count C. de, *The Monks of the West* (Edinburgh, 1861).

Moule, H. C. G., *Outlines of Christian Doctrine* (London, 1899).

Ninove, L. van, *The Capuchin Mission in the Punjab: With Notes on the History, Geography, Ethnology and Religions of the Country* (Mangalore, 1910).

O'Dwyer, M., *India as I Knew It, 1885–1925* (London, 1925).

Orton, D. M., 'Montgomerywala: Past and Present', *Church Missionary Outlook*, 65/770 (May 1938).

Ram, L. G., and Dass, L. C., *The Uplift Movement at Sialkot, Punjab* (Calcutta, 1914).

Ruskin, J., *Unto This Last* (London, 1862).

Singh, J. P., 'The Panchayats in Punjab, 1849–1947', *Punjab Past and Present*, 32/1 (Apr. 2001).

Singh, S. K., *Ham Hindu Nahin* (Amritsar, 1899).

Stock, E., *History of the Church Missionary Society*, 4 vols (London, 1899, 1916).

Venn, H., *The Missionary Life and Labours of Francis Xavier, Taken from his Own Correspondence: With a Sketch of the General Results of Roman Catholic Missions among the Heathen* (London, 1862).

Waskom Pickett, J., *Christian Mass Movements in India: A Study with Recommendations* (New York, 1933).

Whitehead, H., 'Bishop Whitehead in the Punjab: Extracts from his Journal', *CMR* 64/772 (Aug. 1913).

Whitehead, H., 'Mass Movement and Education in India', *CMR* 68/814 (Mar. 1917).

Wigram, E. F. E., 'The Christian Campaign in the Punjab', *CMR* 66/795 (July 1915).

Youngson, J., *Forty Years of the Panjab Mission of the Church of Scotland 1855–1895* (Edinburgh, 1896).

—— 'The Chuhras', *Indian Antiquary*, 35 (1906).

Secondary

Aggarwal, S., *Punjab: A Select Bibliography (including Haryana) 1939–1979* (Chandigarh, 1980).

Ahmad, S., 'Social Stratification in a Punjabi Village', *Contributions to Indian Sociology*, new ser., 4 (1970).

Ahuja, R. L., 'Social Movements in the Punjab', *Punjab Past and Present*, 18/1 (Apr. 1984).

Ali, I., 'Malign Growth? Agricultural Colonization and the Roots of Backwardness in the Punjab', *Past and Present*, 114 (Feb. 1987).

—— *The Punjab under Imperialism, 1885–1947* (Princeton, 1988).

Ambler, R. W., *Ranters, Revivalists and Reformers: Primitive Methodism and Rural Society, South Lincolnshire, 1817–1875* (Hull, 1989).

Andersen, W., *Towards a Theology of Mission: A Study of the Encounter between the Missionary Enterprise and the Church and its Theology* (London, 1955).

Ansari, S. F. D., *Sufi Saints and State Power: The Pirs of Sind, 1843–1947* (Cambridge, 1992).

Appadurai, A., *Worship and Conflict under Colonial Rule: A South Indian Case* (Cambridge, 1981).

Aretin, K. O. von, *The Papacy and the Modern World* (London, 1970).

Asad, T., *Genealogies of Religion: Discipline and Reasons of Power in Christianity and Islam* (Baltimore, 1993).

Aspinwall, B., 'Changing Images of Roman Catholic Religious Orders in the Nineteenth Century', in Ecclesiastical History Society, *Monks, Hermits and the Ascetic Tradition* (Padstow, 1985).

Austin-Broos, D., 'The Anthropology of Conversion: An Introduction', in A. Bucker and S. D. Glazier (eds), *The Anthropology of Religious Conversion* (Oxford, 2003).

Bajaj, S. K., 'Malcolm Lyall Darling: A Study of his Perspective', *Punjab Past and Present*, 14/1 (Apr. 1980).

Bakshi, S. R., *Gandhi and his Social Thought* (New Delhi, 1986).

Barrier, N. G., 'The Formulation and Enactment of the Punjab Alienation of Land Bill', *Indian Economic and Social Review*, 2/2 (1965).

—— *Punjab Alienation of Land Bill of 1900* (Durham, NC, 1966).

—— 'The Punjab Disturbances of 1907: The Response of the British Government in India to Agrarian Unrest', *Modern Asian Studies*, 1/2 (1967).

____ 'The Punjab Government and Communal Politics, 1870–1908', *Journal of Asian Studies*, 27/3 (May 1968).
____ 'Banned Literature in the Punjab', in W. Gustafson and K. W. Jones (eds), *Sources on Punjab History* (Delhi, 1975).
____ (ed.), *The Census in British India: New Perspectives* (New Delhi, 1981).
Bayly, C. A., *Indian Society and the Making of the British Empire* (Cambridge, 1988).
Bayly, S., *Saints, Goddesses and Kings: Muslims and Christians in South Indian Society 1700–1900* (Cambridge, 1989).
____ *Caste, Society and Politics in India from the Eighteenth Century to the Modern Age* (Cambridge, 1999).
Bebbington, D. W., *Evangelicalism in Modern Britain: A History from the 1730s to the 1980s* (London, 1989).
____ *Victorian Non-Conformity* (Bangor, 1992).
Bharucha, R., *The Question of Faith* (New Delhi, 1993).
Bhatti, H. S., *Folk Religion: Change and Continuity* (Jaipur, 2000).
Bhole, L. M., 'A Gandhian Critique of Planned Development in India', in B. P. Pandey (ed.), *Gandhi and Economic Development* (London, 1991).
Billington Harper, S., *In the Shadow of the Mahatma: Bishop V. S. Azariah and the Travails of Christianity in British India* (Richmond, 2000).
Blauw, J., *The Missionary Nature of the Church: A Survey of the Biblical Theology of Mission* (London, 1962).
Blom, J. C. H., and Lamberts, E. (eds), *History of the Low Countries* (New York, 1999).
Bose, S., and Jalal, A., *Modern South Asia: History, Culture, Political Economy* (London, 1998).
Breckenridge, C., and Veer, P. van der (eds), *Orientalism and the Post-Colonial Predicament: Perspectives on South Asia* (Philadelphia, 1993).
Brock, P., 'New Christians as Evangelists', in N. Etherington (ed.), *Missions and Empire* (Oxford, 2005).
Brown, J. M., *Modern India: The Origins of an Asian Democracy* (Oxford, 1985).
____ *Gandhi, Prisoner of Hope* (New Haven, 1989).
____ 'Gandhi—A Victorian Gentleman: An Essay in Imperial Encounter', *Journal of Imperial and Commonwealth History*, 27/2 (May 1999).
____ and Frykenberg, R. E. (eds), *Christians, Cultural Interactions and India's Religious Traditions* (London, 2002).
Brown, K. D., *A Social History of the Non-Conformist Ministry in England and Wales, 1800–1930* (Oxford, 1988).
Bucker, A., and Glazier, S. D. (eds), *The Anthropology of Religious Conversion* (Oxford, 2003).
Bugge, H., *Mission and Tamil Society: Social and Religious Change in South India 1840–1900* (Richmond, 1994).
Cain, P. J., and Hopkins, A. G., *British Imperialism: Innovation and Expansion 1688–1914* (London, 1993).

Cappa, F., *The Modern Papacy since 1789* (New York, 1998).

Cary, O., *A History of Christianity in Japan*, 2 vols (New York, 1909).

Certeau, M. de, *The Practice of Everyday Life* (London, 1984).

Chadwick, O., *The Victorian Church*, 2 vols (London, 1966–70).

—— *The Secularization of the European Mind in the Nineteenth Century* (Cambridge, 1990).

—— *A History of the Popes 1830–1914* (Oxford, 1998).

Chatterjee, P., *The Nation and its Fragments: Colonial and Post-Colonial Histories* (Princeton, 1993).

—— 'Caste and Subaltern Consciousness', in R. Guha (ed.), *Subaltern Studies*, vi: *Writings on South Asian History and Society* (New Delhi, 1989).

Chaudhuri, N. C., *Hinduism* (London, 1979).

Clarke, S., 'Conversion to Christianity in Tamil Nadu: Conscious and Constitutive Community Mobilization towards a Different Symbolic World Vision', in R. Robinson and S. Clarke (eds), *Religious Conversion in India: Modes, Motivations and Meanings* (Oxford, 2003).

Clough, S. B., *A History of the Flemish Movement in Belgium: A Study in Nationalism* (New York, 1930).

Cohn, B. S., 'The Changing Status of a Depressed Caste', in M. Marriott (ed.), *Village India: Studies in the Little Community* (Chicago, 1955).

—— 'Structural Change in Indian Rural Society, 1596–1885', in R. E. Frykenberg (ed.), *Land Control and Social Structure in Indian History* (Madison, 1969).

—— *An Anthropologist among Historians and Other Essays* (Oxford, 1990).

—— 'Representing Authority in Victorian India', in E. Hobsbawm and T. R. Ranger (eds), *The Invention of Tradition* (Cambridge, 1992).

—— *Colonialism and its Forms of Knowledge: The British in India* (Princeton, 1996).

Collini, S., *Public Moralists, Political Thought and Intellectual Life in Britain 1850–1930* (Oxford, 1991).

Comaroff, J., and Comaroff, J., *Of Revelation and Revolution: Christianity, Colonialism and Consciousness in South Africa* (Chicago, 1991).

Conway, M., 'Building the Christian City: Catholics and Politics in Inter-War Francophone Belgium', *Past and Present*, 128 (1990).

Copley, A., *Religions in Conflict: Ideology, Cultural Contact and Conversion in Late Colonial India* (Delhi, 1997).

Cort, J. C., *Christian Socialism: An Informal History* (Maryknoll, NY, 1988).

Cox, J., *Imperial Fault Lines: Christianity and Colonial Power in India, 1818–1940* (Stanford, 2002).

Crook, B. A., *Belgium: A History* (New York, 2002).

Cummings, J., 'Saint Francis and the Missions', *Spirit and Life: A Journal of Contemporary Franciscan Studies*, 6 (1994).

Davies, N., *Europe: A History* (Oxford, 1996).

Davis, R. W., and Helmstadter, R. J. (eds), *Religion and Irreligion in Victorian Society: Essays in Honour of R. K. Webb* (London, 1992).

Dewey, C., 'The Education of a Ruling Caste', *English Historical Review*, 88 (1973).

____ *Anglo-Indian Attitudes: The Mind of the Indian Civil Service* (London, 1993).

Dirks, N. B., 'Colonial Histories and Native Informants: Biography of an Archive', in C. Breckenridge and P. van der Veer (eds), *Orientalism and the Post-Colonial Predicament: Perspectives on South Asia* (Philadelphia, 1993).

Donajgrodski, A. P., *Social Control in Nineteenth Century Britain* (London, 1977).

____ '"Social Police" and the Bureaucratic Elite: A Vision of Order in the Age of Reform', in Donajgrodski (ed.), *Social Control in Nineteenth Century Britain* (London, 1977).

Dowland, D., *Nineteenth-Century Anglican Theological Training: The Redbrick Challenge* (Oxford, 1997).

Downs, F. S., 'Christian Conversion Movements in North East India', in R. Robinson and S. Clarke (eds), *Religious Conversion in India: Modes, Motivations and Meanings* (Oxford, 2003).

D'Souza, D., *Implanting of the Capuchin Order in North India, 1965–80* (Brahmanar, 1996).

____ *Capuchin Missions in India* (Karnataka, 1997).

Dube, S., *Untouchable Pasts: Religion, Identity, and Power among a Central Indian Community, 1780–1950* (New York, 1998).

Dumont, L., *Homo Hierarchicus* (London, 1970).

Dungen, P. van den, *The Punjab Tradition: Influence and Authority in Nineteenth Century India* (London, 1972).

Epstein, S., 'District Officers in Decline: The Erosion of British Authority in the Bombay Countryside, 1919 to 1947', *Modern Asian Studies*, 6/3 (1982).

Esser, C., 'Saint Francis and the Mission Church', *Spirit and Life: A Journal of Contemporary Franciscan Studies*, 6 (1994).

Etherington, N. (ed.), *Missions and Empire* (Oxford, 2005).

Evans, E. L., *The Cross and the Ballot: Catholic Political Parties in Germany, Switzerland, Austria, Belgium and the Netherlands, 1785–1985* (Boston, 1999).

Ewing, A., 'The Indian Civil Service 1919–1924: Service Discontent and the Response in London and Delhi', *Modern Asian Studies*, 8/1 (1984).

Farmer, D. H., *The Oxford Dictionary of Saints* (Oxford, 1983).

Felder, H., *The Ideals of St Francis of Assisi* (Paderborn, 1951).

Finnegan, C. V., 'Franciscan Evangelization: A Brief Historical Overview', *Spirit and Life: A Journal of Contemporary Franciscan Studies*, 6 (1994).

Forrester, D. B., *Caste and Christianity: Attitudes and Policies on Caste of Anglo-Saxon Protestant Missions in India* (London, 1980).

Forrester, D. B., 'The Depressed Castes and Conversion to Christianity, 1860–1960', in G. A. Oddie (ed.), *Religion in South Asia* (New Delhi, 1991).

Foucault, M., *The Archaeology of Knowledge* (London, 1989).

Fox, R. C., *In the Belgian Chateau* (Chicago, 1994).

Fox, R. G., 'Urban Class and Communal Consciousness in Colonial Punjab: The Genesis of India's Intermediate Regime', *Modern Asian Studies*, 8/3 (1984).

Frykenberg, R. E., 'Village Strength in India', in R. E. Frykenberg (ed.), *Land Control and Social Structure in Indian History* (Madison, 1969).

—— 'Christian Missions and the Raj', in N. Etherington (ed.), *Missions and Empire* (Oxford, 2005).

—— (ed.), *Christians and Missionaries in India: Cross-Cultural Communication since 1500* (Cambridge, 2003).

Ghai, R. K., 'Arya Megh Uddhar Sabha, Sialkot', *Punjab Past and Present*, 21/1 (Apr. 1987).

—— 'Swami Shraddhanand and the Untouchables: A Case of Reconversion of Malkana Rajputs', *Punjab Past and Present*, 23/1 (Apr. 1989).

Ghosh, A. (ed.), *Dalits and Peasants: The Emerging Caste-Class Dynamics* (Delhi, 1999).

Gilley, S., and Sheils, W. J., *A History of Religion in Britain: Practice and Belief from Pre-Roman Times to the Present* (Oxford, 1994).

Gooptu, N., 'Caste, Deprivation and Politics', in P. Robb (ed.), *Dalit Movements and the Meanings of Labour in India* (Delhi, 1996).

—— *The Politics of the Urban Poor in Early Twentieth-Century India* (Cambridge, 2001).

Griffiths, G., '"Trained to Tell the Truth": Missionaries, Converts, and Narration', in N. Etherington (ed.), *Missions and Empire* (Oxford, 2005).

Guha, R., 'Dominance without Hegemony and its Historiography', in R. Guha (ed.), *Subaltern Studies VI: Writings on South Asian History and Society* (New Delhi, 1989).

Gupta, S. K., *The Scheduled Castes in Modern Indian Politics: Their Emergence as a Political Power* (New Delhi, 1985).

Gustafson, W., and Jones, K., *Sources on Punjab History* (Delhi, 1975).

Gutierrez, G., *Las Casas: In Search of the Poor of Jesus Christ* (Maryknoll, NY, 1993).

Hales, E. E. Y., *The Catholic Church in the Modern World* (London, 1958).

Harding, S., 'Representing Fundamentalism: The Problem of the Repugnant Cultural Other', *Social Research*, 58 (Summer 1991).

Harford, J. B., and McDonald, F. C., *Handley Carr Glyn Moule, Bishop of Durham: A Biography* (London, 1922).

Harries, P., 'Anthropology', in N. Etherington (ed.), *Missions and Empire* (Oxford, 2005).

Hartnack, C., *Psychoanalysis in Colonial India* (Oxford, 2001).

Hastings, A., *The Church in Africa: 1450–1950* (Oxford, 1994).

Hearder, H., *Europe in the Nineteenth Century: 1830–1880* (New York, 1966).

Heasman, K., *Evangelicals in Action: An Appraisal of their Social Work in the Victorian Era* (London, 1962).

Hedlund, R. E. (ed.), *Christianity's Indian: The Emergence of an Indigenous Community* (Delhi, 2000).

Heeger, G. A., 'The Growth of the Congress Movement in Punjab', *Journal of Asian Studies*, 32/1 (Nov. 1972).

Heimsath, C., *Indian Nationalism and Hindu Social Reform* (Princeton, 1964).

Hewitt, G., *The Problems of Success: A History of the Church Missionary Society, 1910–1942*, 2 vols (London, 1971).

Hilton, B., *Age of Atonement* (Oxford, 1988).

Hobsbawm, E., *Primitive Rebels: Studies of Archaic Forms of Social Movement in the Nineteenth and Twentieth Centuries* (Manchester, 1959).

Holmes, J. D., and Bickers, B. W., *A Short History of the Catholic Church* (London, 1992).

Howkins, A., *Poor Labouring Men: Rural Radicalism in Norfolk, 1872–1923* (London, 1985).

____ *Reshaping Rural England: A Social History* (London, 1991).

Hunt, R., and Harrison, J., *The District Officer in India, 1930–1947* (London, 1980).

Hylson-Smith, K., *The Churches in England from Elizabeth I to Elizabeth II*, 3 vols (London, 1996–8).

Iqbal, M., *The Reconstruction of Religious Thought in Islam* (Lahore, 1930).

Irschick, E., *Dialogue and History: Constructing South India, 1795–1895* (Berkeley, 1994).

Islam, M., *Irrigation, Agriculture and the Raj* (New Delhi, 1997).

Jedin, H., *Crisis and Closure of the Council of Trent: A Retrospective View from the Second Vatican Council* (London, 1967).

____ (ed.), *History of the Church*, 10 vols (London, 1965–81).

Jenkins, P., *The Next Christendom: The Coming of Global Christianity* (Oxford, 2002).

Johnson, P., *A History of Christianity* (London, 1976).

Jones, K. W., *Arya Dharm: Hindu Consciousness in Nineteenth Century Punjab* (New Delhi, 1976).

____ *Socio-Religious Reform Movements in British India* (Cambridge, 1989).

Jones, W. W., '"Mass Movements" as Missionary Dream and Reality: John C. Lowrie, 1842, and J. Wascom [*sic*] Pickett, 1932', *Indian Church History Review*, 28/2 (Dec. 1994).

Judge, P. S., *Scheduled Caste Women in Work Force in Rural Punjab*, Occasional Paper, Centre for Social Studies, Surat, Oct. 1990.

Juergensmeyer, M., *Religion as Social Vision: The Movement against Untouchability in Twentieth Century Punjab* (Berkeley, 1982).

Kalu, O. U. (ed.), *The History of Christianity in West Africa* (London, 1980).

Kessinger, T. G., *Vilyatpur 1848–1968: Social and Economic Change in a North Indian Village* (Berkeley, 1974).

—— 'Sources for the Social and Economic History of Rural Punjab', in W. Gustafson and K. W. Jones (eds), *Sources on Punjab History* (Delhi, 1975).

Kidd, A., *State, Society and the Poor in Nineteenth Century England* (London, 1999).

Kitson Clark, G., *Churchmen and the Condition of England, 1832–1885* (London, 1973).

Kossman, E. H., *The Low Countries 1780–1940* (Oxford, 1978).

Kuriakose, M. K., *History of Christianity in India: Source Materials* (Delhi, 1982).

Latourette, K. S., *A History of the Expansion of Christianity*, 7 vols (London, 1939–47).

Lehmann, A., *Mission zwischen Gestern und Morgen* (Stuttgart, 1952).

Lewis, O., *Village Life in Northern India: Studies in a Delhi Village* (Urbana, Ill., 1958).

Liebau, H., 'Country Priests, Catechists and Schoolmasters as Cultural, Religious, and Social Middlemen in the Context of the Tranquebar Mission', in R. E. Frykenberg (ed.), *Christians and Missionaries in India: Cross-Cultural Communication since 1500* (Cambridge, 2003).

Lis, C., *Social Change and the Labouring Poor: Antwerp, 1770–1860* (New Haven, 1986).

Loehlin, C. H., 'History of Christianity in the Panjab', *Punjab Past and Present*, 7/1 (Apr. 1973).

Lucas, E. D., and Thakur Das, F., *The Rural Church in the Punjab* (Lahore, 1938).

Ludden, D., 'Orientalist Empiricism: Transformations of Colonial Knowledge', in C. Breckenridge and P. van der Veer (eds), *Orientalism and the Post-Colonial Predicament: Perspectives on South Asia* (Philadelphia, 1993).

Luria, K. P., 'The Politics of Protestant Conversion to Catholicism in Seventeenth Century France', in P. van der Veer (ed.), *Conversion to Modernities: The Globalization of Christianity* (New York, 1996).

MacCulloch, D., *Groundwork of Christian History* (London, 1987).

—— *Reformation: Europe's House Divided, 1490–1700* (London, 2003).

MacKenzie, J. M., *Empire of Nature: Hunting, Conservation and British Imperialism* (Manchester, 1988).

Manela, E., *The Wilsonian Moment: Self-Determination and the International Origins of Anti-Colonial Nationalism* (Oxford, 2007).

Marriott, M. (ed.), *Village India: Studies in the Little Community* (Chicago, 1955).

Massey, J., *Dalits in India: Religion as a Source of Bondage or Liberation with Special Reference to Christians* (Delhi, 1995).

Metcalf, T., *Ideologies of the Raj* (Cambridge, 1994).

Misner, P., *Social Catholicism in Europe: From the Onset of Industrialization to the First World War* (London, 1991).

Morris, M. D. (ed.), *The Indian Economy in the Nineteenth Century* (Delhi, 1969).

Nanda, B. R., *Mahatma Gandhi: A Biography* (London, 1958).

Nandy, A., *The Intimate Enemy: Loss and Recovery of Self under Colonialism* (Oxford, 1983).

Neill, S., *A History of Christian Missions* (Harmondsworth, 1964).

Nemer, L., *Anglican and Roman Catholic Attitudes on Missions: An Historical Study of Two English Missionary Societies in the Late Nineteenth Century, 1865–1885* (St Augustin, 1981).

Niebuhr, H. R., *The Social Sources of Denominationalism* (Hamden, Conn., 1954).

Obelkevich, J., *Religion and Rural Society: South Lindsey, 1825–1875* (Oxford, 1976).

O'Brien, J., *The Construction of Pakistani Christian Identity* (Lahore, 2006).

Oddie, G. A., 'Protestant Missions, Caste and Social Change in India, 1858–1914', *Indian and Social History Review*, 6 (Sept. 1969).

____ *Social Protest in India: British Protestant Missionaries and Social Reform, 1850–1900* (New Delhi, 1979).

____ 'Constructing Hinduism: The Impact of the Protestant Missionary Movement on Hindu Self-Understanding', in R. E. Frykenberg (ed.), *Christians and Missionaries in India: Cross-Cultural Communication since 1500* (Cambridge, 2003).

____ (ed.), *Religion in South Asia* (New Delhi, 1991).

OFM International Mission Council, Brady, M., Moons, A., Müller, A., and Walsh, F., 'Listening to Francis of Assisi on Mission', *Spirit and Life: A Journal of Contemporary Franciscan Studies*, 6 (1994).

O'Hanlon, R., *Caste, Conflict and Ideology: Mahatma Jotirao Phule and Low Caste Protest in Nineteenth-Century Western India* (Cambridge, 1985).

____ 'Recovering the Subject: Subaltern Studies and Histories of Resistance in Colonial South Asia', *Modern Asian Studies*, 22 (1988).

____ and Washbrook, D., 'After Orientalism: Culture, Criticism and Politics in the Third World', *Comparative Studies in Society and History*, 34 (1992).

Pagden, A., Introduction, in B. de Las Casas, *A Short Account of the Destruction of the Indies* (Harmondsworth, 1992).

Pandey, B. P. (ed.), *Gandhi and Economic Development* (London, 1991).

Parekh, B., *Colonialism, Tradition and Reform: An Analysis of Gandhi's Political Discourse* (New Delhi, 1989).

Parel, A. (ed.), *Hind Swaraj and Other Writings* (Cambridge, 1997).

Parry, J. H., *The Spanish Seaborne Empire* (London, 1966).

Pastor, L. F. von, *The History of the Popes from the Close of the Middle Ages*, 40 vols (London, 1901–53).

Paustian, P. W., *Canal Irrigation in the Punjab* (New York, 1930).

Pelikan, J., *The Christian Tradition: A History of the Development of Doctrine*, 5 vols (Chicago, 1971–89).

Pemble, J., *The Mediterranean Passion: Victorians and Edwardians in the South* (Oxford, 1987).

Piggin, S., *Making Evangelical Missionaries, 1789–1858* (Abingdon, 1984).

Pinto, A., *Dalit Christians* (Bangalore, 1992).

Pollock, S., 'Deep Orientalism? Notes on Sanskrit and Power beyond the Raj', in C. Breckenridge and P. van der Veer (eds), *Orientalism and the Post-Colonial Predicament: Perspectives on South Asia* (Philadelphia, 1993).

Porter, A., 'Cambridge, Keswick and Late Nineteenth Century Attitudes to Africa', *Journal of Imperial and Commonwealth History*, 5/1 (1976).

—— 'Evangelical Enthusiasm, Missionary Motivation and West Africa in the Late Nineteenth Century: The Career of G. W. Brooke', *Journal of Imperial and Commonwealth History*, 6/1 (1977).

—— 'Religion and Empire: British Expansion in the Long Nineteenth Century, 1780–1914', *Journal of Imperial and Commonwealth History*, 2/20 (1992).

Potter, D. C., *India's Political Administrators* (Oxford, 1986).

Powell, A. A., ' "Pillar of a New Faith": Christianity in Late-Nineteenth-Century Punjab from the Perspective of a Convert from Islam', in R. E. Frykenberg (ed.), *Christians and Missionaries in India: Cross-Cultural Communication since 1500* (Cambridge, 2003).

Prashad, V., *Untouchable Freedom: A Social History of a Dalit Community* (New Delhi, 2000).

Radhakrishnan, S., *The Hindu View of Life* (London, 1927).

Robinson, R., and Clarke, S., *Religious Conversion in India: Modes, Motivations and Meanings* (Oxford, 2003).

Rooney, J., *The Hesitant Dawn: Christianity in Pakistan, 1579–1760* (Rawalpindi, 1984).

—— *Into Deserts: A History of the Catholic Diocese of Lahore, 1886–1986* (Rawalpindi, 1986).

—— *On Heels of Battles: A History of the Catholic Church in Pakistan* (Rawalpindi, 1986).

Rosman, D. M., *Evangelicalism and Culture* (London, 1984).

Rowntree, R. S., *Land and Labour: Lessons from Belgium* (London, 1911).

Royle, E., 'Evangelicals and Education', in J. Wolffe (ed.), *Evangelical Faith and Public Zeal: Evangelicals and Society in Britain, 1780–1980* (London, 1995).

Sanneh, L., *Translating the Message: The Missionary Impact on Culture* (Maryknoll, NY, 1989).

—— *Whose Religion is Christianity? The Gospel Beyond the West* (Grand Rapids, Mich., 2003).

Sarkar, S., *Modern India: 1885–1947* (Delhi, 1983).

Sen Gupta, K. P., *The Christian Missionaries in Bengal, 1793–1833* (Calcutta, 1971).

Shah, D., 'Gandhian Approach to Rural Development', in B. P. Pandey (ed.), *Gandhi and Economic Development* (London, 1991).

Sharma, A., *Caste, Class and Politics in Rural India: A Comparative Study of Village Panchayats, Bihar and West Bengal* (New Delhi, 1993).

Sharma, S. K., *Social Movements and Social Change: A Study of Arya Samaj and Untouchables in Punjab* (Delhi, 1985).

Shenk, W. R., *Henry Venn: Missionary Statesman* (New York, 1983).

Singh, J. P., 'The Panchayats in Punjab, 1849–1947', *Punjab Past and Present*, 32/1 (Apr. 2001).

Singh, S., 'The Socio-Economic Effects of the Canal Colonies in the Punjab, 1886–1947', *Punjab Past and Present*, 21/2 (Oct. 1987).

Sobhanan, B. (ed.), *A History of the Christian Missions in South India* (Thiruvananthapuram, 1996).

Sookhdeo, P., *A People Betrayed: The Impact of Islamization on the Christian Community in Pakistan* (Fearn, 2002).

Srinivas, M. N., 'The Social System of a Mysore Village', in M. Marriott (ed.), *Village India: Studies in the Little Community* (Chicago, 1955).

Stokes, E., *The English Utilitarians and India* (Oxford, 1959).

—— *The Peasant and the Raj: Studies in Agrarian Society and Peasant Rebellion in Colonial India* (Cambridge, 1978).

Stone, I., *Canal Irrigation in British India* (Cambridge, 1984).

Strikwerda, C., *A House Divided: Catholics, Socialists and Flemish Nationalists in Nineteenth-Century Belgium* (Oxford, 1997).

Studdert-Kennedy, G., *British Christians, Indian Nationalists and the Raj* (Delhi, 1991).

—— *Providence and the Raj: Imperial Mission and Missionary Imperialism* (New Delhi, 1998).

Sunquist, S. (ed.), *Dictionary of Asian Christianity* (Grand Rapids, Mich., 2001).

Talbot, I., *Punjab and the Raj, 1849–1947* (New Delhi, 1988).

—— and Tatla, D. S., *Punjab* (Oxford, 1995).

Tandon, P., *Punjabi Century, 1857–1947* (London, 1961).

Teuns, S., *Historische Ledenlijst Minderbroeders-Kapucijnen, 1802–1995* (Sint-Truiden, 1996).

Thomas, G., *Christian Indians and Indian Nationalism, 1885–1950: An Interpretation in Historical and Theological Perspectives* (Frankfurt, 1979).

Tomlinson, B., 'The Historical Roots of Indian Poverty', *Modern Asian Studies*, 22/1 (1988).

Viswanathan, G., *Outside the Fold: Conversion, Modernity and Belief* (Princeton, 1998).

Walbridge, L. S., *The Christians of Pakistan: The Passion of Bishop John Joseph* (Richmond, 2003).

Wallis, F. H., *Popular Anti-Catholicism in Mid-Victorian Britain* (New York, 1993).

Ward, K., and Stanley, B. (eds), *The Church Mission Society and World Christianity. 1799–1999* (Richmond, 2000).
Warren, M., *Social History and Christian Mission* (London, 1967).
Watt, C., 'Education for National Efficiency: Constructive Nationalism in North India, 1909–1916', *Modern Asian Studies*, 31/2 (May 1997).
Webster, J. C. B, 'Competing Systems of Western Education in the Punjab, 1858–1882', *Indian Church History Review*, 1 (June 1967).
—— *The Christian Community and Change in Nineteenth Century North India* (Delhi, 1976).
—— 'British Missions in India', in T. Christensen and W. R. Hutchison (eds), *Missionary Ideologies in the Imperialist Era: 1880–1920* (Aarhus, 1982).
—— 'Punjabi Christians and the Indian Nationalist Movement, 1919–1947', *Indo-British Review*, Special Issue, 15/1 (1988).
—— *A History of the Dalit Christians in India* (San Francisco, 1992).
—— *Religion and Dalit Liberation* (New Delhi, 1999).
—— 'Dalits and Christianity in Colonial Punjab: Cultural Interactions', in J. M. Brown and R. E. Frykenberg (eds), *Christians, Cultural Interactions and India's Religious Traditions* (London, 2002).
—— 'Christian Conversion in the Punjab: What Has Changed?', in R. Robinson and S. Clarke (eds), *Religious Conversion in India: Modes, Motivations and Meanings* (Oxford, 2003).
—— *A Social History of Christianity: North-West India since 1800* (Delhi, 2007).
Winks, R. W. (ed.), *Historiography*, vol. v of *The Oxford History of the British Empire* (Oxford, 1999).
Wiser, W. H., and Wiser, C. V., *Behind Mud Walls, 1930–1960* (Berkeley, 1969).
Witte, E., 'The Battle for Monasteries, Cemeteries and Schools: Belgium', in C. Clark and W. Kaiser (eds), *Culture Wars: Secular–Catholic Conflict in Nineteenth-Century Europe* (Cambridge, 2003).
Wolffe, J. (ed.), *Evangelical Faith and Public Zeal: Evangelicals and Society in Britain, 1780–1980* (London, 1995).
Veer, P. van der, *Imperial Encounters: Religion and Modernity in India and Britain* (Princeton, 2001).
—— *Religious Nationalism: Hindus and Muslims in India* (Berkeley, 1994).
—— (ed.), *Conversion to Modernities: The Globalization of Christianity* (New York, 1996).
Zelliot, E., *From Untouchable to Dalit: Essays on the Ambedkar Movement* (New Delhi, 1996).

THESES

Reid-Graham, J., 'The Arya Samaj as a Reformation in Hinduism: With Special Reference to Caste', Ph.D. thesis (Yale University, 1943).

Index

Page numbers in **bold** refer to photographs